NUMERICAL MATHEMATICS AND SCIENTIFIC
COMPUTATION

NUMERICAL MATHEMATICS AND SCIENTIFIC COMPUTATION

Fortran 95/2003 Explained

Michael Metcalf
Formerly of CERN, Geneva, Switzerland

John Reid
JKR Associates, Oxfordshire

and

Malcolm Cohen
The Numerical Algorithms Group
Oxfordshire

OXFORD
UNIVERSITY PRESS

OXFORD

UNIVERSITY PRESS

Great Clarendon Street, Oxford OX2 6DP

Oxford University Press is a department of the University of Oxford.
It furthers the University's objective of excellence in research, scholarship,
and education by publishing worldwide in

Oxford New York

Auckland Cape Town Dar es Salaam Hong Kong Karachi
Kuala Lumpur Madrid Melbourne Mexico City Nairobi
New Delhi Shanghai Taipei Toronto

With offices in

Argentina Austria Brazil Chile Czech Republic France Greece
Guatemala Hungary Italy Japan South Korea Poland Portugal
Singapore Switzerland Thailand Turkey Ukraine Vietnam

Oxford is a registered trade mark of Oxford University Press
in the UK and in certain other countries

Published in the United States
by Oxford University Press Inc., New York

First published 2004
Reprinted 2004 (with corrections), 2005 (with corrections)

A catalogue record for this title is available from the British Library

Library of Congress Cataloging in Publication Data
(Data available)

ISBN 0 19 852692 X (Hbk)
ISBN 0 19 852693 8 (Pbk)

10 9 8 7 6 5 4 3

Printed in Great Britain
on acid-free paper by
Biddles Ltd., King's Lynn, Norfolk

Preface

Fortran remains one of the principal languages used in the fields of scientific, numerical, and engineering programming, and a series of revisions to the standard defining successive versions of the language has progressively enhanced its power and kept it competitive with several generations of rivals.

Beginning in 1978, the technical committee responsible for the development of Fortran standards, X3J3 (now called J3), laboured to produce a new, much-needed modern version of the language, Fortran 90. Its purpose was to 'promote portability, reliability, maintainability, and efficient execution... on a variety of computing systems'. That standard was published in 1991, and work began in 1993 on a minor revision, known informally as Fortran 95. Subsequently, and with the same purpose, a further major upgrade to the language has been prepared by J3 and the international committee, WG5. This revision, which includes object-oriented programming features, is now known as Fortran 2003 and, once again, it seems appropriate to prepare a definitive informal description of the language that it defines. This continues the series of editions of this book — the two editions of *Fortran 8x Explained* that described the two drafts of the standard (1987 and 1989), *Fortran 90 Explained* that described the Fortran 90 standard (1990), and two editions of *Fortran 90/95 Explained* that included Fortran 95 too (1996 and 1999). In this new endeavour, a third co-author is welcomed.

In this book, an initial chapter sets out the background to the work on new standards, and the nine following chapters describe Fortran 95 (less its obsolescent features) in a manner suitable both for grasping the implications of its features, and for writing programs. Some knowledge of programming concepts is assumed. In order to reduce the number of forward references and also to enable, as quickly as possible, useful programs to be written based on material already absorbed, the order of presentation does not always follow that of the standard. In particular, we have chosen to defer to the very last chapter of the book the description of features that are redundant in Fortran 95 and whose use we deprecate. It would impair the flow of the exposition if we were to describe them in the main body of the text. They may be encountered in old programs, but are not needed in new ones.

This edition has two chapters, 11 and 12, on official extensions of Fortran 95, each specified by an ISO Technical Report, and now part of Fortran 2003. These are followed, in Chapters 13 to 19, by descriptions of the new features defined by the Fortran 2003 standard, although, formally, Chapter 13 is an extension of the standard rather than part of it. The structure of the book thus allows the reader to distinguish clearly between Fortran 95, its extensions, and the new Fortran 2003 features.

In order to make the book a complete reference work, it concludes with six appendices. They contain, successively, a list of the intrinsic procedures, a description of the obsolescent features, an extended example illustrating the use of pointers and recursion, advice on avoiding compilation cascades, a glossary of Fortran terms, and solutions to most of the exercises.

The whole of Fortran 77 was contained in Fortran 90, but certain of its features were labelled 'obsolescent' in the standard, and their use was not recommended. The obsolescent features of Fortran 90 had replacements in Fortran 77 and some were deleted from the Fortran 95 standard. Other Fortran 77 features, with replacements in Fortran 90, were labelled obsolescent in Fortran 95. We have relegated the description of the surviving obsolescent features to Appendix B; they have fallen into disuse and an understanding of them is required only when dealing with old programs, although they remain part of the standard. This appendix includes advice on how to avoid their use, and the same is true for those features whose use we deprecate, and which are described only in Chapter 20.

It is our hope that this book, by providing complete descriptions of Fortran 95 and Fortran 2003, will continue the helpful role that earlier editions played for the Fortran 90 and 95 standards, and will serve as a long-term reference work for the Fortran programming language.

***

Malcolm Cohen wishes to thank the Numerical Algorithms Group (NAG) for its encouragement during the writing of this book.

Conventions used in this book

Fortran displayed text is set in typewriter font:

```
integer :: i, j
```

and a line consisting of a colon indicates omitted lines:

```
subroutine sort
    :
end subroutine sort
```

Informal BNF terms are in italics:

    if (*scalar-logical-expr*) *action-stmt*

Square brackets indicate optional items:

    end if [*name*]

and an ellipsis represents an arbitrary number of repeated items:

    [case *selector* [*name*]
            block] ...

The italic letter *b* signifies a blank character.

    Corrections to any significant errors detected in this book will be made available in the files *edits.ps* and *edits.pdf* at ftp://ftp.numerical.rl.ac.uk/pub/MRandC.

Contents

1. Whence Fortran?

1.1 Introduction

This book is concerned with the Fortran 95 and Fortran 2003 programming languages, setting out a reasonably concise description of the whole of each. The form chosen for its presentation is that of a textbook intended for use in teaching or learning the language.

The description of Fortran 95 occupies Chapters 2 to 10 and Chapter 20, which are written in such a way that simple programs can already be coded after the first three of these chapters (on language elements, expressions and assignments, and control) have been read. Successively more complex programs can be written as the information in each subsequent chapter is absorbed. Chapter 5 describes the important concept of the module and the many aspects of procedures, Chapter 6 completes the description of the powerful array features, Chapter 7 considers the details of specifying data objects and derived types, and Chapter 8 details the intrinsic procedures. Chapters 9 and 10 cover the whole of the input/output features in a manner such that the reader can also approach this more difficult area feature by feature, but always with a useful subset already covered. Finally, Chapter 20 describes those features that are redundant in the language, and whose use we choose to deprecate. Here we emphasize that this deprecation represents our own opinion, and is completely unofficial.

Chapters 11 and 12 describe official extensions to Fortran 95. Chapter 13 describes an official extension to Fortran 2003 that we expect to be widely implemented as an extension to Fortran 95.

Fortran 2003 contains all of Fortran 95, including the extensions of Chapters 11 and 12, and Chapters 14 to 19 describe its additional features. Chapter 14 deals with interoperability with the C programming language, Chapter 15 with parameterized data types and procedure pointers, Chapter 16 with object-oriented programming, and Chapter 17 with establishing and manipulating data. Chapter 18 covers some miscellaneous enhancements, while Chapter 19 concludes with enhancements in the area of input/output.

This introductory chapter has the task of setting the scene for those that follow. Section 1.2 presents the early history of Fortran, starting with its introduction about fifty years ago. Section 1.3 continues with the development of the Fortran 90 standard, summarizes its important new features, and outlines how standards are developed; Section 1.4 looks at the mechanism that has been adopted to permit the language to evolve. Sections 1.5 to 1.7 consider the development of Fortran 95, extensions to Fortran 95, and Fortran 2003. The final section considers the requirements on programs and processors for conformance with the standard.

1.2   Fortran's early history

Programming in the early days of computing was tedious in the extreme. Programmers required a detailed knowledge of the instructions, registers, and other aspects of the central processing unit (CPU) of the computer for which they were writing code. The *source code* itself was written in a numerical notation, so-called *octal code*. In the course of time mnemonic codes were introduced, a form of coding known as *machine* or *assembly code*. These codes were translated into the instruction words by programs known as *assemblers*. In the 1950s it became increasingly apparent that this form of programming was highly inconvenient, although it did enable the CPU to be used in a very efficient way.

These difficulties spurred a team led by John Backus of IBM to develop one of the earliest high-level languages, Fortran. Their aim was to produce a language which would be simple to understand but almost as efficient in execution as assembly language. In this they succeeded beyond their wildest dreams. The language was indeed simple to learn, as it was possible to write mathematical formulae almost as they are usually written in mathematical texts. (In fact, the name Fortran is a contraction of Formula Translation.) This enabled working programs to be written faster than before, for only a small loss in efficiency, as a great deal of care was devoted to the construction of the compiler.

But Fortran was revolutionary as well as innovatory. Programmers were relieved of the tedious burden of using assembler language, and were able to concentrate more on the problem in hand. Perhaps more important, however, was the fact that computers became accessible to any scientist or engineer willing to devote a little effort to acquiring a working knowledge of Fortran; no longer was it necessary to be an expert on computers to be able to write application programs.

Fortran spread rapidly as it fulfilled a real need. Inevitably dialects of the language developed, which led to problems in exchanging programs between computers, and so, in 1966 the then American Standards Association (later the American National Standards Institute, ANSI) brought out the first ever standard for a programming language, now known as Fortran 66.

Fortran brought with it several other advances, apart from its ease of learning combined with a stress on efficient execution of code. It was, for instance, a language which remained close to, and exploited, the available hardware rather than being an abstract concept. It also brought with it the possibility for programmers to control storage allocation in a simple way, a feature which was very necessary in those early days of small memories, even if it is now regarded as being potentially dangerous.

The proliferation of dialects remained a problem after the publication of the 1966 standard. There was a widespread implementation in compilers of features which were essential for large-scale programs, but which were ignored by the standard. Different compilers implemented such facilities in different ways.

These difficulties were partially resolved by the publication of a new standard, in 1978, known as Fortran 77. It included several new features that were based on vendor extensions or pre-processors and it was, therefore, not simply a common subset of existing dialects.

1.3 The drive for the Fortran 90 standard

After thirty years' existence, Fortran was far from being the only programming language available on most computers. In the course of time new languages had been developed, and where they were demonstrably more suitable for a particular type of application they had been adopted in preference to Fortran for that purpose. Fortran's superiority had always been in the area of numerical, scientific, engineering, and technical applications and, in order that it be brought properly up to date, the ANSI-accredited technical committee J3 (then known as X3J3), working as a development body for the ISO committee ISO/IEC JTC1/SC22/WG5 (which we abbreviate to WG5), once again prepared a new standard, formerly known as Fortran 8x and now as Fortran 90.

J3 itself is a body composed of representatives of computer hardware and software vendors, users, and academia. It is now accredited to NCITS (National Council for Information Technology Standards). J3 acts as the development body for the corresponding international group, WG5, consisting of international experts responsible for recommending that a draft standard become an international standard. J3 maintains other close contacts with the international community by welcoming foreign members, including the present authors over several years.

What were the justifications for continuing to revise the definition of the Fortran language? As well as standardizing vendor extensions, there was a need to modernize it in response to the developments in language design which had been exploited in other languages, such as APL, Algol 68, Pascal, Ada, C, and C++. Here, J3 could draw on the obvious benefits of concepts like data hiding. In the same vein was the need to begin to provide an alternative to dangerous storage association, to abolish the rigidity of the outmoded source form, and to improve further on the regularity of the language, as well as to increase the safety of programming in the language and to tighten the conformance requirements. To preserve the vast investment in Fortran 77 codes, the whole of Fortran 77 was retained as a subset. However, unlike the previous standard, which resulted almost entirely from an effort to standardize *existing practices*, the Fortran 90 standard was much more a *development* of the language, introducing features which were new to Fortran, but were based on experience in other languages.

The main features of Fortran 90 were, first and foremost, the array language and abstract data types. The former is built on whole array operations and assignments, array sections, intrinsic procedures for arrays, and dynamic storage. It was designed with optimization in mind. The latter is built on modules and module procedures, derived data types, operator overloading, and generic interfaces, together with pointers. Also important were the new facilities for numerical computation including a set of numeric inquiry functions, the parameterization of the intrinsic types, new control constructs — select case and new forms of do — internal and recursive procedures and optional and keyword arguments, improved I/O facilities, and many new intrinsic procedures. Last but not least were the new free source form, an improved style of attribute-oriented specifications, the implicit none statement, and a mechanism for identifying redundant features for subsequent removal from the language. The requirement on compilers to be able to identify, for example, syntax extensions, and to report why a program has been rejected, are also significant. The resulting language was not only a far more powerful tool than its predecessor, but a safer and more reliable one too. Storage association, with its attendant dangers, was not abolished, but rendered unnecessary. Indeed, experience showed that compilers detected errors far more frequently than before, resulting in a faster development cycle. The array syntax and recursion also allowed quite compact code to be written, a further aid to safe programming.

1.4   Language evolution

The procedures under which J3 works require that a period of notice be given before any existing feature is removed from the language. This means, in practice, a minimum of one revision cycle, which for Fortran means at least five years. The need to remove features is evident: if the only action of the committee is to add new features, the language will become grotesquely large, with many overlapping and redundant items. The solution finally adopted by J3 was to publish as an appendix to a standard a set of two lists showing which items have been removed or are candidates for eventual removal.

One list contains the *deleted features*, those that have been removed. Since Fortran 90 contained the whole of Fortran 77, this list was empty for Fortran 90 but was not for Fortran 95.

The second list contains the *obsolescent features*, those considered to be outmoded and redundant, and which are candidates for deletion in the next revision. The Fortran 95 obsolescent features are described in Appendix B.

For Fortran 2003, there are no new obsolescent features and none of the Fortran 95 obsolescent features have been deleted. Furthermore, the Fortran 90 obsolescent features that were deleted from Fortran 95 are still supported by compilers, because of the demand for old tried and tested programs to continue to work. Thus, the concept of obsolescence is really not working as intended, but at least it gives a clear signal that certain features are outmoded, and should be avoided in new programs and should not be taught to new programmers.

1.5   Fortran 95

Following the publication of the Fortran 90 standard in 1991, two further significant developments concerning the Fortran language occurred. The first was the continued operation of the two Fortran standards committees, J3 and WG5, and the second was the founding of the High Performance Fortran Forum (HPFF).

Early on in their deliberations, the standards committees decided on a strategy whereby a minor revision of Fortran 90 would be prepared by the mid-1990s and a major revision by about the year 2000. The first revision, Fortran 95, is the subject of the first part of this book.

The HPFF was set up in an effort to define a set of extensions to Fortran, such that it would be possible to write portable code when using parallel computers for handling problems involving large sets of data that can be represented by regular grids. This version of Fortran was to be known as High Performance Fortran (HPF), and it was quickly decided, given the array features of Fortran 90, that it, and not Fortran 77, should be its base language. The final form of HPF[1] is of a superset of Fortran 90, the main extensions being in the form of directives

---

[1] *The High Performance Fortran Handbook*, C. Koebel *et al.*, MIT Press, Cambridge, MA, 1994.

that take the form of Fortran 90 comment lines, and are thus recognized as directives only by an HPF processor. However, it did become necessary also to add some additional syntax, as not all the desired features could be accommodated in the form of such directives.

The work of J3 and WG5 went on at the same time as that of HPFF, and the bodies liaised closely. It was evident that, in order to avoid the development of divergent dialects of Fortran, it would be desirable to include the new syntax defined by HPFF in Fortran 95 and, indeed, the HPF features are the most significant new features. Beyond this, a small number of other pressing but minor language changes were made, mainly based on experience with the use of Fortran 90.

Fortran 95 was backwards compatible with Fortran 90, apart from a minor change in the definition of sign (Section 8.3.2) and the deletion of some Fortran 77 features declared obsolete in Fortran 90. However, there were two new intrinsic procedures, null and cpu_time, which might also be names of external procedures in an existing Fortran 90 program.

The details of Fortran 95 were finalized in 1995, and the new ISO standard, replacing Fortran 90, was adopted in 1997, following successful ballots, as ISO/IEC 1539-1 : 1997.

1.6   Extensions to Fortran 95

Soon after the publication of Fortran 90, an auxiliary standard for varying length strings was developed. A minority felt that this should have been part of Fortran 90, but were satisfied with this alternative. The auxiliary standard defines the interface and semantics for a module that provides facilities for the manipulation of character strings of arbitrary and dynamically variable length. It has been revised for Fortran 95 as ISO/IEC 1539-2 : 2000(E). An annex references a possible implementation[2] in Fortran 95, which demonstrates its feasibility, but the intention was that vendors provide equivalent features that execute more efficiently.

Further, in 1995, WG5 decided that these three features:

   i) handling floating-point exceptions,

  ii) permitting allocatable arrays as structure components, dummy arguments, and function results, and

 iii) interoperability with C,

were so urgently needed in Fortran that it established development bodies to develop 'Technical Reports of Type 2'. The intent was that the material of these technical reports be integrated into the next revision of the Fortran standard, apart from any defects found in the field. It is essentially a beta-test facility for a language feature. In the event, the first two have been completed and are the subjects of Chapters 11 and 12. Difficulties were encountered with the third, so the report mechanism was abandoned for interoperability with C, but it was subsequently included in Fortran 2003 (see Chapter 14).

Another auxiliary standard, ISO/IEC 1539-3 : 1999(E), was developed to meet the need of programmers to maintain several versions of code to allow for different systems and different applications. Keeping several copies of the source code is error prone. It is far better to

---

[2]ftp://ftp.nag.co.uk/sc22wg5/ISO_VARYING_STRING/

maintain a master code from which any of the versions may be selected. This standard is for a very simple form of conditional compilation, which selects some of the Fortran lines from the source and omits the rest or converts them to comments. The process is controlled by 'coco lines' in the source that are also omitted or converted to comments. It is hoped that the facilities will be built into compilers, but they may also be implemented by a pre-processor.

1.7   Fortran 2003

The next full language revision was published in November 2004 and is known as Fortran 2003 since the details were finalized in 2003. It is the subject of the second part of this book. Unlike Fortran 95, it is a major revision. Its main new features are:

- Derived type enhancements: parameterized derived types, improved control of accessibility, improved structure constructors, and finalizers.

- Object-oriented programming support: type extension and inheritance, polymorphism, dynamic type allocation, and type-bound procedures.

- Data manipulation enhancements: allocatable components, deferred type parameters, volatile attribute, explicit type specification in array constructors and allocate statements, pointer enhancements, extended initialization expressions, and enhanced intrinsic procedures.

- Input/output enhancements: asynchronous transfer, stream access, user-specified transfer operations for derived types, user-specified control of rounding during format conversions, named constants for preconnected units, the flush statement, regularization of keywords, and access to error messages.

- Procedure pointers.

- Support of IEC 60559 (IEEE 754) exceptions.

- Interoperability with the C programming language.

- Support for international usage: access to ISO 10646 4-byte characters and choice of decimal point or comma in numeric formatted I/O.

- Enhanced integration with the host operating system: access to command line arguments, environment variables, and processor error messages.

Fortran 2003 has not yet been implemented in any compilers, but even now, new ideas are being collected for a further revision cycle. The standard is augmented by a further Technical Report, published in February 2005, that defines how the use of modules can be enhanced by the use of submodules (see Chapter 13). All this activity provides a means of ensuring that Fortran remains a powerful and well-honed tool for numerical and scientific applications.

1.8 Conformance

The standards are almost exclusively concerned with the rules for programs rather than processors. A processor is required to accept a standard-conforming program and to interpret it according to the standard, subject to limits that the processor may impose on the size and complexity of the program. The processor is allowed to accept further syntax and to interpret relationships that are not specified in the standard, provided they do not conflict with the standard. Of course, the programmer must avoid such syntax extensions if portability is desired.

The interpretation of some of the standard syntax is *processor dependent*, that is, may vary from processor to processor. For example, the set of characters allowed in character strings is processor dependent. Care must be taken whenever a processor-dependent feature is used in case it leads to the program not being portable to a desired processor.

A drawback of the Fortran 77 standard was that it made no statement about requiring processors to provide a means to detect any departure from the allowed syntax by a program, as long as that departure did not conflict with the syntax rules defined by the standard. The new standards are written in a different style to the old one. The syntax rules are expressed in a form of BNF with associated constraints, and the semantics are described by the text. This semi-formal style is not used in this book, so an example is perhaps helpful:

R609	*substring*	**is**	*parent-string (substring-range)*
R610	*parent-string*	**is**	*scalar-variable-name*
		or	*array-element*
		or	*scalar-structure-component*
		or	*scalar-constant*
R611	*substring-range*	**is**	[*scalar-int-expr*] : [*scalar-int-expr*]

Constraint: *parent-string* shall be of type character.

> The value of the first *scalar-int-expr* in *substring-range* is called the **starting point** and the value of the second one is called the **ending point**. The length of a substring is the number of characters in the substring and is $\mathrm{MAX}(\ell - f + 1, 0)$, where f and ℓ are the starting and ending points, respectively.

Here, the three production rules and the associated constraint for a character substring are defined, and the meaning of the length of such a substring explained.

The standard is written in such a way that a processor, at compile-time, may check that the program satisfies all the constraints. In particular, the processor must provide a capability to detect and report the use of any

- obsolescent feature,

- additional syntax,

- kind type parameter (Section 2.5) that it does not support,

- non-standard source form or character,

- name that is inconsistent with the scoping rules, or

- non-standard intrinsic procedure.

Furthermore, it must be able to report the reason for rejecting a program. These capabilities are of great value in producing correct and portable code.

2. Language elements

2.1 Introduction

Written prose in a natural language, such as an English text, is composed firstly of basic elements — the letters of the alphabet. These are combined into larger entities, words, which convey the basic concepts of objects, actions, and qualifications. The words of the language can be further combined into larger units, phrases and sentences, according to certain rules. One set of rules defines the grammar. This tells us whether a certain combination of words is correct in that it conforms to the *syntax* of the language, that is those acknowledged forms which are regarded as correct renderings of the meanings we wish to express. Sentences can in turn be joined together into paragraphs, which conventionally contain the composite meaning of their constituent sentences, each paragraph expressing a larger unit of information. In a novel, sequences of paragraphs become chapters and the chapters together form a book, which usually is a self-contained work, largely independent of all other books.

2.2 Fortran character set

Analogies to these concepts are found in a programming language. In Fortran 95, the basic elements, or character set, are the 26 letters of the English alphabet, the 10 Arabic numerals, 0 to 9, the underscore, _, and the so-called special characters listed in Table 2.1. The standard does not require the support of lower-case letters, but almost all computers nowadays support them. Within the Fortran syntax, the lower-case letters are equivalent to the corresponding upper-case letters; they are distinguished only when they form part of character sequences. In this book, syntactically significant characters will always be written in lower case. The letters, numerals, and underscore are known as *alphanumeric* characters.

Except for the currency symbol, whose graphic may vary (for example, to be £ in the United Kingdom), the graphics are fixed, though their styles are not fixed. The special characters $ and ? have no specific meaning within the Fortran language.

In the course of this and the following chapters, we shall see how further analogies with natural language may be drawn. The unit of Fortran information is the *lexical token*, which corresponds to a word or punctuation mark. Adjacent tokens are usually separated by spaces or the end of a line, but sensible exceptions are allowed just as for a punctuation mark in prose. Sequences of tokens form *statements*, corresponding to sentences. Statements, like sentences, may be joined to form larger units like paragraphs. In Fortran these are known

Table 2.1. The special characters of the Fortran 95 language.

Character	Name	Character	Name
=	Equals sign	:	Colon
+	Plus sign		Blank
–	Minus sign	!	Exclamation mark
*	Asterisk	"	Quotation mark
/	Slash	%	Percent
(	Left parenthesis	&	Ampersand
)	Right parenthesis	;	Semicolon
,	Comma	<	Less than
.	Decimal point	>	Greater than
$	Currency symbol	?	Question mark
'	Apostrophe		

as *program units*, and out of these may be built a *program*. A program forms a complete set of instructions to a computer to carry out a defined sequence of operations. The simplest program may consist of only a few statements, but programs of more than 100 000 statements are now quite common.

2.3 Tokens

Within the context of Fortran, alphanumeric characters (the letters, the underscore, and the numerals) may be combined into sequences that have one or more meanings. For instance, one of the meanings of the sequence 999 is a constant in the mathematical sense. Similarly, the sequence date might represent, as one possible interpretation, a variable quantity to which we assign the calendar date.

The special characters are used to separate such sequences and also have various meanings. We shall see how the asterisk is used to specify the operation of multiplication, as in x*y, and also has a number of other interpretations.

Basic significant sequences of alphanumeric characters or of special characters are referred to as *tokens*; they are labels, keywords, names, constants (other than complex literal constants), operators (listed in Table 3.4, Section 3.8), and *separators*, which are

$$/ \quad (\quad) \quad (/ \quad /) \quad , \quad = \quad => \quad : \quad :: \quad ; \quad \%$$

For example, the expression x*y contains the three tokens x, *, and y.

Apart from within a character string or within a token, blanks may be used freely to improve the layout. Thus, whereas the variable date may not be written as d a t e, the sequence x * y is syntactically equivalent to x*y. In this context, multiple blanks are syntactically equivalent to a single blank.

A name, constant, or label must be separated from an adjacent keyword, name, constant, or label by one or more blanks or by the end of a line. For instance, in

```
      real x
      read 10
 30 do k=1,3
```

the blanks are required after real, read, 30, and do. Likewise, adjacent keywords must normally be separated, but some pairs of keywords, such as else if, are not required to be separated. Similarly, some keywords may be split; for example inout may be written in out. We do not use these alternatives, but the exact rules are given in Table 2.2.

Table 2.2. Adjacent keywords where separating blanks are optional.

block data	double precision	else if
else where*	end associate*	end block data
end do	end enum*	end file
end forall	end function	end if
end interface	end module	end program
end select	end subroutine	end type
end where	go to	in out
select case	select type*	

* = applies to Fortran 2003 only.

2.4 Source form

The statements of which a source program is composed are written on *lines*. Each line may contain up to 132 characters,[1] and usually contains a single statement. Since leading spaces are not significant, it is possible to start all such statements in the first character position, or in any other position consistent with the user's chosen layout. A statement may thus be written as

```
  x = (-y + root_of_discriminant)/(2.0*a)
```

In order to be able to mingle suitable comments with the code to which they refer, Fortran allows any line to carry a trailing comment field, following an exclamation mark (!). An example is

```
  x = y/a - b    ! Solve the linear equation
```

Any comment always extends to the end of the source line and may include processor-dependent characters (it is not restricted to the Fortran character set, Section 2.2). Any line whose first non-blank character is an exclamation mark, or contains only blanks, or which is empty, is purely commentary and is ignored by the compiler. Such comment lines may appear anywhere in a program unit, including ahead of the first statement (but not after the final program unit). A *character context* (those contexts defined in Sections 2.6.4 and 9.12.4)

---

[1]Lines containing characters of non-default kind (Section 2.6.4) are subject to a processor-dependent limit.

is allowed to contain !, so the ! does not initiate a comment in this case; in all other cases it does.

Since it is possible that a long statement might not be accommodated in the 132 positions allowed in a single line, up to 39 additional continuation lines are allowed (more in Fortran 2003, see Section 18.8). The so-called *continuation mark* is the ampersand (&) character, and this is appended to each line that is followed by a continuation line. Thus, the first statement of this section (considerably spaced out) could be written as

```
x =                                                    &
    (-y + root_of_discriminant)                        &
    /(2.0*a)
```

In this book, the ampersands will normally be aligned to improve readability. On a non-comment line, if & is the last non-blank character or the last non-blank character ahead of the comment symbol !, the statement continues from the character immediately preceding the &. Normally, continuation is to the first character of the next non-comment line, but if the first non-blank character of the next non-comment line is &, continuation is to the character following the &. For instance, the above statement may be written

```
x =                                                    &
    &(-y + root_of_discriminant)/(2.0*a)
```

In particular, if a token cannot be contained at the end of a line, the first non-blank character on the next non-comment line must be an & followed immediately by the remainder of the token.

Comments are allowed to contain any characters, including &, so they cannot be continued since a trailing & is taken as part of the comment. However, comment lines may be freely interspersed among continuation lines and do not count towards the limit of 39 lines.

In a character context, continuation must be from a line without a trailing comment and to a line with a leading ampersand. This is because both ! and & are permitted both in character contexts and in comments.

No line is permitted to have & as its only non-blank character, or as its only non-blank character ahead of !. Such a line is really a comment and becomes a comment if & is removed.

When writing short statements one after the other, it can be convenient to write several of them on one line. The semicolon (;) character is used as a *statement separator* in these circumstances, for example:

```
a = 0; b = 0; c = 0
```

Since commentary always extends to the end of the line, it is not possible to insert commentary between statements on a single line. In principle, it is possible to write even long statements one after the other in a solid block of lines, each 132 characters long and with the appropriate semicolons separating the individual statements. In practice, such code is unreadable, and the use of multiple-statement lines should be reserved for trivial cases such as the one shown in this example.

Any Fortran statement (that is not part of a compound statement) may be labelled, in order to be able to identify it. For some statements a label is mandatory. A statement *label* precedes the statement, and is regarded as a token. The label consists of from one to five digits, one of which must be nonzero. An example of a labelled statement is

```
100 continue
```

Leading zeros are not significant in distinguishing between labels. For example, 10 and 010 are equivalent.

2.5   Concept of type

In Fortran, it is possible to define and manipulate various types of data. For instance, we may have available the value 10 in a program, and assign that value to an integer scalar variable denoted by i. Both 10 and i are of type integer; 10 is a fixed or *constant* value, whereas i is a *variable* which may be assigned other values. Integer expressions, such as i+10, are available too.

A *data type* consists of a set of data values, a means of denoting those values, and a set of operations that are allowed on them. For the integer data type, the values are $\ldots, -3, -2, -1, 0, 1, 2, 3, \ldots$ between some limits depending on the kind of integer and computer system being used. Such tokens as these are *literal constants*, and each data type has its own form for expressing them. Named scalar variables, such as i, may be established. During the execution of a program, the value of i may change to any valid value, or may become *undefined*, that is have no predictable value. The operations which may be performed on integers are those of usual arithmetic; we can write 1+10 or i-3 and obtain the expected results. Named constants may be established too; these have values that do not change during a given execution of the program.

Properties like those just mentioned are associated with all the data types of Fortran, and will be described in detail in this and the following chapters. The language itself contains five data types whose existence may always be assumed. These are known as the *intrinsic data types*, whose literal constants form the subject of the next section. Of each intrinsic type there is a default kind and a processor-dependent number of other kinds. Each kind is associated with a non-negative integer value known as the *kind type parameter*. This is used as a means of identifying and distinguishing the various kinds available.

In addition, it is possible to define other data types based on collections of data of the intrinsic types, and these are known as *derived data types*. The ability to define data types of interest to the programmer — matrices, geometrical shapes, lists, interval numbers — is a powerful feature of the language, one which permits a high level of *data abstraction*, that is the ability to define and manipulate data objects without being concerned about their actual representation in a computer.

2.6   Literal constants of intrinsic type

The intrinsic data types are divided into two classes. The first class contains three *numeric* types which are used mainly for numerical calculations — integer, real, and complex. The second class contains the two *non-numeric* types which are used for such applications as text-processing and control — character and logical. The numerical types are used in conjunction with the usual operators of arithmetic, such as + and –, which will be described in Chapter 3. Each includes a zero and the value of a signed zero is the same as that of an unsigned zero.[2] The non-numeric types are used with sets of operators specific to each type; for instance, character data may be concatenated. These too will be described in Chapter 3.

2.6.1   Integer literal constants

The first type of literal constant is the *integer literal constant*. The default kind is simply a signed or unsigned integer value, for example

```
1
0
-999
32767
+10
```

The *range* of the default integers is not specified in the language, but on a computer with a word size of n bits, is often from -2^{n-1} to $+2^{n-1} - 1$. Thus on a 32-bit computer the range is often from -2147483648 to $+2147483647$.

To be sure that the range will be adequate on any computer requires the specification of the kind of integer by giving a value for the kind type parameter. This is best done through a named integer constant. For example, if the range -999999 to 999999 is desired, k6 may be established as a constant with an appropriate value by the statement, fully explained later,

```
integer, parameter :: k6=selected_int_kind(6)
```

and used in constants thus:

```
-123456_k6
+1_k6
 2_k6
```

Here, selected_int_kind(6) is an intrinsic inquiry function call, and it returns a kind parameter value that yields the range -999999 to 999999 with the least margin (see Section 8.7.4).

On a given processor, it might be known that the kind value needed is 3. In this case, the first of our constants can be written

```
-123456_3
```

but this form is less portable. If we move the code to another processor, this particular value may be unsupported, or might correspond to a different range.

Many implementations use kind values that indicate the number of bytes of storage occupied by a value, but the standard allows greater flexibility. For example, a processor might have hardware only for 4-byte integers, and yet support kind values 1, 2, and 4 with

---

[2]Although the representation of data is processor dependent, for the numeric data types the standard defines model representations and means to inquire about the properties of those models. The details are deferred to Section 8.7.

this hardware (to ease portability from processors that have hardware for 1-, 2-, and 4-byte integers). However, the standard makes no statement about kind values or their order, except that the kind value is never negative.

The value of the kind type parameter for a given data type on a given processor can be obtained from the kind intrinsic function (Section 8.2):

```
kind(1)        for the default value
kind(2_k6)     for the example
```

and the decimal exponent range (number of decimal digits supported) of a given entity may be obtained from another function (Section 8.7.2), as in

```
range(2_k6)
```

which in this case would return a value of at least 6.

In addition to the usual integers of the decimal number system, for some applications it is very convenient to be able to represent positive whole numbers in binary, octal, or hexadecimal form. Unsigned constants of these forms exist in Fortran, and are represented as illustrated in these examples:

```
binary (base 2):        b'01100110'
octal (base 8):         o'076543'
hexadecimal (base 16):  z'10fa'
```

In the hexadecimal form, the letters a to f represent the values beyond 9; they may be used also in upper case. The delimiters may be quotation marks or apostrophes. The use of these forms of constants is limited to their appearance as implicit integers in the data statement (Section 7.5.2). A binary, octal, or hexadecimal constant may also appear in an internal or external file as a digit string, without the leading letter and the delimiters (see Section 9.12.2).

Bits stored as an integer representation may be manipulated by the intrinsic procedures described in Section 8.8.

2.6.2 Real literal constants

The second type of literal constant is the *real literal constant*. The default kind is a floating-point form built of some or all of: a signed or unsigned integer part, a decimal point, a fractional part, and a signed or unsigned exponent part. One or both of the integer part and fractional part must be present. The exponent part is either absent or consists of the letter e followed by a signed or unsigned integer. One or both of the decimal point and the exponent part must be present. An example is

```
-10.6e-11
```

meaning -10.6×10^{-11}, and other legal forms are

```
1.
-0.1
1e-1
3.141592653
```

The default real literal constants are representations of a subset of the real numbers of mathematics, and the standard specifies neither the allowed range of the exponent nor the number of significant digits represented by the processor. Many processors conform to the IEEE standard for floating-point arithmetic and have values of 10^{-37} to 10^{+37} for the range, and a precision of six decimal digits.

To be sure to obtain a desired range and significance requires the specification of a kind parameter value. For example,

```
integer, parameter :: long = selected_real_kind(9, 99)
```

ensures that the constants

```
1.7_long
12.3456789e30_long
```

have a precision of at least nine significant decimals, and an exponent range of at least 10^{-99} to 10^{+99}. The number of digits specified in the significand has no effect on the kind. In particular, it is permitted to write more digits than the processor can in fact use.

As for integers, many implementations use kind values that indicate the number of bytes of storage occupied by a value, but the standard allows greater flexibility. It specifies only that the kind value is never negative. If the desired kind value is known it may be used directly, as in the case

```
1.7_4
```

but the resulting code is then less portable.

The processor must provide at least one representation with more precision than the default, and this second representation may also be specified as double precision. We defer the description of this alternative but outmoded syntax to Section 20.7.

The kind function is valid also for real values:

```
kind(1.0)        for the default value
kind(1.0_long)   for the example
```

In addition, there are two inquiry functions available which return the actual precision and range, respectively, of a given real entity (see Section 8.7.2). Thus, the value of

```
precision(1.7_long)
```

would be at least 9, and the value of

```
range(1.7_long)
```

would be at least 99.

2.6.3 Complex literal constants

Fortran, as a language intended for scientific and engineering calculations, has the advantage of having as third literal constant type the *complex literal constant*. This is designated by a pair of literal constants, which are either integer or real, separated by a comma and enclosed in parentheses. Examples are

```
(1., 3.2)
(1, .99e-2)
(1.0, 3.7_8)
```

where the first constant of each pair is the real part of the complex number, and the second constant is the imaginary part. If one of the parts is integer, the kind of the complex constant is that of the other part. If both parts are integer, the kind of the constant is that of the default real type. If both parts are real and of the same kind, this is the kind of the constant. If both parts are real and of different kinds, the kind of the constant is that of one of the parts: the part with the greater decimal precision, or the part chosen by the processor if the decimal precisions are identical.

A default complex constant is one whose kind value is that of default real.

The kind, precision, and range functions are equally valid for complex entities.

Note that if an implementation uses the number of bytes needed to store a real as its kind value, the number of bytes needed to store a complex value of the corresponding kind is twice the kind value. For example, if the default real type has kind 4 and needs four bytes of storage, the default complex type has kind 4 but needs eight bytes of storage.

2.6.4 Character literal constants

The fourth type of literal constant is the *character literal constant*. The default kind consists of a string of characters enclosed in a pair of either apostrophes or quotation marks, for example

```
'Anything goes'
```

```
"Nuts & bolts"
```

The characters are not restricted to the Fortran set (Section 2.2). Any graphic character supported by the processor is permitted, but not control characters such as 'newline'. The apostrophes and quotation marks serve as *delimiters*, and are not part of the value of the constant. The value of the constant

```
'STRING'
```

is STRING. We note that in character constants the blank character is significant. For example

```
'a string'
```

is not the same as

```
'astring'
```

A problem arises with the representation of an apostrophe or a quotation mark in a character constant. Delimiter characters of one sort may be embedded in a string delimited by the other, as in the examples

```
'He said "Hello"'
"This contains an ' "
```

Alternatively, a doubled delimiter without any embedded intervening blanks is regarded as a single character of the constant. For example

```
'Isn''t it a nice day'
```

has the value `Isn't it a nice day`.

The number of characters in a string is called its *length*, and may be zero. For instance, `''` and `""` are character constants of length zero.

We mention here the particular rule for the source form concerning character constants that are written on more than one line (needed because constants may include the characters ! and &): not only must each line that is continued be without a trailing comment, but each continuation line must *begin* with a continuation mark. Any blanks following a trailing ampersand or preceding a leading ampersand are not part of the constant, nor are the ampersands themselves part of the constant. Everything else, including blanks, is part of the constant. An example is

```
long_string =                                               &
      'Were I with her, the night would post too soon;      &
    & But now are minutes added to the hours;               &
    & To spite me now, each minute seems a moon;            &
    & Yet not for me, shine sun to succour flowers!         &
    &   Pack night, peep day; good day, of night now borrow:   &
    &   Short, night, to-night, and length thyself tomorrow.'
```

On any computer, the characters have a property known as their *collating sequence*. One may ask the question whether one character occurs before or after another in the sequence. This question is posed in a natural form such as 'Does C precede M?', and we shall see later how this may be expressed in Fortran terms. Fortran requires the computer's collating sequence to satisfy the following conditions:

- A is less than B is less than C ... is less than Y is less than Z;

- 0 is less than 1 is less than 2 ... is less than 8 is less than 9;

- blank is less than A and Z is less than 0, or blank is less than 0 and 9 is less than A;

and, if the lower-case letters are available,

- a is less than b is less than c ... is less than y is less than z;

- blank is less than a and z is less than 0, or blank is less than 0 and 9 is less than a.

Thus we see that there is no rule about whether the numerals precede or succeed the letters, nor about the position of any of the special characters or the underscore, apart from the rule that blank precedes both partial sequences. Any given computer system has a complete collating sequence, and most computers nowadays use the collating sequence of the ASCII standard (also known as ISO/IEC 646 : 1991). However, Fortran is designed to accommodate other sequences, notably EBCDIC, so for portability, no program should ever depend on any ordering beyond that stated above. Alternatively, Fortran provides access to the ASCII collating sequence on any computer through intrinsic functions (Section 8.5.1), but this access is not so convenient and is less efficient on some computers.

A processor is required to provide access to the default kind of character constant just described. In addition, it may support other kinds of character constants, in particular those of non-European languages, which may have more characters than can be provided in a single byte. For example, a processor might support Kanji with the kind parameter value 2; in this case, a Kanji character constant may be written

2_'国内'

or

kanji_"標準"

where `kanji` is an integer named constant with the value 2. We note that, in this case, the kind type parameter exceptionally *precedes* the constant. This is necessary in order to enable compilers to parse statements simply.

There is no requirement on a processor to provide more than one kind of character, and the standard does not require any particular relationship between the kind parameter values and the character sets and the number of bytes needed to represent them. In fact, all that is required is that each kind of character set includes a blank character. As for the other data types, the `kind` function gives the actual value of the kind type parameter, as in

kind('ASCII')

Non-default characters are permitted in comments.

2.6.5 Logical literal constants

The fifth type of literal constant is the *logical literal constant*. The default kind has one of two values, `.true.` and `.false.`. These logical constants are normally used only to initialize logical variables to their required values, as we shall see in Section 3.6.

The default kind has a kind parameter value which is processor dependent. The actual value is available as `kind(.true.)`. As for the other intrinsic types, the kind parameter may be specified by an integer constant following an underscore, as in

.false._1
.true._long

Non-default logical kinds are useful for storing logical arrays compactly; we defer further discussion until Section 6.17.

2.7 Names

A Fortran program references many different entities by name. Such names must consist of between 1 and 31 alphanumeric characters (letters, underscores, and numerals) of which the first must be a letter. There are no other restrictions on the names; in particular there are no reserved words in Fortran. We thus see that valid names are, for example,

```
a
a_thing
x1
mass
q123
real
time_of_flight
```

and invalid names are

```
1a              First character is not alphabetic
a thing         Contains a blank
$sign           Contains a non-alphanumeric character
```

Within the constraints of the syntax, it is important for program clarity to choose names that have a clear significance — these are known as *mnemonic names*. Examples are day, month, and year, for variables to store the calendar date.

The use of names to refer to constants, already met in Section 2.6.1, will be fully described in Section 7.4.

2.8   Scalar variables of intrinsic type

We have seen in the section on literal constants that there exist five different intrinsic data types. Each of these types may have variables too. The simplest way by which a variable may be declared to be of a particular type is by specifying its name in a *type declaration statement* such as

```
integer   :: i
real      :: a
complex   :: current
logical   :: pravda
character :: letter
```

Here all the variables have default kind, and letter has default length, which is 1. Explicit requirements may also be specified through *type parameters*, as in the examples

```
integer(kind=4)              :: i
real(kind=long)              :: a
character(len=20, kind=1)    :: english_word
character(len=20, kind=kanji) :: kanji_word
```

Character is the only type to have two parameters, and here the two character variables each have length 20. Where appropriate, just one of the parameters may be specified, leaving the other to take its default value, as in the cases

```
character(kind=kanji) :: kanji_letter
character(len=20)     :: english_word
```

The shorter forms

```
integer(4)             :: i
real(long)             :: a
character(20, 1)       :: english_word
character(20, kanji)   :: kanji_word
character(20)          :: english_word
```

are available, but note that

```
character(kanji) :: kanji_letter        ! Beware
```

is not an abbreviation for

```
character(kind=kanji) :: kanji_letter
```

because a single unnamed parameter is taken as the length parameter.

2.9   Derived data types

When programming, it is often useful to be able to manipulate objects that are more sophisticated than those of the intrinsic types. Imagine, for instance, that we wished to specify objects representing persons. Each person in our application is distinguished by a name, an age, and an identification number. Fortran allows us to define a corresponding data type in the following fashion:

```
type person
   character(len=10) :: name
   real              :: age
   integer           :: id
end type person
```

This is the *definition* of the type. A scalar object of such a type is called a *structure*. In order to create a structure of that type, we write an appropriate type declaration statement, such as

```
type(person) :: you
```

The scalar variable you is then a composite object of type person containing three separate components, one corresponding to the name, another to the age, and a third to the identification number. As will be described in Sections 3.8 and 3.9, a variable such as you may appear in expressions and assignments involving other variables or constants of the same or different types. In addition, each of the components of the variable may be referenced individually using the *component selector* character percent (%). The identification number of you would, for instance, be accessed as

```
you%id
```

and this quantity is an integer variable which could appear in an expression such as

```
you%id + 9
```

Similarly, if there were a second object of the same type:

```
type(person) :: me
```

the differences in ages could be established by writing

```
you%age - me%age
```

It will be shown in Section 3.8 how a meaning can be given to an expression such as

```
you - me
```

Just as the intrinsic data types have associated literal constants, so too may literal constants of derived type be specified. Their form is the name of the type followed by the constant values of the components, in order and enclosed in parentheses. Thus, the constant

```
person( 'Smith', 23.5, 2541)
```

may be written assuming the derived type defined at the beginning of this section, and could be *assigned* to a variable of the same type:

```
you = person( 'Smith', 23.5, 2541)
```

Any such *structure constructor* can appear only after the definition of the type.

A derived type may have a component that is of a previously defined derived type. This is illustrated in Figure 2.1. A variable of type triangle may be declared thus

```
type(triangle) :: t
```

and t has components t%a, t%b, and t%c all of type point, and t%a has components t%a%x and t%a%y of type real.

Figure 2.1

```
type point
   real :: x, y
end type point
type triangle
   type(point) :: a, b, c
end type triangle
```

2.10   Arrays of intrinsic type

Another compound object supported by Fortran is the *array*. An array consists of a rectangular set of elements, all of the same type and type parameters. There are a number of ways in which arrays may be declared; for the moment we shall consider only the declaration of arrays of fixed sizes. To declare an array named a of 10 real elements, we add the dimension attribute to the type declaration statement thus:

```
real, dimension(10) :: a
```

The successive elements of the array are a(1), a(2), a(3), ..., a(10). The number of elements of an array is called its *size*. Each array element is a scalar.

Many problems require a more elaborate declaration than one in which the first element is designated 1, and it is possible in Fortran to declare a lower as well as an upper *bound*:

```
real, dimension(-10:5) :: vector
```

This is a vector of 16 elements, vector(-10), vector(-9), ..., vector(5). We thus see that whereas we always need to specify the upper bound, the lower bound is optional, and by default has the value 1.

An array may extend in more than one dimension, and Fortran allows up to seven dimensions to be specified. For instance

```
real, dimension(5,4) :: b
```

declares an array with two dimensions, and

```
real, dimension(-10:5, -20:-1, 0:1, -1:0, 2, 2, 2) :: grid
```

declares seven dimensions, the first four with explicit lower bounds. It may be seen that the size of this second array is

$$16 \times 20 \times 2 \times 2 \times 2 \times 2 \times 2 = 10240,$$

and that arrays of many dimensions can thus place large demands on the memory of a computer. The number of dimensions of an array is known as its *rank*. Thus, grid has a rank of seven. Scalars are regarded as having rank zero. The number of elements along a dimension of an array is known as the *extent* in that dimension. Thus, grid has extents 16, 20, ...

The sequence of extents is known as the *shape*. For example, grid has the shape $(16, 20, 2, 2, 2, 2, 2)$.

A derived type may contain an array component. For example, the following type

```
type triplet
   real                :: u
   real, dimension(3)  :: du
   real, dimension(3,3) :: d2u
end type triplet
```

might be used to hold the value of a variable in three dimensions and the values of its first and second derivatives. If t is of type triplet, t%du and t%d2u are arrays of type real.

Some statements treat the elements of an array one by one in a special order which we call the *array element order*. It is obtained by counting most rapidly in the early dimensions. Thus, the elements of grid in array element order are

```
grid(-10, -20, 0, -1, 1, 1, 1)
grid( -9, -20, 0, -1, 1, 1, 1)
    :
grid(  5,  -1, 1,  0, 2, 2, 2)
```

This is illustrated for an array of two dimensions in Figure 2.2. Most implementations actually store arrays in contiguous storage in array element order, but we emphasize that the standard does not require this.

Figure 2.2 The ordering of elements in the array b(5,4).

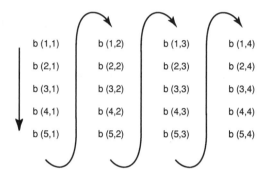

We reference an individual element of an array by specifying, as in the examples above, its *subscript* values. In the examples we used integer constants, but in general each subscript may be formed of a *scalar integer expression*, that is, any arithmetic expression whose value is scalar and of type integer. Each subscript must be within the corresponding ranges defined in the array declaration and the number of subscripts must equal the rank. Examples are

```
a(1)
a(i*j)            ! i and j are of type integer
a(nint(x+3.))     ! x is of type real
t%d2u(i+1,j+2)    ! t is of derived type triplet
```

where nint is an intrinsic function to convert a real value to the nearest integer (see Section 8.3.1). In addition subarrays, called *sections*, may be referenced by specifying a range for one or more subscripts. The following are examples of array sections:

```
a(i:j)            ! Rank-one array of size j-i+1
b(k, 1:n)         ! Rank-one array of size n
c(1:i, 1:j, k)    ! Rank-two array with extents i and j
```

We describe array sections in more detail in Section 6.13. An array section is itself an array, but its individual elements must not be accessed through the section designator. Thus, b(k, 1:n)(1) cannot be written; it must be expressed as b(k, 1).
    A further form of subscript is shown in

```
a(ipoint)         ! ipoint is an integer array
```

where ipoint is an array of indices, pointing to array elements. It may thus be seen that a(ipoint), which identifies as many elements of a as ipoint has elements, is an example of another *array-valued object*, and ipoint is referred to as a *vector subscript*. This will be met in greater detail in Section 6.13.

It is often convenient to be able to define an array constant. In Fortran, a rank-one array may be constructed as a list of elements enclosed between the tokens (/ and /). A simple example is

```
(/ 1, 2, 3, 5, 10 /)
```

which is an array of rank one and size five. To obtain a series of values, the individual values may be defined by an expression that depends on an integer variable having values in a range, with an optional stride. Thus, the constructor

```
(/1, 2, 3, 4, 5/)
```

can be written as

```
(/ (i, i = 1,5) /)
```

and

```
(/2, 4, 6, 8/)
```

as

```
(/ (i, i = 2,8,2) /)
```

and

```
(/ 1.1, 1.2, 1.3, 1.4, 1.5 /)
```

as

```
(/ (i*0.1, i=11,15) /)
```

An array constant of rank greater than one may be constructed by using the function reshape (see Section 8.13.3) to reshape a rank-one array constant.

A full description of array constructors is reserved for Section 6.16.

2.11 Character substrings

It is possible to build arrays of characters, just as it is possible to build arrays of any other type:

```
character, dimension(80) :: line
```

declares an array, called line, of 80 elements, each one character in length. Each character may be addressed by the usual reference, line(i) for example. In this case, however, a more appropriate declaration might be

```
character(len=80) :: line
```

which declares a scalar data object of 80 characters. These may be referenced individually or in groups using a *substring* notation

```
line(i:j)    ! i and j are of type integer
```

which references all the characters from i to j in line. The colon is used to separate the two substring subscripts, which may be any scalar integer expressions. The colon is obligatory in substring references, so that referencing a single character requires line(i:i). There are default values for the substring subscripts. If the lower one is omitted, the value 1 is assumed; if the upper one is omitted, a value corresponding to the character length is assumed. Thus,

```
line(:i)    is equivalent to line(1:i)
line(i:)    is equivalent to line(i:80)
line(:)     is equivalent to line or line(1:80)
```

If i is greater than j in line(i:j), the value is a zero-sized string.

We may now combine the length declaration with the array declaration to build arrays of character objects of specified length, as in

```
character(len=80), dimension(60) :: page
```

which might be used to define storage for the characters of a whole page, with 60 elements of an array, each of length 80. To reference the line j on a page we may write page(j), and to reference character i on that line we could combine the array subscript and character substring notations into

```
page(j)(i:i)
```

A substring of a character constant or of a structure component may also be formed:

```
'ABCDEFGHIJKLMNOPQRSTUVWXYZ'(j:j)
you%name(1:2)
```

At this point we must note a limitation associated with character variables, namely that character variables must have a declared maximum length, making it impossible to manipulate character variables of variable length, unless they are defined appropriately as of a derived data type.[3] Nevertheless, this data type is adequate for most character manipulation applications.

2.12 Objects and subobjects

We have seen that derived types may have components that are arrays, as in

```
type triplet
   real, dimension(3) :: vertex
end type triplet
```

and arrays may be of derived type as in the example

---

[3]But see first paragraph of Section 1.6.

```
type(triplet), dimension(10) :: t
```

A single structure (for example, t(2)) is always regarded as a scalar, but it may have a component (for example, t(2)%vertex) that is an array. Derived types may have components of other derived types.

An object referenced by an unqualified name (up to 31 alphanumeric characters) is called a *named object* and is not part of a bigger object. Its subobjects have *designators* that consist of the name of the object followed by one or more qualifiers (for example, t(1:7) and t(1)%vertex). Each successive qualifier specifies a part of the object specified by the name or designator that precedes it.

Because of these possibilities, the terms *array* and *variable* are now used with a more general meaning than in Fortran 77. The term 'array' is used for any object that is not scalar, including an array section or an array-valued component of a structure. The term 'variable' is used for any named object that is not specified to be a constant and for any part of such an object, including array elements, array sections, structure components, and substrings.

2.13 Pointers

In everyday language, nouns are often used in a way that makes their meaning precise only because of the context. 'The chairman said that ...' will be understood precisely by the reader who knows that the context is the Fortran Committee developing Fortran 90 and that its chairman was then Jeanne Adams.

Similarly, in a computer program it can be very useful to be able to use a name that can be made to refer to different objects during execution of the program. One example is the multiplication of a vector by a sequence of square matrices. We might write code that calculates

$$y_i = \sum_{j=1}^{n} a_{ij} x_j, \quad i = 1, 2, \ldots, n$$

from the vector $x_j, j = 1, 2, \ldots, n$. In order to use this to calculate

$$BCz$$

we might first make x refer to z and A refer to C, thereby using our code to calculate $y = Cz$, then make x refer to y and A refer to B so that our code calculates the result vector we finally want.

An object that can be made to refer to other objects in this way is called a *pointer*, and must be declared with the pointer attribute, for example

```
real, pointer              :: son
real, pointer, dimension(:)    :: x, y
real, pointer, dimension(:,:) :: a
```

In the case of an array, only the rank (number of dimensions) is declared, and the bounds (and hence shape) are taken from that of the object to which it points. Given such a declaration, the compiler arranges storage for a descriptor that will later hold the address of the actual object (known as the *target*) and holds, if it is an array, its bounds and strides.

Besides pointing to existing variables, a pointer may be made explicitly to point at nothing:

```
nullify (son, x, y, a)    ! Further details are in Section 6.5.4
```

or may be given fresh storage by an `allocate` statement such as

```
allocate (son, x(10), y(-10:10), a(n, n))
```

In the case of arrays, the lower and upper bounds are specified just as for the `dimension` attribute (Section 2.10) except that any scalar integer expression is permitted. Permitting such expressions remedies one of the major deficiencies of Fortran 77, namely that areas of only static storage may be defined, and we will discuss this use further in Section 6.5.

By default, pointers are initially undefined (see also final paragraph of Section 3.3). This is a very undesirable state since there is no way to test for it. However, it may be avoided by using the declaration:

```
real, pointer :: son => null()
```

and we recommend that this always be employed. Alternatively, pointers may be defined as soon as they come into scope by execution of a nullify statement or a pointer assignment.

Components of derived types are permitted to have the pointer attribute. This enables a major application of pointers: the construction of linked lists. As a simple example, we might decide to hold a sparse vector as a chain of variables of the type shown in Figure 2.3, which allows us to access the entries one by one; given

```
type(entry), pointer :: chain
```

where `chain` is a scalar of this type and holds a chain that is of length two, its entries are `chain%index` and `chain%next%index`, and `chain%next%next` will have been nullified. Additional entries may be created when necessary by an appropriate allocate statement. We defer the details to Section 3.12.

Figure 2.3

```
      type entry
         real                 :: value
         integer              :: index
         type(entry), pointer :: next
      end type entry
```

When a pointer is of derived type and a component such as `chain%index` is selected, it is actually a component of the pointer's target that is selected.

A subobject is not a pointer unless it has a final component selector for the name of a pointer component, for example, `chain%next`.

Pointers will be discussed in detail in later chapters (especially Sections 3.12, 5.7.1, 6.14, 6.15, 7.5.3, 7.5.4, and 8.2) and a major application is given in Appendix C.

2.14 Summary

In this chapter, we have introduced the elements of the Fortran language. The character set has been listed, and the manner in which sequences of characters form literal constants and names explained. In this context, we have encountered the five intrinsic data types defined in Fortran, and seen how each data type has corresponding literal constants and named objects. We have seen how derived types may be constructed from the intrinsic types. We have introduced one method by which arrays may be declared, and seen how their elements may be referenced by subscript expressions. The concepts of the array section, character substring, and pointer have been presented, and some important terms defined. In the following chapter we shall see how these elements may be combined into expressions and statements, Fortran's equivalents of 'phrases' and 'sentences'.

With respect to Fortran 77, there are many changes in this area: the larger character set; a new source form; the significance of blanks; the parameterization of the intrinsic types; the binary, octal, and hexadecimal constants; the ability to obtain a desired precision and range; quotes as well as apostrophes as character constant delimiters; longer names; derived data types; new array subscript notations; array constructors; and last, but not least, pointers. Together they represent a substantial improvement in the ease of use and power of the language.

2.15 Exercises

1. For each of the following assertions, state whether it is true, false, or not determined, according to the Fortran collating sequences:

```
b is less than m
8 is less than 2
* is greater than T
$ is less than /
blank is greater than A
blank is less than 6
```

2. Which of the Fortran lines in Figure 2.4 are correctly written according to the requirements of the Fortran source form? Which ones contain commentary? Which lines are initial lines and which are continuation lines?

Figure 2.4

```
      x = y
3     a = b+c ! add
      word = 'string'
      a = 1.0; b = 2.0
      a = 15. ! initialize a; b = 22. ! and b
      song = "Life is just&
         & a bowl of cherries"
      chide = 'Waste not,
         want not!'
0     c(3:4) = 'up"
```

3. Classify the following literal constants according to the five intrinsic data types of Fortran. Which are not legal literal constants?

```
-43                 'word'
4.39                1.9-4
0.0001e+20          'stuff & nonsense'
4 9                 (0.,1.)
(1.e3,2)            'I can''t'
'(4.3e9, 6.2)'      .true._1
e5                  'shouldn' 't'
1_2                 "O.K."
z10                 z'10'
```

4. Which of the following names are legal Fortran names?

```
name        name32
quotient    123
a182c3      no-go
stop!       burn_
no_go       long__name
```

5. What are the first, tenth, eleventh, and last elements of the following arrays?

```
real, dimension(11)       :: a
real, dimension(0:11)     :: b
real, dimension(-11:0)    :: c
real, dimension(10,10)    :: d
real, dimension(5,9)      :: e
real, dimension(5,0:1,4)  :: f
```

Write an array constructor of eleven integer elements.

6. Given the array declaration

```
character(len=10), dimension(0:5,3) :: c
```

which of the following subobject designators are legal?

```
c(2,3)          c(4:3)(2,1)
c(6,2)          c(5,3)(9:9)
c(0,3)          c(2,1)(4:8)
c(4,3)(:)       c(3,2)(0:9)
c(5)(2:3)       c(5:6)
c(5,3)(9)       c(,)
```

7. Write derived type definitions appropriate for:

 a) a vehicle registration;

 b) a circle;

 c) a book (title, author, and number of pages).

Give an example of a derived type constant for each one.

8. Given the declaration for t in Section 2.12, which of the following objects and subobjects are arrays?

```
t                  t(4)%vertex(1)
t(10)              t(5:6)
t(1)%vertex        t(5:5)
```

9. Write specifications for these entities:

  a) an integer variable inside the range -10^{20} to 10^{20};

  b) a real variable with a minimum of 12 decimal digits of precision and a range of 10^{-100} to 10^{100};

  c) a Kanji character variable on a processor that supports Kanji with kind=2.

3. Expressions and assignments

3.1 Introduction

We have seen in the previous chapter how we are able to build the 'words' of Fortran — the constants, keywords, and names — from the basic elements of the character set. In this chapter we shall discover how these entities may be further combined into 'phrases' or *expressions*, and how these, in turn, may be combined into 'sentences' or *statements*.

In an expression, we describe a computation that is to be carried out by the computer. The result of the computation may then be assigned to a variable. A sequence of assignments is the way in which we specify, step by step, the series of individual computations to be carried out, in order to arrive at the desired result. There are separate sets of rules for expressions and assignments, depending on whether the operands in question are numeric, logical, character, or derived in type, and whether they are scalars or arrays. There are also separate rules for pointer assignments. We shall discuss each set of rules in turn, including a description of the relational expressions which produce a result of type logical and are needed in control statements (see next chapter). To simplify the initial discussion, we commence by considering expressions and assignments that are intrinsically defined and involve neither arrays nor entities of derived data types.

An expression in Fortran is formed of operands and operators, combined in a way which follows the rules of Fortran syntax. A simple expression involving a *dyadic* (or binary) operator has the form

operand *operator* operand

an example being

    x+y

and a unary or *monadic* operator has the form

operator operand

an example being

    -y

The operands may be constants, variables, or functions (see Chapter 5), and an expression may itself be used as an operand. In this way, we can build up more complicated expressions such as

>   operand *operator* operand *operator* operand

where consecutive operands are separated by a single operator. Each operand must have a defined value and the result must be mathematically defined; for example, raising a negative real value to a real power is not permitted.

The rules of Fortran state that the parts of expressions without parentheses are evaluated successively from left to right for operators of equal precedence, with the exception of ** (see Section 3.2). If it is necessary to evaluate part of an expression, or *subexpression,* before another, parentheses may be used to indicate which subexpression should be evaluated first. In

>   operand *operator* (operand *operator* operand)

the subexpression in parentheses will be evaluated, and the result used as an operand to the first operator.

If an expression or subexpression has no parentheses, the processor is permitted to evaluate an equivalent expression, that is an expression that always has the same value apart, possibly, from the effects of numerical round-off. For example, if a, b, and c are real variables, the expression

```
a/b/c
```

might be evaluated as

```
a/(b*c)
```

on a processor that can multiply much faster than it can divide. Usually, such changes are welcome to the programmer since the program runs faster, but when they are not (for instance, because they would lead to more round-off) parentheses should be inserted because the processor is required to respect them.

If two operators immediately follow each other, as in

>   operand *operator operator* operand

the only possible interpretation is that the second operator is unary. Thus, there is a general rule that a binary operator must not follow immediately after another operator.

3.2   Scalar numeric expressions

A *numeric expression* is an expression whose operands are one of the three numeric types — integer, real, and complex — and whose operators are

>   **   exponentiation
>   * /   multiplication, division
>   + -   addition, subtraction

These operators are known as *numeric intrinsic* operators, and are listed here in their order of precedence. In the absence of parentheses, exponentiations will be carried out before multiplications and divisions, and these before additions and subtractions.

We note that the minus sign (–) and the plus sign (+) can be used as a unary operators, as in

```
-tax
```

Because it is not permitted in ordinary mathematical notation, a unary minus or plus must not follow immediately after another operator. When this is needed, as for x^{-y}, parentheses must be placed around the operator and its operand:

```
x** (-y)
```

The type and kind type parameter of the result of a unary operation are those of the operand.

The exception to the left-to-right rule noted in Section 3.1 concerns exponentiations. Whereas the expression

```
-a+b+c
```

will be evaluated from left to right as

```
((-a)+b)+c
```

the expression

```
a**b**c
```

will be evaluated as

```
a** (b**c)
```

For integer data, the result of any division will be truncated towards zero, that is to the integer value whose magnitude is equal to or just less than the magnitude of the exact result. Thus, the result of

```
 6/3   is    2
 8/3   is    2
-8/3   is   -2
```

This fact must always be borne in mind whenever integer divisions are written. Similarly, the result of

```
2**3   is   8
```

whereas the result of

```
2** (-3)   is   1/(2**3)
```

which is zero.

The rules of Fortran allow a numeric expression to contain numeric operands of differing types or kind type parameters. This is known as a *mixed-mode expression*. Except when raising a real or complex value to an integer power, the object of the weaker (or simpler) of the two data types will be converted, or *coerced*, into the type of the stronger one. The result will also be that of the stronger type. If, for example, we write

```
a*i
```

when a is of type real and i is of type integer, then i will be converted to a real data type before the multiplication is performed, and the result of the computation will also be of type real. The rules are summarized for each possible combination for the operations +, −, *, and / in Table 3.1, and for the operation ** in Table 3.2. The functions real and cmplx that they reference are defined in Section 8.3.1. In both Tables, I stands for integer, R for real, and C for complex.

Table 3.1. Type of result of a .op. b, where .op. is +, −, *, or /.

Type of a	Type of b	Value of a used	Value of b used	Type of result
I	I	a	b	I
I	R	real(a,kind(b))	b	R
I	C	cmplx(a,0,kind(b))	b	C
R	I	a	real(b,kind(a))	R
R	R	a	b	R
R	C	cmplx(a,0,kind(b))	b	C
C	I	a	cmplx(b,0,kind(a))	C
C	R	a	cmplx(b,0,kind(a))	C
C	C	a	b	C

Table 3.2. Type of result of $a**b$.

Type of a	Type of b	Value of a used	Value of b used	Type of result
I	I	a	b	I
I	R	real(a,kind(b))	b	R
I	C	cmplx(a,0,kind(b))	b	C
R	I	a	b	R
R	R	a	b	R
R	C	cmplx(a,0,kind(b))	b	C
C	I	a	b	C
C	R	a	cmplx(b,0,kind(a))	C
C	C	a	b	C

If both operands are of type integer, the kind type parameter of the result is that of the operand with the greater decimal exponent range, or is processor dependent if the kinds differ but the decimal exponent ranges are the same. If both operands are of type real or complex, the kind type parameter of the result is that of the operand with the greater decimal precision, or is processor dependent if the kinds differ but the decimal precisions are the same. If one operand is of type integer and the other is of real or complex, the type parameter of the result is that of the real or complex operand.

Note that a literal constant in a mixed-mode expression is held to its own precision, which may be less than that of the expression. For example, given a variable a of kind long (Section 2.6.2), the result of a/1.7 will be less precise than that of a/1.7_long.

In the case of raising a complex value to a complex power, the principal value[1] is taken.

3.3 Defined and undefined variables

In the course of the explanations in this and the following chapters, we shall often refer to a variable becoming *defined* or *undefined*. In the previous chapter, we showed how a scalar variable may be called into existence by a statement like

```
real :: speed
```

In this simple case, the variable speed has, at the beginning of the execution of the program, no defined value. It is undefined. No attempt must be made to reference its value since it has none. A common way in which it might become defined is for it to be assigned a value:

```
speed = 2.997
```

After the execution of such an *assignment statement* it has a value, and that value may be referenced, for instance in an expression:

```
speed*0.5
```

For a compound object, all of its subobjects that are not pointers must be individually defined before the object as a whole is regarded as defined. Thus, an array is said to be defined only when each of its elements is defined, an object of a derived data type is defined only when each of its non-pointer components is defined, and a character variable is defined only when each of its characters is defined.

A variable that is defined does not necessarily retain its state of definition throughout the execution of a program. As we shall see in Chapter 5, a variable that is local to a single subprogram usually becomes undefined when control is returned from that subprogram. In certain circumstances, it is even possible that a single array element becomes undefined and this causes the array considered as a whole to become undefined; a similar rule holds for entities of derived data type and for character variables.

A means to specify the initial value of a variable is explained in Section 7.5.

In the case of a pointer, the pointer association status may be *undefined*, *associated* with a target, or *disassociated*, which means that it is not associated with a target but has a definite status that may be tested by the function associated (Section 8.2). Even though a pointer is associated with a target, the target itself may be defined or undefined. A means to specify the initial status of disassociated is provided (see Section 7.5.3).

---

[1]The principal value of a^b is $\exp(b(\log|a| + i\arg a))$, with $-\pi < \arg a \leq \pi$.

3.4   Scalar numeric assignment

The general form of a scalar numeric assignment is

> *variable* = *expr*

where *variable* is a scalar numeric variable and *expr* is a scalar numeric expression. If *expr* is not of the same type or kind as *variable*, it will be converted to that type and kind before the assignment is carried out, according to the set of rules given in Table 3.3 (the function int is defined in Section 8.3.1).

Table 3.3. Numeric conversion for assignment statement *variable* = *expr*.

Type of *variable*	Value assigned
integer	int(*expr*, kind(*variable*))
real	real(*expr*, kind(*variable*))
complex	cmplx(*expr*, kind=kind(*variable*))

We note that if the type of *variable* is integer but *expr* is not, then the assignment will result in a loss of precision unless *expr* happens to have an integral value. Similarly, assigning a real expression to a real variable of a kind with less precision will also cause a loss of precision to occur, and the assignment of a complex quantity to a non-complex variable involves the loss of the imaginary part. Thus, the values in i and a following the assignments

```
i = 7.3                  ! i of type default integer
a = (4.01935, 2.12372)   ! a of type default real
```

are 7 and 4.01935, respectively. Also, if a literal constant is assigned to a variable of greater precision, the result will have the accuracy of the constant. For example, given a variable a of kind long (Section 2.6.2), the result of a = 1.7 will be less precise than that of a = 1.7_long.

3.5   Scalar relational operators

It is possible in Fortran to test whether the value of one numeric expression bears a certain relation to that of another, and similarly for character expressions. The relational operators are

```
.lt. or  <     less than
.le. or  <=    less than or equal
.eq. or  ==    equal
.ne. or  /=    not equal
.gt. or  >     greater than
.ge. or  >=    greater than or equal
```

If either or both of the expressions are complex, only the operators == and /= (or .eq. and .ne.) are available.

The result of such a comparison is one of the default logical values .true. or .false., and we shall see in the next chapter how such tests are important in controlling the flow of a program. Examples of relational expressions (for i and j of type integer, a and b of type real, and char1 of type default character) are

`i < 0`	integer relational expression
`a < b`	real relational expression
`a+b > i-j`	mixed-mode relational expression
`char1 == 'Z'`	character relational expression

In the third expression above, we note that the two components are of different numeric types. In this case, and whenever either or both of the two components consist of numeric expressions, the rules state that the components are to be evaluated separately, and converted to the type and kind of their sum before the comparison is made. Thus, a relational expression such as

```
a+b <= i-j
```

will be evaluated by converting the result of (i-j) to type real.

For character comparisons, the kinds must be the same and the letters are compared from the left until a difference is found or the strings are found to be identical. If the lengths differ, the shorter one is regarded as being padded with blanks[2] on the right. Two zero-sized strings are considered to be identical.

No other form of mixed-mode relational operator is intrinsically available, though such an operator may be defined (Section 3.8). The numeric operators take precedence over the relational operators.

3.6 Scalar logical expressions and assignments

Logical constants, variables, and functions may appear as operands in logical expressions. The logical operators, in decreasing order of precedence, are:

unary operator:
      .not.   logical negation

binary operators:
`.and.`	logical intersection
`.or.`	logical union
`.eqv. and .neqv.`	logical equivalence and non-equivalence

If we assume a logical declaration of the form

```
logical i,j,k,l
```

then the following are valid logical expressions:

---

[2]Here and elsewhere, the blank padding character used for a non-default type is processor dependent.

```
.not.j
j .and. k
i .or. l .and.  .not.j
( .not.k .and. j .neqv. .not.l) .or. i
```

In the first expression we note the use of .not. as a unary operator. In the third expression, the rules of precedence imply that the subexpression l.and..not.j will be evaluated first, and the result combined with i. In the last expression, the two subexpressions .not.k.and.j and .not.l will be evaluated and compared for non-equivalence. The result of the comparison, .true. or .false., will be combined with i.

The kind type parameter of the result is that of the operand for .not., and for the others is that of the operands if they have the same kind or processor dependent otherwise.

We note that the .or. operator is an inclusive operator; the .neqv. operator provides an exclusive logical or (a.and..not.b .or. .not.a.and.b).

The result of any logical expression is the value true or false, and this value may then be assigned to a logical variable such as element 3 of the logical array flag in the example

```
flag(3) = ( .not. k .eqv. l) .or. j
```

The kind type parameter values of the variable and expression need not be identical.

A logical variable may be set to a predetermined value by an assignment statement:

```
flag(1) = .true.
flag(2) = .false.
```

In the foregoing examples, all the operands and results were of type logical — no other data type is allowed to participate in an intrinsic logical operation or assignment.

The results of several relational expressions may be combined into a logical expression, and assigned, as in

```
real     :: a, b, x, y
logical :: cond
:
cond = a>b .or. x<0.0 .and. y>1.0
```

where we note the precedence of the relational operators over the logical operators. If the value of such a logical expression can be determined without evaluating a subexpression, a processor is permitted not to evaluate the subexpression. An example is

```
i<=10 .and. ary(i)==0
```

when i has the value 11. However, the programmer must not rely on such behaviour. For example, when ary has size 10, an out-of-bounds subscript might be referenced if the processor chooses to evaluate the right-hand subexpression before the left-hand one. We return to this topic in Section 5.10.1.

3.7 Scalar character expressions and assignments

The only intrinsic operator for character expressions is the concatenation operator //, which has the effect of combining two character operands into a single character result. For example, the result of concatenating the two character constants AB and CD, written as

```
'AB'//'CD'
```

is the character string ABCD. The operands must have the same kind parameter values, but may be character variables, constants, or functions. For instance, if word1 and word2 are both of default kind and length 4, and contain the character strings LOOP and HOLE, respectively, the result of

```
word1(4:4)//word2(2:4)
```

is the string POLE.

The length of the result of a concatenation is the sum of the lengths of the operands. Thus, the length of the result of

```
word1//word2//'S'
```

is 9, which is the length of the string LOOPHOLES.

The result of a character expression may be assigned to a character variable of the same kind. Assuming the declarations

```
character(len=4) :: char1, char2
character(len=8) :: result
```

we may write

```
char1 = 'any '
char2 = 'book'
result = char1//char2
```

In this case, result will now contain the string any book. We note in these examples that the lengths of the left- and right-hand sides of the three assignments are in each case equal. If, however, the length of the result of the right-hand side is shorter than the length of the left-hand side, then the result is placed in the left-most part of the left-hand side and the rest is filled with blank characters. Thus, in

```
character(len=5) :: fill
fill(1:4) = 'AB'
```

fill(1:4) will have the value ABbb (where b stands for a blank character). The value of fill(5:5) remains undefined, that is, it contains no specific value and should not be used in an expression. As a consequence, fill is also undefined. On the other hand, when the left-hand side is shorter than the result of the right-hand side, the right-hand end of the result is truncated. The result of

```
character(len=5) :: trunc8
trunc8 = 'TRUNCATE'
```

is to place in `trunc8` the character string `TRUNC`. If a left-hand side is of zero length, no assignment takes place.

The left- and right-hand sides of an assignment may overlap. In such a case, it is always the old values that are used in the right-hand side expression. For example, the assignment

```
result(3:5) = result(1:3)
```

is valid and if `result` began with the value `ABCDEFGH`, it would be left with the value `ABABCFGH`.

Other means of manipulating characters and strings of characters, via intrinsic functions, are described in Sections 8.5 and 8.6.

3.8   Structure constructors and scalar defined operators

No operators for derived types are automatically available, but a structure may be constructed from expressions for its components, just as a constant structure may be constructed from constants (Section 2.9). The general form of a *structure constructor* is

type-name (*expr-list*)

where the *expr-list* specifies the values of the components. For example, given the type

```
type string
   integer          :: length
   character(len=10) :: value
end type string
```

and the variables

```
character(len=4) :: char1, char2
```

the following is a value of type `string`:

```
string(8, char1//char2)
```

Each expression in *expr-list* corresponds to a component of the structure; if it is not a pointer component, the value is assigned to the component under the rules of intrinsic assignment; if it is a pointer component, the expression must be a valid target for it,[3] as in a pointer assignment statement (Section 3.12).

When a programmer defines a derived type and wishes operators to be available, he or she must define the operators, too. For a binary operator this is done by writing a function, with two intent `in` arguments, that specifies how the result depends on the operands, and an interface block that associates the function with the operator token (functions, intent, and interface blocks will be explained fully in Chapter 5). For example, given the type

```
type interval
   real :: lower, upper
end type interval
```

---

[3] In particular, it must not be a constant.

that represents intervals of numbers between a lower and an upper bound, we may define addition by a module (Section 5.5) containing the procedure

```
function add_interval(a,b)
   type(interval)                :: add_interval
   type(interval), intent(in) :: a, b
   add_interval%lower = a%lower + b%lower ! Production code
   add_interval%upper = a%upper + b%upper ! would allow for
end function add_interval                 ! roundoff.
```

and the interface block (Section 5.18)

```
interface operator(+)
   module procedure add_interval
end interface
```

This function would be invoked in an expression such as

```
y + z
```

to perform this programmer-defined add operation for scalar variables y and z of type interval. A unary operator is defined by an interface block and a function with one intent in argument.

The operator token may be any of the tokens used for the intrinsic operators or may be a sequence of up to 31 letters enclosed in decimal points other than .true. or .false. . An example is

```
.sum.
```

In this case, the header line of the interface block would be written as

```
interface operator(.sum.)
```

and the expression as

```
y.sum.z
```

If an intrinsic token is used, the number of arguments must be the same as for the intrinsic operation, the priority of the operation is as for the intrinsic operation, and a unary minus or plus must not follow immediately after another operator. Otherwise, it is of highest priority for defined unary operators and lowest priority for defined binary operators. The complete set of priorities is given in Table 3.4. Where another priority is required within an expression, parentheses must be used.

Retaining the intrinsic priorities is helpful both to the readability of expressions and to the efficiency with which a compiler can interpret them. For example, if + is used for set union and * for set intersection, we can interpret the expression

```
i*j + k
```

Table 3.4. Relative precedence of operators (in decreasing order).

Type of operation when intrinsic	Operator
—	monadic (unary) defined operator
Numeric	`**`
Numeric	`* or /`
Numeric	monadic `+ or –`
Numeric	dyadic `+ or –`
Character	`//`
Relational	`.eq. .ne. .lt. .le. .gt. .ge.`
	`== /= < <= > >=`
Logical	`.not.`
Logical	`.and.`
Logical	`.or.`
Logical	`.eqv. or .neqv.`
—	dyadic (binary) defined operator

for sets i, j, and k without difficulty.

If either of the intrinsic tokens .eq. and == is used, the definition applies to both tokens so that they are always equivalent. The same is true for the other equivalent pairs of relational operators.

Note that a defined unary operator not using an intrinsic token may follow immediately after another operator as in

```
y .sum. .inverse. x
```

Operators may be defined for any types of operands, except where there is an intrinsic operation for the operator and types. For example, we might wish to be able to add an interval number to an ordinary real, which can be done by adding the procedure

```
function add_interval_real(a,b)
    type(interval)            :: add_interval_real
    type(interval), intent(in) :: a
    real, intent(in)          :: b
    add_interval_real%lower = a%lower + b ! Production code would
    add_interval_real%upper = a%upper + b ! allow for roundoff.
end function add_interval_real
```

and changing the interface block to

```
interface operator(+)
    module procedure add_interval, add_interval_real
end interface
```

The result of a defined operation may have any type. The type of the result, as well as its value, must be specified by the function.

Note that an operation that is defined intrinsically cannot be redefined; thus in

```
real :: a, b, c
:
c = a + b
```

the meaning of the operation is always unambiguous.

3.9 Scalar defined assignments

Assignment of an expression of derived type to a variable of the same type is automatically available and takes place component by component. For example, if a is of the type `interval` defined at the start of Section 3.8, we may write

```
a = interval(0.0, 1.0)
```

(structure constructors were met in Section 3.8, too).

In other circumstances, however, we might wish to define a different action for an assignment involving an object of derived type, and indeed this is possible. An assignment may be redefined or another assignment may be defined by a subroutine with two arguments, the first having intent `out` or intent `inout` and corresponding to the variable and the second having intent `in` and corresponding to the expression (subroutines will also be dealt with fully in Chapter 5). In the case of an assignment involving an object of derived type and an object of a different type, such a definition must be provided. For example, assignment of reals to intervals and vice versa might be defined by a module containing the subroutines

```
subroutine real_from_interval(a,b)
    real, intent(out)            :: a
    type(interval), intent(in) :: b
    a = (b%lower + b%upper)/2
end subroutine real_from_interval
```

and

```
subroutine interval_from_real(a,b)
    type(interval), intent(out) :: a
    real, intent(in)             :: b
    a%lower = b
    a%upper = b
end subroutine interval_from_real
```

and the interface block

```
interface assignment(=)
    module procedure real_from_interval, interval_from_real
end interface
```

Given this, we may write

```
type(interval) :: a
a = 0.0
```

A defined assignment must not redefine the meaning of an intrinsic assignment for intrinsic types, that is an assignment between two objects of numeric type, of logical type, or of character type with the same kind parameter, but may redefine the meaning of an intrinsic assignment for two objects of the same derived type. For instance, for an assignment between two variables of the type string (Section 3.8) that copies only the relevant part of the character component, we might write

```
subroutine assign_string (left, right)
   type(string), intent(out) :: left
   type(string), intent(in)  :: right
   left%length = right%length
   left%value(1:left%length) = right%value(1:right%length)
end subroutine assign_string
```

Intrinsic assignment for a derived-type object always involves intrinsic assignment for all its non-pointer components, even if a component is of a derived type for which assignment has been redefined.

3.10   Array expressions

So far in this chapter, we have assumed that all the entities in an expression are scalar. However, any of the unary intrinsic operations may also be applied to an array to produce another array of the same shape (identical rank and extents, see Section 2.10) and having each element value equal to that of the operation applied to the corresponding element of the operand. Similarly, binary intrinsic operations may be applied to a pair of arrays of the same shape to produce an array of that shape, with each element value equal to that of the operation applied to corresponding elements of the operands. One of the operands to a binary operation may be a scalar, in which case the result is as if the scalar had been broadcast to an array of the same shape as the array operand. Given the array declarations

```
real, dimension(10,20) :: a,b
real, dimension(5)     :: v
```

the following are examples of array expressions:

```
a/b          ! Array of shape (10,20), with elements a(i,j)/b(i,j)
v+1.         ! Array of shape (5), with elements v(i)+1.0
5/v+a(1:5,5) ! Array of shape (5), with elements 5/v(i)+a(i,5)
a.eq.b       ! Logical array of shape (10,20), with elements
             ! .true. if a(i,j).eq.b(i,j), and .false. otherwise
```

Two arrays of the same shape are said to be *conformable* and a scalar is conformable with any array.

Note that the correspondence is by position in the extent and not by subscript value. For example,

```
a(2:9,5:10) + b(1:8,15:20)
```

has element values

```
a(i+1,j+4) + b(i,j+14), i=1,2,...,8, j=1,2,...,6
```

This may be represented pictorially as in Figure 3.1.

Figure 3.1 The sum of two array sections.

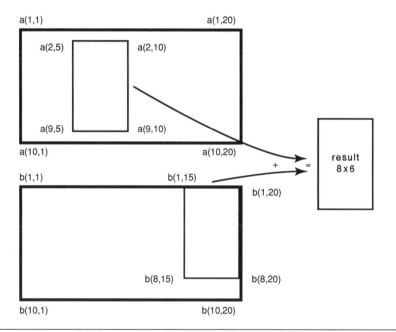

The order in which the scalar operations in any array expression are executed is not specified in the standard, thus enabling a compiler to arrange efficient execution on a vector or parallel computer.

Any scalar intrinsic operator may be applied in this way to arrays and array–scalar pairs. For derived operators, the programmer may define an elemental procedure with these properties (see Section 6.11). He or she may also define operators directly for certain ranks or pairs of ranks. For example, the type

```
type matrix
    real :: element
end type matrix
```

might be defined to have scalar operations that are identical to the operations for reals, but for arrays of ranks one and two the operator * defined to mean matrix multiplication. The type matrix would therefore be suitable for matrix arithmetic, whereas reals are not suitable because multiplication for real arrays is done element by element. This is further discussed in Section 6.7.

3.11   Array assignment

By intrinsic assignment, an array expression may be assigned to an array variable of the same shape, which is interpreted as if each element of the expression were assigned to the corresponding element of the variable. For example, with the declarations of the beginning of the last section, the assignment

```
a = a + 1.0
```

replaces a(i,j) by a(i,j)+1.0 for i = 1, 2, ... , 10 and j = 1, 2, ... , 20. Note that, as for expressions, the element correspondence is by position within the extent rather than by subscript value. This is illustrated by the example

```
a(1,11:15) = v      ! a(1,j+10) is assigned from
                    ! v(j), j=1,2,...,5
```

A scalar expression may be assigned to an array, in which case the scalar value is broadcast to all the array elements.

If the expression includes a reference to the array variable or to a part of it, the expression is interpreted as being fully evaluated before the assignment commences. For example, the statement

```
v(2:5) = v(1:4)
```

results in each element v(i) for i = 2, 3, 4, 5 having the value that v(i-1) had prior to the commencement of the assignment. This rule exactly parallels the rule for substrings that was explained in Section 3.7. The order in which the array elements are assigned is not specified by the standard, to allow optimizations.

Sets of numeric and mathematical intrinsic functions, whose results may be used as operands in scalar or array expressions and in assignments, are described in Sections 8.3 and 8.4.

If a defined assignment (Section 3.9) is defined by an elemental subroutine (Section 6.11), it may be used to assign a scalar value to an array or an array value to an array of the same shape. A separate subroutine may be provided for any particular combination of ranks and will override the elemental assignment. If there is no elemental defined assignment, intrinsic assignment is still available for those combinations of ranks for which there is no corresponding defined assignment. A form of array assignment expressed with the help of indices is provided (Section 6.9).

3.12   Pointers in expressions and assignments

A pointer may appear as a variable in the expressions and assignments that we have considered so far in this chapter, provided it has a valid association with a target. The target is accessed without any need for an explicit dereferencing symbol. In particular, if both sides of an assignment statement are pointers, data are copied from one target to the other target.

Sometimes the need arises for another sort of assignment. We may want the left-hand pointer to point to another target, rather than that its current target acquire fresh data. That is, we want the descriptor to be altered. This is called *pointer assignment* and takes place in a pointer assignment statement:

> *pointer* => *target*

where *pointer* is the name of a pointer or the designator of a structure component that is a pointer, and *target* is usually a variable but may also be a reference to a pointer-valued function (see Section 5.10). For example, the statements

```
x => z
a => c
```

have variables as targets and are needed for the first matrix multiplication of Section 2.13, in order to make x refer to z and a to refer to c. The statement

```
x => null()
```

nullifies x. Pointer assignment also takes place for a pointer component of a structure when the structure appears on the left-hand side of an ordinary assignment. For example, suppose we have used the type entry of Section 2.13 to construct a chain of entries and wish to add a fresh entry at the front. If first points to the first entry and current is a scalar pointer of type entry, the statements

```
allocate (current)
current = entry(new_value, new_index, first)
first => current
```

allocate a new entry and link it into the top of the chain. The assignment statement has the effect

```
current%next => first
```

and establishes the link. The pointer assignment statement gives first the new entry as its target without altering the old first entry. An ordinary assignment would be incorrect because the target would be copied, destroying the old first entry, corresponding to the component assignments

```
first%value = current%value    ! Components of the
first%index = current%index    ! old first are lost.
first%next => current%next
```

In the case where the chain began with length two and consisted of

```
first :      (1.0, 10, associated)
first%next : (2.0, 15, null)
```

following the execution of the first set of statements it would have length three and consist of

```
first :           (4.0, 16, associated)
first%next :      (1.0, 10, associated)
first%next%next : (2.0, 15, null)
```

If the *target* in a pointer assignment statement is a variable that is not itself a pointer or a subobject of a pointer target, it must have the target attribute. For example, the statement

```
real, dimension(10), target :: y
```

declares y to have the target attribute. Any non-pointer subobject of an object with the target attribute also has the target attribute. The target attribute is required for the purpose of code optimization by the compiler. It is very helpful to the compiler to know that a variable that is not a pointer or a target may not be accessed by a pointer target.

The target in a pointer assignment statement may be a subobject of a pointer target. For example, given the declaration

```
character(len=80), dimension(:), pointer :: page
```

and an appropriate association, the following are all permitted targets:

```
page, page(10), page(2:4), page(2)(3:15)
```

Note that it is sufficient for there to be a pointer at any level of component selection. For example, given the declaration

```
type(entry) :: node ! This has a pointer component next,
                    ! see Section 2.13.
```

and an appropriate association, node%next%value is a permitted target.

If the *target* in a pointer assignment statement is itself a pointer target, then a straightforward copy of the descriptor takes place. If the pointer association status is undefined or disassociated, this state is copied.

If the *target* is a pointer or a subobject of a pointer target, the new association is with that pointer's target and is not affected by any subsequent changes to its pointer association status. This is illustrated by the following example. The sequence

```
b => c    ! c has the target attribute
a => b
nullify (b)
```

will leave a still pointing to c.

The type, type parameters, and rank of the *pointer* and *target* in a pointer assignment statement must each be the same. If the *pointer* is an array, it takes its shape and bounds from the *target*. The bounds are as would be returned by the functions lbound and ubound (Section 8.12.2) for the target, which means that an array section or array expression is always taken to have the value 1 for a lower bound and the extent for the corresponding upper bound.

Fortran is unusual in not requiring a special character for a reference to a pointer target, but requiring one for distinguishing pointer assignment from ordinary assignment. The reason for this choice was the expectation that most engineering and scientific programs will refer to target data far more often than they change targets.

3.13 Summary

In this chapter, we have seen how scalar and array expressions of numeric, logical, character, and derived types may be formed, and how the corresponding assignments of the results may be made. The relational expressions and the use of pointers have also been presented. We now have the information required to write short sections of code forming a sequence of statements to be performed one after the other. In the following chapter we shall see how more complicated sequences, involving branching and iteration, may be built up.

3.14 Exercises

1. If all the variables are numeric scalars, which of the following are valid numeric expressions?

```
a+b              -c
a+-c             d+(-f)
(a+c)**(p+q)     (a+c)(p+q)
-(x+y)**i        4.((a-d)-(a+4.*x)+1)
```

2. In the following expressions, add the parentheses which correspond to Fortran's rules of precedence (assuming a, c-f are real scalars, i-n are logical scalars, and b is a logical array), for example

```
a+d**2/c      becomes      a+((d**2)/c)

c+4.*f
4.*g-a+d/2.
a**e**c**d
a*e-c**d/a+e
i .and. j .or. k
.not. l .or. .not. i .and. m .neqv. n
b(3).and.b(1).or.b(6).or..not.b(2)
```

3. What are the results of the following expressions?

```
3+4/2        6/4/2
3.*4**2      3.**3/2
-1.**2       (-1.)**3
```

4. A scalar character variable r has length eight. What are the contents of r after each of the following assignments?

```
r = 'ABCDEFGH'
r = 'ABCD'//'01234'
r(:7) = 'ABCDEFGH'
r(:6) = 'ABCD'
```

5. Which of the following logical expressions are valid if b is a logical array?

```
.not.b(1).and.b(2)      .or.b(1)
b(1).or..not.b(4)       b(2)(.and.b(3).or.b(4))
```

6. If all the variables are real scalars, which of the following relational expressions are valid?

```
d .le. c                 p .lt. t > 0
x-1 /= y                 x+y < 3 .or. > 4.
d.lt.c.and.3.0           q.eq.r .and. s>t
```

7. Write expressions to compute:

a) the perimeter of a square of side l;

b) the area of a triangle of base b and height h;

c) the volume of a sphere of radius r.

8. An item costs n cents. Write a declaration statement for suitable variables and assignment statements which compute the change to be given from a \$1 bill for any value of n from 1 to 99, using coins of denomination 1, 5, 10, and 25 cents.

9. Given the type declaration for `interval` in Section 3.8, the definitions of + given in Section 3.8, the definitions of assignment given in Section 3.9, and the declarations

```
type(interval) :: a,b,c,d
real           :: r
```

which of the following statements are valid?

```
a = b + c
c = b + 1.0
d = b + 1
r = b + c
a = r + 2
```

10. Given the type declarations

```
real, dimension(5,6) :: a, b
real, dimension(5)   :: c
```

which of the following statements are valid?

```
a = b                    c = a(:,2) + b(5,:5)
a = c+1.0                c = a(2,:) + b(:,5)
a(:,3) = c               b(2:,3) = c + b(:5,3)
```

4. Control constructs

4.1 Introduction

We have learnt in the previous chapter how assignment statements may be written, and how these may be ordered one after the other to form a sequence of code which is executed step by step. In most computations, however, this simple sequence of statements is by itself inadequate for the formulation of the problem. For instance, we may wish to follow one of two possible paths through a section of code, depending on whether a calculated value is positive or negative. We may wish to sum 1000 elements of an array, and to do this by writing 1000 additions and assignments is clearly tedious; the ability to iterate over a single addition is required instead. We may wish to pass control from one part of a program to another, or even stop processing altogether.

For all these purposes, we have available in Fortran various facilities to enable the logical flow through the program statements to be controlled. The facilities contained in Fortran correspond to those now widely regarded as being the most appropriate for a modern programming language. Their general form is that of a *block* construct, that is a construct which begins with an initial keyword statement, may have intermediate keyword statements, and ends with a matching terminal statement, and that may be entered only at the initial statement. Each sequence of statements between keywords is called a *block*. A block may be empty, though such cases are rare.

Block constructs may be *nested*, that is a block may contain another block construct. In such a case, the block must contain the whole of the inner construct. Execution of a block always begins with its first statement.

However, we begin by describing the simple go to statement.

4.2 The go to statement

In this section, we consider the most disputed statement in programming languages — the go to statement. It is generally accepted that it is difficult to understand a program which is interrupted by many branches, especially if there is a large number of backward branches — those returning control to a statement preceding the branch itself. At the same time there are certain occasions, especially when dealing with error conditions, when go to statements are required in even the most advanced languages.

The form of the unconditional go to statement is

```
go to label
```

where *label* is a statement label. This statement label must be present on an *executable statement* (a statement which can be executed, as opposed to one of an informative nature, like a declaration). An example is

```
    x = y+3.0
    go to 4
  3 x = x+2.0
  4 z = x+y
```

in which we note that after execution of the first statement, a branch is taken to the last statement, labelled 4. This is a *branch target statement*. The statement labelled 3 is jumped over, and can be executed only if there is a branch to the label 3 somewhere else. If the statement following an unconditional go to is unlabelled it can never be reached and executed, creating *dead code*, normally a sign of incorrect coding.

A go to statement must never specify a branch into a block, though it may specify a branch

- from within a block to another statement in the block,

- to the terminal statement of its construct, or

- to a statement outside its construct.

4.3   The if statement and construct

The if statement and if construct provide a mechanism for branching depending on a condition. They are powerful tools, the if construct being a generalized form of the if statement.

In the if statement, the value of a scalar logical expression is tested, and a single statement executed if its value is true. The general form is

> if (*scalar-logical-expr*) *action-stmt*

where *scalar-logical-expr* is any scalar logical expression, and *action-stmt* is any executable statement other than one that marks the beginning or end of a block (for instance, if, else if, else, end if, see next subsection), another if statement, or an end statement (see Chapter 5). Examples are

```
    if (flag) go to 6
    if (x-y > 0.0) x = 0.0
    if (cond .or. p<q .and. r<=1.0) s(i,j) = t(j,i)
```

The if statement is normally used either to perform a single assignment depending on a condition, or to branch depending on a condition. The *action-stmt* may not be labelled separately.

The if construct allows either the execution of a sequence of statements (a block) to depend on a condition, or the execution of alternative sequences of statements (blocks) to depend on alternative conditions. The simplest of its three forms is

```
[name:] if (scalar-logical-expr) then
            block
        end if [name]
```

where *scalar-logical-expr* is any scalar logical expression and *block* is any sequence of executable statements (except an end statement or an incomplete construct). The *block* is executed if *scalar-logical-expr* evaluates to the value true, and is not executed if it evaluates to the value false. The if construct may be optionally named: the first and last statements may bear the same name, which may be any valid and distinct Fortran name (see Section 5.15 for a discussion on the scope of names). The fact that the name is optional is indicated here by the square brackets, a convention that will be followed throughout the book.

We notice that the if construct is a compound statement, the beginning being marked by the if...then, and the end by the end if. An example is

```
swap: if (x < y) then
          temp = x
          x = y
          y = temp
      end if swap
```

in which we notice also that the block inside the if construct is indented with respect to its beginning and end. This is not obligatory, but makes the logic easier to understand, especially in nested if constructs as we shall see at the end of this section.

In the second form of the if construct, an alternative block of statements is executable, for the case where the condition is false. The general form is

```
[name:]   if (scalar-logical-expr) then
              block1
          else [name]
              block2
          end if [name]
```

in which the first block of statements (*block1*) is executed if the condition is true and the second block (*block2*), following the else statement, is executed if the condition is false. An example is

```
if (x < y) then
    x = -x
else
    y = -y
end if
```

in which the sign of x is changed if x is less than y, and the sign of y is changed if x is greater than or equal to y.

The third and most general type of if construct uses the else if statement to make a succession of tests, each of which has its associated block of statements. The tests are made one after the other until one is fulfilled, and the associated statements of the relevant if or else if block are executed. Control then passes to the end of the if construct. If no test is fulfilled, no block is executed, unless there is a final 'catch-all' else clause. The general form is shown in Figure 4.1. There can be any number (including zero) of else if statements, and zero or one else statements. An else or else if statement may be named only if the corresponding if and end if statements are named, and must be given the same name.

Figure 4.1
```
[name:] if (scalar-logical-expr) then
            block
        [else if (scalar-logical-expr) then [name]
            block]...
        [else [name]
            block]
        end if [name]
```

The statements within an if construct may be labelled, but the labels must never be referenced in such a fashion as to pass control into the range of an if construct from outside it, to an else if or else statement, or into a block of the construct from outside the block. For example, the following if construct is illegal:

```
    if (temp > 100.0) then
        go to 1                      ! illegal branch
        boil = .true.
        steam = .true.
    else
1       boil = .false.
        liquid = .true.
    end if
```

It is permitted to pass control to an end if statement from within its construct. Execution of an end if statement has no effect.

It is permitted to nest if constructs within one another to an arbitrary depth, as shown to two levels in Figure 4.2, in which we see again the necessity to indent the code in order to be able to understand the logic easily. For even deeper nesting, naming is to be recommended. The constructs must be properly nested, that is each construct must be wholly contained in a block of the next outer construct.

4.4   The case construct

Fortran provides another means of selecting one of several options, rather similar to that of the if construct. The principal differences between the two constructs are that, for the case construct, only *one* expression is evaluated for testing, and the evaluated expression may belong to no more than one of a series of pre-defined sets of values. The form of the case construct is shown by:

Figure 4.2

```
     if (i < 0) then
        if (j < 0) then
           x = 0.0
           y = 0.0
        else
           z = 0.0
        end if
     else if (k < 0) then
        z = 1.0
     else
        x = 1.0
        y = 1.0
     end if
```

```
[name:]   select case (expr)
            [case selector [name]
                  block]...
          end select [name]
```

As for the if construct, the leading and trailing statements must either both be unnamed or both bear the same name; a case statement within it may be named only if the leading statement is named and bears the same name. The expression *expr* must be scalar and of type character, logical, or integer, and the specified values in each *selector* must be of this type. In the character case, the lengths are permitted to differ, but not the kinds. In the logical and integer cases, the kinds may differ. The simplest form of *selector* is a scalar initialization expression[1] in parentheses, such as in the statement

```
     case(1)
```

For character or integer *expr*, a range may be specified by a lower and an upper scalar initialization expression separated by a colon:

```
     case (low:high)
```

Either *low* or *high*, but not both, may be absent; this is equivalent to specifying that the case is selected whenever *expr* evaluates to a value that is less than or equal to *high*, or greater than or equal to *low*, respectively. An example is shown in Figure 4.3.

The general form of *selector* is a list of non-overlapping values and ranges, all of the same type as *expr*, enclosed in parentheses, such as

```
     case (1, 2, 7, 10:17, 23)
```

---

[1]An initialization expression is a restricted form of constant expression (the restrictions being chosen for ease of implementation). The details are tedious and are deferred to Section 7.4. In this section, all examples employ the simplest form of initialization expression: the literal constant.

Figure 4.3

```
select case (number)      ! number is of type integer
case (:-1)                ! all values below 0
   n_sign = -1
case (0)                  ! only 0
   n_sign = 0
case (1:)                 ! all values above 0
   n_sign = 1
end select
```

The form

```
case default
```

is equivalent to a list of all the possible values of *expr* that are not included in the other selectors of the construct. Though we recommend that the values be in order, as in this example, this is not required. Overlapping values are not permitted within one *selector*, nor between different ones in the same construct.

There may be only a single case default *selector* in a given case construct as shown in Figure 4.4. The case default clause does not necessarily have to be the last clause of the case construct.

Figure 4.4

```
select case (ch)          ! ch of type character
case ('c', 'd', 'r':)
   ch_type = .true.
case ('i':'n')
   int_type = .true.
case default
   real_type = .true.
end select
```

Since the values of the selectors are not permitted to overlap, at most one selector may be satisfied; if none is satisfied, control passes to the next executable statement following the end select statement.

Like the if construct, case constructs may be nested inside one another. Branching to a statement in a case block is permitted only from another statement in the block, it is not permitted to branch to a case statement, and any branch to an end select statement must be from within the case construct which it terminates.

4.5   The do construct

Many problems in mathematics require the ability to *iterate*. If we wish to sum the elements of an array a of length 10, we could write

```
sum = a(1)
sum = sum+a(2)
    :
sum = sum+a(10)
```

which is clearly laborious. Fortran provides a facility known as the do construct which allows us to reduce these ten lines of code to

```
sum = 0.0
do  i = 1,10 ! i is of type integer
    sum = sum+a(i)
end do
```

In this fragment of code we first set sum to zero, and then require that the statement between the do statement and the end do statement shall be executed ten times. For each iteration there is an associated value of an index, kept in i, which assumes the value 1 for the first iteration through the loop, 2 for the second, and so on up to 10. The variable i is a normal integer variable, but is subject to the rule that it must not be explicitly modified within the do construct.

The do statement has more general forms. If we wished to sum the fourth to ninth elements we would write

```
do  i = 4, 9
```

thereby specifying the required first and last values of i. If, alternatively, we wished to sum all the odd elements, we would write

```
do  i = 1, 9, 2
```

where the third of the three loop *parameters,* namely the 2, specifies that i is to be incremented in steps of 2, rather than by the default value of 1, which is assumed if no third parameter is given. In fact, we can go further still, as the parameters need not be constants at all, but integer expressions, as in

```
do  i = j+4, m, -k(j)**2
```

in which the first value of i is j+4, and subsequent values are decremented by k(j)**2 until the value of m is reached. Thus, do indices may run 'backwards' as well as 'forwards'. If any of the three parameters is a variable or is an expression that involves a variable, the value of the variable may be modified within the loop without affecting the number of iterations, as the *initial* values of the parameters are used for the control of the loop.

The general form of this type of bounded do construct control clause is

```
[name:]   do [,]  variable = expr1, expr2 [,expr3]
                block
          end do [name]
```

where *variable* is a named scalar integer variable, *expr1, expr2,* and *expr3* (*expr3* is optional but must be nonzero when present) are any valid scalar integer expressions, and *name* is the optional construct name. The do and end do statements must either both bear the same *name*, or both be unnamed.

The number of iterations of a do construct is given by the formula

max((*expr2-expr1+expr3*)/*expr3*, 0)

where max is a function which we shall meet in Section 8.3.2 and which returns either the value of the expression or zero, whichever is the larger. There is a consequence following from this definition, namely that if a loop begins with the statement

```
do  i = 1, n
```

then its body will not be executed at all if the value of n on entering the loop is zero or less. This is an example of the *zero-trip loop*, and results from the application of the max function.

A very simple form of the do statement is the unbounded

```
[name:] do
```

which specifies an endless loop. In practice, a means to exit from an endless loop is required, and this is provided in the form of the exit statement:

```
exit [name]
```

where *name* is optional and is used to specify from which do construct the exit should be taken in the case of nested constructs. Execution of an exit statement causes control to be transferred to the next executable statement after the end do statement to which it refers. If no name is specified, it terminates execution of the innermost do construct in which it is enclosed. As an example of this form of the do, suppose we have used the type entry of Section 2.13 to construct a chain of entries in a sparse vector, and we wish to find the entry with index 10, known to be present. If first points to the first entry, the code in Figure 4.5 is suitable.

Figure 4.5

```
type(entry), pointer :: first, current
:
current => first
do
   if (current%index == 10) exit
   current => current%next
end do
```

The exit statement is also useful in a bounded loop when all iterations are not always needed.

A related statement is the cycle statement

```
cycle [name]
```

which transfers control to the end do statement of the corresponding construct. Thus, if further iterations are still to be carried out, the next one is initiated.

The value of a do construct index (if present) is incremented at the end of every loop iteration for use in the subsequent iteration. As the value of this index is available outside the loop after its execution, we have three possible situations, each illustrated by the following loop:

```
do  i = 1, n
    :
    if (i==j) exit
    :
end do
l = i
```

The situations are as follows.

i) If, at execution time, n has the value zero or less, i is set to 1 but the loop is not executed, and control passes to the statement following the end do statement.

ii) If n has a value which is greater than or equal to j, an exit will be taken at the if statement, and l will acquire the last value of i, which is of course j.

iii) If the value of n is greater than zero but less than j, the loop will be executed n times, with the successive values of i being $1, 2, \ldots$, *etc.* up to n. When reaching the end of the loop for the n*th* time, i will be incremented a final time, acquiring the value n+1, which will then be assigned to l.

We see how important it is to make careful use of loop indices outside the do block, especially when there is the possibility of the number of iterations taking on the boundary value of the maximum for the loop.

The do block, just mentioned, is the sequence of statements between the do statement and the end do statement. From anywhere outside a do block, it is prohibited to jump into the block or to its end do statement.

It is similarly illegal for the block of a do construct (or an if, case, or where construct, see Section 6.8), to be only partially contained in a block of another construct. The construct must be completely contained in the block. The following two sequences are legal:

```
if (scalar-logical-expr) then
    do i = 1, n
        :
    end do
else
    :
end if
```

and

```
do i = 1, n
   if (scalar-logical-expr) then
      :
   end if
end do
```

Any number of do constructs may be nested provided that the range of each nested loop is completely contained within the range of another. We may thus write a matrix multiplication as shown in Figure 4.6.

Figure 4.6

```
do  i = 1, n
   do  j = 1, m
      a(i,j) = 0.0
      do  l = 1, k
         a(i,j) = a(i,j)+b(i,l)*c(l,j)
      end do
   end do
end do
```

A final form of the do construct makes use of a statement label to identify the end of the construct. In this case, the terminating statement may be either a labelled end do statement or a labelled continue ('do nothing') statement.[2] The label is, in each case, the same as that on the do statement itself. The label on the do statement may be followed by a comma. Simple examples are

```
do 10 i = 1, n
   :
10 end do
```

and

```
do 20 i = 1, j
   do, 10 k = 1, l
      :
10    continue
20 continue
```

As shown in the second example, each loop must have a separate label. Additional, but redundant, do syntax is described in Section 20.6 (and Appendix B.2.2).

Finally, it should be noted that many short do-loops can be expressed alternatively in the form of array expressions and assignments. However, this is not always possible, and a particular danger to watch for is where one iteration of the loop depends upon a previous one. Thus, the loop

---

[2]The continue statement is not limited to being the last statement of a do construct; it may appear anywhere among the executable statements.

```
do i = 2, n
   a(i) = a(i-1) + b(i)
end do
```

cannot be replaced by the statement

```
a(2:n) = a(1:n-1) + b(2:n)        ! Beware
```

4.6 Summary

In this chapter we have introduced the four main features by which the control in Fortran code may be programmed — the go to statement, the if statement and construct, the case construct, and the do construct. The effective use of these features is the key to sound code.

We have touched upon the concept of a *program unit* as being like the chapter of a book. Just as a book may have just one chapter, so a complete program may consist of just one program unit, which is known as a *main program*. In its simplest form it consists of a series of statements of the kinds we have been dealing with so far, and terminates with an end statement, which acts as a signal to the computer to stop processing the current program. In order to test whether a program unit of this type works correctly, we need to be able to output, to a terminal or printer, the values of the computed quantities. This topic will be fully explained in Chapter 9, and for the moment we need to know only that this can be achieved by a statement of the form

```
print * , ' var1 = ', var1 , ' var2 = ', var2
```

which will output a line such as

```
var1 = 1.0   var2 = 2.0
```

Similarly, input data can be read by statements like

```
read *, val1, val2
```

This is sufficient to allow us to write simple programs like that in Figure 4.7, which outputs the converted values of a temperature scale between specified limits. Valid inputs are shown at the end of the example.

Figure 4.7

```
!    Print a conversion table of the Fahrenheit and Celsius
!    temperature scales between specified limits.
!
   real      :: celsius, fahrenheit
   integer   :: low_temp, high_temp, temperature
   character :: scale
!
read_loop: do
!
!    Read scale and limits
      read *, scale, low_temp, high_temp
!
!    Check for valid data
      if (scale /= 'C' .and. scale /= 'F') exit read_loop
!
!    Loop over the limits
      do  temperature = low_temp, high_temp
!
!    Choose conversion formula
          select case (scale)
          case ('C')
             celsius = temperature
             fahrenheit = 9.0/5.0*celsius + 32.0
!    Print table entry
             print *, celsius, ' degrees C correspond to',   &
                 fahrenheit, ' degrees F'
          case ('F')
             fahrenheit = temperature
             celsius = 5.0/9.0*(fahrenheit-32.0)
!    Print table entry
             print *, fahrenheit, ' degrees F correspond to',&
                 celsius, ' degrees C'
          end select
      end do
   end do read_loop
!
!    Termination
print *, ' End of valid data'
   end
C  90    100
F  20    32
*   0    0
```

4.7 Exercises

1. Write a program which

    a) defines an array to have 100 elements;

    b) assigns to the elements the values $1, 2, 3, \ldots, 100$;

    c) reads two integer values in the range 1 to 100;

    d) reverses the order of the elements of the array in the range specified by the two values.

2. The first two terms of the Fibonacci series are both 1, and all subsequent terms are defined as the sum of the preceding two terms. Write a program which reads an integer value `limit` and which computes and prints the coefficients of the first `limit` terms of the series.

3. The coefficients of successive orders of the binomial expansion are shown in the normal Pascal triangle form as

$$1$$
$$1 \ 1$$
$$1 \ 2 \ 1$$
$$1 \ 3 \ 3 \ 1$$
$$1 \ 4 \ 6 \ 4 \ 1$$
$$\text{etc.}$$

Write a program which reads an integer value `limit` and prints the coefficients of the first `limit` lines of this Pascal triangle.

4. Define a character variable of length 80. Write a program which reads a value for this variable. Assuming that each character in the variable is alphabetic, write code which sorts them into alphabetic order, and prints out the frequency of occurrence of each letter.

5. Write a program to read an integer value `limit` and print the first `limit` prime numbers, by any method.

6. Write a program which reads a value x, and calculates and prints the corresponding value `x/(1.+x)`. The case `x=-1.` should produce an error message and be followed by an attempt to read a new value of x.

7. Given a chain of entries of the type `entry` of Section 2.13, modify the code in Figure 4.5 (Section 4.5) so that it removes the entry with index 10, and makes the previous entry point to the following entry.

5. Program units and procedures

5.1 Introduction

As we saw in the previous chapter, it is possible to write a complete Fortran program as a single unit, but it is preferable to break the program down into manageable units. Each such *program unit* corresponds to a program task that can be readily understood and, ideally, can be written, compiled, and tested in isolation. We will discuss the three kinds of program unit, the main program, external subprogram, and module.

A complete program must, as a minimum, include one *main program*. This may contain statements of the kinds that we have met so far in examples, but normally its most important statements are invocations or *calls* to subsidiary programs known as *subprograms*. A subprogram defines a *function* or a *subroutine*.[1] They differ in that a function returns a single object and usually does not alter the values of its arguments (so that it represents a function in the mathematical sense), whereas a subroutine usually performs a more complicated task, returning several results through its arguments and by other means. Functions and subroutines are known collectively as *procedures*.

There are various kinds of subprograms. A subprogram may be a program unit in its own right, in which case it is called an *external subprogram* and defines an *external procedure*. External procedures may also be defined by means other than Fortran (usually assembly language). A subprogram may be a member of a collection in a program unit called a *module*, in which case we call it a *module subprogram* and it defines a *module procedure*. A subprogram may be placed inside a module subprogram, an external subprogram, or a main program, in which case we call it an *internal subprogram* and it defines an *internal procedure*. Internal subprograms may not be nested, that is they may not contain further subprograms, and we expect them normally to be short sequences of code, say up to about twenty lines. We illustrate the nesting of subprograms in program units in Figure 5.1. If a program unit or subprogram contains a subprogram, it is called the *host* of that subprogram.

Besides containing a collection of subprograms, a module may contain data definitions, derived type definitions, interface blocks (Section 5.11), and namelist groups (Section 7.15). This collection may provide facilities associated with some particular task, such as providing matrix arithmetic, a library facility, or a data base. It may sometimes be large.

---

[1] It is possible to write a subprogram that defines more than one function or more than one subroutine (see Section 20.4), but we do not recommend this practice.

Figure 5.1 Nesting of subprograms in program units.

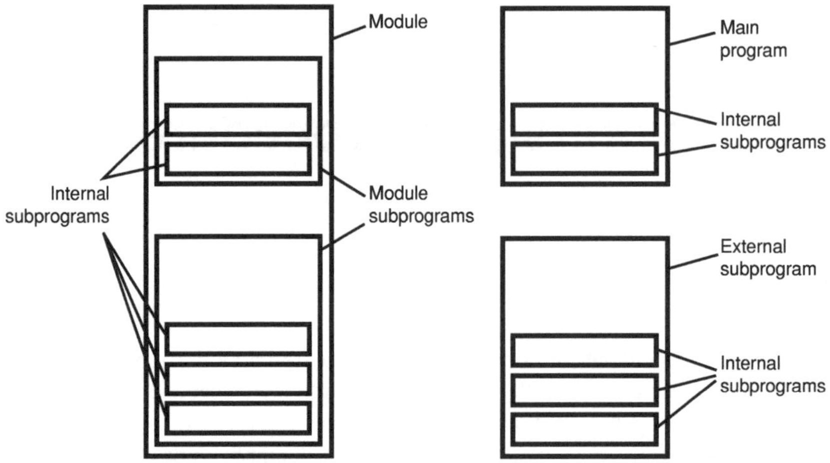

In this chapter, we will describe program units and the statements that are associated with them. Within a complete program, they may appear in any order, but many compilers require a module to precede other program units that use it.

5.2   Main program

Every complete program must have one, and only one, main program. Optionally, it may contain calls to subprograms. A main program has the following form:

```
[program program-name]
    [specification-stmts]
    [executable-stmts]
[contains
    internal-subprograms]
end [program [program-name]]
```

The program statement is optional, but we recommend its use. The *program-name* may be any valid Fortran name such as model. The only non-optional statement is the end statement which has two purposes. It acts as a signal to the compiler that it has reached the end of the program unit and, when executed, it causes the complete program to stop. If it includes *program-name*, this must be the name on the program statement. We recommend using the full form so that it is clear both to the reader and to the compiler exactly what is terminated by the end statement.

A main program without calls to subprograms is usually used only for short tests, as in

```
program test
   print *, 'Hello world!'
end program test
```

The specification statements define the environment for the executable statements. So far, we have met the type declaration statement (`integer`, `real`, `complex`, `logical`, `character`, and `type(`*type-name*`)`) that specifies the type and other properties of the entities that it lists, and the type definition block (bounded by `type` *type-name* and `end type` statements). We will meet other specification statements in this and the next two chapters.

The executable statements specify the actions that are to be performed. So far, we have met the assignment statement, the pointer assignment statement, the `go to` statement, the `if` statement and construct, the `do` and `case` constructs, and the `read` and `print` statements. We will meet other executable statements in this and later chapters. Execution of a program always commences with the first executable statement of the main program.

The `contains` statement flags the presence of one or more internal subprograms. We will describe internal subprograms in Section 5.6. If the execution of the last statement ahead of the `contains` statement does not result in a branch, control passes over the internal subprograms to the `end` statement and the program stops. The `end` statement may be labelled and may be the target of a branch from one of the executable statements. If such a branch is taken, again the program stops.

5.3 The stop statement

Another way to stop program execution is to execute a `stop` statement. This statement may be labelled, may be part of an `if` statement, and is an executable statement that may appear in the main program or any subprogram. A well-designed program normally returns control to the main program for program termination, so the `stop` statement should appear there. However, in applications where several `stop` statements appear in various places in a complete program, it is possible to distinguish which of the `stop` statements has caused the termination by adding to each one an *access code* consisting of a default character constant or a string of up to five digits whose leading zeros are not significant. This might be used by a given processor to indicate the origin of the `stop` in a message. Examples are

```
stop
stop 'Incomplete data. Program terminated.'
stop 12345
```

5.4 External subprograms

External subprograms are called from a main program or elsewhere, usually to perform a well-defined task within the framework of a complete program. Apart from the leading statement, they have a form that is very like that of a main program:

> *subroutine-stmt*
>   [*specification-stmts*]
>   [*executable-stmts*]
> [contains
>   *internal-subprograms*]
> end [subroutine [*subroutine-name*]]

or

> *function-stmt*
>   [*specification-stmts*]
>   [*executable-stmts*]
> [contains
>   *internal-subprograms*]
> end [function [*function-name*]]

The contains statement plays exactly the same role as within a main program (see Section 5.2). The effect of executing an end statement in a subprogram is to return control to the caller, rather than to stop execution. As for the end program statement, we recommend using the full form for the end statement so that it is clear both to the reader and to the compiler exactly what it terminates.

The simplest form of external subprogram defines a subroutine without any arguments and has a *subroutine-stmt* of the form

> subroutine *subroutine-name*

Such a subprogram is useful when a program consists of a sequence of distinct phases, in which case the main program consists of a sequence of call statements that invoke the subroutines as in the example

```
program game         ! Main program to control a card game
   call shuffle      ! First shuffle the cards.
   call deal         ! Now deal them.
   call play         ! Play the game.
   call display      ! Display the result.
end program game     ! Cease execution.
```

But how do we handle the flow of information between the subroutines? How does play know which cards deal has dealt? There are, in fact, two methods by which information may be passed. The first is via data held in a module (Section 5.5) and accessed by the subprograms, and the second is via arguments (Section 5.7) in the procedure calls.

5.5   Modules

The third type of program unit, the module, provides a means of packaging global data, derived types and their associated operations, subprograms, interface blocks (Section 5.11), and namelist groups (Section 7.15). Everything associated with some task (such as interval arithmetic, see later in this section) may be collected into a module and accessed whenever it is needed. Those parts that are associated with the internal working and are of no interest to the user may be made 'invisible' to the user, which allows the internal design to be altered without the need to alter the program that uses it and prevents accidental alteration of internal data. We expect Fortran libraries to consist of sets of modules.

The module has the form

```
module module-name
    [specification-stmts]
[contains
    module-subprograms]
end [module [module-name]]
```

As for the end program, end subroutine, and end function statements, we recommend using the full form for the end statement.

In its simplest form, the body consists only of data specifications. For example

```
module state
    integer, dimension(52) :: cards
end module state
```

might hold the state of play of the game of Section 5.4. It is accessed by the statement

```
use state
```

appearing at the beginnings of the main program game and subprograms shuffle, deal, play, and display. The array cards is set by shuffle to contain the integer values 1 to 52 in a random order, where each integer value corresponds to a pre-defined playing card. For instance, 1 might stand for the ace of clubs, 2 for the two of clubs, etc. up to 52 for the king of spades. The array cards is changed by the subroutines deal and play, and finally accessed by subroutine display.

A further example of global data in a module would be the definitions of the values of the kind type parameters that might be required throughout a program (Sections 2.6.1 and 2.6.2). They can be placed in a module and used wherever they are required. On a processor that supports all the kinds listed, an example might be:

```
module numeric_kinds
    ! named constants for 4, 2, and 1 byte integers:
    integer, parameter ::                                    &
        i4b = selected_int_kind(9),                          &
        i2b = selected_int_kind(4),                          &
        i1b = selected_int_kind(2)
    ! and for single, double and quadruple precision reals:
    integer, parameter ::                                    &
        sp = kind(1.0),                                      &
        dp = selected_real_kind(2*precision(1.0_sp)),  &
        qp = selected_real_kind(2*precision(1.0_dp))
end module numeric_kinds
```

A very useful role for modules is to contain definitions of types and their associated operators. For example, a module might contain the type `interval` of Section 3.8, as shown in Figure 5.2. Given this module, any program unit needing this type and its operators need only include the statement

```
use interval_arithmetic
```

at the head of its specification statements.

Figure 5.2

```
module interval_arithmetic
    type interval
        real :: lower, upper
    end type interval
    interface operator(+)
        module procedure add_intervals
    end interface
    :
contains
    function add_intervals(a,b)
        type(interval)                :: add_intervals
        type(interval), intent(in) :: a, b
        add_intervals%lower = a%lower + b%lower
        add_intervals%upper = a%upper + b%upper
    end function add_intervals
    :
end module interval_arithmetic
```

A module subprogram has exactly the same form as an external subprogram, except that `function` or `subroutine` *must* be present on the `end` statement, so there is no need for a separate description. It always has access to other entities of the module, including the ability to call other subprograms of the module, rather as if it contained a `use` statement for its module.

A module may contain `use` statements that access other modules. It must not access itself directly or indirectly through a chain of `use` statements, for example a accessing b and b accessing a. No ordering of modules is required by the standard, but normal practice is to require each module to precede its use. We recommend this practice, which will make it impossible for a module to access itself through other modules. It is required by many compilers.

It is possible within a module to specify that some of the entities are private to it and cannot be accessed from other program units. Also there are forms of the `use` statement that allow access to only part of a module and forms that allow renaming of the entities accessed. These features will be explained in Sections 7.6 and 7.10. For the present, we assume that the whole module is accessed without any renaming of the entities in it.

Besides data definitions, type definitions, subprograms, and interface blocks, a module may contain namelist groups (Section 7.15). The ability to make single definitions of interface blocks will be seen to be important in the context of constructing large libraries of reusable software.

5.6 Internal subprograms

We have seen that internal subprograms may be defined inside main programs and external subprograms, and within module subprograms. They have the form

> *subroutine-stmt*
>   [*specification-stmts*]
>   [*executable-stmts*]
>   end subroutine [*subroutine-name*]

or

> *function-stmt*
>   [*specification-stmts*]
>   [*executable-stmts*]
>   end function [*function-name*]

that is, the same form as a module subprogram, except that they may not contain further internal subprograms. Note that function or subroutine must be present on the end statement. An internal subprogram automatically has access to all the host's entities, including the ability to call its other internal subprograms. Internal subprograms must be preceded by a contains statement in the host.

In the rest of this chapter, we describe several properties of subprograms that apply to external, module, and internal subprograms. We therefore do not need to describe internal subprograms separately. An example is given in Figure 5.11 (Section 5.15).

5.7 Arguments of procedures

Procedure arguments provide an alternative means for two program units to access the same data. Returning to our card game example, instead of placing the array cards in a module, we might declare it in the main program and pass it as an actual argument to each subprogram, as shown in Figure 5.3.

Each subroutine receives cards as a dummy argument. For instance, shuffle has the form shown in Figure 5.4.

We can, of course, imagine a card game in which deal is going to deal only three cards to each of four players. In this case, it would be a waste of time for shuffle to prepare a deck of 52 cards when only the first 12 cards are needed. This can be achieved by requesting shuffle to limit itself to a number of cards that is transmitted in the calling sequence thus:

```
call shuffle(3*4, cards(1:12))
```

Figure 5.3

```
program game          ! Main program to control a card game
   integer, dimension(52) :: cards
   call shuffle(cards)       ! First shuffle the cards.
   call deal(cards)          ! Now deal them.
   call play(cards)          ! Play the game.
   call display(cards)       ! Display the result.
end program game             ! Cease execution.
```

Figure 5.4

```
subroutine shuffle(cards)
   ! Subroutine that places the values 1 to 52 in cards
   ! in random order.
   integer, dimension(52) :: cards
   ! Statements that fill cards
   :
end subroutine shuffle    ! Return to caller.
```

Inside shuffle, we would define the array to be of the given length and the algorithm to fill cards would be contained in a do construct with this number of iterations, as shown in Figure 5.5.

Figure 5.5

```
subroutine shuffle(ncards, cards)
   integer                   :: ncards, icard
   integer, dimension(ncards) :: cards
   do icard = 1, ncards
      :
      cards(icard) = ...
   end do
end subroutine shuffle
```

We have seen how it is possible to pass an array and a constant expression between two program units. An actual argument may be any variable or expression (or a procedure name, see Section 5.12). Each dummy argument of the called procedure must agree with the corresponding actual argument in type, type parameters, and shape (the requirements on character length and shape agreement are relaxed in Section 20.3). However, the names do not have to be the same. For instance, if two decks had been needed, we might have written the code thus:

```
program game
   integer, dimension(52) :: acards, bcards
   call shuffle(acards)          ! First shuffle the a deck.
   call shuffle(bcards)          ! Next shuffle the b deck.
   :
end program game
```

The important point is that subprograms can be written independently of one another, the association of the dummy arguments with the actual arguments occurring each time the call is executed. We can imagine shuffle being used in other programs which use other names. In this manner, libraries of subprograms may be built up.

Being able to have different names for actual and dummy arguments provides a useful flexibility, but it should only be used when it is actually needed. When the same name can be used, the code is more readable.

As the type of an actual argument and its corresponding dummy argument must agree, care must be taken when using component selection within an actual argument. Thus, supposing the type definitions point and triangle of Figure 2.1 (Section 2.9) are available in a module def, we might write

```
use def
type(triangle) :: t
:
call sub(t%a)
:
contains
   subroutine sub(p)
      type(point) :: p
```

5.7.1 Pointer arguments

A dummy argument is permitted to have the attribute pointer. In this case, the actual argument must also have the attribute pointer. When the subprogram is invoked, the rank of the actual argument must match that of the dummy argument, and its pointer association status is passed to the dummy argument. On return, the actual argument normally takes its pointer association status from that of the dummy argument, but it becomes undefined if the dummy argument is associated with a target that becomes undefined when the return is executed (for example, if the target is a local variable that does not have the save attribute, Section 7.9).

In the case of a module or internal procedure, the compiler knows when the dummy argument is a pointer. In the case of an external or dummy procedure, the compiler assumes that the dummy argument is not a pointer unless it is told otherwise in an interface block (Section 5.11).

A pointer actual argument is also permitted to correspond to a non-pointer dummy argument. In this case, the pointer must have a target and the target is associated with the dummy argument, as in

```
    real, pointer :: a(:,:)
    :
    allocate ( a(80,80) )
    call find (a)
    :
subroutine find (c)
    real :: c(:,:) ! Assumed-shape array, see Section 6.3
```

5.7.2   Restrictions on actual arguments

There are two important restrictions on actual arguments, which are designed to allow the compiler to optimize on the assumption that the dummy arguments are distinct from each other and from other entities that are accessible within the procedure. For example, a compiler may arrange for an array to be copied to a local variable on entry, and copied back on return. While an actual argument is associated with a dummy argument the following statements hold.

i) Action that affects the allocation status or pointer association status of the argument or any part of it (any pointer assignment, allocation, deallocation, or nullification) must be taken through the dummy argument. If this is done, then throughout the execution of the procedure, the argument may be referenced only through the dummy argument.

ii) Action that affects the value of the argument or any part of it must be taken through the dummy argument unless

    a) the dummy argument has the `pointer` attribute,

    b) the part is all or part of a pointer subobject, or

    c) the dummy argument has the `target` attribute, the dummy argument does not have intent in (Section 5.9), the dummy argument is scalar or an assumed-shape array, and the actual argument is a target other than an array section with a vector subscript.

If the value of the argument or any part of it is affected through a dummy argument for which neither a), b), or c) holds, then throughout the execution of the procedure, the argument may be referenced only through that dummy argument.

An example of i) is a pointer that is nullified (Section 6.5.4) while still associated with the dummy argument. As an example of ii), consider

```
call modify(a(1:5), a(3:9))
```

Here, a(3:5) may not be changed through either dummy argument since this would violate the rule for the other argument. However, a(1:2) may be changed through the first argument and a(6:9) may be changed through the second. Another example is an actual argument that is an object being accessed from a module; here, the same object must not be accessed from the module by the procedure and redefined. As a third example, suppose an internal procedure call associates a host variable h with a dummy argument d. If d is defined during the call, then at no time during the call may h be referenced directly.

5.7.3   Arguments with the target attribute

In most circumstances, an implementation is permitted to make a copy of an actual argument on entry to a procedure and copy it back on return. This may be desirable on efficiency grounds, particularly when the actual argument is not held in contiguous storage. In any case, if a dummy argument has neither the `target` nor `pointer` attribute, any pointers associated with the actual argument do not become associated with the corresponding dummy argument but remain associated with the actual argument.

However, copy in / copy out is not allowed when

i) a dummy argument has the `target` attribute and is either scalar or is an assumed-shaped array, and

ii) the actual argument is a target other than an array section with a vector subscript.

In this case, the dummy and actual arguments must have the same shape, any pointer associated with the actual argument becomes associated with the dummy argument on invocation, and any pointer associated with the dummy argument on return remains associated with the actual argument.

When a dummy argument has the `target` attribute, but the actual argument is not a target or is an array section with a vector subscript, any pointer associated with the dummy argument obviously becomes undefined on return.

In other cases where the dummy argument has the `target` attribute, whether copy in / copy out occurs is processor dependent. No reliance should be placed on the pointer associations with such an argument after the invocation.

5.8   The return statement

We saw in Section 5.2 that if the last executable statement in a main program is executed and does not cause a branch, the end statement is executed and the program stops. Similarly, if the last executable statement in a subprogram is executed and does not cause a branch, the `end` statement is executed and control returns to the point of invocation. Just as the `stop` statement is an executable statement that provides an alternative means of stopping execution, so the `return` statement provides an alternative means of returning control from a subprogram. It has the form

```
return
```

Like the `stop` statement, this statement may be labelled, may be part of an `if` statement, and is an executable statement. It must not appear among the executable statements of a main program.

5.9   Argument intent

In Figure 5.5, the dummy argument `cards` was used to pass information out from `shuffle` and the dummy argument `ncards` was used to pass information in. A third possibility is for a dummy argument to be used for both. We can specify the intent on the type declaration statement for the argument, for example:

```
subroutine shuffle(ncards, cards)
    integer, intent(in)                        :: ncards
    integer, intent(out), dimension(ncards) :: cards
```

For input–output arguments, intent inout may be specified.

If a dummy argument is specified with intent in, it (or any part of it) must not be redefined by the procedure, say by appearing on the left-hand side of an assignment or by being passed on as an actual argument to a procedure that redefines it. For the specification intent inout, the corresponding actual argument must be a variable because the expectation is that it will be redefined by the procedure. For the specification intent out, the corresponding actual argument must again be a variable; in this case, it becomes undefined on entry to the procedure because the intention is that it be used only to pass information out.

If a function specifies a defined operator (Section 3.8), the dummy arguments must have intent in. If a subroutine specifies defined assignment (Section 3.9), the first argument must have intent out or inout, and the second argument must have intent in.

If a dummy argument has no intent, the actual argument may be a variable or an expression, but the actual argument must be a variable if the dummy argument is redefined. It has been traditional for Fortran compilers not to check this rule, since they usually compile each program unit separately. Breaching the rule can lead to program errors at execution time that are very difficult to find. We recommend that all dummy arguments be given a declared intent. Not only is this good documentation, but it allows compilers to make more checks at compile time.

If a dummy argument has the pointer attribute, its intent is not allowed to be specified in Fortran 95. This is because of the ambiguity of whether the intent applies to the target data object or to the pointer association. In Fortran 2003, intent is allowed and refers to the pointer association status (see Section 18.2).

If a dummy argument is of a derived type with pointer components, its intent attribute also refers to the pointer association status of those components. For example, if the intent is in, no pointer assignment, allocation, or deallocation is permitted.

The Fortran 95 standard is unclear as to whether the intent attribute applies to the target of a pointer component; some vendors believe it does, though they apply no restriction to the target of a local pointer that is pointer associated with such a component, as in the example

```
subroutine sub(a)
    type (t), intent(in) :: a ! type t has a real pointer component, p
    real, pointer :: ap
    ap => a%p
    ap = 0 ! target of local pointer overwritten
end subroutine sub
```

Fortran 2003 is clear that the intent attribute does not apply to such targets and that the assignment statement a%p = 0 is also valid.

5.10   Functions

Functions are similar to subroutines in many respects, but they are invoked within an expression and return a value that is used within the expression. For example, the subprogram in Figure 5.6 returns the distance between two points in space and the statement

```
if (distance(a, c) > distance(b, c) ) then
```

invokes the function twice in the logical expression that it contains.

Figure 5.6

```
function distance(p, q)
   real                            :: distance
   real, intent(in), dimension(3) :: p, q
   distance = sqrt( (p(1)-q(1))**2 + (p(2)-q(2))**2 +    &
                    (p(3)-q(3))**2 )
   ! The intrinsic function sqrt is defined in Section 8.4.
end function distance
```

Note the type declaration for the function result. The result behaves just like a dummy argument with intent out. It is initially undefined, but once defined it may appear in an expression and it may be redefined. The type may also be defined on the function statement thus:

```
real function distance(p, q)
```

It is permissible to write functions that change the values of their arguments, modify values in modules, rely on saved local data (Section 7.9), or perform input–output operations. However, these are known as *side-effects* and conflict with good programming practice. Where they are needed, a subroutine should be used. It is reassuring to know that when a function is called, nothing else goes on 'behind the scenes', and it may be very helpful to an optimizing compiler, particularly for internal and module subprograms. A formal mechanism for avoiding side-effects is provided, but we defer its description to Section 6.10.

A function result may be an array, in which case it must be declared as such. It may also be a pointer,[2] which is very useful when the size of the result depends on a calculation in the function itself. The result is initially undefined. Within the function, it must become associated or defined as disassociated. We expect the function reference usually to be such that a pointer assignment takes place for the result, that is, the reference occurs as the right-hand side of a pointer assignment (Section 3.12) or as a pointer component of a structure constructor. For example, the statements

---

[2]However, it is not possible for a pointer to have a function as its target. In other words, *dynamic binding*, or association of a pointer with a function at run time, is not available. This deficiency is remedied in Fortran 2003 (see Section 15.6).

```
use data_handler
real           :: x(100)
real, pointer :: y(:)
  :
y => compact(x)
```

might be used to reference the pointer function in Figure 5.7 in the module data_handler. The reference may also occur as a primary of an expression or as the right-hand side of an ordinary assignment, in which case the result must become associated with a target that is defined and the value of the target is used. We do not recommend this practice, however, since it is likely to lead to memory leakage, discussed at the end of Section 6.5.3.

Figure 5.7

```
function compact(x) ! a procedure to remove duplicates from
                    ! the array x
   real, pointer :: compact(:)
   real          :: x(:) ! Assumed-shape array, see Section 6.3
   integer       :: n
   :                     ! find the number of distinct values, n
   allocate(compact(n))
   :                     ! copy the distinct values into compact
end function compact
```

The value returned by a non-pointer function must always be defined.

As well as being a scalar or array value of intrinsic type, a function result may also be a scalar or array value of a derived type, as we have seen already in Section 3.8. When the function is invoked, the function value must be used as a whole, that is, it is not permitted to be qualified by substring, array-subscript, array-section, or structure-component selection.

Although this is not very useful, a function is permitted to have an empty argument list. In this case, the brackets are obligatory both within the function statement and at every invocation.

5.10.1 Prohibited side-effects

In order to assist an optimizing compiler, the standard prohibits reliance on certain side-effects. It specifies that it is not necessary for a processor to evaluate all the operands of an expression, or to evaluate entirely each operand, if the value of the expression can be determined otherwise. For example, in evaluating

```
x>y .or. l(z)   ! x, y, and z are real; l is a logical function
```

the function reference need not be made if x is greater than y. Since some processors will make the call and others will not, any variable (for example z) that is redefined by the function becomes undefined following such an expression evaluation. Similarly, it is not necessary for a processor to evaluate any subscript or substring expressions for an array of zero size or character object of zero character length.

Another prohibition is that a function reference must not redefine the value of a variable that appears in the same statement or affect the value of another function reference in the same statement. For example, in

```
d = max(distance(p,q), distance(q,r))
```

`distance` is required not to redefine its arguments. This rule allows any expressions that are arguments of a single procedure call to be evaluated in any order. With respect to this rule, an `if` statement,

```
if (lexpr) stmt
```

is treated as the equivalent `if` construct

```
if (lexpr) then
    stmt
end if
```

and the same is true for the `where` statement (Section 6.8).

5.11   Explicit and implicit interfaces

A call to an internal subprogram must be from a statement within the same program unit. It may be assumed that the compiler will process the program unit as a whole and will therefore know all about any internal subprogram. In particular, it will know about its *interface*, that is whether it defines a function or a subroutine, the names and properties of the arguments, and the properties of the result if it defines a function. This, for example, permits the compiler to check whether the actual and dummy arguments match in the way that they should. We say that the interface is *explicit*.

A call to a module subprogram must either be from another statement in the module or from a statement following a use statement for the module. In both cases, the compiler will know all about the subprogram, and again we say that the interface is explicit. Similarly, intrinsic procedures (Chapter 8) always have explicit interfaces.

When compiling a call to an external or dummy procedure (Section 5.12), the compiler normally does not have a mechanism to access its code. We say that the interface is *implicit*. To specify that a name is that of an external or dummy procedure, the `external` statement is available. It has the form

```
external external-name-list
```

and appears with other specification statements, after any use or implicit statements (Section 7.2) and before any executable statements. The type and type parameters of a function with an implicit interface are usually specified by a type declaration statement for the function name; an alternative is by the rules of implicit typing (Section 7.2) applied to the name, but this is not available in a module unless the function has the `private` attribute (see Section 7.6).

The `external` statement merely specifies that each *external-name* is the name of an external or dummy procedure. It does not specify the interface, which remains implicit. However, a mechanism is provided for the interface to be specified. It may be done through an interface block of the form

```
interface
     interface-body
end interface
```

Normally, the *interface-body* is an exact copy of the subprogram's header, the specifications of its arguments and function result, and its `end` statement. However,

- the names of the arguments may be changed;

- other specifications may be included (for example, for a local variable), but not internal procedures, `data` statements, or `format` statements;

- the information may be given by a different combination of statements;[3]

- in the case of an array argument or function result, the expressions that specify a bound may differ as long as their values can never differ; and

- a recursive procedure (Sections 5.16 and 5.17) or a pure procedure (Section 6.10) need not be specified as such if it is not called as such.

An *interface-body* may be provided for a call to an external procedure defined by means other than Fortran (usually C or assembly language).

Naming a procedure in an `external` statement or giving it an interface body (doing both is not permitted) ensures that it is an external or dummy procedure. We strongly recommend the practice for external procedures, since otherwise the processor is permitted to interpret the name as that of an intrinsic procedure. It is needed for portability since processors are permitted to provide additional intrinsic procedures. Naming a procedure in an `external` statement makes all versions of an intrinsic procedure having the same name unavailable. The same is true for giving it an interface body in the way described in the next section (but not when the interface is generic, Section 5.18).

The interface block is placed in a sequence of specification statements and this suffices to make the interface explicit. Perhaps the most convenient way to do this is to place the interface block among the specification statements of a module and then `use` the module. We imagine subprogram libraries being written as sets of external subprograms together with modules holding interface blocks for them. This keeps the modules of modest size. Note that if a procedure is accessible in a scoping unit, its interface is either explicit or implicit there. An external procedure may have an explicit interface in some scoping units and an implicit interface in others.

Interface blocks may also be used to allow procedures to be called as defined operators (Section 3.8), as defined assignments (Section 3.9), or under a single generic name. We

---

[3] A practice that is permitted by the standard, but which we do not recommend, is for a dummy argument to be declared implicitly as a procedure by invoking it in an executable statement. If the subprogram has such a dummy procedure, the interface will need an `external` statement for that dummy procedure.

therefore defer description of the full generality of the interface block until Section 5.18, where overloading is discussed.

An explicit interface is required to invoke a procedure with a pointer or target dummy argument or a pointer function result, and is required for several useful features that we will meet later in this and the next chapter. It is needed so that the processor can make the appropriate linkage. Even when not strictly required, it gives the compiler an opportunity to examine data dependencies and thereby improve optimization. Explicit interfaces are also desirable because of the additional security that they provide. It is straightforward to ensure that all interfaces are explicit and we recommend the practice.

5.12 Procedures as arguments

So far, we have taken the actual arguments of a procedure invocation to be variables and expressions, but another possibility is for them to be procedures. Let us consider the case of a minimization subprogram to perform function minimization. It needs to receive the user's function, just as the subroutine shuffle in Figure 5.5 needs to receive the required number of cards. The minimization code might look like the code in Figure 5.8. Notice the way the procedure argument is declared by an interface block playing a similar role to that of the type declaration statement for a data object. Although such an interface block is not required, we recommend its use.

Figure 5.8

```
real function minimum(a, b, func) ! Returns the minimum
        ! value of the function func(x) in the interval (a,b)
    real, intent(in) :: a, b
    interface
       real function func(x)
          real, intent(in) :: x
       end function func
    end interface
    real :: f,x
    :
    f = func(x)    ! invocation of the user function.
    :
end function minimum
```

Just as the type and shape of actual and dummy data objects must agree, so must the properties of the actual and dummy procedures. The agreement is exactly as for a procedure and an interface body for that procedure (see Section 5.11). It would make no sense to specify an intent attribute (Section 5.9) for a dummy procedure, and this is not permitted.

On the user side, the code may look like that in Figure 5.9. Notice that the structure is rather like a sandwich: user-written code invokes the minimization code which in turn invokes user-written code. Again, we recommend the use of an interface block. As a minimum, the procedure name must be declared in an external statement.

Figure 5.9

```
program main
   real :: a, b, f
   interface
      real function fun(x)
         real, intent(in) :: x
      end function fun
   end interface
   f = minimum(1.0, 2.0, fun)
   :
end program main
real function fun(x)
   :
end function fun
```

The procedure that is passed must be an external or module procedure and its specific name must be passed when it also has a generic name (Section 5.18). Internal procedures are not permitted because it is anticipated that they may be implemented quite differently (for example, by in-line code), and because of the need to identify the depth of recursion when the host is recursive (Section 5.16) and the procedure involves host variables.

5.13   Keyword and optional arguments

In practical applications, argument lists can get long and many of the arguments may often not be needed. For example, a subroutine for constrained minimization might have the form

```
subroutine mincon(n, f, x, upper, lower,                    &
             equalities, inequalities, convex, xstart)
```

On many calls, there may be no upper bounds, or no lower bounds, or no equalities, or no inequalities, or it may not be known whether the function is convex, or a sensible starting point may not be known. All the corresponding dummy arguments may be declared `optional` (see also Section 7.8). For instance, the bounds might be declared by the statement

```
real, optional, dimension(n) :: upper,lower
```

If the first four arguments are the only wanted ones, we may use the statement

```
call mincon(n, f, x, upper)
```

but usually the wanted arguments are scattered. In this case, we may follow a (possibly empty) ordinary positional argument list for leading arguments by a keyword argument list, as in the statement

```
call mincon(n, f, x, equalities=q, xstart=x0)
```

The keywords are the dummy argument names and there must be no further positional arguments after the first keyword argument.

This example also illustrates the merits of both positional and keyword arguments as far as readability is concerned. A small number of leading positional arguments (for example, n, f, and x) are easily linked in the reader's mind to the corresponding dummy arguments. Beyond this, the keywords are very helpful to the reader in making these links. We recommend their use for long argument lists even when there are no gaps caused by optional arguments that are not present.

A non-optional argument must appear exactly once, either in the positional list or in the keyword list. An optional argument may appear at most once, either in the positional list or in the keyword list. An argument must not appear in both lists.

The called subprogram needs some way to detect whether an argument is present so that it can take appropriate action when it is not. This is provided by the intrinsic function present (see Section 8.2). For example

```
present(xstart)
```

returns the value .true. if the current call has provided a starting point and .false. otherwise. When it is absent, the subprogram might use a random number generator to provide a starting point.

A slight complication occurs if an optional dummy argument is used within the subprogram as an actual argument in a procedure invocation. For example, our minimization subroutine might start by calling a subroutine that handles the corresponding equality problem by the call

```
call mineq(n, f, x, equalities, convex, xstart)
```

In such a case, an absent optional argument is also regarded as absent in the second-level subprogram. For instance, when convex is absent in the call of mincon, it is regarded as absent in mineq too. Such absent arguments may be propagated through any number of calls, provided the dummy argument is optional in each case. An absent argument further supplied as an actual argument must be specified as a whole, and not as a subobject. Furthermore, an absent pointer is not permitted to be associated with a non-pointer dummy argument (the target is doubly absent).

Since the compiler will not be able to make the appropriate associations unless it knows the keywords (dummy argument names), the interface must be explicit (Section 5.11) if any of the dummy arguments are optional or keyword arguments are in use. Note that an interface block may be provided for an external procedure to make the interface explicit. In all cases where an interface block is provided, it is the names of the dummy arguments in the block that are used to resolve the associations.

5.14 Scope of labels

Execution of the main program or a subprogram always starts at its first executable statement and any branching always takes place from one of its executable statements to another. Indeed, each subprogram has its own independent set of labels. This includes the case of a host subprogram with several internal subprograms. The same label may be used in the host and the internal subprograms without ambiguity.

This is our first encounter with *scope*. The scope of a label is a main program or a subprogram, excluding any internal subprograms that it contains. The label may be used unambiguously anywhere among the executable statements of its scope. Notice that the host end statement may be labelled and be a branch target from a host statement, that is the internal subprograms leave a hole in the scope of the host (see Figure 5.10).

5.15   Scope of names

In the case of a named entity, there is a similar set of statements within which the name may always be used to refer to the entity. Here, type definitions and interface blocks as well as subprograms can knock holes in scopes. This leads us to regard each program unit as consisting of a set of non-overlapping scoping units. A *scoping unit* is one of the following:

- a derived-type definition,

- a procedure interface body, excluding any derived-type definitions and interface bodies contained within it, or

- a program unit or subprogram, excluding derived-type definitions, interface bodies, and subprograms contained within it.

An example containing five scoping units is shown in Figure 5.10.

Figure 5.10

```
module scope1              ! scope 1
       :                   ! scope 1
contains                   ! scope 1
    subroutine scope2      ! scope 2
        type scope3        ! scope 3
              :            ! scope 3
        end type scope3    ! scope 3
        interface          ! scope 2
              :            ! scope 4
        end interface      ! scope 2
          :                ! scope 2
    contains               ! scope 2
        function scope5(...) ! scope 5
              :            ! scope 5
        end function scope5 ! scope 5
    end subroutine scope2  ! scope 2
end module scope1          ! scope 1
```

Once an entity has been declared in a scoping unit, its name may be used to refer to it in that scoping unit. An entity declared in another scoping unit is always a different entity even if it has the same name and exactly the same properties.[4] Each is known as a *local* entity. This is very helpful to the programmer, who does not have to be concerned about the possibility of accidental name clashes. Note that this is true for derived types, too. Even if two derived types have the same name and the same components, entities declared with them are treated as being of different types.[5]

A use statement of the form

    use *module-name*

is regarded as a re-declaration of all the module entities inside the local scoping unit, with exactly the same names and properties. The module entities are said to be accessible by *use association*. Names of entities in the module may not be used to declare local entities (but see Section 7.10 for a description of further facilities provided by the use statement when greater flexibility is required).

Figure 5.11

```
subroutine outer
   real :: x, y
   :
contains
   subroutine inner
      real :: y
      y = f(x) + 1.
      :
   end subroutine inner
   function f(z)
      real              :: f
      real, intent(in) :: z
      :
   end function f
end subroutine outer
```

In the case of a derived-type definition, a module subprogram, or an internal subprogram, the name of an entity in the host (including an entity accessed by use association) is similarly treated as being automatically re-declared with the same properties, provided no entity with this name is declared locally, is a local dummy argument or function result, or is accessed by use association. The host entity is said to be accessible by *host association*. For example, in the subroutine inner of Figure 5.11, x is accessible by host association, but y is a separate local variable and the y of the host is inaccessible. We note that inner calls another internal procedure that is a function, f; it must not contain a type specification for that function, as the interface is already explicit. Such a specification would, in fact, declare a different, *external*

---

[4] Apart from the effect of storage association, which is not discussed until Chapter 20 and whose use we strongly discourage.

[5] Apart from storage association effects (Chapter 20).

function of that name. The same remark applies to a module procedure calling a function in the same module.

Note that the host does not have access to the local entities of a subroutine that it contains.

Host association does not extend to interface blocks. This allows an interface body to be constructed mechanically from the specification statements of an external procedure. Note, however, that if a derived type needed for the interface is accessed from a module, the interface block constructed from the procedure cannot be placed in the module that defines the type since a module is not permitted to access itself. For example, the attempted access in Figure 5.12 is not permitted.

Figure 5.12

```
module m
    type t
        integer :: i, j, k
    end type t
    interface g
        subroutine s(a)
            use m        ! Illegal module access.
            type(t) :: a
        end subroutine s
    end interface
end module m
```

Within a scoping unit, each named data object, procedure, derived type, named construct, and namelist group (Section 7.15) must have a distinct name, with the one exception of generic names of procedures (to be described in Section 5.18). Note that this means that any appearance of the name of an intrinsic procedure in another rôle makes the intrinsic procedure inaccessible by its name (the renaming facility described in Section 7.10 allows an intrinsic procedure to be accessed from a module and renamed). Within a type definition, each component of the type, each intrinsic procedure referenced, and each derived type or named constant accessed by host association, must have a distinct name. Apart from these rules, names may be reused. For instance, a name may be used for the components of two types, or the arguments of two procedures referenced with keyword calls.

The names of program units and external procedures are *global*, that is available anywhere in a complete program. Each must be distinct from the others and from any of the local entities of the program unit.

At the other extreme, the do variable of an implied-do in a data statement (Section 7.5.2) or an array constructor (Section 6.16) has a scope that is just the implied-do. It is different from any other entity with the same name.

5.16 Direct recursion

Normally, a subprogram may not invoke itself, either directly or indirectly, through a sequence of other invocations. However, if the leading statement is prefixed recursive, this is allowed. Where the subprogram is a function that calls itself directly in this fashion, the function name cannot be used for the function result and another name is needed. This is done by adding a further clause to the function statement as in Figure 5.13, which illustrates the use of a recursive function to sum the entries in a chain (see Section 2.13).

Figure 5.13

```
recursive function sum(top) result(s)
   type(node), pointer :: top
   real             :: s
   if (associated(top)) then
      s = top%value + sum(top%next)
   else
      s = 0.0
   end if
end function sum
```

The type of the function (and its result) may be specified on the function statement, either before or after the token recursive:

```
    integer recursive function factorial(n) result(res)
```
or
```
    recursive integer function factorial(n) result(res)
```

or in a type declaration statement for the result name (as in Figure 5.13). In fact, the result name, rather than the function name, must be used in any specification statement. In the executable statements, the function name refers to the function itself and the result name must be used for the result variable. If there is no result clause, the function name is used for the result, and is not available for a recursive function call.

The result clause may also be used in a non-recursive function.

Just as in Figure 5.13, any recursive procedure that calls itself directly must contain a conditional test that terminates the sequence of calls at some point, otherwise it will call itself indefinitely.

Each time a recursive procedure is invoked, a fresh set of local data objects is created, which ceases to exist on return. They consist of all data objects declared in its specification statements or declared implicitly (see Section 7.2), but excepting those with the data or save attribute (see Sections 7.5 and 7.9) and any dummy arguments. The interface is explicit within the procedure.

5.17   Indirect recursion

A procedure may also be invoked by indirect recursion, that is it may call itself through calls to other procedures. To illustrate that this may be useful, suppose we wish to perform a two-dimensional integration but have only the procedure for one-dimensional integration shown in Figure 5.14.

Figure 5.14

```
recursive function integrate(f, bounds)
   ! Integrate f(x) from bounds(1) to bounds(2)
   real :: integrate
   interface
      function f(x)
         real             :: f
         real, intent(in) :: x
      end function f
   end interface
   real, dimension(2), intent(in) :: bounds
   :
end function integrate
```

Figure 5.15

```
module func
   real             :: yval
   real, dimension(2) :: xbounds, ybounds
contains
   function f(xval)
      real             :: f
      real, intent(in) :: xval
      f = ...      ! Expression involving xval and yval
   end function f
end module func
```

Figure 5.16

```
function fy(y)
   use func
   real             :: fy
   real, intent(in) :: y
   yval = y
   fy = integrate(f, xbounds)
end function fy
```

For example, suppose that it is desired to integrate a function f of x and y over a rectangle. We might write a Fortran function in a module to receive the value of x as an argument and the value of y from the module itself by host association, as shown in Figure 5.15. We can then integrate over x for a particular value of y, as shown in Figure 5.16, where `integrate` might be as shown in Figure 5.14. We may now integrate over the whole rectangle thus

```
volume = integrate(fy, ybounds)
```

Note that `integrate` calls `fy`, which in turn calls `integrate`.

5.18 Overloading and generic interfaces

We saw in Section 5.11 how to use a simple interface block to provide an explicit interface to an external or dummy procedure. Another use is for overloading, that is being able to call several procedures by the same generic name. Here the interface block contains several interface bodies and the `interface` statement specifies the generic name. For example, the code in Figure 5.17 permits both the functions `sgamma` and `dgamma` to be invoked using the generic name `gamma`.

Figure 5.17

```
interface gamma
   function sgamma(x)
      real (selected_real_kind( 6))              :: sgamma
      real (selected_real_kind( 6)), intent(in) :: x
   end function sgamma
   function dgamma(x)
      real (selected_real_kind(12))              :: dgamma
      real (selected_real_kind(12)), intent(in) :: x
   end function dgamma
end interface
```

A specific name for a procedure may be the same as its generic name. For example, the procedure `sgamma` could be renamed `gamma` without invalidating the interface block.

Furthermore, a generic name may be the same as another accessible generic name. In such a case, all the procedures that have this generic name may be invoked through it. This capability is important, since a module may need to extend the intrinsic functions such as `sin` to a new type such as `interval` (Section 3.8).

If it is desired to overload a module procedure, the interface is already explicit so it is inappropriate to specify an interface body. Instead, the statement

```
module procedure procedure-name-list
```

is included in the interface block in order to name the module procedures for overloading; if the functions `sgamma` and `dgamma` above were defined in a module, the interface block becomes

```
interface gamma
   module procedure sgamma, dgamma
end interface
```

It is probably most convenient to place such a block in the module itself.

Any generic specification on an `interface` statement may be repeated on the corresponding `end interface` statement, for example,

```
end interface gamma
```

As for other `end` statements, we recommend use of this fuller form.

Another form of overloading occurs when an interface block specifies a defined operation (Section 3.8) or a defined assignment (Section 3.9) to *extend* an intrinsic operation or assignment. The scope of the defined operation or assignment is the scoping unit that contains the interface block, but it may be accessed elsewhere by use or host association. If an intrinsic operator is extended, the number of arguments must be consistent with the intrinsic form (for example, it is not possible to define a unary *).

The general form of the interface block is

```
interface [generic-spec]
   [interface-body ]...
   [module procedure procedure-name-list]...
      ! Interface bodies and module
      ! procedure statements may appear in any order.
end interface [generic-spec]
```

where *generic-spec* is

generic-name
operator(*defined-operator*)

or

assignment(=)

A `module procedure` statement is permitted only when a *generic-spec* is present, and all the procedures must be accessible module procedures (as shown in the complete module in Figure 5.19 below). No procedure name may be given a particular *generic-spec* more than once in the interface blocks accessible within a scoping unit. An interface body must be provided for an external or dummy procedure.

If `operator` is specified on the interface statement, all the procedures in the block must be functions with one or two non-optional arguments having intent `in`.[6] If `assignment` is specified, all the procedures must be subroutines with two non-optional arguments, the first having intent `out` or `inout` and the second intent `in`. In order that invocations are always unambiguous, if two procedures have the same generic operator and the same number of arguments or both define assignment, one must have a dummy argument that corresponds

---

[6]Since intent must not be specified in Fortran 95 for a pointer dummy argument (Section 5.7.1), this implies that if an operand of derived data type also has the pointer attribute, it is the value of its target that is passed to the function defining the operator, and not the pointer itself. The pointer status is inaccessible within the function. In Fortran 2003, `intent` may be specified for a pointer dummy argument.

by position in the argument list to a dummy argument of the other that has a different type, different kind type parameter, or different rank.

All procedures that have a given generic name must be subroutines or all must be functions, including the intrinsic ones when an intrinsic procedure is extended. Any two non-intrinsic procedures with the same generic name must have arguments that differ sufficiently for any invocation to be unambiguous. The rule is that either

i) one of them has more non-optional data-object arguments of a particular data type, kind type parameter, and rank than the other has data-object arguments (including optional data-object arguments) of that data type, kind type parameter, and rank; or

ii) at least one of them has a non-optional dummy argument that both

- corresponds by position in the argument list to a dummy argument that is not present in the other, is present with a different type or kind type parameter, or is present with a different rank, and

- corresponds by name to a dummy argument that is not present in the other, is present with a different type or kind type parameter, or is present with a different rank.

For case ii), both rules are needed in order to cater for both keyword and positional dummy argument lists. For instance, the interface in Figure 5.18 is invalid because the two functions are always distinguishable in a positional call, but not on a keyword call such as f(i=int, x=posn). If a generic invocation is ambiguous between a non-intrinsic and an intrinsic procedure, the non-intrinsic procedure is invoked.

Figure 5.18

```
!  Example of a broken overloading rule
   interface f
      function fxi(x,i)
         real              :: fxi
         real, intent(in) :: x
         integer           :: i
      end function fxi
      function fix(i,x)
         real              :: fix
         real, intent(in) :: x
         integer           :: i
      end function fix
   end interface
```

Note that the presence or absence of the pointer attribute is insufficient to ensure an unambiguous invocation since a pointer actual argument may be associated with a non-pointer dummy argument, see Section 5.7.1.

Figure 5.19

```
module sorts
   type time
      real :: seconds
   end type time
   type velocity
      real :: metres_per_second
   end type velocity
   type length
      real :: metres
   end type length
   type length_squared
      real :: metres_squared
   end type length_squared
   interface operator(/)
      module procedure length_by_time
   end interface
   interface operator(+)
      module procedure time_plus_time
   end interface
   interface sqrt
      module procedure sqrt_metres_squared
   end interface
contains
   function length_by_time(s, t)
      type(length), intent(in) :: s
      type(time), intent(in)    :: t
      type(velocity)            :: length_by_time
      length_by_time%metres_per_second = s%metres / t%seconds
   end function length_by_time
   function time_plus_time(t1, t2)
      type(time), intent(in)    :: t1, t2
      type(time)                :: time_plus_time
      time_plus_time%seconds = t1%seconds + t2%seconds
   end function time_plus_time
   function sqrt_metres_squared(l2)
      type(length_squared), intent(in) :: l2
      type(length)                      :: sqrt_metres_squared
      sqrt_metres_squared%metres = sqrt(l2%metres_squared)
   end function sqrt_metres_squared
end module sorts
```

There are many scientific applications in which it is useful to keep a check on the sorts of quantities involved in a calculation. For instance, in dimensional analysis, whereas it might be sensible to divide length by time to obtain velocity, it is not sensible to add time to velocity. There is no intrinsic way to do this, but we conclude this section with an outline example, see Figures 5.19 and 5.20, of how it might be achieved using derived types.

Figure 5.20

```
program test
   use sorts
   type(length)          :: s  = length(10.0), l
   type(length_squared)  :: s2 = length_squared(10.0)
   type(velocity)        :: v
   type(time)            :: t  = time(3.0)
   v = s / t
! Note: v = s + t    or    v = s * t   would be illegal
   t = t + time(1.0)
   l = sqrt(s2)
   print *, v, t, l
end program test
```

Note that definitions for operations between like entities are also required, as shown by time_plus_time. Similarly, any intrinsic function that might be required, here sqrt, must be overloaded appropriately. Of course, this can be avoided if the components of the variables are referenced directly, as in

```
t%seconds = t%seconds + 1.0
```

5.19   Assumed character length

A character dummy argument may be declared with an asterisk for the value of the length type parameter, in which case it automatically takes the value from the actual argument. For example, a subroutine to sort the elements of a character array might be written thus

```
subroutine sort(n,chars)
   integer, intent(in)                         :: n
   character(len=*), dimension(n), intent(in)  :: chars
   :
end subroutine sort
```

If the length of the associated actual argument is needed within the procedure, the intrinsic function len (Section 8.6) may be invoked, as in Figure 5.21.

An asterisk must not be used for a kind type parameter value. This is because a change of character length is analogous to a change of an array size and can easily be accommodated in the object code, whereas a change of kind probably requires a different machine instruction for every operation involving the dummy argument. A different version of the procedure

---

Figure 5.21

```
integer function count (letter, string)
   character (1), intent(in) :: letter
   character (*), intent(in) :: string
!    Count the number of occurrences of letter in string
   count = 0
   do i = 1, len(string)
      if (string(i:i) == letter) count = count + 1
   end do
end function count
```

---

would need to be generated for each possible kind value of each argument. The overloading feature (previous section) gives the programmer an equivalent functionality with explicit control over which versions are generated.

5.20   The subroutine and function statements

We finish this chapter by giving the syntax of the subroutine and function statements, which have so far been explained through examples. It is

   [*prefix*] subroutine *subroutine-name* [([*dummy-argument-list*])]

and

   [*prefix*] function *function-name* ([*dummy-argument-list*]) &
   [result(*result-name*)]

where *prefix* is

   prefix-spec [*prefix-spec*] ...

and *prefix-spec* is *type*, recursive, pure, or elemental. A *prefix-spec* must not be repeated. For details of *type*, see Section 7.13; this, of course, must not be present on a subroutine statement.

Apart from pure and elemental, which will be explained in Sections 6.10 and 6.11, each feature has been explained separately and the meanings are the same in the combinations allowed by the syntax.

5.21   Summary

A program consists of a sequence of program units. It must contain exactly one main program but may contain any number of modules and external subprograms. We have described each kind of program unit. Modules contain data definitions, type definitions, namelist groups, interface blocks, and module subprograms, all of which may be accessed in other program units with the use statement. The program units may be in any order, but many compilers require modules to precede their use.

Subprograms define procedures, which may be functions or subroutines. They may also be defined intrinsically (Chapter 8) and external procedures may be defined by means other than Fortran. We have explained how information is passed between program units and to procedures through argument lists and through the use of modules. Procedures may be called recursively provided they are correspondingly specified.

The interface to a procedure may be explicit or implicit. If it is explicit, keyword calls may be made, and the procedure may have optional arguments. Interface blocks permit procedures to be invoked as operations or assignments, or by a generic name. The character lengths of dummy arguments may be assumed.

We have also explained about the scope of labels and Fortran names, and introduced the concept of a scoping unit.

5.22 Exercises

1. A subroutine receives as arguments an array of values, x, and the number of elements in x, n. If the mean and variance of the values in x are estimated by

$$\text{mean} = \frac{1}{n}\sum_{i=1}^{n} x(i)$$

and

$$\text{variance} = \frac{1}{n-1}\sum_{i=1}^{n}(x(i) - \text{mean})^2$$

write a subroutine which returns these calculated values as arguments. The subroutine should check for invalid values of n (≤ 1).

2. A subroutine `matrix_mult` multiplies together two matrices A and B, whose dimensions are $i \times j$ and $j \times k$, respectively, returning the result in a matrix C dimensioned $i \times k$. Write `matrix_mult`, given that each element of C is defined by

$$C(m, n) = \sum_{\ell=1}^{J}(A(m, \ell) \times B(\ell, n))$$

The matrices should appear as arguments to `matrix_mult`.

3. The subroutine `random_number` (Section 8.16.3) returns a random number in the range 0.0 to 1.0, that is

```
call random_number(r)    ! 0≤r<1
```

Using this function, write the subroutine `shuffle` of Figure 5.4.

4. A character string consists of a sequence of letters. Write a function to return that letter of the string which occurs earliest in the alphabet; for example, the result of applying the function to DGUMVETLOIC is C.

5. Write an internal procedure to calculate the volume, $\pi r^2 \ell$, of a cylinder of radius r and length ℓ, using as the value of π the result of `acos(-1.0)`, and reference it in a host procedure.

6. Choosing a simple card game of your own choice, and using the random number procedure (Section 8.16.3), write the subroutines `deal` and `play` of Section 5.4, using data in a module to communicate between them.

7. Objects of the intrinsic type `character` are of a fixed length. Write a module containing a definition of a variable-length character string type, of maximum length 80, and also the procedures necessary to:

    i)   assign a character variable to a string;

   ii) assign a string to a character variable;

 iii) return the length of a string;

 iv) concatenate two strings.

6. Array features

6.1   Introduction

In an era when many computers have the hardware capability for efficient processing of array operands, it is self-evident that a numerically-based language such as Fortran should have matching notational facilities. Such facilities provide not only a notational convenience for the programmer, but provide an opportunity to extend the power of the language.

Arrays were introduced in Sections 2.10 to 2.13, their use in simple expressions and in assignments was explained in Sections 3.10 and 3.11, and they were used as procedure arguments in Chapter 5. These descriptions were deliberately restricted because Fortran contains a very full set of array features whose complete description would have unbalanced those chapters. The purpose of this chapter is to describe the array features in detail, but without anticipating the descriptions of the array intrinsic procedures of Chapter 8; the rich set of intrinsic procedures should be regarded as an integral part of the array features.

6.2   Zero-sized arrays

It might be thought that an array would always have at least one element. However, such a requirement would force programs to contain extra code to deal with certain natural situations. For example, the code in Figure 6.1 solves a lower-triangular set of linear equations. When i has the value n, the sections have size zero, which is just what is required.

Figure 6.1

```
do i = 1,n
   x(i) = b(i) / a(i, i)
   b(i+1:n) = b(i+1:n) - a(i+1:n, i) * x(i)
end do
```

Fortran allows arrays to have zero size in all contexts. Whenever a lower bound exceeds the corresponding upper bound, the array has size zero.

There are few special rules for zero-sized arrays because they follow the usual rules, though some care may be needed in their interpretation. For example, two zero-sized arrays of the same rank may have different shapes. One might have shape (0,2) and the other (0,3) or (2,0).

Such arrays of differing shape are not conformable and therefore may not be used together as the operands of a binary operation. However, an array is always conformable with a scalar so the statement

   zero-sized-array = *scalar*

is valid and the scalar is 'broadcast to all the array elements', making this a 'do nothing' statement.

A zero-sized array is regarded as being defined always, because it has no values that can be undefined.

6.3   Assumed-shape arrays

Outside Chapter 20, we require that the shapes of actual and dummy arguments agree, and so far we have achieved this by passing the extents of the array arguments as additional arguments. However, it is possible to require that the shape of the dummy array be taken automatically to be that of the corresponding actual array argument. Such an array is said to be an *assumed-shape* array. When the shape is declared by the `dimension` clause, each dimension has the form

   [*lower-bound*] :

where *lower-bound* is an integer expression that may depend on module data or the other arguments (see Section 7.14 for the exact rules). If *lower-bound* is omitted, the default value is 1. Note that it is the shape that is passed, and not the upper and lower bounds. For example, if the actual array is a, declared thus:

```
real, dimension(0:10, 0:20) :: a
```

and the dummy array is da, declared thus:

```
real, dimension(:, :) :: da
```

then `a(i,j)` corresponds to `da(i+1,j+1)`; to get the natural correspondence, the lower bound must be declared:

```
real, dimension(0:, 0:) :: da
```

In order that the compiler knows that additional information is to be supplied, the interface must be explicit (Section 5.11) at the point of call. A dummy array with the `pointer` attribute is not regarded as an assumed-shape array because its shape is not necessarily assumed.

6.4   Automatic objects

A procedure with dummy arguments that are arrays whose size varies from call to call may also need local arrays whose size varies. A simple example is the array work in the subroutine to interchange two arrays that is shown in Figure 6.2.

An array whose extents vary in this way is called an *automatic array*, and is an example of an *automatic data object*. Such an object is not a dummy argument and its declaration

Figure 6.2

```
subroutine swap(a, b)
   real, dimension(:), intent(inout) :: a, b
   real, dimension(size(a))          :: work
            ! size provides the size of an array,
            ! and is defined in Section 8.12.2.
   work = a
   a = b
   b = work
end subroutine swap
```

contains one or more values that are not known at compile time; that is, not an initialization expression (Section 7.4). An implementation is likely to bring them into existence when the procedure is called and destroy them on return, maintaining them on a stack.[1] The values must be defined by specification expressions (Section 7.14).

The other way that automatic objects arise is through varying character length. The variable word2 in

```
subroutine example(word1)
   character(len = *), intent(inout) :: word1
   character(len = len(word1))       :: word2
```

is an example. If a function result has varying character length, the interface must be explicit at the point of call because the compiler needs to know this, as shown in Figure 6.3.

Figure 6.3

```
program loren
   character (len = *), parameter :: a = 'just a simple test'
   print *, double(a)
contains
   function double(a)
      character (len = *), intent(in) :: a
      character (len = 2*len(a))      :: double
      double = a//a
   end function double
end program loren
```

An array bound or the character length of an automatic object is fixed for the duration of each execution of the procedure and does not vary if the value of the specification expression varies or becomes undefined.

---

[1]A stack is a memory management mechanism whereby fresh storage is established and old storage is discarded on a 'last in, first out' basis, often within contiguous memory.

Some small restrictions on the use of automatic data objects appear in Sections 7.5, 7.9, and 7.15.

6.5   Heap storage

There is an underlying assumption in Fortran that the processor supplies a mechanism for managing heap[2] storage. The statements described in this section are the user interface to that mechanism.

6.5.1   Allocatable arrays

Sometimes an array is required to be of a size that is known only after some data have been read or some calculations performed. An array with the `pointer` attribute might be used for this purpose, but this is really not appropriate if the other properties of pointers are not needed. Instead, an array that is not a dummy argument or function result may be given the `allocatable` attribute by a statement such as

```
real, dimension(:, :), allocatable :: a
```

Such an array is called *allocatable*. Its rank is specified when it is declared, but the bounds are undefined until an `allocate` statement such as

```
allocate(a(n, 0:n+1))      ! n of type integer
```

has been executed for it. Its initial allocation status is 'not currently allocated' and it becomes allocated following successful execution of an `allocate` statement.

An important example is shown in Figure 6.4. The array `work` is placed in a module and is allocated at the beginning of the main program to a size that depends on input data. The array is then available throughout program execution in any subprogram that has a `use` statement for `work_array`.

Figure 6.4

```
module work_array
   integer                       :: n
   real, dimension(:,:,:), allocatable :: work
end module work_array
program main
   use work_array
   read *, n
   allocate(work(n, 2*n, 3*n))
   :
```

When an allocatable array a is no longer needed, it may be deallocated by execution of the statement

---

[2]A heap is a memory management mechanism whereby fresh storage may be established and old storage may be discarded in any order. Mechanisms to deal with the progressive fragmentation of the memory are usually required.

```
deallocate (a)
```

following which the array is 'not currently allocated'. The deallocate statement is described in more detail in Section 6.5.3.

If it is required to make any change to the bounds of an allocatable array, the array must be deallocated and then allocated afresh. It is an error to allocate an allocatable array that is already allocated, or to deallocate an allocatable array that is not currently allocated, but one that can easily be avoided by the use of the allocated intrinsic function (Section 8.12.1).

If a variable-sized array component of a structure is required, unfortunately, an array pointer must be used (see Section 6.14). The prohibition on allocatable arrays here was made to keep the feature simple, but this is now recognized as a mistake that has been corrected in Fortran 2003 (see Section 12.4).

An undefined allocation status cannot occur. On return from a subprogram, an allocated allocatable array without the save attribute is automatically deallocated if it is local to the subprogram, and it is processor dependent as to whether it remains allocated or is deallocated if it is local to a module and is accessed only by the subprogram. This automatic deallocation avoids inadvertent memory leakage.[3]

6.5.2 The allocate statement

We mentioned in Section 2.13 that the allocate statement can also be used to give fresh storage for a pointer target directly. A pointer becomes associated (Section 3.3) following successful execution of the statement. The general form of the allocate statement is

allocate(*allocation-list* [, stat=*stat*])

where *allocation-list* is a list of allocations of the form

allocate-object [(*array-bounds-list*)]

each *array-bound* has the form

[*lower-bound*:] *upper-bound*

and *stat* is a scalar integer variable that must not be part of an object being allocated.

If the stat= specifier is present, *stat* is given either the value zero after a successful allocation or a positive value after an unsuccessful allocation (for example, if insufficient storage is available). After an unsuccessful execution, each array that was not successfully allocated retains its previous allocation or pointer association status. If stat= is absent and the allocation is unsuccessful, program execution stops.

Each *allocate-object* is an allocatable array or a pointer. It may have zero character length and in the case of a pointer may be a structure component.

Each *lower-bound* and each *upper-bound* is a scalar integer expression. The default value for the lower bound is 1. The number of *array-bounds* in a list must equal the rank of the *allocate-object*. They determine the array bounds, which do not alter if the value of a variable in one of the expressions changes subsequently. An array may be allocated to be of size zero.

---

[3]Fortran 90 did not have automatic deallocation, which led to the possibility of an allocation status of undefined, which was highly undesirable since it meant that no further use of the array was allowed.

The bounds of all the arrays being allocated are regarded as undefined during the execution of the allocate statement, so none of the expressions that specify the bounds may depend on any of the bounds or on the value of the stat= variable. For example,

```
allocate (a(size(b)), b(size(a)))   ! illegal
```

or even

```
allocate (a(n), b(size(a)))         ! illegal
```

is not permitted, but

```
allocate (a(n))
allocate (b(size(a)))
```

is valid. This restriction allows the processor to perform the allocations in a single allocate statement in any order.

In contrast to the case with an allocatable array, a pointer may be allocated a new target even if it is currently associated with a target. In this case, the previous association is broken. If the previous target was created by allocation, it becomes inaccessible unless another pointer is associated with it. We expect linked lists normally to be created by using a single pointer in an allocate statement for each node of the list, using pointer components of the allocated object at the node to hold the links from the node. We illustrate this by the addition of an extra nonzero element to the sparse vector held as a chain of entries of the type

```
type entry
   real                  :: value
   integer               :: index
   type(entry), pointer :: next
end type entry
```

of Section 2.13. The code in Figure 6.5 adds the new entry at the front of the chain. Note the importance of the last statement being a pointer assignment: the assignment

```
first = current
```

would overwrite the old leading entry by the new one.

Figure 6.5

```
type(entry), pointer :: first, current
real    :: fill
integer :: fill_index
   :
allocate (current)
current = entry (fill, fill_index, first)
first => current
```

6.5.3 The deallocate statement

When an allocatable array or pointer target is no longer needed, its storage may be recovered by using the `deallocate` statement. Its general form is

deallocate (*allocate-object-list* [, stat=*stat*])

where each *allocate-object* is an allocatable array that is allocated or a pointer that is associated with the whole of a target that was allocated through a pointer in an `allocate` statement.[4] Here *stat* is a scalar integer variable that must not be deallocated by the statement nor depend on an object that is deallocated by the statement. If `stat=` is present, *stat* is given either the value zero after a successful execution or a positive value after an unsuccessful execution (for example, if a pointer is disassociated). After an unsuccessful execution, each array that was not successfully deallocated retains its previous allocation or pointer association status. If `stat=` is absent and the deallocation is unsuccessful, program execution stops.

A pointer becomes disassociated (Section 3.3) following successful execution of the statement. If there is more than one object in the list, there must be no dependencies among them, to allow the processor to deallocate the objects one by one in any order.

A danger in using the `deallocate` statement is that storage may be deallocated while pointers are still associated with the targets it held. Such pointers are left 'dangling' in an undefined state, and must not be reused until they are again associated with an actual target.

In order to avoid an accumulation of unused and unusable storage, all explicitly allocated storage should be explicitly deallocated when it is no longer required (although, as noted at the end of Section 6.5.1, for allocatable arrays, there are circumstances in which this is automatic). This explicit management is required in order to avoid a potentially significant overhead on the part of the processor in handling arbitrarily complex allocation and reference patterns.

Note also that the standard does not specify whether the processor recovers storage allocated through a pointer but no longer accessible through this or any other pointer. This might be important where, for example, a pointer function is referenced within an expression — the programmer cannot rely on the compiler to arrange for deallocation. To ensure that there is no memory leakage, it is necessary to use such functions only on the right-hand side of pointer assignments, as in the example `compact` in Section 5.10, or as pointer component values in structure constructors, and to deallocate the pointer (y in Section 5.10) when it is no longer needed (but see also Section 13.3).

6.5.4 The nullify statement

A pointer may be explicitly disassociated from its target by executing a `nullify` statement. Its general form is

nullify (*pointer-object-list*)

---

[4]Note that this excludes a pointer that is associated with an allocatable array.

There must be no dependencies among the objects, in order to allow the processor to nullify the objects one by one in any order. The statement is also useful for giving the disassociated status to an undefined pointer. An advantage of nullifying pointers rather than leaving them undefined is that they may then be tested by the intrinsic function `associated` (Section 8.2). For example, the end of the chain of Figure 6.5 will be flagged as a disassociated pointer if the statement

```
nullify(first)
```

is executed initially to create a zero-length chain. Because often there are other ways to access a target (for example, through another pointer), the `nullify` statement does not deallocate the targets. If deallocation is also required, a `deallocate` statement should be executed instead.

6.6   Elemental operations and assignments

We saw in Section 3.10 that an intrinsic operator can be applied to conformable operands, to produce an array result whose element values are the values of the operation applied to the corresponding elements of the operands. Such an operation is called *elemental*.

It is not essential to use operator notation to obtain this effect. Many of the intrinsic procedures (Chapter 8) are elemental and have scalar dummy arguments that may be called with array actual arguments provided all the array arguments have the same shape. For a function, the shape of the result is the shape of the array arguments. For example, we may find the square roots of all the elements of a real array thus:

```
a = sqrt(a)
```

For a subroutine, if any argument is array-valued, all the arguments with intent `out` or `inout` must be arrays. If a procedure that references an elemental function has an optional array-valued dummy argument that is absent, that dummy argument must not be used in the elemental reference unless another array of the same rank is associated with a non-optional argument of the elemental procedure (to ensure that the rank does not vary from call to call).

Similarly, an intrinsic assignment may be used to assign a scalar to all the elements of an array, or to assign each element of an array to the corresponding element of an array of the same shape (Section 3.11). Such an assignment is also called *elemental*.

If a similar effect is desired for a defined operator, it is not strictly necessary to provide a function for each rank or pair of ranks for which it is needed, rather, an elemental procedure can be defined for this purpose (Section 6.11). The module in Figure 6.6 would provide summation for scalars and rank-one arrays of intervals (Section 3.8).

Similarly, elemental versions of defined assignments may be provided explicitly but, again, this is not necessary (see Section 6.11).

6.7   Array-valued functions

We mentioned in Section 5.10 that a function may have an array-valued result, and have used this language feature in Figure 6.6 where the interpretation is obvious.

Figure 6.6

```
module interval_addition
   type interval
      real :: lower, upper
   end type interval
   interface operator(+)
      module procedure add00, add11
   end interface
contains
   function add00 (a, b)
      type (interval)              :: add00
      type (interval), intent(in) :: a, b
      add00%lower = a%lower + b%lower   ! Production code would
      add00%upper = a%upper + b%upper   ! allow for roundoff.
   end function add00
   function add11 (a, b)
      type (interval), dimension(:), intent(in)       :: a
      type (interval), dimension(size(a))             :: add11
      type (interval), dimension(size(a)), intent(in) :: b
      add11%lower = a%lower + b%lower   ! Production code would
      add11%upper = a%upper + b%upper   ! allow for roundoff.
   end function add11
end module interval_addition
```

In order that the compiler should know the shape of the result, the interface must be explicit (Section 5.11) whenever such a function is referenced. The shape is specified within the function definition by the dimension attribute for the function name. Unless the function result is a pointer, the bounds must be explicit expressions and they are evaluated on entry to the function. For another example, see the declaration of the function result in Figure 6.7.

An array-valued function is not necessarily elemental. For example, at the end of Section 3.10 we considered the type

```
type matrix
   real :: element
end type matrix
```

Its scalar and rank-one operations might be as for reals, but for multiplying a rank-two array by a rank-one array, we might use the module function shown in Figure 6.7 to provide matrix by vector multiplication.

6.8   The where statement and construct

It is often desired to perform an array operation only for certain elements, say those whose values are positive. The where statement provides this facility. A simple example is

Figure 6.7

```
function mult(a, b)
!
    type(matrix), dimension(:, :)        :: a
    type(matrix), dimension(size(a, 2)) :: b
                   ! size is defined in Section 8.12
    type(matrix), dimension(size(a, 1)) :: mult
    integer                              :: j, n
!
    mult = 0.0     ! A defined assignment from a real
                   ! scalar to a rank-one matrix.
    n = size(a, 1)
    do j = 1, size(a, 2)
       mult = mult + a(1:n, j) * b(j)
                ! Uses defined operations for addition of
                ! two rank-one matrices and multiplication
                ! of a rank-one matrix by a scalar matrix.
    end do
end function mult
```

```
where ( a > 0.0 ) a = 1.0/a     ! a is a real array
```

which reciprocates the positive elements of a and leaves the rest unaltered. The general form
is

```
where (logical-array-expr) array-variable = expr
```

The logical array expression *logical-array-expr* must have the same shape as *array-variable*.
It is evaluated first and then just those elements of *expr* that correspond to elements of *logical-
array-expr* that have the value true are evaluated and are assigned to the corresponding
elements of *array-variable*. All other elements of *array-variable* are left unaltered. The
assignment may be a defined assignment, provided that it is elemental (Section 6.11).

A single logical array expression may be used for a sequence of array assignments all of
the same shape. The general form of this construct is

```
where (logical-array-expr)
    array-assignments
end where
```

The logical array expression *logical-array-expr* is first evaluated and then each array
assignment is performed in turn, under the control of this mask. If any of these assignments
affect entities in *logical-array-expr*, it is always the value obtained when the where statement
is executed that is used as the mask.

The where construct may take the form

```
where (logical-array-expr)
    array-assignments
elsewhere
    array-assignments
end where
```

Here, the assignments in the first block of assignments are performed in turn under the control of *logical-array-expr* and then the assignments in the second block are performed in turn under the control of .not.*logical-array-expr*. Again, if any of these assignments affect entities in *logical-array-expr*, it is always the value obtained when the where statement is executed that is used as the mask. No array assignment in a where construct may be a branch target statement.

A simple example of a where construct is

```
where (pressure <= 1.0)
    pressure = pressure + inc_pressure
    temp = temp + 5.0
elsewhere
    raining = .true.
end where
```

where pressure, inc_pressure, temp, and raining are arrays of the same shape.

If a where statement or construct masks an elemental function reference, the function is called only for the wanted elements. For example,

```
where ( a > 0 ) a = log(a)      ! log is defined in Section 8.4
```

would not lead to erroneous calls of log for negative arguments.

This masking applies to all elemental function references except any that are within an argument of a non-elemental function reference. The masking does not extend to array arguments of such a function. In general, such arguments have a different shape so that masking would not be possible, but the rule applies in such a case as

```
where (a > 0) a = a/sum(log(a)) ! sum is defined in Section 8.11
```

Here the logarithms of each of the elements of a are summed, and the statement will fail if they are not all positive.

If a non-elemental function reference or an array constructor is masked, it is fully evaluated before the masking is applied.

It is permitted to mask not only the where statement of the where construct, but also any elsewhere statement that it contains. The masking expressions involved must be of the same shape. A where construct may contain any number of masked elsewhere statements but at most one elsewhere statement without a mask, and that must be the final one. In addition, where constructs may be nested within one another; the masking expressions of the nested constructs must be of the same shape, as must be the array variables on the left-hand sides of the assignments.

A simple where statement such as that at the start of this section is permitted within a where construct and is interpreted as if it were the corresponding where construct containing one array assignment.

Finally, a where construct may be named in the same way as other constructs.

An example illustrating more complicated where constructs that are named is shown in Figure 6.8.

Figure 6.8

```
assign_1: where (cond_1)
             :                    ! masked by cond_1
          elsewhere (cond_2)
             :                    ! masked by
             :                    ! cond_2.and..not.cond_1
assign_2:    where (cond_4)
                :                 ! masked by
                :                 ! cond_2.and..not.cond_1.and.cond_4
             elsewhere
                :        ! masked by
                :        ! cond_2.and..not.cond_1.and..not.cond_4
             end where assign_2
             :
          elsewhere (cond_3) assign_1
             :           ! masked by
             :           ! cond_3.and..not.cond_1.and..not.cond_2
          elsewhere assign_1
             :       ! masked by
             :       ! not.cond_1.and..not.cond_2.and..not.cond_3
          end where assign_1
```

All the statements of a where construct are executed one by one in sequence, including the where and elsewhere statements. The logical array expressions in the where and elsewhere statements are evaluated once and control of subsequent assignments is not affected by changes to the values of these expressions. Throughout a where construct there is a control mask and a pending mask which change after the evaluation of each where, elsewhere, and end where statement, as illustrated in Figure 6.8.

6.9   The forall statement and construct

When elements of an array are assigned values by a do construct such as

```
do i = 1, n
   a(i, i) = 2.0 * x(i)      ! a is rank-2 and x rank-1
end do
```

the processor is required to perform each successive iteration in order and one after the other. This represents a potentially severe impediment to optimization on a parallel processor so, for this purpose, Fortran has the forall statement. The above loop can be written as

```
forall(i = 1:n) a(i, i) = 2.0 * x(i)
```

which specifies that the set of expressions denoted by the right-hand side of the assignment is first evaluated in any order, and the results are then assigned to their corresponding array elements, again in any order of execution. The `forall` statement may be considered to be an array assignment expressed with the help of indices. In this particular example, we note also that this operation could not otherwise be represented as a simple array assignment. Other examples of the `forall` statement are

```
forall(i = 1:n, j = 1:m)                  a(i, j) = i + j
forall(i = 1:n, j = 1:n, y(i, j) /= 0.) x(j, i) = 1.0/y(i, j)
```

where, in the second statement, we note the masking condition — the assignment is not carried out for zero elements of y.

The `forall` construct also exists. The `forall` equivalent of the array assignments

```
a(2:n-1, 2:n-1) = a(2:n-1, 1:n-2) + a(2:n-1, 3:n)     &
                  + a(1:n-2, 2:n-1) + a(3:n, 2:n-1)
b(2:n-1, 2:n-1) = a(2:n-1, 2:n-1)
```

is

```
forall(i = 2:n-1, j = 2:n-1)
   a(i, j) = a(i, j-1) + a(i, j+1) + a(i-1, j) + a(i+1, j)
   b(i, j) = a(i, j)
end forall
```

This sets each internal element of a equal to the sum of its four nearest neighbours and copies the result to b. The `forall` version is more readable. Note that each assignment in a `forall` is like an array assignment; the effect is as if all the expressions were evaluated in any order, held in temporary storage, then all the assignments performed in any order. The first statement must fully complete before the second can begin.

A `forall` statement or construct may contain pointer assignments. An example is

```
type element
   character(32), pointer :: name
end type element
type(element)           :: chart(200)
character(32), target :: names(200)
:                          ! define names
forall(i =1:200)
   chart(i)%name => names(i)
end forall
```

Note that there is no array syntax for performing, as in this example, an array of pointer assignments.

As with all constructs, `forall` constructs may be nested. The sequence

```
forall (i = 1:n-1)
   forall (j = i+1:n)
      a(i, j) = a(j, i)                ! a is a rank-2 array
   end forall
end forall
```

assigns the transpose of the lower triangle of a to the upper triangle of a.

A forall construct can include a where statement or construct. Each statement of a where construct is executed in sequence. An example with a where statement is

```
forall (i = 1:n)
   where ( a(i, :) == 0) a(i, :) = i
   b(i, :) = i / a(i, :)
end forall
```

Here, each zero element of a is replaced by the value of the row index and, following this complete operation, the elements of the rows of b are assigned the reciprocals of the corresponding elements of a multiplied by the corresponding row index.

The complete syntax of the forall construct is

```
[name:] forall(index = lower: upper [:stride] &
       [, index = lower: upper [:stride]]... [,scalar-logical-expr] )
           [body]
        end forall [name]
```

where *index* is a named integer scalar variable. Its scope is that of the construct; that is, other variables may have the name but are separate and not accessible in the forall. The *index* may not be redefined within the construct. Within a nested construct, each *index* must have a distinct name. The expressions *lower*, *upper*, and *stride* (*stride* is optional but must be nonzero when present) are scalar integer expressions and form a sequence of values as for a section subscript (Section 6.13); they may not reference any *index* of the same statement but may reference an *index* of an outer forall. Once these expressions have been evaluated, the *scalar-logical-expr*, if present, is evaluated for each combination of index values. Those for which it has the value .true. are active in each statement of the construct. The *name* is the optional construct name; if present, it must appear on both the forall and the end forall statements.

The *body* itself consists of one or more: assignment statements, pointer assignment statements, where statements or constructs, and further forall statements or constructs. The subobject on the left-hand side of each assignment in the *body* should reference each *index* of the constructs it is contained in as part of the identification of the subobject, whether it be a non-pointer variable or a pointer object.[5] None of the statements in the *body* may be a branch target, for instance for a go to statement.

---

[5]This is not actually a requirement, but any missing *index* would need to be restricted to a single value to satisfy the requirements of the final paragraph of this section. For example, the statement

```
forall (i = i1:i2, j = j1:j2) a(j) = a(j) + b(i, j)
```

is valid only if i1 and i2 have the same value.

In the case of a defined assignment statement, the subroutine that is invoked must not reference any variable that becomes defined by the statement, nor any pointer object that becomes associated.

A `forall` construct whose body is a single assignment or pointer assignment statement may be written as a single `forall` statement.

Procedures may be referenced within the scope of a `forall`, both in the logical scalar expression that forms the optional mask or, directly or indirectly (for instance as a defined operation or assignment), in the body of the construct. *All such procedures must be pure* (see Section 6.10).

As in assignments to array sections (Section 6.13), it is not allowed to make a many-to-one assignment. The construct

```
forall (i = 1:10)
   a(index(i)) = b(i)        ! a, b and index are arrays
end forall
```

is valid if and only if `index(1:10)` contains no repeated values. Similarly, it is not permitted to associate more than one target with the same pointer.

6.10   Pure procedures

In the description of functions in Section 5.10, we noted the fact that, although it is permissible to write functions with side-effects, this is regarded as undesirable. In fact, used within `forall` statements or constructs (Section 6.9), the possibility that a function or subroutine reference might have side-effects is a severe impediment to optimization on a parallel processor — the order of execution of the assignments could affect the results. In order to control this situation, it is possible for the programmer to assert that a procedure has no side-effects by adding the pure keyword to the subroutine or function statement. In practical terms, this is an assertion that the procedure

   i) if a function, does not alter any dummy argument;

   ii) does not alter any part of a variable accessed by host or use association;

   iii) contains no local variable with the `save` attribute;

   iv) performs no operation on an external file (Chapters 9 and 10); and

   v) contains no `stop` statement.

To ensure that these requirements are met and that a compiler can easily check that this is so, there are the following further rules:

   i) any dummy argument that is a procedure and any procedure referenced must be pure and have an explicit interface;

   ii) the intent of a dummy argument must be declared unless it is a procedure or a pointer, and this intent must be in in the case of a function;

   iii) any procedure internal to a pure procedure must be pure; and

iv) a variable that is accessed by host or use association or is an intent in dummy argument or any part of such a variable must not be the target of a pointer assignment statement; it must not be the right-hand side of an intrinsic assignment if the left-hand side is of derived type with a pointer component at any level of component selection; and it must not be associated as an actual argument with a dummy argument that is a pointer or has intent out or inout.

This last rule ensures that a local pointer cannot cause a side-effect but unfortunately prevents benign uses such as aliasing (Section 6.15) for use within an expression.

The function in Figure 5.6 (Section 5.10) is pure, and this could be specified explicitly:

```
pure function distance(p, q)
```

An external or dummy procedure that is used as a pure procedure must have an interface block that specifies it as pure. However, the procedure may be used in other contexts without the use of an interface block or with an interface block that does not specify it as pure. This allows library procedures to be specified as pure without limiting them to be used as such.

The main reason for allowing pure subroutines is to be able to use a defined assignment in a forall statement or construct and so, unlike pure functions, they may have dummy arguments that have intent out or inout or the pointer attribute. Their existence also gives the possibility of making subroutine calls from within pure functions.

All the intrinsic functions (Chapter 8) are pure, and can thus be referenced freely within pure procedures. Also, the elemental intrinsic subroutine mvbits (Section 8.8.3) is pure.

The pure attribute is given automatically to any procedure that has the elemental attribute (next section).

6.11   Elemental procedures

We have met already the notion of elemental intrinsic procedures (Section 6.6 and, later, Chapter 8) — those with scalar dummy arguments that may be called with array actual arguments provided that the array arguments have the same shape (that is, provided all the arguments are conformable). For a function, the shape of the result is the shape of the array arguments. This feature exists too for non-intrinsic procedures. This requires the elemental prefix on the function or subroutine statement. For example, we could make the function add_intervals of Section 3.8 elemental, as shown in Figure 6.9. This is enormously useful

Figure 6.9

```
   elemental function add_intervals(a,b)
      type(interval)            :: add_intervals
      type(interval), intent(in) :: a, b
      add_intervals%lower = a%lower + b%lower ! Production code
      add_intervals%upper = a%upper + b%upper ! would allow for
   end function add_intervals                 ! roundoff.
```

to the programmer who could get the same effect in Fortran 90 only by writing 22 versions, for ranks 0-0, 0-1, 1-0, 1-1, 0-2, 2-0, 2-2, ..., 0-7, 7-0, 7-7, and is an aid to optimization on parallel processors.

An elemental procedure must satisfy all the requirements of a pure procedure (previous section); in fact, it automatically has the `pure` attribute. In addition, all dummy arguments and function results must be scalar variables without the pointer attribute. A dummy argument or its subobject may be used in a specification expression only as an argument to the intrinsic functions `bit_size`, `kind`, `len` or numeric inquiry functions of Section 8.7.2. An example is

```
elemental real function f(a)
   real, intent(in)                          :: a
   real(selected_real_kind(precision(a)*2)) :: work
   :
end function f
```

This restriction prevents character functions yielding an array result with elements of varying character lengths and permits implementations to create array-valued versions that employ ordinary arrays internally. A simple example that would break the rule is

```
elemental function c(n)
   character (len=n)   :: c       ! Invalid
   integer, intent(in) :: n
   real                :: work(n) ! Invalid
   :
end function c
```

If this were allowed, a rank-one version would need to hold `work` as a ragged-edge array of rank two.

An interface block for an external procedure is required if the procedure itself is non-intrinsic and elemental. The interface must specify it as elemental. This is because the compiler may use a different calling mechanism in order to accommodate the array case efficiently. It contrasts with the case of pure procedures, where more freedom is permitted (see previous section).

For an elemental subroutine, if any argument is array valued, all the arguments with intent `inout` or `out` must be arrays. For example, we can make the subroutine `swap` of Figure 6.2 (Section 6.4) perform its task on arrays of any shape or size, as shown in Figure 6.10. Calling `swap` with an array and a scalar argument is obviously erroneous and is not permitted.

Figure 6.10

```
elemental subroutine swap(a, b)
   real, intent(inout)  :: a, b
   real                 :: work
   work = a
   a = b
   b = work
end subroutine swap
```

If a generic procedure reference (Section 5.18) is consistent with both an elemental and a non-elemental procedure, the non-elemental procedure is invoked. For example, we might write versions of add_intervals (Figure 6.9) for arrays of rank one and rely on the elemental function for other ranks. In general, one must expect the elemental version to execute more slowly for a specific rank than the corresponding non-elemental version.

We note that a non-intrinsic elemental procedure may not be used as an actual argument. A procedure is not permitted to be both elemental and recursive.

6.12   Array elements

In Section 2.10, we restricted the description of array elements to simple cases. In general, an array element is a scalar of the form

   part-ref [*%part-ref*] . . .

where *part-ref* is

   part-name [(*subscript-list*)]

The last *part-ref* must have a *subscript-list*. The number of subscripts in each list must be equal to the rank of the array or array component, and each subscript must be a scalar integer expression whose value is within the bounds of its dimension of the array or array component. To illustrate this, take the type

```
type triplet
    real                :: u
    real, dimension(3)  :: du
    real, dimension(3,3) :: d2u
end type triplet
```

which was considered in Section 2.10. An array may be declared of this type:

```
type(triplet), dimension(10,20,30) :: tar
```

and

```
tar(n,2,n*n)        ! n of type integer
```

is an array element. It is a scalar of type triplet and

```
tar(n, 2, n*n)%du
```

is a real array with

```
tar(n, 2, n*n)%du(2)
```

as one of its elements.

If an array element is of type character, it may be followed by a substring reference:

   (*substring-range*)

for example,

```
page (k*k) (i+1:j-5) ! i, j, k of type integer
```

By convention, such an object is called a substring rather than an array element.

Notice that it is the array *part-name* that the subscript list qualifies. It is not permitted to apply such a subscript list to an array designator unless the designator terminates with an array *part-name*. An array section, a function reference, or an array expression in parentheses must not be qualified by a subscript list.

6.13 Array subobjects

Array sections were introduced in Section 2.10 and provide a convenient way to access a regular subarray such as a row or a column of a rank-two array:

```
a(i, 1:n)    ! Elements 1 to n of row i
a(1:m, j)    ! Elements 1 to m of column j
```

For simplicity of description, we did not explain that one or both bounds may be omitted when the corresponding bound of the array itself is wanted, and that a stride other than one may be specified:

```
a(i, :)       ! The whole of row i
a(i, 1:n:3)   ! Elements 1, 4, ... of row i
```

Another form of section subscript is a rank-one integer expression. All the elements of the expression must be defined with values that lie within the bounds of the parent array's subscript. For example,

```
v( (/ 1, 7, 3, 2 /) )
```

is a section with elements $v(1)$, $v(7)$, $v(3)$, and $v(2)$, in this order. Such a subscript is called a *vector subscript*. If there are any repetitions in the values of the elements of a vector subscript, the section is called a *many–one section* because more than one element of the section is mapped onto a single array element. For example

```
v( (/ 1, 7, 3, 7 /) )
```

has elements 2 and 4 mapped onto $v(7)$. A many–one section must not appear on the left of an assignment statement because there would be several possible values for a single element. For instance, the statement

```
v( (/ 1, 7, 3, 7 /) ) = (/ 1, 2, 3, 4 /)      ! Illegal
```

is not allowed because the values 2 and 4 cannot both be stored in $v(7)$. The extent is zero if the vector subscript has zero size.

When an array section with a vector subscript is an actual argument, it is regarded as an expression and the corresponding dummy argument must not be defined or redefined and must not have intent out or inout. We expect compilers to make a copy as a temporary regular array on entry but to perform no copy back on return. Also, an array section with a vector subscript is not permitted to be a pointer target, since allowing them would seriously complicate the mechanism that compilers would otherwise have to establish for pointers. For similar reasons, such an array section is not permitted to be an internal file (Section 9.6).

In addition to the regular and irregular subscripting patterns just described, the intrinsic circular shift function cshift (Section 8.13.5) provides a mechanism that manipulates array sections in a 'wrap-round' fashion. This is useful in handling the boundaries of certain types of periodic grid problems, although it is subject to similar restrictions to those on vector subscripts. If an array v(5) has the value [1,2,3,4,5], then cshift(v, 2) has the value [3,4,5,1,2].

The general form of a subobject is

   part-ref[%*part-ref*] ... [(*substring-range*)]

where *part-ref* now has the form

   part-name [(*section-subscript-list*)]

where the number of section subscripts in each list must be equal to the rank of the array or array component. Each *section-subscript* is either a *subscript* (Section 6.12), a rank-one integer expression (vector subscript), or a *subscript-triplet* of the form

   [*lower*] : [*upper*] [: *stride*]

where *lower*, *upper*, and *stride* are scalar integer expressions. If *lower* is omitted, the default value is the lower bound for this subscript of the array. If *upper* is omitted, the default value is the upper bound for this subscript of the array. If *stride* is omitted, the default value is one. The stride may be negative so that it is possible to take, for example, the elements of a row in reverse order by specifying a section such as

   a(i, 10:1:-1)

The extent is zero if *stride*>0 and *lower*>*upper*, or if *stride*<0 and *lower*<*upper*. The value of *stride* must not be zero.

Normally, we expect the values of both *lower* and *upper* to be within the bounds of the corresponding array subscript. However, all that is required is that each value actually used to select an element is within the bounds. Thus,

   a(1, 2:11:2)

is legal even if the upper bound of the second dimension of a is only 10.

The *subscript-triplet* specifies a sequence of subscript values,

   *lower, lower + stride, lower + 2*stride, . . .*

going as far as possible without going beyond *upper* (above it when $stride > 0$ or below it when $stride < 0$). The length of the sequence for the ith *subscript-triplet* determines the ith extent of the array that is formed.

The rank of a *part-ref* with a *section-subscript-list* is the number of vector subscripts and subscript triplets that it contains. So far in this section, all the examples have been of rank one; by contrast, the ordinary array element

```
a(1,7)
```

is an example of a *part-ref* of rank zero, and the section

```
a(:,1:7)
```

is an example of a *part-ref* of rank two. The rank of a *part-ref* without a *section-subscript-list* is the rank of the object or component. A *part-ref* may be an array; for example,

```
tar%du(2)
```

for the array `tar` of Section 6.12 is an array section with elements `tar(1)%du(2)`, `tar(2)%du(2)`, `tar(3)%du(2)`, ... Being able to form sections in this way from arrays of derived type, as well as by selecting sets of elements, is a very useful feature of the language. A more prosaic example, given the specification

```
type(person), dimension(1:50) :: my_group
```

for the type `person` of Section 2.9, is the subobject `my_group%id` which is an integer array section of size 50.

Unfortunately, it is not permissible for more than one *part-ref* to be an array; for example, it is not permitted to write

```
tar%du    ! Illegal
```

for the array `tar` of Section 6.12. The reason for this is that if `tar%du` were considered to be an array, its element (1,2,3,4) would correspond to

```
tar(2,3,4)%du(1)
```

which would be too confusing a notation.

The *part-ref* with nonzero rank determines the rank and shape of the subobject. If any of its extents is zero, the subobject itself has size zero. It is called an array section if the final *part-ref* has a *section-subscript-list* or another *part-ref* has a nonzero rank.

A *substring-range* may be present only if the last *part-ref* is of type character and is either a scalar or has a *section-subscript-list*. By convention, the resulting object is called a section rather than a substring. It is formed from the unqualified section by taking the specified substring of each element. Note that, if c is a rank-one character array,

```
c(i:j)
```

is the section formed from elements i to j; if substrings of all the array elements are wanted, we may write the section

```
c(:)(k:l)
```

An array section that ends with a component name is also called a *structure component*. Note that if the component is scalar, the section cannot be qualified by a trailing subscript list or section subscript list. Thus, using the example of Section 6.12,

```
tar%u
```

is such an array section and

```
tar(1, 2, 3)%u
```

is a component of a valid element of `tar`. The form

```
tar%u(1, 2, 3)   ! not permitted
```

is not allowed.

Additionally, a *part-name* to the right of a *part-ref* with nonzero rank must not have the `pointer` attribute. This is because such an object would represent an array of pointers and require a very different implementation mechanism from that needed for an ordinary array. For example, consider the array

```
type(entry), dimension(n) :: rows  ! n of type integer
```

for the type `entry` defined near the end of Section 6.5.2. If we were allowed to write the object `rows%next`, it would be interpreted as another array of size n and type `entry`, but its elements are likely to be stored without any regular pattern (each having been separately given storage by an `allocate` statement) and indeed some will be null if any of the pointers are disassociated. Note that there is no problem over accessing individual pointers such as `rows(i)%next`.

6.14 Arrays of pointers

Although arrays of pointers as such are not allowed in Fortran, the equivalent effect can be achieved by creating a type containing a pointer component. For example, a lower-triangular matrix may be held by using a pointer for each row. Consider the type

```
type row
   real, dimension(:), pointer :: r
end type row
```

and the arrays

```
type(row), dimension(n) :: s, t     ! n of type integer
```

Storage for the rows can be allocated thus

```
do i = 1, n                ! i of type integer
   allocate (t(i)%r(1:i)) ! Allocate row i of length i
end do
```

The array assignment

```
s = t
```

would then be equivalent to the pointer assignments

```
s(i)%r => t(i)%r
```

for all the components.

A type containing just a pointer component is useful also when constructing a linked list that is more complicated than the chain described in Section 2.13. For instance, if a variable number of links are needed at each entry, the recursive type entry of Figure 2.3 might be expanded to the pair of types:

```
type ptr
    type(entry), pointer :: point
end type ptr
type entry
    real                 :: value
    integer              :: index
    type(ptr), pointer   :: children(:)
end type entry
```

After appropriate allocations and pointer associations, it is then possible to refer to the index of child j of node as

```
node%children(j)%point%index
```

This extra level of indirection is necessary because the individual elements of children do not, themselves, have the pointer attribute — this is a property only of the whole array. For example, we can take two existing nodes, say a and b, each of which is a tree root, and make a big tree thus

```
tree%children(1)%point => a
tree%children(2)%point => b
```

which would not be possible with the original type entry.

6.15   Pointers as aliases

If an array section without vector subscripts, such as

```
table(m:n, p:q)
```

is wanted frequently while the integer variables m, n, p, and q do not change their values, it is convenient to be able to refer to the section as a named array such as

```
window
```

Such a facility is provided in Fortran by pointers and the pointer assignment statement. Here window would be declared thus

```
real, dimension(:, :), pointer :: window
```

and associated with table, which must of course have the target or pointer attribute, by the execution of the statement

```
window  => table(m:n, p:q)
```

If, later on, the size of `window` needs to be changed, all that is needed is another pointer assignment statement. Note, however, that the subscript bounds for `window` in this example are (1:n-m+1, 1:q-p+1) since they are as provided by the functions `lbound` and `ubound` (Section 8.12.2).

The facility provides a mechanism for subscripting or sectioning arrays such as

```
tar%u
```

where `tar` is an array and `u` is a scalar component, discussed in Section 6.13. Here we may perform the pointer association

```
taru => tar%u
```

if `taru` is a rank-three pointer of the appropriate type. Subscripting as in

```
taru(1, 2, 3)
```

is then permissible. Here the subscript bounds for `taru` will be those of `tar`.

6.16   Array constructors

The syntax that we introduced in Section 2.10 for array constants may be used to construct more general rank-one arrays. The general form of an *array-constructor* is

```
(/ array-constructor-value-list /)
```

where each *array-constructor-value* is one of *expr* or *constructor-implied-do*. The array thus constructed is of rank one with its sequence of elements formed from the sequence of scalar expressions and elements of the array expressions in array element order. A *constructor-implied-do* has the form

```
(array-constructor-value-list, variable = expr1, expr2 [,expr3])
```

where *variable* is a named integer scalar variable, and *expr1*, *expr2*, and *expr3* are scalar integer expressions. Its interpretation is as if the *array-constructor-value-list* had been written

```
max ( (expr2 - expr1 + expr3)/expr3, 0 )
```

times, with *variable* replaced by *expr1*, *expr1+expr3*,..., as for the do construct (Section 4.5). A simple example is

```
(/ (i,i=1,10) /)
```

which is equal to

```
(/ 1, 2, 3, 4, 5, 6, 7, 8, 9, 10 /)
```

Note that the syntax permits nesting of one *constructor-implied-do* inside another, as in the example

```
(/ ((i,i=1,3), j=1,3) /)
```

which is equal to

```
(/ 1, 2, 3, 1, 2, 3, 1, 2, 3 /)
```

and the nesting of structure constructors within array constructors (and vice versa), for instance, for the type in Section 6.7,

```
(/ (matrix(0.0), i = 1, 100) /)
```

The sequence may be empty, in which case a zero-sized array is constructed. The scope of the *variable* is the *constructor-implied-do*. Other statements, or even other parts of the array constructor, may refer to another variable having the same name. The value of the other variable is unaffected by execution of the array constructor and is available except within the *constructor-implied-do*.

The type and type parameters of an array constructor are those of the first *expr*, and each *expr* must have the same type and type parameters. If every *expr*, *expr1*, *expr2*, and *expr3* is an initialization expression (Section 7.4), the array constructor is an initialization expression.

An array of rank greater than one may be constructed from an array constructor by using the intrinsic function reshape (Section 8.13.3). For example,

```
reshape( source = (/ 1,2,3,4,5,6 /), shape = (/ 2,3 /) )
```

has the value

```
1   3   5
2   4   6
```

6.17 Mask arrays

Logical arrays are needed for masking in where statements and constructs (Section 6.8), and they play a similar role in many of the array intrinsic functions (Chapter 8). Often, such arrays are large, and there may be a worthwhile storage gain from using non-default logical types, if available. For example, some processors may use bytes to store elements of logical(kind=1) arrays, and bits to store elements of logical(kind=0) arrays. Unfortunately, there is no *portable* facility to specify such arrays, since there is no intrinsic function comparable to selected_int_kind and selected_real_kind.

Logical arrays are formed implicitly in certain expressions, usually as compiler-generated temporary variables. In

```
where (a > 0.0) a = 2.0 * a
```

or

```
if (any(a > 0.0)) then    ! any is described in Section 8.11.1
```

the expression a > 0.0 is a logical array. In such a case, an optimizing compiler can be expected to choose a suitable kind type parameter for the temporary array.

6.18   Summary

We have explained that arrays may have zero size and that no special rules are needed for them. A dummy array may assume its shape from the corresponding actual argument. Storage for an array may be allocated automatically on entry to a procedure and automatically deallocated on return, or the allocation may be controlled in detail by the program. Functions may be array-valued either through the mechanism of an elemental reference that performs the same calculation for each array element, or through the truly array-valued function. Array assignments may be masked through the use of the where statement and construct. Structure components may be arrays if the parent is an array or the component is an array, but not both. A subarray may either be formulated directly as an array section, or indirectly by using pointer assignment to associate it with a pointer. An array may be constructed from a sequence of expressions. A logical array may be used as a mask.

The intrinsic functions are an important part of the array features and will be described in Chapter 8.

We conclude this chapter with a complete program, Figures 6.12 and 6.13, that illustrates the use of array expressions, array assignments, allocatable arrays, automatic arrays, and array sections. The module linear contains a subroutine for solving a set of linear equations, and this is called from a main program that prompts the user for the problem and then solves it.

Figure 6.12

```
module linear
   integer, parameter, public :: kind=selected_real_kind(10)
   public :: solve

contains
   subroutine solve(a, piv_tol, b, ok)
   ! arguments
      real(kind), intent(inout), dimension(:,:) :: a
                        ! The matrix a.
      real(kind), intent(in) :: piv_tol
                        ! Smallest acceptable pivot.
      real(kind), intent(inout), dimension(:) :: b
                        ! The right-hand side vector on
                        ! entry. Overwritten by the solution.
      logical, intent(out)      :: ok
                        ! True after a successful entry
                        ! and false otherwise.

   ! Local variables
      integer :: i      ! Row index.
      integer :: j      ! Column index.
      integer :: n      ! Matrix order.
      real(kind), dimension(size(b)) :: row
                        ! Automatic array needed for workspace;
                        ! size is described in Section 8.12.2.
      real(kind) :: element ! Workspace variable.

      n = size(b)
      ok = size(a, 1) == n .and. size(a, 2) == n
      if (.not.ok) then
         return
      end if

      do j = 1, n

!        Update elements in column j.
         do i = 1, j - 1
            a(i+1:n, j) = a(i+1:n, j) - a(i,j) * a(i+1:n, i)
         end do

!        Find pivot and check its size
         i = maxloc(abs(a(j:n, j)), dim=1) + j - 1
            ! maxloc is described in Section 8.14.
         if (abs(a(i, j)) < piv_tol) then
            ok = .false.
            return
         end if
```

Figure 6.13

```
!      If necessary, apply row interchange
         if (i/=j) then
             row = a(j, :); a(j, :) = a(i, :); a(i, :) = row
             element = b(j); b(j) = b(i); b(i) = element
         end if

!      Compute elements j+1 : n of j-th column.
         a(j+1:n, j) = a(j+1:n, j)/a(j, j)
      end do

!  Forward substitution
      do i = 1, n-1
         b(i+1:n) = b(i+1:n) - b(i)*a(i+1:n, i)
      end do

!   Back-substitution
      do j = n, 1, -1
         b(j) = b(j)/a(j, j)
         b(1:j-1) =  b(1:j-1) - b(j)*a(1:j-1, j)
      end do
   end subroutine solve
end module linear

program main
   use linear
   integer :: i, n
   real(kind), allocatable :: a(:, :), b(:)
   logical :: ok

   print *, ' Matrix order?'
   read *,  n
   allocate ( a(n, n), b(n) )
   do i = 1, n
      write(*,'(a, i2, a)') ' Elements of row ', i, ' of a?'
             ! Edit descriptors are described in Section 9.12
      read *, a(i,:)
      write(*,'(a, i2, a)') ' Component ', i, ' of b?'
      read *, b(i)
   end do

   call solve(a, maxval(abs(a))*1.0e-10, b, ok)
   if (ok) then
      write(*, '(/,a,/,(5f12.4))') ' Solution is', b
   else
      print *, ' The matrix is singular'
   end if
end program main
```

6.19 Exercises

1. Given the array declaration

```
real, dimension(50,20) :: a
```

write array sections representing

    i) the first row of a;

    ii) the last column of a;

    iii) every second element in each row and column;

    iv) as for (iii) in reverse order in both dimensions;

    v) a zero-sized array.

2. Write a where statement to double the value of all the positive elements of an array z.

3. Write an array declaration for an array j which is to be completely defined by the statement

```
j = (/ (3, 5, i=1,5), 5,5,5, (i, i =  5,3,-1 ) /)
```

4. Classify the following arrays:

```
subroutine example(n, a, b)
   real, dimension(n, 10) :: w
   real                   :: a(:), b(0:)
   real, pointer          :: d(:, :)
```

5. Write a declaration and a pointer assignment statement suitable to reference as an array all the third elements of component du in the elements of the array tar having all three subscript values even (Section 6.12).

6. Given the array declarations

```
integer, dimension(100, 100), target :: l, m, n
integer, dimension(:, :), pointer     :: ll, mm, nn
```

rewrite the statements

```
l(j:k+1, j-1:k) = l(j:k+1, j-1:k) + l(j:k+1, j-1:k)
l(j:k+1, j-1:k) = m(j:k+1, j-1:k) + n(j:k+1, j-1:k) + n(j:k+1, j:k+1)
```

as they could appear following execution of the statements

```
ll => l(j:k+1, j-1:k)
mm => m(j:k+1, j-1:k)
nn => n(j:k+1, j-1:k)
```

7. Complete Exercise 1 of Chapter 4 using array syntax instead of do constructs.

8. Write a module to maintain a data structure consisting of a linked list of integers, with the ability to add and delete members of the list, efficiently.

9. Write a module that contains the example in Figure 6.7 (Section 6.7) as a module procedure and supports the defined operations and assignments that it contains.

7. Specification statements

7.1 Introduction

In the preceding chapters we have learnt the elements of the Fortran language, how they may be combined into expressions and assignments, how we may control the logic flow of a program, how to divide a program into manageable parts, and have considered how arrays may be processed. We have seen that this knowledge is sufficient to write programs, when combined with a rudimentary print statement and with the end statement.

Already in Chapters 2 to 6, we met some specification statements when declaring the type and other properties of data objects, but to ease the reader's task we did not always explain all the available options. In this chapter we fill this gap. To begin with, however, it is necessary to recall the place of specification statements in a programming language. A program is processed by a computer in stages. In the first stage, *compilation*, the source code (text) of the program is read by a program known as a *compiler* which analyses it, and generates files containing *object code*. Each program unit of the complete program is usually processed separately. The object code is a translation of the source code into a form which can be understood by the computer hardware, and contains the precise instructions as to what operations the computer is to perform. Using these files, an executable program is constructed. The final stage consists of the *execution*, whereby the coded instructions are performed and the results of the computations made available.

During the first stage, the compiler requires information about the entities involved. This information is provided at the beginning of each program unit or subprogram by specification statements. The description of most of these is the subject of this chapter. The specification statements associated with procedure interfaces, including interface blocks and the interface statement and also the external statement, were explained in Chapter 5. The intrinsic statement is explained in Chapter 8. The statements connected with storage association (common, equivalence, and sequence) are deferred to Chapter 20.

7.2 Implicit typing

Many programming languages require that all typed entities have their types specified explicitly. Any data entity that is encountered in an executable statement without its type having been declared will cause the compiler to indicate an error. This, and a prohibition on mixing types, is known as *strong typing*. In the case of Fortran, an entity appearing in the code without having been explicitly typed is normally *implicitly* typed, being assigned a type according to its initial letter. The default in a program unit or an interface block is that entities whose names begin with one of the letters i, j,...,n are of type default integer, and variables beginning with the letters a,b,...,h or o,p,...,z are of type default real. This absence of strong typing can lead to program errors; for instance, if a variable name is misspelt, the misspelt name will give rise to a separate variable. For this reason, we recommend that implicit typing be avoided.

Implicit typing does not apply to an entity accessed by use or host association because its type is the same as in the module or the host.

If a different rule for implicit typing is desired in a given scoping unit, the implicit statement may be employed. For no implicit typing whatsoever, the statement

```
implicit none
```

is available (our recommendation), and for changing the mapping between the letters and the types, statements such as

```
implicit integer (a-h)
implicit real(selected_real_kind(10)) (r,s)
implicit type(entry) (u,x-z)
```

are available. The letters are specified as a list in which a set of adjacent letters in the alphabet may be abbreviated, as in a-h. No letter may appear twice in the implicit statements of a scoping unit and, if there is an implicit none statement, there must be no other implicit statement in the scoping unit. For a letter not included in the implicit statements, the mapping between the letter and a type is the default mapping.

In the case of a scoping unit other than a program unit or an interface block, for example a module subprogram, the default mapping for each letter in an inner scoping unit is the mapping for the letter in the immediate host. If the host contains an implicit none statement, the default mapping is null and the effect may be that implicit typing is available for some letters, because of an additional implicit statement in the inner scope, but not for all of them. The mapping may be to a derived type even when that type is not otherwise accessible in the inner scoping unit because of a declaration there of another type with the same name.

Figure 7.1 provides a comprehensive illustration of the rules of implicit typing.

The general form of the implicit statement is

```
implicit none
```

or

```
implicit type (letter-spec-list) [,type (letter-spec-list)]...
```

where *type* specifies the type and type parameters (Section 7.13) and each *letter-spec* is *letter* [- *letter*].

The implicit statement may be used for a derived type. For example, given access to the type

Figure 7.1

```
module example_mod
   implicit none
   :
   interface
      function fun(i)      ! i is implicitly
         integer :: fun    ! declared integer.
      end function fun
   end interface
contains
   function jfun(j)        ! All data entities must
      integer :: jfun, j   ! be declared explicitly.
      :
   end function jfun
end module example_mod
subroutine sub
   implicit complex (c)
   c = (3.0,2.0)                ! c is implicitly declared complex
   :
contains
   subroutine sub1
      implicit integer (a,c)
      c = (0.0,0.0) ! c is host associated and of type complex
      z = 1.0        ! z is implicitly declared real.
      a = 2          ! a is implicitly declared integer.
      cc = 1.0       ! cc is implicitly declared integer.
      :
   end subroutine sub1
   subroutine sub2
      z = 2.0        ! z is implicitly declared real and is
                     ! different from the variable z in sub1.
      :
   end subroutine sub2
   subroutine sub3
   use example_mod             ! Access the integer function fun.
      q = fun(k)               ! q is implicitly declared real and
                               ! k is implicitly declared integer.
      :
   end subroutine sub3
end subroutine sub
```

```
type posn
   real    :: x, y
   integer :: z
end type posn
```

and given the statement

```
implicit type(posn) (a,b), integer (c-z)
```

variables beginning with the letters a and b are implicitly typed posn and variables beginning with the letters c,d,...,z are implicitly typed integer.

An implicit none statement may be preceded within a scoping unit only by use (and format) statements, and other implicit statements may be preceded only by use, parameter, and format statements. We recommend that all implicit statements be at the start of the specifications, immediately following any use statements.

7.3   Declaring entities of differing shapes

So far, we have used separate type declaration statements such as

```
integer              :: a, b
integer, dimension(10)  :: c, d
integer, dimension(8,7) :: e
```

to declare several entities of the same type but differing shapes. In fact, Fortran permits the convenience of using a single statement. Whether or not there is a dimension attribute present, arrays may be declared by placing the shape information after the name of the array:

```
integer :: a, b, c(10), d(10), e(8, 7)
```

If the dimension attribute is present, it provides a default shape for the entities that are not followed by their own shape information, and is ignored for those that are:

```
integer, dimension(10) :: c, d, e(8, 7)
```

7.4   Named constants and initialization expressions

Inside a program, we often need to define a constant or set of constants. For instance, in a program requiring repeated use of the speed of light, we might use a real variable c that is given its value by the statement

```
c = 2.99792458
```

A danger in this practice is that the value of c may be overwritten inadvertently, for instance because another programmer reuses c as a variable to contain a different quantity, failing to notice that the name is already in use.

It might also be that the program contains specifications such as

```
real    :: x(10), y(10), z(10)
integer :: mesh(10, 10), ipoint(100)
```

where all the dimensions are 10 or 10^2. Such specifications may be used extensively, and 10 may even appear as an explicit constant, say as a parameter in a do-construct which processes these arrays:

```
do i = 1, 10
```

Later, it may be realised that the value 20 rather than 10 is required, and the new value must be substituted everywhere the old one occurs, an error-prone undertaking.

Yet another case was met in Section 2.6, where named constants were needed for kind type parameter values.

In order to deal with all of these situations, Fortran contains what are known as *named constants*. These may never appear on the left-hand side of an assignment statement, but may be used in expressions in any way in which a literal constant may be used, except within a complex constant (Section 2.6.3).[1] A type declaration statement may be used to specify such a constant:

```
real, parameter :: c = 2.99792458
```

The value is protected, as c is now the name of a constant and may not be used as a variable name in the same scoping unit. Similarly, we may write

```
integer, parameter :: length = 10
real               :: x(length), y(length), z(length)
integer            :: mesh(length, length), ipoint(length**2)
:
do i = 1, length
```

which has the clear advantage that in order to change the value of 10 to 20 only a single line need be modified, and the new value is then correctly propagated.

In this example, the expression length**2 appeared in one of the array bound specifications. This is a particular example of an initialization expression. Such an expression is expected to be evaluated at compile time, so it is restricted in its form. An *initialization expression* is an expression in which each operation is intrinsic, each exponentiation operator has an integer power and each primary is

i) a constant or a subobject of a constant,

ii) an array constructor whose expressions (including bounds and strides) have primaries that are initialization expressions,

iii) a structure constructor whose components are initialization expressions,

iv) an integer or character elemental intrinsic function reference whose arguments are initialization expressions of type integer or character,

---

[1]This irregularity is corrected in Fortran 2003.

v) a reference to one of the transformational intrinsic functions `repeat`, `reshape`, `selected_int_kind`, `selected_real_kind`, `transfer`, and `trim` with actual arguments that are initialization expressions,

vi) a reference to the transformational intrinsic function `null` with an argument that is either of type other than character or has character length that is defined by an initialization expression and is not assumed,

vii) a reference to

an array inquiry function (Section 8.12) other than `allocated`, the bit inquiry function `bit_size`, the character inquiry function `len`, the kind inquiry function `kind`, or a numeric inquiry function (Section 8.7.2)

where each argument is either an initialization expression or a variable whose type parameters or bounds inquired about are neither assumed, defined by an expression other than an initialization expression, defined by an `allocate` statement, nor defined by a pointer assignment,

viii) an implied-do variable with initialization expressions as bounds and strides, or

ix) an initialization expression enclosed in parentheses,

and where each subscript, section subscript, or substring bound is an initialization expression.

If an initialization expression invokes an inquiry function for a type parameter or an array bound of an object, the type parameter or array bound must be specified in a prior specification statement or to the left in the same specification statement.

In the definition of a named constant we may use any initialization expression, and the constant becomes defined with the value of the expression according to the rules of intrinsic assignment. This is illustrated by the example

```
integer, parameter :: length=10, long=selected_real_kind(12)
real, parameter    :: lsq = length**2
```

Note from this example that it is possible in one statement to define several named constants, in this case two, separated by commas.

A named constant may be an array, as in the case

```
real, dimension(3), parameter :: field = (/ 0.0, 10.0, 20.0 /)
```

For an array of rank greater than one, the `reshape` function described in Section 8.13.3 must be applied.

A named constant may be of derived type, as in the case

```
type(posn), parameter :: a = posn(1.0,2.0,0)
```

for the type defined at the end of Section 7.2. Note that a subobject of a constant need not necessarily have a constant value. For example, if i is an integer variable, `field(i)` may have the value 0.0, 10.0, or 20.0. Note also that a constant may not be a pointer, allocatable array, dummy argument, or function result, since these are always variables. However, it may be of a derived type with a pointer component that is disassociated (Section 7.5.4):

```
type(entry), parameter :: e = entry(0.0, null())
```

Clearly, since such a pointer component is part of a constant, it is not permitted to be allocated or pointer assigned.

Any named constant used in an initialization expression must either be accessed from the host, be accessed from a module, be declared in a preceding statement, or be declared to the left of its use in the same statement. An example using a constant expression including a named constant that is defined in the same statement is

```
integer, parameter :: apple = 3, pear = apple**2
```

Finally, there is an important point concerning the definition of a scalar named constant of type `character`. Its length may be specified as an asterisk and taken directly from its value, which obviates the need to count the length of a character string, making modifications to its definition much easier. An example of this is

```
character(len=*), parameter :: string = 'No need to count'
```

Unfortunately, there *is* a need to count when a character array is defined using an array constructor, since all the elements must be of the same length:

```
character(len=7), parameter, dimension(3) ::             &
                c=(/'Cohen  ', 'Metcalf', 'Reid   '/)
```

would not be correct without the two blanks in `'Cohen  '` and the three in `'Reid   '` (a restriction that can be circumvented in Fortran 2003, see Section 17.9).

The `parameter` attribute is an important means whereby constants may be protected from overwriting, and programs modified in a safe way. It should be used for these purposes on every possible occasion.

7.5   Initial values for variables

7.5.1   Initialization in type declaration statements

A variable may be assigned an initial value in a type declaration statement, simply by following the name of the variable by an initialization expression (Section 7.4), as in the examples

```
real            :: a = 0.0
real, dimension(3) :: b = (/ 0.0, 1.2, 4.5 /)
```

The initial value is defined by the value of the corresponding expression according to the rules of intrinsic assignment. The variable automatically acquires the `save` attribute (Section 7.9). It must not be a dummy argument, a pointer, an allocatable array, an automatic object, or a function result.

7.5.2   The data statement

An alternative way to specify an initial value for a variable is by the `data` statement. It has the general form

```
data object-list /value-list/ [[,] object-list /value-list/]...
```

where *object-list* is a list of variables and implied-do loops; and *value-list* is a list of scalar constants and structure constructors. A simple example is

```
real    :: a, b, c
integer :: i, j, k
data      a,b,c/1.,2.,3./, i,j,k/1,2,3/
```

in which a variable a acquires the initial value 1., b the value 2., etc.

If any part of a variable is initialized in this way, the variable automatically acquires the save atribute. The variable must not be a dummy argument, an allocatable array, an automatic object, or a function result. It may be a pointer and the corresponding value must be a reference to the intrinsic function null with no arguments.

After any array or array section in *object-list* has been expanded into a sequence of scalar elements in array element order, there must be as many constants in each *value-list* as scalar elements in the corresponding *object-list*. Each scalar element is assigned the corresponding scalar constant.

Constants which repeat may be written once and combined with a scalar integer *repeat count* which may be a named or literal constant:

```
data i,j,k/3*0/
```

The value of the repeat count must be positive or zero. As an example consider the statement

```
data r(1:length)/length*0./
```

where r is a real array and length is a named constant which might take the value zero.

Arrays may be initialized in three different ways: as a whole, by element, or by an implied-do loop. These three ways are shown below for an array declared by

```
real :: a(5, 5)
```

Firstly, for the whole array, the statement

```
data a/25*1.0/
```

sets each element of a to 1.0.

Secondly, individual elements and sections of a may be initialized, as in

```
data a(1,1), a(3,1), a(1,2), a(3,3) /2*1.0, 2*2.0/
data a(2:5,4) /4*1.0/
```

in each of which only the four specified elements and the section are initialized. Each array subscript must be an initialization expression, as must any character substring subscript.

When the elements to be selected fall into a pattern which can be represented by do-loop indices, it is possible to write data statements a third way, like

```
data ((a(i,j), i=1,5,2), j=1,5) /15*0./
```

The general form of an implied-do loop is

$(dlist, \; do\text{-}var = expr, \; expr[, \; expr])$

where *dlist* is a list of array elements, scalar structure components, and implied-do loops, *do-var* is a named integer scalar variable, and each *expr* is a scalar integer expression. It is interpreted as for a do construct (Section 4.5), except that the do variable has the scope of the implied-do as in an array constructor (Section 6.16). A variable in an *expr* must be a *do-var* of an outer implied-do:

```
integer             :: j, k
integer, parameter :: l=5, l2=((l+1)/2)**2
real                :: a(l,l)
data ((a(j,k), k=1,j), j=1,l,2) / l2 * 1.0 /
```

This example sets to 1.0 the first element of the first row of a, the first three elements of the third row, and all the elements of the last row, as shown in Figure 7.2.

Figure 7.2 Result of an implied-do loop in a data statement.

1.0	.	.	.	.
.	.	.	.	.
1.0	1.0	1.0	.	.
.	.	.	.	.
1.0	1.0	1.0	1.0	1.0

The only variables permitted in subscript expressions in data statements are do indices of the same or an outer-level loop, and all operations must be intrinsic.

An object of derived type may appear in a data statement. In this case, the corresponding value must be a structure constructor having an initialization expression for each component. Using the type definition of posn in Section 7.2, we can write

```
type(posn) :: position1, position2
data position1 /posn(2., 3., 0)/, position2%z /4/
```

In the examples given so far, the types and type parameters of the constants in a *value-list* have always been the same as the type of the variables in the *object-list*. This need not be the case, but they must be compatible for intrinsic assignment since the entity is initialized following the rules for intrinsic assignment. It is thus possible to write statements such as

```
data q/1/, i/3.1/, b/(0.,1.)/
```

(where b and q are real and i is integer). Integer values may be binary, octal, or hexadecimal constants (Section 2.6.1).

Each variable must either have been typed in a previous type declaration statement in the scoping unit, or its type is that associated with the first letter of its name according to the implicit typing rules of the scoping unit. In the case of implicit typing, the appearance of the name of the variable in a subsequent type declaration statement in the scoping unit must confirm the type and type parameters. Similarly, any array variable must have previously been declared as such.

No variable or part of a variable may be initialized more than once in a scoping unit.

We recommend using the type declaration statement rather than the data statement, but the data statement *must* be employed when only part of a variable is to be initialized.

7.5.3   Pointer initialization and the function null

Means are available to avoid the initial status of a pointer being undefined. This would be a most undesirable status since such a pointer cannot even be tested by the intrinsic function associated (Section 8.2). Pointers may be given the initial status of disassociated in a type declaration statement such as

```
real, pointer, dimension(:) :: vector => null()
```

or a data statement

```
real, pointer, dimension(:) :: vector
data vector/ null() /
```

This, of course, implies the save attribute, which applies to the pointer association status. The pointer must not be a dummy argument or function result. Here, or if the save attribute is undesirable (for a local variable in a recursive procedure, for example), the variable may be explicitly nullified early in the subprogram.

Our recommendation is that all pointers be so initialized to reduce the risk of bizarre effects from the accidental use of undefined pointers. This is an aid too in writing code that avoids memory leaks.

The function null is an intrinsic function (Section 8.15), whose simple form null(), as used in the above example, is almost always suitable since the attributes are immediately apparent from the context. For example, given the type entry of Section 6.5.2, the structure constructor

```
entry (0.0, 0, null())
```

is available. Also, for a pointer vector, the statement

```
vector => null()
```

is equivalent to

```
nullify(vector)
```

The form with the argument is needed when null is an actual argument that corresponds to a dummy argument with assumed character length (Section 5.19) or is in a reference to a generic procedure and the type, type parameter, or rank is needed to resolve the reference (Section 5.18).

There is no mechanism to initialize a pointer as associated.

7.5.4 Default initialization of components

Means are available to specify that any object of a derived type is given a default initial value for a component. The value must be specified when the component is declared as part of the type definition (Section 2.9). If the component is not a pointer, this is done in the usual way (Section 7.5.1) with the equals sign followed by an initialization expression and the rules of intrinsic assignment apply (including specifying a scalar value for all the elements of an array component). If the component is a pointer, the only initialization allowed is the pointer assignment symbol followed by a reference to the intrinsic function `null` with no arguments.

Initialization does not have to apply to all components of a given derived type. An example for the type defined in Section 6.5.2 is

```
type entry
   real              :: value = 2.0
   integer           :: index
   type(entry), pointer :: next => null()
end type entry
```

Given an array declaration such as

```
type(entry), dimension(100) :: matrix
```

subobjects such as `matrix(3)%value` will have the initial value 2.0, and the reference `associated(matrix(3)%next)` will return the value false.

For an object of a nested derived type, the initializations associated with components at all levels are recognized. For example, given the specifications

```
type node
   integer     :: counter
   type(entry) :: element
end type node
type (node) :: n
```

the component `n%element%value` will have the initial value 2.0.

Unlike explicit initialization in a type declaration or `data` statement, default initialization does not imply that the objects have the `save` attribute. However, an object of such a type that is declared in a module is required to have the `save` attribute unless it is a pointer or an allocatable array. This is because of the difficulty that some implementations would have with determining when a non-saved object would need to be re-initialized.

Objects may still be explicitly initialized in a type declaration statement, as in

```
type(entry), dimension(100) :: matrix=entry(huge(0.0),   &
                                  huge(0),null())
```

in which case the default initialization is ignored. Similarly, default initialization may be overridden in a nested type definition such as

```
type node
   integer     :: counter
   type(entry) :: element=entry(0.0, 0 , null())
end type node
```

However, no part of a non-pointer object with default initialization is permitted in a data statement (Section 7.5.2).

As well as applying to the initial values of static data, default initialization also applies to any data that is dynamically created during program execution. This includes allocation with the allocate statement. For example, the statement

```
allocate (matrix(1)%next)
```

creates a partially initialized object of type entry. It also applies to unsaved local variables (including automatic objects), function results, and dummy arguments with intent out.

It applies even if the type definition is private or the components are private.

7.6   The public and private attributes

Modules (Section 5.5) permit specifications to be 'packaged' into a form that allows them to be accessed elsewhere in the program. So far, we have assumed that all the entities in the module are to be accessible, that is have the public attribute, but sometimes it is desirable to limit the access. For example, several procedures in a module may need access to a work array containing the results of calculations that they have performed. If access is limited to only the procedures of the module, there is no possibility of an accidental corruption of these data by another procedure and design changes can be made within the module without affecting the rest of the program. In cases where entities are not to be accessible outside their own module, they may be given the private attribute.

These two attributes may be specified with the public and private attributes on type declaration statements in the module, as in

```
real, public    :: x, y, z
integer, private :: u, v, w
```

or in public and private statements, as in

```
public  :: x, y, z, operator(.add.)
private :: u, v, w, assignment(=), operator(*)
```

which have the general forms

```
public [ [ :: ] access-id-list]
private [ [ :: ] access-id-list]
```

where *access-id* is a name or a *generic-spec* (Section 5.18).

Note that if a procedure has a generic identifier, the accessibility of its specific name is independent of the accessibility of its generic identifier. One may be public while the other is private, which means that it is accessible only by its specific name or only by its generic identifier.

If a `public` or `private` statement has no list of entities, it confirms or resets the default. Thus the statement

```
public
```

confirms `public` as the default value, and the statement

```
private
```

sets the default value for the module to `private` accessibility. For example,

```
private
public :: means
```

gives the entity `means` the `public` attribute whilst all others are `private`. There may be at most one accessibility statement without a list in a scoping unit.

The entities that may be specified by name in `public` or `private` lists are named variables, procedures (including generic procedures), derived types, named constants, and namelist groups. Thus, to make a generic procedure name accessible but the corresponding specific names inaccessible, we might write

```
module example
   private specific_int, specific_real
   interface generic_name
      module procedure specific_int, specific_real
   end interface
contains
   subroutine specific_int(i)
      :
   subroutine specific_real(a)
      :
end module example
```

An entity with a type must not have the `public` attribute if its type is declared with the `private` attribute (because there is little one can do with such an entity without access to its type). However, a type that is accessed from a module may be given the `private` attribute in the accessing module (see Section 7.10). If an entity of this type has the `public` attribute, a subsequent use statement for it may be accompanied by a use statement for the type from the original module. Therefore, the restriction in the first sentence of this paragraph refers only to types originally declared to be `private`.

For similar reasons, if a module procedure has a dummy argument or function result of a type declared with the `private` attribute, the procedure must be given the attribute `private` and must not have a generic identifier that is `public`.

The use of the `private` statement for components of derived types in the context of defining an entity's access within a module will be described in Section 7.11.

The `public` and `private` attributes may appear only in the specifications of a module.

7.7 The pointer, target, and allocatable statements

For the sake of regularity in the language, there are statements for specifying the pointer, target, and allocatable attributes of entities. They take the forms:

```
pointer [::]  object-name[(array-spec)]
                        [,object-name [(array-spec)]]...
target [::]  object-name[(array-spec)]
                        [,object-name [(array-spec)]]...
```

and

```
allocatable [::]  array-name[(array-spec)]
                            [,array-name [(array-spec)]]...
```

as in

```
real         :: a, son, y
allocatable :: a(:,:)
pointer     :: son
target      :: a, y(10)
```

We believe that it is much clearer to specify these attributes on the type declaration statements, and therefore do not use these forms.

7.8 The intent and optional statements

The intent attribute (Section 5.9) for a dummy argument that is not a dummy procedure or pointer may be specified in a type declaration statement or in an intent statement of the form

```
intent( inout ) [::] dummy-argument-name-list
```

where *inout* is in, out, or inout. Examples are

```
subroutine solve (a, b, c, x, y, z)
    real         :: a, b, c, x, y, z
    intent(in)  :: a, b, c
    intent(out) :: x, y, z
```

The optional attribute (Section 5.13) for a dummy argument may be specified in a type declaration statement or in an optional statement of the form

```
optional [::] dummy-argument-name-list
```

An example is

```
optional :: a, b, c
```

The optional attribute is the only attribute which may be specified for a dummy argument that is a procedure.

Note that the intent and optional attributes may be specified only for dummy arguments. As for the statements of Section 7.7, we believe that it is much clearer to specify these attributes on the type declaration statements, and therefore do not use these forms.

7.9 The save attribute

Let us suppose that we wish to retain the value of a local variable in a subprogram, for example to count the number of times the subprogram is entered. We might write a section of code as in Figure 7.3. In this example, the local variables, a and counter, are initialized to zero, and it is assumed that their current values are available each time the subroutine is called. This is not necessarily the case. Fortran allows the computer system being used to 'forget' a new value, the variable becoming undefined on each return unless it has the save attribute. In Figure 7.3, it is sufficient to change the declaration of a to

```
real, save :: a
```

to be sure that its value is always retained between calls. This may be done for counter, too, but is not necessary as all variables with initial values acquire the save attribute automatically (Section 7.5).

Figure 7.3

```
subroutine anything(x)
    real    :: a, x
    integer :: counter = 0 ! Initialize the counter
    :
    counter = counter + 1
    if (counter==1) then
       a = 0.0
    else
       a = a + x
    end if
    :
```

A similar situation arises with the use of variables in modules (Section 5.5). On return from a subprogram that accesses a variable in a module, the variable becomes undefined unless the main program accesses the module, another subprogram in execution accesses the module, or the variable has the save attribute.

If a variable that becomes undefined has a pointer associated with it, the pointer's association status becomes undefined.

The save attribute must not be specified for a dummy argument, a function result, or an automatic object (Section 6.4). It may be specified for a pointer, in which case the pointer association status is saved. It may be specified for an allocatable array, in which case the allocation status and value are saved. A saved variable in a recursive subprogram is shared by all instances of the subprogram.

An alternative to specifying the save attribute on a type declaration statement is the save statement:

```
save [ [::] variable-name-list ]
```

A save statement with no list is equivalent to a list containing all possible names, and in this case the scoping unit must contain no other save statements and no save attributes in type declaration statements. Our recommendation is against this form of save. If a programmer tries to give the save attribute explicitly to an automatic object, a diagnostic will result. On the other hand, he or she might think that save without a list would do this too, and not get the behaviour intended. Also, there is a loss of efficiency associated with save on some processors, so it is best to restrict it to those objects for which it is really needed.

The save statement or save attribute may appear in the declaration statements in a main program but has no effect.

7.10   The use statement

In Section 5.5, we introduced the use statement in its simplest form

   use *module-name*

which provides access to all the public named data objects, derived types, interface blocks, procedures, generic identifiers, and namelist groups in the module named.   Any use statements must precede other specification statements in a scoping unit. The only attribute of an accessed entity that may be specified afresh is public or private (and this only in a module), but the entity may be included in one or more namelist groups (Section 7.15).

If access is needed to two or more modules that have been written independently, the same name may be used in more than one module. This is the main reason for permitting accessed entities to be renamed by the use statement. Renaming is also available to resolve a name clash between a local entity and an entity accessed from a module, though our preference is to use a text editor or other tool to change the local name. With renaming, the use statement has the form

   use *module-name, rename-list*

where each *rename* has the form

   local-name => *use-name*

and refers to a public entity in the module that is to be accessed by a different local name.
   As an example,

```
use stats_lib, sprod => prod
use maths_lib
```

makes all the public entities in both stats_lib and maths_lib accessible. If maths_lib contains an entity called prod, it is accessible by its own name while the entity prod of stats_lib is accessible as sprod.

Renaming is not needed if there is a name clash between two entities that are not required. A name clash is permitted if there is no reference to the name in the scoping unit.

A name clash is also permissible for a generic name that is required. Here, all generic interfaces accessed by the name are treated as a single concatenated interface block. This is true also for defined operators and assignments, where no renaming facility is available. In all these cases, any two procedures having the same generic identifier must differ as explained in Section 5.18. We imagine that this will usually be exactly what is needed. For example, we might access modules for interval arithmetic and matrix arithmetic, both needing the functions sqrt, sin, etc., the operators +, -, etc., and assignment, but for different types.

For cases where only a subset of the names of a module is needed, the only option is available, having the form

    use *module-name*, only : [*only-list*]

where each *only* has the form

    access-id

or

    [*local-name* =>] *use-name*

where each *access-id* is a public entity in the module, and is either a *use-name* or a *generic-spec* (Section 5.18). This provides access to an entity in a module only if the entity is public and is specified as a *use-name* or *access-id*. Where a *use-name* is preceded by a *local-name*, the entity is known locally by the *local-name*. An example of such a statement is

    use stats_lib, only : sprod => prod, mult

which provides access to prod by the local name sprod and to mult by its own name.

We would recommend that only one use statement for a given module be placed in a scoping unit, but more are allowed. If there is a use statement without an only qualifier, all public entities in the module are accessible and the *rename-lists* and *only-lists* are interpreted as if concatenated into a single *rename-list* (with the form *use-name* in an *only-list* being treated as the rename *use-name* => *use-name*). If all the statements have the only qualification, only those entities named in one or more of the *only-lists* are accessible, that is all the *only-lists* are interpreted as if concatenated into a single *only-list*.

The form

    use *module-name*, only :

might appear redundant. It is provided for the situation where a scoping unit calls a set of procedures that communicate with each other through shared data in a module. It ensures that the data are available throughout the execution of the scoping unit.

An only list will be rather clumsy if almost all of a module is wanted. The effect of an 'except' clause can be obtained by renaming unwanted entities. For example, if a large program (such as one written in Fortran 77) contains many external procedures, a good practice is to collect interface blocks for them all into a module that is referenced in each program unit for complete mutual checking. In an external procedure, we might then write:

    use all_interfaces, except_this_one => name

to avoid having two explicit interfaces for itself (where all_interfaces is the module name and name is the procedure name).

When a module contains use statements, the entities accessed are treated as entities in the module. They may be given the private or public attribute explicitly or through the default

---

Figure 7.4

```
module one
    integer :: i
end module one
module two
    use one
    private
    :
end module two
```

---

rule in effect in the module. Thus, given the two modules in Figure 7.4 and a third program unit containing a use statement for two, the variable i is accessible there only if it also contains a use statement for one *or* if i is made public explicitly in two.

An entity may be accessed by more than one local name. This is illustrated in Figure 7.5, where module b accesses s of module a by the local name bs; if a subprogram such as c accesses both a and b, it will access s by both its original name and by the name bs. Figure 7.5 also illustrates that an entity may be accessed by the same name by more than one route (see variable t).

Figure 7.5

```
module a
    real :: s, t
    :
end module a
module b
    use a, bs => s
    :
end module b
subroutine c
    use a
    use b
    :
end subroutine c
```

A more direct way for an entity to be accessed by more than one local name is for it to appear more than once as a *use-name*. This is not a practice that we recommend.

Of course, all the local names of entities accessed from modules must differ from each other and from names of local entities. If a local entity is accidentally given the same name as an accessible entity from a module, this will be noticed at compile time if the local entity is declared explicitly (since no accessed entity may be given any attribute locally, other than private or public, and that only in a module). However, if the local entity is intended to be implicitly typed (Section 7.2) and appears in no specification statements, then each appearance of the name will be taken, incorrectly, as a reference to the accessed variable. To avoid this, we recommend the use of

```
implicit none
```

in a scoping unit containing one or more use statements. For greater safety, the `only` option may be employed on a `use` statement to ensure that all accesses are intentional.

7.11   Derived-type definitions

When derived types were introduced in Section 2.9, some simple example definitions were given, but the full generality was not included. An example illustrating more features is

```
type, public :: lock
   private
   integer, pointer :: key(:)
   logical          :: state
end type lock
```

The general form (apart from redundant features, see Sections 20.2 and B.1.3) is

```
type [[,access]:: ] type-name
    [ private ]
    component-def-stmt
    [component-def-stmt] . . .
end type [ type-name ]
```

Each *component-def-stmt* has the form

```
type [ [ ,component-attr-list] :: ]component-decl-list
```

where *type* specifies the type and type parameters (Section 7.13), each *component-attr* is either `pointer` or `dimension`(*bounds-list*), and each *component-decl* is

```
component-name [ (bounds-list)][ *char-len ]
```

or

```
component-name [ (bounds-list)][ *char-len ] [ comp-int ]
```

The meaning of *char-len* is explained in Section 7.13 and *comp-int* represents component initialization, as explained in Section 7.5.4. If the *type* is a derived type and the `pointer` attribute is not specified, the type must be previously defined in the host scoping unit or accessible there by use or host association.   If the `pointer` attribute is specified, the type may also be the one being defined (for example, the type `entry` of Section 2.13), or one defined elsewhere in the scoping unit.

A *type-name* must not be the same as the name of any intrinsic type or a derived type accessed from a module.

The bounds of an array component are declared by a *bounds-list*, where each *bounds* is just

        :

for a pointer component (see example in Section 6.14) or

        [*lower-bound*:] *upper-bound*

for a non-pointer component, and *lower-bound* and *upper-bound* are constant expressions that are restricted to specification expressions (Section 7.14). Similarly, the character length of a component of type character must be a constant specification expression. If there is a *bounds-list* attached to the *component-name*, this defines the bounds. If a dimension attribute is present in the statement, its *bounds-list* applies to any component in the statement without its own *bounds-list*.

Only if the host scoping unit is a module may the *access* qualifier or private statement appear. The *access* qualifier on a type statement may be public or private and specifies the accessibility of the type. If it is private, then the type name, the structure constructor for the type, any entity of the type, and any procedure with a dummy argument or function result of the type are all inaccessible outside the host module. The accessibility may also be specified in a private or public statement in the host. In the absence of both of these, the type takes the default accessibility of the host module. If a private statement appears for a type with public accessibility, the components of the type are inaccessible in any scoping unit accessing the host module, so that neither component selection nor structure construction are available there. Also, if any component is of a derived type that is private, the type being defined must be private or have private components.

We can thus distinguish three levels of access:

  i) all public, where the type and all its components are accessible, and the components of any object of the type are accessible wherever the object is accessible;

  ii) a public type with private components, where the type is accessible but its components are hidden;

  iii) all private, where both the type and its components are used only within the host module, and are hidden to an accessing procedure.

Case ii) has, where appropriate, the advantage of enabling changes to be made to the type without in any way affecting the code in the accessing procedure. Case iii) offers this advantage and has the additional merit of not cluttering the name space of the accessing procedure. The use of private accessibility for the components or for the whole type is thus recommended whenever possible.

We note that, even if two derived-type definitions are identical in every respect except their names, then entities of those two types are *not* equivalent and are regarded as being of different types. Even if the names, too, are identical, the types are different (unless they have the sequence attribute, a feature that we do not recommend and whose description is left to Section 20.2.1). If a type is needed in more than one program unit, the definition should be placed in a module and accessed by a use statement wherever it is needed. Having a single definition is far less prone to errors.

7.12 The type declaration statement

We have already met many simple examples of the declarations of named entities by integer, real, complex, logical, character, and type(*type-name*) statements. The general form is

> *type* [[, *attribute*]... ::] *entity-list*

where *type* specifies the type and type parameters (Section 7.13), *attribute* is one of the following:

parameter	dimension(*bounds-list*)
public	intent(*inout*)
private	optional
pointer	save
target	external
allocatable	intrinsic

and each *entity* is

> *object-name* [(*bounds-list*)] [*char-len*] [=*initialization-expr*]

or

> *function-name* [*char-len*]

or

> *pointer-name* [(*bounds-list*)] [*char-len*] [=> *null-init*]

where *null-init* is a reference to the intrinsic function null with no arguments. The meaning of *char-len* is explained in Section 7.13; a *bounds-list* specifies the rank and possibly bounds of array-valued entities.

No attribute may appear more than once in a given type declaration statement. The double colon :: need not appear in the simple case without any *attribute*s and without any =*initialization-expr*; for example

```
real a, b, c(10)
```

If the statement specifies a parameter attribute, =*initialization-expr* must appear.

If a pointer attribute is specified, the target, intent, external, and intrinsic attributes must not be specified. The target and parameter attributes may not be specified for the same entity, and the pointer and allocatable attributes may not be specified for the same array. If the target attribute is specified, neither the external nor the intrinsic attribute may also be specified.

If an object is specified with the intent or parameter attribute, this is shared by all its subobjects. The pointer attribute is not shared in this manner, but note that a derived-data type component may itself be a pointer. However, the target attribute is shared by all its subobjects, except for any that are pointer components.

The allocatable, parameter, or save attribute must not be specified for a dummy argument or function result.

The intent and optional attributes may be specified only for dummy arguments.

For a function result, specifying the external attribute is an alternative to the external statement (Section 5.11) for declaring the function to be external, and specifying the intrinsic attribute is an alternative to the intrinsic statement (Section 8.1.3) for declaring the function to be intrinsic. These two attributes are mutually exclusive.

Each of the attributes may also be specified in statements (such as save) that list entities having the attribute. This leads to the possibility of an attribute being specified explicitly more than once for a given entity, but this is not permitted. Our recommendation is to avoid such statements because it is much clearer to have all the attributes for an entity collected in one place.

7.13   Type and type parameter specification

We have used *type* to represent one of the following

```
integer [( [kind=] kind-value)]
real   [( [kind=] kind-value)]
complex   [( [kind=] kind-value)]
character [(actual-parameter-list)]
logical [([kind=] kind-value) ]
type ( type-name )
```

in the function statement (Section 5.20), the implicit statement (Section 7.2), the component definition statement (Section 7.11), and the type declaration statement (Section 7.12). A *kind-value* must be an initialization expression (Section 7.4) and must have a value that is valid on the processor being used.

For character, each *actual-parameter* has the form

[len=] *len-value*

or

[kind=] *kind-value*

and provides a value for one of the parameters. It is permissible to omit kind= from a kind *actual-parameter* only when len= is omitted and *len-value* is both present and comes first, just as for an actual argument list (Section 5.13). Neither parameter may be specified more than once.

For a scalar named constant or for a dummy argument of a subprogram, a *len-value* may be specified as an asterisk, in which case the value is assumed from that of the constant itself or the associated actual argument. In both cases, the len intrinsic function (Section 8.6.1) is available if the actual length is required directly, for instance as a do-construct iteration count. A combined example is

```
character(len=len(char_arg)) function line(char_arg)
   character(len=*)              :: char_arg
   character(len=*), parameter :: char_const = 'page'
   if ( len(char_arg) < len(char_const) ) then
   :
```

A *len-value* that is not an asterisk must be a specification expression (Section 7.14). Negative values declare character entities to be of zero length.

In addition, it is possible to attach an alternative form of *len-value* to individual entities in a type declaration statement using the syntax *entity*char-len*, where *char-len* is either (*len-value*) or *len* and *len* is a scalar integer literal constant which specifies a length for the entity. The constant *len* must not have a kind type parameter specified for it. An illustration of this form is

```
character(len=8) :: word(4), point*1, text(20)*4
```

where, `word`, `point`, and `text` have character length 8, 1, and 4, respectively. Similarly, the alternative form may be used for individual components in a component definition statement.

7.14   Specification expressions

Non-constant scalar integer expressions may be used to specify the array bounds (examples in Section 6.4) and character lengths of data objects in a subprogram, and of function results. Such an expression may depend only on data values that are defined on entry to the subprogram. It must not depend on an optional argument, even if present. Any variable referenced must not have its type and type parameters specified later in the same sequence of specification statements, unless they are those implied by the implicit typing rules.

Array constructors and derived-type constructors are permitted. The expression may reference an inquiry function for an array bound or for a type parameter of an entity which either is accessed by use or host association, or is specified earlier in the same specification sequence, but not later in the sequence.[2] An element of an array specified in the same specification sequence can be referenced only if the bounds of the array are specified earlier in the sequence.[3] Such an expression is called a *specification expression*.

An array whose bounds are declared using specification expressions is called an *explicit-shape array*.

A variety of possibilities are shown in Figure 7.6.

The bounds and character lengths are not affected by any redefinitions or undefinitions of variables in the expressions during execution of the procedure.

---

[2] This avoids such a case as

```
character (len=len(a)) :: fun
character (len=len(fun)) ::  a
```

[3] This avoids such a case as

```
integer, parameter, dimension (j(1):j(1)+1) ::  i = (/0,1/)
integer, parameter, dimension (i(1):i(1)+1) ::  j = (/1,2/)
```

Figure 7.6

```
subroutine sample(arr, value, string)
   use definitions  ! Contains the real a
   real, dimension(:,:), intent(out) :: arr    ! Assumed-shape array
   integer, intent(in)               :: value
   character(len=*), intent(in)      :: string ! Assumed length
   real, dimension(ubound(arr, 1)+5) :: x      ! Automatic array
   character(len=value+len(string))  :: cc     ! Automatic object
   integer, parameter :: pa2 =  selected_real_kind(2*precision(a))
   real(kind=pa2)      :: z       ! Precision of z is at least twice
                                  ! the precision of a
   :
   :
```

7.14.1   Specification functions

Any of the intrinsic functions defined by the standard may be used in a specification expression. In addition, a non-intrinsic pure function may be used provided that such a function is neither an internal function nor recursive, it does not have a dummy procedure argument, and the interface is explicit. Functions that fulfil these conditions are termed *specification functions*. The arguments of a specification function when used in a specification expression are subject to the same restrictions as those on specification expressions themselves, except that they do not necessarily have to be scalar.

As the interfaces of specification functions must be explicit yet they cannot be internal functions,[4] such functions are probably most conveniently written as module procedures.

This feature is a great convenience for specification expressions that cannot be written as simple expressions. Here is an example,

```
function solve (a, ...
   use matrix_ops
   type(matrix), intent(in) :: a
   real                     :: work(wsize(a))
```

where matrix is a type defined in the module matrix_ops and intended to hold a sparse matrix and its LU factorization:

```
type matrix
   integer :: n           ! Matrix order.
   integer :: nz          ! Number of nonzero entries.
   logical :: new = .true. ! Whether this is a new, unfactorized
                           ! matrix.
   :
end type matrix
```

---

[4]This prevents them enquiring, via host association, about objects being specified in the set of statements in which the specification function itself is referenced.

and `wsize` is a module procedure that calculates the required size of the array `work`:

```
pure integer function wsize(a)
   type(matrix), intent(in) :: a
   wsize = 2*a%n + 2
   if(a%new) wsize = a%nz + wsize
end function wsize
```

7.15 The namelist statement

It is sometimes convenient to gather a set of variables into a single group, in order to facilitate input/output (I/O) operations on the group as a whole. The actual use of such groups is explained in Section 9.10. The method by which a group is declared is via the `namelist` statement which in its simple form has the syntax

```
namelist namelist-spec
```

where *namelist-spec* is

```
/namelist-group-name/ variable-name-list
```

The *namelist-group-name* is the name given to the group for subsequent use in the I/O statements. A variable named in the list must not be a dummy array with a non-constant bound, a variable with non-constant character length, an automatic object, an allocatable array, a pointer, or have a component at any depth of component selection that is a pointer or is inaccessible. An example is

```
real :: carpet, tv, brushes(10)
namelist /household_items/ carpet, tv, brushes
```

It is possible to declare several namelist groups in one statement, with the syntax

```
namelist namelist-spec [[,]namelist-spec]...
```

as in the example

```
namelist /list1/ a, b, c /list2/ x, y, z
```

It is possible to continue a list within the same scoping unit by repeating the namelist name on more than one statement. Thus,

```
namelist /list/ a, b, c
namelist /list/ d, e, f
```

has the same effect as a single statement containing all the variable names in the same order. A namelist group object may not appear more than once in a namelist group but may belong to more than one namelist group.

If the type, type parameters, or shape of a namelist variable is specified in a specification statement in the same scoping unit, the specification statement must either appear before the `namelist` statement, or be a type declaration statement that confirms the implicit typing rule in force in the scoping unit for the initial letter of the variable. Also, if the namelist group has the `public` attribute, no variable in the list may have the `private` attribute or have private components.

7.16   Summary

In this chapter most of the specification statements of Fortran have been described. The following concepts have been introduced: implicit typing and its attendant dangers, named constants, constant expressions, data initialization, control of the accessibility of entities in modules, saving data between procedure calls, selective access of entities in a module, renaming entities accessed from a module, specification expressions that may be used when specifying data objects and function results, and the formation of variables into namelist groups. We have also explained alternative ways of specifying attributes.

We conclude this chapter with a complete program, Figures 7.7 and 7.8, that uses a module to sort US-style addresses (name, street, town, and state with a numerical zip code) by order of zip code. It illustrates the interplay between many of the features described so far, but note that it is not a production code since the sort routine is not very efficient and the full range of US addresses is not handled. Suitable test data are:

```
Prof. James Bush,
206 Church St. SE,
Minneapolis,
MN 55455

J. E. Dougal,
Rice University,
Houston,
TX 77251

Jack Finch,
104 Ayres Hall,
Knoxville,
TN 37996
```

Figure 7.7

```
module sort              ! To sort postal addresses by zip code.
   implicit none
   private
   public :: selection_sort
   integer, parameter :: string_length = 30
   type, public :: address
      character(len = string_length) :: name, street, town, &
                                        state*2
      integer                        :: zip_code
   end type address
contains
   recursive subroutine selection_sort (array_arg)
      type (address), dimension (:), intent (inout)         &
                                     :: array_arg
      integer                        :: current_size
      integer                        :: big
      current_size = size (array_arg)
      if (current_size > 0) then
                     ! maxloc is described in Section 8.14.
         big = maxloc (array_arg(:)%zip_code, dim=1)
         call swap (big, current_size)
         call selection_sort (array_arg(1: current_size - 1))
      end if
   contains
      subroutine swap (i, j)
         integer, intent (in) :: i, j
         type (address)       :: temp
         temp = array_arg(i)
         array_arg(i) = array_arg(j)
         array_arg(j) = temp
      end subroutine swap
   end subroutine selection_sort
end module sort
```

Figure 7.8

```
program zippy
   use sort
   implicit none
   integer, parameter                      :: array_size = 100
   type (address), dimension (array_size)  :: data_array
   integer                                 :: i, n
   do i = 1, array_size
      read  (*, '(/a/a/a/a2,i8)', end=10) data_array(i)
                           ! For end= see Section 9.7;
      write (*, '(/a/a/a/a2,i8)')          data_array(i)
   end do                  ! for editing see Section 9.12.
10 n = i - 1
   call selection_sort (data_array(1: n))
   write(*, '(//a)') 'after sorting:'
   do i = 1, n
      write (*, '(/a/a/a/a2,i8)') data_array(i)
   end do
end program zippy
```

7.17 Exercises

1. Write suitable type statements for the following quantities:

   i) an array to hold the number of counts in each of the 100 bins of a histogram numbered from 1 to 100;

   ii) an array to hold the temperature to two significant decimal places at points, on a sheet of iron, equally spaced at 1cm intervals on a rectangular grid 20 cm square, with points in each corner (the melting point of iron is $1530°C$);

   iii) an array to describe the state of 20 on/off switches;

   iv) an array to contain the information destined for a printed page of 44 lines, each of 70 letters or digits.

2. Explain the difference between the following pair of declarations:

```
real :: i = 3.1
```

and

```
real, parameter :: i = 3.1
```

What is the value of i in each case?

3. Write type declaration statements which initialize:

    i) all the elements of an integer array of length 100 to the value zero;

    ii) all the odd elements of the same array to 0 and the even elements to 1;

    iii) the elements of a real 10×10 square array to 1.0;

    iv) a character string to the digits 0 to 9.

4. In the following module, identify all the scoping units and list the mappings for implicit typing for all the letters in all of them:

```
module mod
    implicit character(10, 2) (a-b)
    :
contains
    subroutine outer
        implicit none
        :
    contains
        subroutine inner(fun)
            implicit complex (z)
            interface
                function fun(x)
                    implicit real (f, x)
                    :
                end function fun
            end interface
        end subroutine inner
    end subroutine outer
end module mod
```

5.   i) Write a type declaration statement that declares and initializes a variable of derived type `person` (Section 2.9).

    ii) Either

        a) write a type declaration statement that declares and initializes a variable of type `entry` (Section 2.13), or

        b) write a type declaration statement for such a variable and a `data` statement to initialize its non-pointer components.

6. Which of the following are initialization expressions:

    i) `kind(x)`, for x of type real

    ii) `selected_real_kind(6, 20)`

    iii) `1.7**2`

    iv) `1.7**2.0`

    v) `(1.7, 2.3)**(-2)`

    vi) `(/ (7*i, i=1, 10) /)`

    vii) `person("Reid", 25*2.0, 22**2)`

    viii) `entry(1.7, 1, null_pointer)`

8. Intrinsic procedures

8.1 Introduction

In a language that has a clear orientation towards scientific applications there is an obvious requirement for the most frequently required mathematical functions to be provided as part of the language itself, rather than expecting each user to code them afresh. When provided with the compiler, they are normally coded to be very efficient and will have been well tested over the complete range of values that they accept. It is difficult to compete with the high standard of code provided by the vendors.

The efficiency of the intrinsic procedures when handling arrays is likely to be particularly marked because a single call may cause a large number of individual operations to be performed, during the execution of which advantage may be taken of the specific nature of the hardware.

Another feature of a substantial number of the intrinsic procedures is that they extend the power of the language by providing access to facilities that are not otherwise available in the language. Examples are inquiry functions for the presence of an optional argument, the parts of a floating-point number, and the length of a character string.

There are over a hundred intrinsic procedures in all, a particularly rich set. They fall into distinct groups, which we describe in turn. A list in alphabetical order, with one-line descriptions, is given in Appendix A. Some processors may offer additional intrinsic procedures. Note that a program containing references to such procedures is portable only to other processors that provide those same procedures. In fact, such a program does not conform to the standard.

8.1.1 Keyword calls

The procedures may be called with keyword actual arguments, using the dummy argument names as keywords. This facility is not very useful for those with a single non-optional argument, but is useful for those with several optional arguments. For example

```
call date_and_time (date=d)
```

returns the date in the scalar character variable d. The rules for positional and keyword argument lists were explained in Section 5.13. In this chapter, the dummy arguments that are optional are indicated with square brackets. We have taken some 'poetic licence' with this notation, which might suggest to the reader that the positional form is permitted following an absent argument (this is not the case).

8.1.2   Categories of intrinsic procedures

There are four categories of intrinsic procedures.

i) *Elemental procedures.*

ii) *Inquiry functions* return properties of their principal arguments that do not depend on their values; indeed, for variables, their values may be undefined.

iii) *Transformational functions* are functions that are neither elemental nor inquiry; they usually have array arguments and an array result whose elements depend on many of the elements of the arguments.

iv) *Non-elemental subroutines.*

All the functions are pure.

8.1.3   The intrinsic statement

A name may be specified to be that of an intrinsic procedure in an `intrinsic` statement, which has the general form

        intrinsic [::] *intrinsic-name-list*

where *intrinsic-name-list* is a list of intrinsic procedure names. A name must not appear more than once in the `intrinsic` statements of a scoping unit and must not appear in an `external` statement there (but may appear as a generic name on an interface block if an intrinsic procedure is being extended, see Section 5.18). We believe that it is good programming practice to include such a statement in every scoping unit that contains references to intrinsic procedures, because this makes the use clear to the reader. We particularly recommend it when referencing intrinsic procedures that are not defined by the standard, for then a clear diagnostic message should be produced if the program is ported to a processor that does not support the extra intrinsic procedures.

8.1.4   Argument intents

Since all the functions are pure, their arguments all have intent `in`. For the subroutines, the intents vary from case to case (see the descriptions given later in the chapter).

8.2   Inquiry functions for any type

The following are inquiry functions whose arguments may be of any type.

associated (pointer [,target]), when target is absent, returns the value true if the pointer pointer is associated with a target and false otherwise. The pointer association status of pointer must not be undefined. If target is present, it must have the same type, type parameters, and rank as pointer. The value is true if pointer is associated with target, and false otherwise. In the array case, true is returned only if the shapes are identical and corresponding array elements, in array element order, are associated with each other. If the character length or array size is zero, false is returned. A different bound, as in the case of associated(p,a) following the pointer assignment p => a(:) when lbound(a) = 0, is insufficient to cause false to be returned. The argument target may itself be a pointer, in which case its target is compared with the target of pointer; the pointer association status of target must not be undefined and if either pointer or target is disassociated, the result is false.

present (a) may be called in a subprogram that has an optional dummy argument a or accesses such a dummy argument from its host. It returns the value true if the corresponding actual argument is present in the current call to it, and false otherwise. If an absent dummy argument is used as an actual argument in a call of another subprogram, it is regarded as also absent in the called subprogram.

There is an inquiry function whose argument may be of any intrinsic type:

kind (x) has type default integer and value equal to the kind type parameter value of x.

8.3 Elemental numeric functions

There are 17 elemental functions for performing simple numerical tasks, many of which perform type conversions for some or all permitted types of arguments.

8.3.1 Elemental functions that may convert

If kind is present in the following elemental functions, it must be a scalar integer initialization expression and provide a kind type parameter that is supported on the processor.

abs (a) returns the absolute value of an argument of type integer, real, or complex. The result is of type integer if a is of type integer and otherwise it is real. It has the same kind type parameter as a.

aimag (z) returns the imaginary part of the complex value z. The type is real and the kind type parameter is that of z.

aint (a [,kind]) truncates a real value a towards zero to produce a real that is a whole number. The value of the kind type parameter is the value of the argument kind if it is present, or that of a otherwise.

anint (a [,kind]) returns a real whose value is the nearest whole number to the real value a. The value of the kind type parameter is the value of the argument kind, if it is present, or that of a otherwise.

ceiling (a [,kind]) returns the least integer greater than or equal to its real argument. If kind is present, the value of the kind type parameter of the result is the value of kind, otherwise it is that of the default integer type.

cmplx (x [,y][,kind]) converts x or (x, y) to complex type with the value of the kind type parameter being the value of the argument kind if it is present or that of default complex otherwise. If y is absent, x may be of type integer, real, or complex. If y is present, it must be of type integer or real and x must be of type integer or real.

floor (a [,kind]) returns the greatest integer less than or equal to its real argument. If kind is present, the value of the kind type parameter of the result is the value of kind, otherwise it is that of the default integer type.

int (a [,kind]) converts to integer type with the value of the kind type parameter being the value of the argument kind, if it is present, or that of the default integer otherwise. The argument a may be

- integer, in which case int(a)=a,
- real, in which case the value is truncated towards zero, or
- complex, in which case the real part is truncated towards zero.

nint (a [,kind]) returns the integer value that is nearest to the real a. If kind is present, the value of the kind type parameter of the result is the value of kind, otherwise it is that of the default integer type.

real (a [,kind]) converts to real type with the value of the kind type parameter being that of kind if it is present. If kind is absent, the kind type parameter is that of default real when a is of type integer or real, and is that of a when a is type complex. The argument a may be of type integer, real, or complex. If it is complex, the imaginary part is ignored.

8.3.2 Elemental functions that do not convert

The following are elemental functions whose result is of type and kind type parameter that are those of the first or only argument. For those having more than one argument, all arguments must have the same type and kind type parameter.

conjg (z) returns the conjugate of the complex value z.

dim (x, y) returns max(x-y, 0.) for arguments that are both integer or both real.

max (a1, a2 [,a3,...]) returns the maximum of two or more integer or real values.

min (a1, a2 [,a3,...]) returns the minimum of two or more integer or real values.

mod (a, p) returns the remainder of a modulo p, that is a-int(a/p)*p. The value of p must not be zero; a and p must be both integer or both real.

modulo (a, p) returns a modulo p when a and p are both integer or both real, that is a-floor(a/p)*p in the real case, and a-floor(a÷p)*p in the integer case, where ÷ represents ordinary mathematical division. The value of p must not be zero.

sign (a, b) returns the absolute value of a times the sign of b. The arguments a and b must be both integer or both real. If b is zero, its sign is taken as positive. However, if b is real with the value zero and the processor can distinguish between a negative and a positive real zero, the result has the sign of b (see also Section 8.7.1).

8.4 Elemental mathematical functions

The following are elemental functions that evaluate elementary mathematical functions. The type and kind type parameter of the result are those of the first argument, which is usually the only argument.

acos (x) returns the arc cosine (inverse cosine) function value for real values x such that $|x| \leq 1$, expressed in radians in the range $0 \leq \text{acos}(x) \leq \pi$.

asin (x) returns the arc sine (inverse sine) function value for real values x such that $|x| \leq 1$, expressed in radians in the range $-\frac{\pi}{2} \leq \text{asin}(x) \leq \frac{\pi}{2}$.

atan (x) returns the arc tangent (inverse tangent) function value for real x, expressed in radians in the range $-\frac{\pi}{2} \leq \text{atan}(x) \leq \frac{\pi}{2}$.

atan2 (y, x) returns the arc tangent (inverse tangent) function value for pairs of reals, x and y, of the same type and type parameter. The result is the principal value of the argument of the complex number (x, y), expressed in radians in the range $-\pi < \text{atan2}(y, x) \leq \pi$. The values of x and y must not both be zero.

cos (x) returns the cosine function value for an argument of type real or complex that is treated as a value in radians.

cosh (x) returns the hyperbolic cosine function value for a real argument x.

exp (x) returns the exponential function value for a real or complex argument x.

log (x) returns the natural logarithm function for a real or complex argument x. In the real case, x must be positive. In the complex case, x must not be zero, and the imaginary part w of the result lies in the range $-\pi < w \leq \pi$.

log10 (x) returns the common (base 10) logarithm of a real argument whose value must be positive.

sin (x) returns the sine function value for a real or complex argument that is treated as a value in radians.

sinh (x) returns the hyperbolic sine function value for a real argument.

sqrt (x) returns the square root function value for a real or complex argument x. If x is real, its value must not be negative. In the complex case, the real part of the result is not negative, and when it is zero the imaginary part of the result is not negative.

tan (x) returns the tangent function value for a real argument that is treated as a value in radians.

tanh (x) returns the hyperbolic tangent function value for a real argument.

8.5 Elemental character and logical functions

8.5.1 Character–integer conversions

The following are elemental functions for conversions from a single character to an integer, and vice versa.

achar (i) is of type default character with length one and returns the character in the position in the ASCII collating sequence that is specified by the integer i. The value of i must be in the range $0 \le i \le 127$, otherwise the result is processor dependent.

char (i[,kind]) is of type character and length one, with a kind type parameter value that of the value of kind if present, or default otherwise. It returns the character in position i in the processor collating sequence associated with the relevant kind parameter. The value of i must be in the range $0 \le i \le n-1$, where n is the number of characters in the processor's collating sequence. If kind is present, it must be a scalar integer initialization expression and provide a kind type parameter that is supported on the processor.

iachar (c) is of type default integer and returns the position in the ASCII collating sequence of the default character c. If c is not in the sequence, the result is processor dependent.

ichar (c) is of type default integer and returns the position of the character c in the processor collating sequence associated with the kind parameter of c.

8.5.2 Lexical comparison functions

The following elemental functions accept default character strings as arguments, make a lexical comparison based on the ASCII collating sequence, and return a default logical result. If the strings have different lengths, the shorter one is padded on the right with blanks.

lge (string_a, string_b) returns the value true if string_a follows string_b in the ASCII collating sequence or is equal to it, and the value false otherwise.

lgt (string_a, string_b) returns the value true if string_a follows string_b in the ASCII collating sequence, and the value false otherwise.

lle (string_a, string_b) returns the value true if string_b follows string_a in the ASCII collating sequence or is equal to it, and the value false otherwise.

llt (string_a, string_b) returns the value true if string_b follows string_a in the ASCII collating sequence, and false otherwise.

8.5.3 String-handling elemental functions

The following are elemental functions that manipulate strings. The arguments string, substring, and set are always of type character, and where two are present have the same kind type parameter. The kind type parameter value of the result is that of string.

adjustl (string) adjusts left to return a string of the same length by removing all leading blanks and inserting the same number of trailing blanks.

adjustr (string) adjusts right to return a string of the same length by removing all trailing blanks and inserting the same number of leading blanks.

index (string, substring [,back]) has type default integer and returns the starting position of substring as a substring of string, or zero if it does not occur as a substring. If back is absent or present with value false, the starting position of the first such substring is returned; the value 1 is returned if substring has zero length. If back is present with value true, the starting position of the last such substring is returned; the value len(string)+1 is returned if substring has zero length.

len_trim (string) returns a default integer whose value is the length of string without trailing blank characters.

scan (string, set [,back]) returns a default integer whose value is the position of a character of string that is in set, or zero if there is no such character. If the logical back is absent or present with value false, the position of the leftmost such character is returned. If back is present with value true, the position of the rightmost such character is returned.

verify (string, set [,back]) returns the default integer value 0 if each character in string appears in set, or the position of a character of string that is not in set. If the logical back is absent or present with value false, the position of the leftmost such character is returned. If back is present with value true, the position of the rightmost such character is returned.

8.5.4 Logical conversion

The following elemental function converts from a logical value with one kind type parameter to another.

logical (l [,kind]) returns a logical value equal to the value of the logical l. The value of the kind type parameter of the result is the value of kind if it is present or that of default logical otherwise. If kind is present, it must be a scalar integer initialization expression and provide a kind type parameter that is supported on the processor.

8.6   Non-elemental string-handling functions

8.6.1   String-handling inquiry function

len (string) is an inquiry function that returns a scalar default integer holding the number of characters in string if it is scalar, or in an element of string if it is array valued. The value of string need not be defined.

8.6.2   String-handling transformational functions

There are two functions that cannot be elemental because the length type parameter of the result depends on the value of an argument.

repeat (string, ncopies) forms the string consisting of the concatenation of ncopies copies of string, where ncopies is of type integer and its value must not be negative. Both arguments must be scalar.

trim (string) returns string with all trailing blanks removed. The argument string must be scalar.

8.7   Numeric inquiry and manipulation functions

8.7.1   Models for integer and real data

The numeric inquiry and manipulation functions are defined in terms of a model set of integers and a model set of reals for each kind of integer and real data type implemented. For each kind of integer, it is the set

$$i = s \times \sum_{k=1}^{q} w_k \times r^{k-1}$$

where s is ± 1, q is a positive integer, r is an integer exceeding 1 (usually 2), and each w_k is an integer in the range $0 \leq w_k < r$. For each kind of real, it is the set

$$x = 0$$

and

$$x = s \times b^e \times \sum_{k=1}^{p} f_k \times b^{-k}$$

where s is ± 1, p and b are integers exceeding 1, e is an integer in a range $e_{\min} \leq e \leq e_{\max}$, and each f_k is an integer in the range $0 \leq f_k < b$ except that f_1 is also nonzero.

   Values of the parameters in these models are chosen for the processor so as best to fit the hardware with the proviso that all model numbers are representable. Note that it is quite likely that there are some machine numbers that lie outside the model. For example, many computers represent the integer $-r^q$, and the IEEE standard for Binary Floating-point Arithmetic (IEEE 754-1985 or IEC 60559 : 1989) contains reals with $f_1 = 0$ (called denormalized numbers) and register numbers with increased precision and range.

In Section 2.6, we noted that the value of a signed zero is regarded as being the same as that of an unsigned zero. However, many processors distinguish at the hardware level between a negative real zero value and a positive real zero value, and the IEEE standard makes use of this where possible. For example, when the exact result of an operation is nonzero but the rounding produces a zero, the sign is retained.

In Fortran, the two zeros are treated identically in all relational operations, as input arguments to all intrinsic functions (except `sign`), or as the scalar expression in the arithmetic `if` statement (Appendix B.2.1). However, the function `sign` (Section 8.3.2) is such that the sign of the second argument may be taken into account even if its value is zero. On a processor that has IEEE arithmetic, the value of `sign(2.0, -0.0)` is -2.0. Also, a Fortran processor is required to represent all negative numbers on output, including zero, with a minus sign.

8.7.2 Numeric inquiry functions

There are nine inquiry functions that return values from the models associated with their arguments. Each has a single argument that may be scalar or array-valued and each returns a scalar result. The value of the argument need not be defined.

digits (x), for real or integer x, returns the default integer whose value is the number of significant digits in the model that includes x, that is p or q.

epsilon (x), for real x, returns a real result with the same type parameter as x that is almost negligible compared with the value one in the model that includes x, that is b^{1-p}.

huge (x), for real or integer x, returns the largest value in the model that includes x. It has the type and type parameter of x. The value is

$$(1 - b^{-p})b^{e_{\max}}$$

or

$$r^q - 1$$

maxexponent (x), for real x, returns the default integer $e_{\max}$, the maximum exponent in the model that includes x.

minexponent (x), for real x, returns the default integer $e_{\min}$, the minimum exponent in the model that includes x.

precision (x), for real or complex x, returns a default integer holding the equivalent decimal precision in the model representing real numbers with the same type parameter value as x. The value is
$$\mathrm{int}((p-1) * \mathrm{log10}(b)) + k$$

where k is 1 if b is an integral power of 10 and 0 otherwise.

radix **(x)**, for real or integer x, returns the default integer that is the base in the model that includes x, that is b or r.

range **(x)**, for integer, real, or complex x, returns a default integer holding the equivalent decimal exponent range in the models representing integer or real numbers with the same type parameter value as x. The value is int(log10(*huge*)) for integers and

$$\text{int}(\min(\log 10(\textit{huge}), -\log 10(\textit{tiny})))$$

for reals, where *huge* and *tiny* are the largest and smallest positive numbers in the models.

tiny **(x)**, for real x, returns the smallest positive number

$$b^{e_{\min}-1}$$

in the model that includes x. It has the type and type parameter of x.

8.7.3   Elemental functions to manipulate reals

There are seven elemental functions whose first or only argument is of type real and that return values related to the components of the model values associated with the actual value of the argument. For the functions exponent, fraction, and set_exponent, if the value of x lies outside the range of model numbers, its e value is determined as if the model had no exponent limits.

exponent **(x)** returns the default integer whose value is the exponent part e of x when represented as a model number. If x=0, the result has value zero.

fraction **(x)** returns a real with the same type parameter as x whose value is the fractional part of x when represented as a model number, that is $x\, b^{-e}$.

nearest **(x, s)** returns a real with the same type parameter as x whose value is the nearest different machine number in the direction given by the sign of the real s. The value of s must not be zero.

rrspacing **(x)** returns a real with the same type parameter as x whose value is the reciprocal of the relative spacing of model numbers near x. If the value of x is a model number this is $|x\, b^{-e}|b^p$.

scale **(x, i)** returns a real with the same type parameter as x, whose value is $x\, b^i$, where b is the base in the model for x, and i is of type integer.

set_exponent **(x, i)** returns a real with the same type parameter as x, whose fractional part is the fractional part of the model representation of x and whose exponent part is i, that is $x\, b^{i-e}$.

spacing **(x)** returns a real with the same type parameter as x whose value is the absolute spacing of model numbers near x.

8.7.4 Transformational functions for kind values

There are two functions that return the least kind type parameter value that will meet a given numeric requirement. They have scalar arguments and results, so are classified as transformational.

selected_int_kind (r) returns the default integer scalar that is the kind type parameter value for an integer data type able to represent all integer values n in the range $-10^r < n < 10^r$, where r is a scalar integer. If more than one is available, a kind with least decimal exponent range is chosen (and least kind value if several have least decimal exponent range). If no corresponding kind is available, the result is -1.

selected_real_kind ([p] [, r]) returns the default integer scalar that is the kind type parameter value for a real data type with decimal precision (as returned by the function precision) at least p, and decimal exponent range (as returned by the function range) at least r. If more than one is available, a kind with the least decimal precision is chosen (and least kind value if several have least decimal precision). Both p and r are scalar integers; at least one of them must be present. If no corresponding kind value is available, the result is -1 if sufficient precision is unavailable, -2 if sufficient exponent range is unavailable, and -3 if both are unavailable.

8.8 Bit manipulation procedures

There are eleven procedures for manipulating bits held within integers. They are based on those in the US Military Standard MIL-STD 1753. They differ only in that here they are elemental, where appropriate, whereas the original procedures accepted only scalar arguments.

These intrinsics are based on a model in which an integer holds s bits w_k, $k = 0, 1, \ldots, s - 1$, in a sequence from right to left, based on the non-negative value

$$\sum_{k=0}^{s-1} w_k \times 2^k$$

This model is valid only in the context of these intrinsics. It is identical to the model for integers in Section 8.7.1 when $r = 2$ and $w_{s-1} = 0$, but when $r \neq 2$ or $w_{s-1} = 1$ the models do not correspond, and the value expressed as an integer may vary from processor to processor.

8.8.1 Inquiry function

bit_size (i) returns the number of bits in the model for bits within an integer of the same type parameter as i. The result is a scalar integer having the same type parameter as i.

8.8.2 Elemental functions

btest (i, pos) returns the default logical value true if bit pos of the integer i has
value 1 and false otherwise. pos must be an integer with value in the range $0 \leq$ pos $<$
bit_size(i).

iand (i, j) returns the logical and of all the bits in i and corresponding bits in j,
according to the truth table

```
i            1   1   0   0
j            1   0   1   0
iand(i, j)   1   0   0   0
```

The arguments i and j must have the same type parameter value, which is the type
parameter value of the result.

ibclr (i, pos) returns an integer, with the same type parameter as i, and value equal
to that of i except that bit pos is cleared to 0. The argument pos must be an integer
with value in the range $0 \leq$ pos $<$ bit_size(i).

ibits (i, pos, len) returns an integer, with the same type parameter as i, and
value equal to the len bits of i starting at bit pos right adjusted and all other bits
zero. The arguments pos and len must be integers with non-negative values such that
pos+len $\leq$ bit_size(i).

ibset (i, pos) returns an integer, with the same type parameter as i, and value equal
to that of i except that bit pos is set to 1. The argument pos must be an integer with
value in the range $0 \leq$ pos $<$ bit_size(i).

ieor (i, j) returns the logical exclusive or of all the bits in i and corresponding bits in
j, according to the truth table

```
i            1   1   0   0
j            1   0   1   0
ieor(i, j)   0   1   1   0
```

The arguments i and j must have the same type parameter value, which is the type
parameter value of the result.

ior (i, j) returns the logical inclusive or of all the bits in i and corresponding bits in
j, according to the truth table

```
i            1   1   0   0
j            1   0   1   0
ior(i, j)    1   1   1   0
```

The arguments i and j must have the same type parameter value, which is the type
parameter value of the result.

ishft (i, shift) returns an integer, with the same type parameter as i, and value equal to that of i except that the bits are shifted shift places to the left (-shift places to the right if shift is negative). Zeros are shifted in from the other end. The argument shift must be an integer with value satisfying the inequality |shift| ≤ bit_size(i).

ishftc (i, shift [, size]) returns an integer, with the same type parameter as i, and value equal to that of i except that the size rightmost bits (or all the bits if size is absent) are shifted circularly shift places to the left (-shift places to the right if shift is negative). The argument shift must be an integer with absolute value not exceeding the value of size (or bit_size(i) if size is absent).

not (i) returns the logical complement of all the bits in i, according to the truth table

i	0	1
not(i)	1	0

8.8.3 Elemental subroutine

call mvbits (from, frompos, len, to, topos) copies the sequence of bits in from that starts at position frompos and has length len to to, starting at position topos. The other bits of to are not altered. The arguments from, frompos, len, and topos are all integers with intent in, and they must have values that satisfy the inequalities: frompos+len ≤ bit_size(from), len ≥ 0, frompos ≥ 0, topos+len ≤ bit_size(to), and topos ≥ 0. The argument to is an integer with intent inout; it must have the same kind type parameter as from. The same variable may be specified for from and to.

8.9 Transfer function

The transfer function allows data of one type to be transferred to another without the physical representation being altered. This would be useful, for example, in writing a data storage and retrieval system. The system itself could be written for one type, default integer say, and other types handled by transfers to and from that type, for example:

```
integer           :: store
character(len=4)  :: word          ! To be stored and retrieved
:
store = transfer(word, store)      ! Before storage
:
word  = transfer(store, word)      ! After retrieval
:
```

transfer (source, mold [,size]) returns a result of type and type parameters those of mold. When size is absent, the result is scalar if mold is scalar, and it is of rank one and size just sufficient to hold all of source if mold is array-valued. When size is present, the result is of rank one and size size. If the physical representation of

the result is as long as or longer than that of source, the result contains source as its
leading part and the value of the rest is processor dependent; otherwise the result is the
leading part of source. As the rank of the result can depend on whether or not size
is specified, the corresponding actual argument must not itself be an optional dummy
argument.

8.10   Vector and matrix multiplication functions

There are two transformational functions that perform vector and matrix multiplications.
They each have two arguments that are both of numeric type (integer, real, or complex) or
both of logical type. The result is of the same type and type parameter as for the multiply or
and operation between two such scalars. The functions sum and any, used in the definitions,
are defined in Section 8.11.1.

dot_product (vector_a, vector_b) requires two arguments each of rank one
and the same size. If vector_a is of type integer or type real, it returns sum(vector_a * vector_b); if vector_a is of type complex, it returns
sum(conjg(vector_a) * vector_b); and if vector_a is of type logical, it returns
any(vector_a .and. vector_b).

matmul (matrix_a, matrix_b) performs matrix multiplication. For numeric arguments, three cases are possible:

   i) matrix_a has shape (n, m) and matrix_b has shape (m, k). The result has shape
   (n, k) and element (i, j) has the value
   sum(matrix_a(i, :) * matrix_b(:, j)).

   ii) matrix_a has shape (m) and matrix_b has shape (m, k). The result has shape
   (k) and element (j) has the value
   sum(matrix_a * matrix_b(:, j)).

   iii) matrix_a has shape (n, m) and matrix_b has shape (m). The result has shape
   (n) and element (i) has the value
   sum(matrix_a(i, :) * matrix_b).

For logical arguments, the shapes are as for numeric arguments and the values are
determined by replacing 'sum' and '*' in the above expressions by 'any' and '.and.'.

8.11   Transformational functions that reduce arrays

There are seven transformational functions that perform operations on arrays such as
summing their elements.

8.11.1   Single argument case

In their simplest form, these functions have a single array argument and return a scalar result.
All except count have a result of the same type and type parameter as the argument. The

mask array mask, used as an argument in any, all, count, and optionally in others, is described also in Section 6.17.

all (mask) returns the value true if all elements of the logical array mask are true or mask has size zero, and otherwise returns the value false.

any (mask) returns the value true if any of the elements of the logical array mask is true, and returns the value false if no elements are true or if mask has size zero.

count (mask) returns the default integer value that is the number of elements of the logical array mask that have the value true.

maxval (array) returns the maximum value of an element of an integer or real array. If array has size zero, it returns the negative value of largest magnitude supported by the processor.

minval (array) returns the minimum value of an element of an integer or real array. If array has size zero, it returns the largest positive value supported by the processor.

product (array) returns the product of the elements of an integer, real, or complex array. It returns the value one if array has size zero.

sum (array) returns the sum of the elements of an integer, real, or complex array. It returns the value zero if array has size zero.

8.11.2 Optional argument dim

All these functions have an optional second argument dim that is a scalar integer. If this is present, the operation is applied to all rank-one sections that span right through dimension dim to produce an array of rank reduced by one and extents equal to the extents in the other dimensions, or a scalar if the original rank is one. For example, if a is a real array of shape (4,5,6), sum(a,dim=2) is a real array of shape (4,6) and element (i, j) has value sum(a(i,:,j)).

As the rank of the result depends on whether dim is specified (unless the original is rank one), the corresponding actual argument must not itself be an optional dummy argument.

8.11.3 Optional argument mask

The functions maxval, minval, product, and sum have a third optional argument, a logical array mask. If this is present, it must have the same shape as the first argument and the operation is applied to the elements corresponding to true elements of mask; for example, sum(a, mask = a>0) sums the positive elements of the array a. The argument mask affects only the value of the function and does not affect the evaluation of arguments that are array expressions. The argument mask is permitted as the second positional argument when dim is absent.

8.12 Array inquiry functions

There are five functions for inquiries about the bounds, shape, size, and allocation status of an array of any type. Because the result depends on only the array properties, the value of the array need not be defined.

8.12.1 Allocation status

allocated (array) returns, when the allocatable array array is currently allocated, the value true; otherwise it returns the value false.

8.12.2 Bounds, shape, and size

The following functions enquire about the bounds of an array. In the case of an allocatable array, it must be allocated; and in the case of a pointer, it must be associated with a target. An array section or an array expression is taken to have lower bounds 1 and upper bounds equal to the extents (like an assumed-shape array with no specified lower bounds). If a dimension has size zero, the lower bound is taken as 1 and the upper bound is taken as 0.

lbound (array [,dim]), when dim is absent, returns a rank-one default integer array holding the lower bounds. When dim is present, it must be a scalar integer and the result is a scalar default integer holding the lower bound in dimension dim. As the rank of the result depends on whether dim is specified, the corresponding actual argument must not itself be an optional dummy argument.

shape (source) returns a rank-one default integer array holding the shape of the array or scalar source. In the case of a scalar, the result has size zero.

size (array [,dim]) returns a scalar default integer that is the size of the array array or extent along dimension dim if the scalar integer dim is present.

ubound (array [,dim]) is similar to lbound except that it returns upper bounds.

8.13 Array construction and manipulation functions

There are eight functions that construct or manipulate arrays of any type.

8.13.1 The merge elemental function

merge (tsource, fsource, mask) is an elemental function. The argument tsource may have any type and fsource must have the same type and type parameters. The argument mask must be of type logical. The result is tsource if mask is true and fsource otherwise.

The principal application of merge is when the three arguments are arrays having the same shape, in which case tsource and fsource are merged under the control of mask. Note, however, that tsource or fsource may be scalar in which case the elemental rules effectively broadcast it to an array of the correct shape.

8.13.2 Packing and unpacking arrays

The transformational function pack packs into a rank-one array those elements of an array that are selected by a logical array of conforming shape, and the transformational function unpack performs the reverse operation. The elements are taken in array element order.

pack (array, mask [,vector]), when vector is absent, returns a rank-one array containing the elements of array corresponding to true elements of mask in array element order; mask may be scalar with value true, in which case all elements are selected. If vector is present, it must be a rank-one array of the same type and type parameters as array and size at least equal to the number t of selected elements; the result has size equal to the size n of vector; if $t < n$, elements i of the result for $i > t$ are the corresponding elements of vector.

unpack (vector, mask, field) returns an array of the type and type parameters of vector and shape of mask. The argument mask must be a logical array and vector must be a rank-one array of size at least the number of true elements of mask. field must be of the same type and type parameters as vector and must either be scalar or be of the same shape as mask. The element of the result corresponding to the ith true element of mask, in array element order, is the ith element of vector; all others are equal to the corresponding elements of field if it is an array or to field if it is a scalar.

8.13.3 Reshaping an array

The transformational function reshape allows the shape of an array to be changed, with possible permutation of the subscripts.

reshape (source, shape [,pad] [,order]) returns an array with shape given by the rank-one integer array shape, and type and type parameters those of the array source. The size of shape must be constant, and its elements must not be negative. If pad is present, it must be an array of the same type and type parameters as source. If pad is absent or of size zero, the size of the result must not exceed the size of source. If order is absent, the elements of the result, in array element order, are the elements of source in array element order followed by copies of pad in array element order. If order is present, it must be a rank-one integer array with a value that is a permutation of $(1,2,...,n)$; the elements $r(s_1,...,s_n)$ of the result, taken in subscript order for the array having elements $r(s_{\text{order}(1)},..., s_{\text{order}(n)})$, are those of source in array element order followed by copies of pad in array element order. For example, if order has the value (/3,1,2/), the elements r(1,1,1), r(1,1,2), ..., r(1,1,k), r(2,1,1), r(2,1,2), ... correspond to the elements of source and pad in array element order.

8.13.4 Transformational function for replication

spread (source, dim, ncopies) returns an array of type and type parameters those of source and of rank increased by one. The argument source may be scalar or array-valued. The arguments dim and ncopies are integer scalars. The result contains max(ncopies, 0) copies of source, and element $(r_1, \ldots, r_{n+1})$ of the result is source$(s_1, \ldots, s_n)$ where $(s_1, \ldots, s_n)$ is $(r_1, \ldots, r_{n+1})$ with subscript dim omitted (or source itself if it is scalar).

8.13.5 Array shifting functions

cshift (array, shift [,dim]) returns an array of the same type, type parameters, and shape as array. The argument shift is of type integer and must be scalar if array is of rank one. If shift is scalar, the result is obtained by shifting every rank-one section that extends across dimension dim circularly shift times. The argument dim is an integer scalar and, if it is omitted, it is as if it were present with the value 1. The direction of the shift depends on the sign of shift, being to the left for a positive value and to the right for a negative value. Thus, for the case with shift=1 and array of rank one and size m, the element i of the result is array(i+1), where $i = 1, 2, \ldots, m-1$, and element m is array(1). If shift is an array, it must have the same shape as that of array with dimension dim omitted, and it supplies a separate value for each shift. For example, if array is of rank three and shape (k, l, m) and dim has the value 2, shift must be of shape (k, m) and supplies a shift for each of the $k \times m$ rank-one sections in the second dimension of array.

eoshift (array, shift [,boundary] [,dim]) is identical to cshift except that an end-off shift is performed and boundary values are inserted into the gaps so created. The argument boundary may be omitted when array has intrinsic type, in which case the value zero is inserted for the integer, real, and complex cases; false in the logical case; and blanks in the character case. If boundary is present, it must have the same type and type parameters as array; it may be scalar and supply all needed values or it may be an array whose shape is that of array with dimension dim omitted and supply a separate value for each shift.

8.13.6 Matrix transpose

The transpose function performs a matrix transpose for any array of rank two.

transpose (matrix) returns an array of the same type and type parameters as the rank-two array matrix. Element (i, j) of the result is matrix(j, i).

8.14 Transformational functions for geometric location

There are two transformational functions that find the locations of the maximum and minimum values of an integer or real array.

`maxloc (array [,mask])` returns a rank-one default integer array of size equal to the rank of `array`. Its value is the sequence of subscripts of an element of maximum value (among those corresponding to true values of the conforming logical array `mask` if it is present), as though all the declared lower bounds of `array` were 1. If there is more than one such element, the first in array element order is taken.

`maxloc (array, dim [,mask])` returns a default integer array of shape equal to that of `array` with dimension `dim` omitted, where `dim` is a scalar integer with value in the range $1 \leq$ `dim` $\leq$ rank(`array`), or a scalar if the original rank is one. The value of each element of the result is the position of the first element of maximum value in the corresponding rank-one section spanning dimension `dim`, among those elements corresponding to true values of the conforming logical array `mask` when it is present.

`minloc (array [,mask])` is identical to `maxloc (array [,mask])` except that the position of an element of minimum value is obtained.

`minloc (array, dim [,mask])` is identical to `maxloc (array, dim [,mask])` except that positions of elements of minimum value are obtained.

8.15 Transformational function for pointer disassociation

The function `null` is available to give the disassociated status to pointer entities.

`null ([mold])` returns a disassociated pointer. The argument `mold` is a pointer of any type and may have any association status, including undefined. The type, type parameter, and rank of the result are those of `mold` if it is present and otherwise are those of the object with which it is associated. In an actual argument associated with a dummy argument of assumed character length, `mold` must be present.

8.16 Non-elemental intrinsic subroutines

There are also in Fortran non-elemental intrinsic subroutines, which were chosen to be subroutines rather than functions because of the need to return information through the arguments.

8.16.1 Real-time clock

There are two subroutines that return information from the real-time clock, the first based on the ISO standard IS 8601 (Representation of dates and times). It is assumed that there is a basic system clock that is incremented by one for each clock count until a maximum `count_max` is reached and on the next count is set to zero. Default values are returned on systems without a clock. All the arguments have intent `out`.

`call date_and_time ([date] [,time] [,zone] [,values])` returns the following (with default values blank or `-huge(0)`, as appropriate, when there is no clock).

date is a scalar character variable holding the date in the form *ccyymmdd*, corresponding to century, year, month, and day.

time is a scalar character variable holding the time in the form *hhmmss.sss*, corresponding to hours, minutes, seconds, and milliseconds.

zone is a scalar character variable that is set to the difference between local time and Coordinated Universal Time (UTC, also known as Greenwich Mean Time) in the form *Shhmm*, corresponding to sign, hours, and minutes. For example, a processor in New York in winter would return the value -0500.

values is a rank-one default integer array of size at least 8 holding the sequence of values: the year, the month of the year, the day of the month, the time difference in minutes with respect to UTC, the hour of the day, the minutes of the hour, the seconds of the minute, and the milliseconds of the second.

call system_clock ([count][,count_rate][,count_max]) returns the following.

count is a scalar default integer holding a processor-dependent value based on the current value of the processor clock, or $-huge(0)$ if there is no clock. On the first call, the processor may set an initial value that may be zero.

count_rate is a scalar default integer holding the number of clock counts per second, or zero if there is no clock.

count_max is a scalar default integer holding the maximum value that count may take, or zero if there is no clock.

8.16.2 CPU time

There is a non-elemental intrinsic subroutine that returns the processor time.

call cpu_time (time) returns the following:

time is a scalar real that is assigned a processor-dependent approximation to the processor time in seconds, or a processor-dependent negative value if there is no clock.

The exact definition of time is left imprecise because of the variability in what different processors are able to provide. The primary purpose is to compare different algorithms on the same computer or discover which parts of a calculation on a computer are the most expensive.

The start time is left imprecise because the purpose is to time sections of code, as in the example

```
real :: t1, t2
:
call cpu_time(t1)
:                       ! Code to be timed.
call cpu_time(t2)
write (*,*) 'Time taken by code was ', t2-t1, ' seconds'
```

8.16.3 Random numbers

A sequence of pseudorandom numbers is generated from a seed that is held as a rank-one array of integers. The subroutine `random_number` returns the pseudorandom numbers and the subroutine `random_seed` allows an inquiry to be made about the size or value of the seed array, and the seed to be reset. The subroutines provide a portable interface to a processor-dependent sequence.

call random_number (harvest) returns a pseudorandom number from the uniform distribution over the range $0 \leq x < 1$ or an array of such numbers. `harvest` has intent out, may be a scalar or an array, and must be of type real.

call random_seed ([size] [put] [get]) has the following arguments.

  size has intent out and is a scalar default integer that the processor sets to the size n of the seed array.

  put has intent in and is a default integer array of rank one and size n that is used by the processor to reset the seed. A processor may set the same seed value for more than one value of put.

  get has intent out and is a default integer array of rank one and size n that the processor sets to the current value of the seed.

No more than one argument may be specified; if no argument is specified, the seed is set to a processor-dependent value.

8.17 Summary

In this chapter, we introduced the four categories of intrinsic procedures, explained the `intrinsic` statement, and gave detailed descriptions of all the procedures.

Some of the intrinsic procedures have names that might also be names of external functions in existing Fortran 77 programs. Appendix B15 of the Fortran 77 standard recommended that external procedures be identified as such by using the `external` statement. For any external procedure with a name contained in the following list, it is essential to provide an interface body or to use the `external` statement.

achar	all	any	btest	count	cshift
digits	floor	huge	iachar	iand	ibclr
ibits	ibset	ieor	ior	ishft	ishftc
kind	lbound	matmul	maxloc	maxval	merge
minloc	minval	modulo	mvbits	not	null
pack	radix	range	repeat	scale	scan
shape	size	spread	sum	tiny	trim
ubound	unpack	verify			

8.18 Exercises

1. Write a program to calculate the real roots or pairs of complex-conjugate roots of the quadratic equation $ax^2 + bx + c = 0$ for any real values of a, b, and c. The program should read these three values and print the results. Use should be made of the appropriate intrinsic functions.

2. Repeat Exercise 1 of Chapter 5, avoiding the use of do constructs.

3. Given the rules explained in Sections 3.12 and 8.2, what are the values printed by the following program?

```
program main
   real, target  :: a(3:10)
   real, pointer :: p1(:), p2(:)
   p1 => a(3:9:2)
   p2 => a(9:3:-2)
   print *, associated(p1, p2)
   print *, associated(p1, p2(4:1:-1))
end program main
```

4. In the following program, two pointer assignments, one to an array and the other to an array section, are followed by a subroutine call. Bearing in mind the rules given in Sections 3.12, 6.3, and 8.12.2, what values does the program print?

```
program main
   real, target  :: a(5:10)
   real, pointer :: p1(:), p2(:)
   p1 => a
   p2 => a(:)
   print *, lbound (a), lbound (a(:))
   print *, lbound (p1), lbound (p2)
   call what (a, a(:))
contains
   subroutine what (x, y)
      real, intent (in) :: x(:), y(:)
      print *, lbound (x), lbound (y)
   end subroutine what
end program main
```

9. Data transfer

9.1 Introduction

Fortran has, in comparison with most other high-level programming languages, a particularly rich set of facilities for input/output (I/O), but it is an area of Fortran into which not all programmers need to delve very deeply. For most small-scale programs it is sufficient to know how to read a few data records containing input variables, and how to transmit to a terminal or printer the results of a calculation. In large-scale data processing, on the other hand, the programs often have to deal with huge streams of data to and from many files; in these cases it is essential that great attention be paid to the way in which the I/O is designed and coded, as otherwise both the execution time and the real time spent in the program can suffer dramatically. The term *file* is used for a collection of data outside the main memory and a file is always organized into a sequence of *records*.

This chapter begins by discussing the various forms of formatted I/O, that is I/O which deals with records that do not use the internal number representation of the computer, but rather a character string which can be displayed for visual inspection by the human eye. It is also the form usually needed for transmitting data between different kinds of computers. The so-called *edit descriptors*, which are used to control the translation between the internal number representation and the external format, are then explained. Finally, the topics of unformatted (or binary) I/O and direct-access files are covered.

9.2 Number conversion

The ways in which numbers are stored internally by a computer are the concern of neither the Fortran standard nor this book. However, if we wish to output values — to display them on a terminal or to print them — then their internal representations must be converted into a character string which can be read in a normal way. For instance, the contents of a given computer word may be (in hexadecimal) be1d7dbf and correspond to the value -0.000450. For our particular purpose, we may wish to display this quantity as $-.000450$, or as $-4.5E-04$, or rounded to one significant digit as $-5E-04$. The conversion from the internal representation to the external form is carried out according to the information specified by an edit descriptor contained in a *format specification*. These will both be dealt with fully later in this chapter; for the moment, it is sufficient to give a few examples. For instance, to print an integer value in a field of 10 characters width, we would use the edit descriptor i10, where i stands for integer conversion, and 10 specifies the width of the output field. To print a real quantity in a field of 10 characters, 5 of which are reserved for the fractional part of the number, we specify f10.5. The edit descriptor f stands for floating-point (real) conversion, 10 is the total width of the output field, and 5 is the width of the fractional part of the field. If the number given above were to be converted according to this edit descriptor, it would appear as *bb*-0.00045, where *b* represents a blank. To print a character variable in a field of 10 characters, we would specify a10, where a stands for alphanumeric conversion.

A format specification consists of a list of edit descriptors enclosed in parentheses, and can be coded either as a default character expression, for instance

```
'(i10, f10.3, a10)'
```

or as a separate format statement, referenced by a statement label, for example

```
10 format(i10, f10.3, a10)
```

To print the scalar variables j, b, and c, of types integer, real, and character, respectively, we may then write either

```
      print '(i10, f10.3, a10)', j,b,c
```
or
```
      print 10, j,b,c
10 format(i10, f10.3, a10)
```

The first form is normally used when there is only a single reference in a scoping unit to a given format specification, and the second when there are several or when the format is complicated. The part of the statement designating the quantities to be printed is known as the *output list* and forms the subject of the following section.

9.3   I/O lists

The quantities to be read or written by a program are specified in an I/O list. For output they may be expressions, but for input they must be variables. In both cases, list items may be implied-do lists of quantities. Examples are shown in Figure 9.1, where we note the use of a *repeat count* in front of those edit descriptors that are required repeatedly. A repeat count must be a positive integer literal constant and must not have a kind type parameter. Function references are permitted in an I/O list, provided they do not themselves cause further I/O to occur.

In all these examples, except the last one, the expressions consist of single variables and would be equally valid in input statements using the read statement, for example

```
      read '(i10)', i
```

Such statements may be used to read values which are then assigned to the variables in the input list.

If an array appears as an item, it is treated as if the elements were specified in array element order. For example, the third of the print statements in Figure 9.1 could have been written

```
      print '(3f10.3)', a(1:3)
```

Figure 9.1

```
integer           :: i
real, dimension(10) :: a
character(len=20)   :: word
print '(i10)',    i
print '(10f10.3)', a
print '(3f10.3)',  a(1),a(2),a(3)
print '(a10)',     word(5:14)
print '(5f10.3)',  (a(i), i=1,9,2)
print '(2f10.3)',  a(1)*a(2)+i, sqrt(a(3))
```

Figure 9.2

```
integer :: j(10), k(3)
:
k = (/ 1, 2, 1 /)
read '(3i10)', j(k)      ! Illegal because j(1) appears twice
```

However, no element of the array may appear more than once in an input item. Thus, the case in Figure 9.2 is not allowed.

If an allocatable array appears as an item, it must be currently allocated.

Any pointers in an I/O list must be associated with a target, and transfer takes place between the file and the targets.

An item of derived type is treated as if the components were specified in the same order as in the type declaration. This rule is applied repeatedly for components of derived type, so that it is as if we specified the list of items of intrinsic type that constitute its ultimate components. For example, if p and t are of the types point and triangle of Figure 2.1, the statement

```
read '(8f10.5)', p, t
```

has the same effect as the statement

```
read '(8f10.5)', p%x, p%y, t%a%x, t%a%y, t%b%x,      &
                 t%b%y, t%c%x, t%c%y
```

Each ultimate component must be accessible (it may not, for example, be a private component of a public type).

An object in an I/O list is not permitted to be of a derived type that has a pointer component at any level of component selection. One reason for this restriction is because of the problems associated with recursive data structures. For example, supposing chain is a data object of the type entry of Figure 2.3 (in Section 2.13) and is set up to hold a chain of length three, then it has as its ultimate components chain%index, chain%next%index, chain%next%next%index, and chain%next%next%next, the last of which is a disassociated pointer. Another reason is that Fortran 2003 allows edit descriptors to be defined for data structures (see Section 19.2). Programmers can write procedures that are called as part of the I/O processing. Such a procedure is much better able to handle structures whose size and composition vary dynamically, the usual case for pointer components.

An I/O list may include an implied-do list, as illustrated by the fifth print statement in Figure 9.1. The general form is

   (do-object-list, do-var = expr, expr [, expr])

where each *do-object* is a variable (for input), an expression (for output), or is itself an implied-do list; *do-var* is a named scalar integer variable and each *expr* is a scalar integer expression. The loop initialization and execution is the same as for a (possibly nested) set of do constructs (Section 4.5). In an input list, a variable that is an item in a *do-object-list* must not be a *do-var* of any implied-do list in which it is contained, nor be associated[1] with such a *do-var*. In an input or output list, no *do-var* may be a *do-var* of any implied-do list in which it is contained or be associated with such a *do-var*.

Note that a zero-sized array, or an implied-do list with a zero iteration count, may occur as an item in an I/O list. Such an item corresponds to no actual data transfer.

9.4   Format definition

In the print and read statements of the previous section, the format specification was given each time in the form of a character constant immediately following the keyword. In fact, there are three ways in which a format specification may be given. They are as follows.

i) As a statement label referring to a format statement containing the relevant specification between parentheses:

```
      print 100, q
          :
  100 format(f10.3)
```

The format statement must appear in the same scoping unit, before the contains statement if it has one.   It is customary either to place each format statement immediately after the first statement which references it, or to group them all together just before the contains or end statement. It is also customary to have a separate sequence of numbers for the statement labels used for format statements. A given format statement may be used by any number of formatted I/O statements, whether for input or for output.

ii) As a default character expression whose value commences with a format specification in parentheses:

```
      print '(f10.3)', q
```

   or

---
[1]Such an illegal association could be established by pointer association.

```
character(len=*), parameter :: form='(f10.3)'
:
print form, q
```

or

```
character :: carray(7)=(/ '(','f','1','0','.','3',')' /)
:
print carray, q ! Elements of an array expression
                ! are concatenated.
```

or

```
character(4) :: carr1(10)
character(3) :: carr2(10)
integer      :: i, j
:
carr1(10) = '(f10'
carr2(3)  = '.3)'
:
i = 10
j = 3
:
print carr1(i)//carr2(j), q
```

>From these examples it may be seen that it is possible to program formats in a flexible way, and particularly that it is possible to use arrays, expressions, and also substrings in a way which allows a given format to be built up dynamically at execution time from various components. Any character data that might follow the trailing right parenthesis are ignored and may be undefined. In the case of an array, its elements are concatenated in array element order. However, on input *no* component of the format specification may appear also in the input list, or be associated with it. This is because the standard requires that the whole format specification be established *before* any I/O takes place. Further, no redefinition or undefinition of any characters of the format is permitted during the execution of the I/O statement.

iii) As an asterisk. This is a type of I/O known as *list-directed* I/O, in which the format is defined by the computer system at the moment the statement is executed, depending on both the type and magnitude of the entities involved. This facility is particularly useful for the input and output of small quantities of values, especially in temporary code which is used for test purposes, and which is removed from the final version of the program:

```
print *, 'Square-root of q = ', sqrt(q)
```

This example outputs a character constant describing the expression which is to be output, followed by the value of the expression under investigation. On the terminal screen, this might appear as

```
Square-root of q = 4.392246
```

the exact format being dependent on the computer system used. Character strings in this form of output are normally undelimited, as if an a edit descriptor were in use, but an option in the open statement (Section 10.3) may be used to require that they be delimited by apostrophes or quotation marks. Except for adjacent undelimited strings, values are separated by spaces or commas. Logical variables are represented as T for true and F for false. The processor may represent a sequence of r identical values c by the form $r*c$. Further details of list-directed input/output are deferred until Section 9.9.

Blank characters may precede the left parenthesis of a format specification, and may appear at any point within a format specification with no effect on the interpretation, except within a character string edit descriptor (Section 9.12.4).

9.5 Unit numbers

Input/output operations are used to transfer data between the variables of an executing program, as stored in the computer, and an external medium. There are many types of external media: the terminal, printer, disc drive, and CD are perhaps the most familiar. Whatever the device, a Fortran program regards each one from which it reads or to which it writes as a *unit*, and each unit, with two exceptions, has associated with it a *unit number*. This number must not be negative and is often in the range 1 to 99. Thus we might associate with a disc drive from which we are reading the unit number 10, and to a hard disc drive to which we are writing the unit number 11. All program units of an executable program that refer to a particular unit number are referencing the same file.

There are two I/O statements, print and a variant of read, that do not reference any unit number; these are the statements that we have used so far in examples, for the sake of simplicity. A read statement without a unit number will normally expect to read from the terminal, unless the program is working in batch (non-interactive) mode, in which case there will be a disc file with a reserved name from which it reads. A print statement will normally expect to output to the terminal, unless the program is in batch mode, in which case another disc file with a reserved name will be used. Such files are usually suitable for subsequent output on a physical output device. The system may implicitly associate unit numbers to these default units (usually 5 for input and 6 for output).

Apart from these two special cases, all I/O statements must refer explicitly to a unit in order to identify the device to which or from which data are to be transferred. The unit may be given in one of three forms. These are shown in the following examples which use another form of the read containing a unit specifier, u, and format specifier, *fmt*, in parentheses and separated by a comma, where *fmt* is a format specification as described in the previous section:

```
read (u, fmt) list
```

The three forms of *u* are as follows.

i) As a scalar integer expression that gives the unit number:

```
read (4, '(f10.3)') q
read (nunit, '(f10.3)') q
read (4*i+j, 100) a
```

where the value may be any non-negative integer allowed by the system for this purpose.

ii) As an asterisk:

```
read (*, '(f10.3)') q
```

where the asterisk implies the standard input unit designated by the system, the same as that used for read without a unit number.

iii) As a default character variable identifying an *internal file* (see next section).

9.6 Internal files

Internal files allow format conversion between various representations to be carried out by the program in a storage area defined within the program itself. There are two particularly useful applications, one to read data whose format is not properly known in advance, and the other to prepare output lists containing mixed character and numerical data, all of which has to be prepared in character form, perhaps to be displayed as a caption on a graphics display. The character data must be of default kind. The first application will now be described; the second will be dealt with in Section 9.8.

Imagine that we have to read a string of 30 digits, which might correspond to 30 one-digit integers, 15 two-digit integers, or 10 three-digit integers. The information as to which type of data is involved is given by the value of an additional digit, which has the value 1, 2, or 3, depending on the number of digits each integer contains. An internal file provides us with a mechanism whereby the 30 digits can be read into a character buffer area. The value of the final digit can be tested separately, and 30, 15, or 10 values read from the internal file, depending on this value. The basic code to achieve this might read as follows (no error recovery or data validation is included, for simplicity):

```
integer      :: ival(30), key, i
character(30):: buffer
character(6) :: form(3) = (/ '(30i1)', '(15i2)', '(10i3)' /)
read (*, '(a30,i1)')     buffer, key
read (buffer, form (key)) (ival(i), i=1,30/key)
```

Here, ival is an array which will receive the values, buffer a character variable of a length sufficient to contain the 30 input digits, and form a character array containing the three possible formats to which the input data might correspond. The first read statement reads 30 digits into buffer as character data, and a final digit into the integer variable key. The second read statement reads the data from buffer into ival, using the appropriate conversion as specified by the edit descriptor selected by key. The number of variables read from buffer to ival is defined by the implied-do loop, whose second specifier is an integer expression depending also on key. After execution of this code, ival will contain 30/key values, their number and exact format not having been known in advance.

If an internal file is a scalar, it has a single record whose length is that of the scalar. If it is an array, its elements, in array element order, are treated as successive records of the file and each has length equal to that of an array element. It may not be an array section with a vector subscript.

A record becomes defined when it is written. The number of characters sent must not exceed the length of the record. It may be less, in which case the rest of the record is padded with blanks. For list-directed output (Section 9.4), character constants are not delimited. A record may be read only if it is defined (which need not only be by an output statement). Records are padded with blanks, if necessary.

An internal file is always positioned at the beginning of its first record prior to data transfer (the array section notation may be used to start elsewhere in an array). Of course, if an internal file is an allocatable array or pointer, it must be allocated or associated with a target. Also, no item in the input/output list may be in the file or associated with the file.

An internal file must be of default character type and non-default character items are not permitted in input/output lists. It may be used for list-directed I/O (Section 9.9), but not for namelist I/O (Section 9.10).

9.7   Formatted input

In the previous sections we have given complete descriptions of the ways that formats and units may be specified, using simplified forms of the read and print statements as examples. There are, in fact, two forms of the formatted read statement. Without a unit, it has the form

    read *fmt* [, *list*]

and with a unit it may take the form

    read ([unit=]*u*, [fmt=]*fmt* [,iostat=*ios*]   &
              [, err=*error-label*] [,end=*end-label*]) [*list*]

where *u* and *fmt* are the unit and format specifiers described in Sections 9.4 and 9.5, iostat=, err=, and end= are optional specifiers which allow a user to specify how a read statement shall recover from various exceptional conditions, and *list* is a list of variables and implied-do lists of variables. The keyword items may be specified in any order, although it is usual to keep the unit number and format specification as the first two. The unit number must be first if it does not have its keyword. If the format does not have its keyword, it must be second, following the unit number without its keyword. Note that this parallels the rules for keyword calls of procedures, except that the positional list is limited to two items.

For simplicity of exposition, we have so far limited ourselves to formats that correspond to a single record in the file, but we will meet later in this chapter cases that lead to the input of a part of a record or of several successive records.

The meanings of the optional specifiers are as follows. If the `iostat=` is specified, then *ios* must be a scalar integer variable of default kind which, after execution of the `read` statement, has a negative value if an end-of-record condition is encountered during non-advancing input (Section 9.11), a different negative value if an endfile condition was detected on the input device (Section 10.2.3), a positive value if an error was detected (for instance a formatting error), or the value zero otherwise. The actual values assigned to *ios* in the event of an exception occurring are not defined by the standard, only the signs.

If the `end=` is specified, then *end-label* must be a statement label of a statement in the same scoping unit, to which control will be transferred in the event of the end of the file being reached.

If the `err=` is specified, then *error-label* is a statement label in the same scoping unit, to which control will be transferred in the event of any other exception occurring. The labels *error-label* and *end-label* may be the same. If they are not specified and an exception occurs, execution will stop, unless `iostat` is specified. An example of a `read` statement with its associated error recovery is given in Figure 9.3, in which `error` and `last_file` are subroutines to deal with the exceptions. They will normally be system dependent.

Figure 9.3

```
      read (nunit, '(3f10.3)', iostat=ios, err=110, end=120) a,b,c
   !
   !   Successful read - continue execution.
   :
   :
   !
   !   Error condition - take appropriate action.
  110   call error (ios)
        go to 999
   !
   !   End-of-file condition - test whether more
   !   files follow.
  120   call last_file
   :
  999   end
```

If an error or end-of-file condition occurs on input, the statement terminates and all list items and any implied-do variables become undefined. If an end-of-file condition occurs for an external file, the file is positioned following the endfile record (Section 10.2.3); if there is otherwise an error condition, the file position is indeterminate. An end-of-file condition occurs also if an attempt is made to read beyond the end of an internal file.

It is a good practice to include some sort of error recovery in all `read` statements which are included permanently in a program. On the other hand, input for test purposes is normally sufficiently well handled by the simple form of `read` without unit number, and without error recovery.

9.8   Formatted output

There are two types of formatted output statements, the print statement which has appeared in many of the examples so far in this chapter, and the write statement whose syntax is similar to that of the read statement:

```
print fmt [, list]
```

and

```
write ([unit=]u, [fmt=]fmt [,iostat=ios]              &
             [,err=error-label] ) [list]
```

where all the components have the same meanings as described for the read statement (Section 9.7). An asterisk for *u* specifies the standard output unit, as used by print. If an error condition occurs on output, execution of the statement terminates, any implied-do variables become undefined, and the file position becomes indeterminate.

An example of a write statement is

```
write (nout, '(10f10.3)', iostat=ios, err=110) a
```

An example using an internal file is given in Figure 9.4, which builds a character string from numeric and character components. The final character string might be passed to another subroutine for output, for instance as a caption on a graphics display.

Figure 9.4

```
integer          :: day
real             :: cash
character(len=50) :: line
   :
!   write into line
write (line,'(a, i2, a, f8.2, a)')                        &
      'Takings for day ', day, ' are ', cash, ' dollars'
```

In this example, we declare a character variable that is long enough to contain the text to be transferred to it. (The write statement contains a format specification with a edit descriptors without a field width. These assume a field width corresponding to the actual length of the character strings to be converted.) After execution of the write statement, line might contain the character string

```
Takings for day  3 are   4329.15 dollars
```

and this could be used as a string for further processing.

The number of characters written to line must not exceed its length.

9.9   List-directed I/O

In Section 9.4, the list-directed output facility using an asterisk as format specifier was introduced. We assumed that the list was short enough to fit into a single record, but for long lists the processor is free to output several records. Character constants may be split between records, and complex constants that are as long as, or longer than, a record may be split after the comma that separates the two parts. Apart from these cases, a value always lies within a single record. For the sake of carriage control (which is described in Appendix B.2), the first character of each record is blank unless a delimited character constant is being continued. Note that when an undelimited character constant is continued, the first character of the continuation record is blank. The only blanks permitted in a numeric constant are within a split complex constant after the comma.

This facility is equally useful for input, especially of small quantities of test data. On the input record, the various constants may appear in any of their usual forms, just as if they were being read under the usual edit descriptors, as defined in Section 9.12. Exceptions are that complex values must be enclosed in parentheses, character constants may be delimited, a blank must not occur except in a delimited character constant or in a complex constant before or after a numeric field, blanks are never interpreted as zeros, and the optional characters which are allowed in a logical constant (those following t or f, see Section 9.12.2) must include neither a comma nor a slash.

Character constants that are enclosed in apostrophes or quotation marks may be spread over as many records as necessary to contain them, except that a doubled quotation mark or apostrophe must not be split between records. Delimiters may be omitted for a default character constant if:

- it is of nonzero length;

- the constant does not contain a blank, comma, or slash;

- it is contained in one record;

- the first character is neither a quotation mark nor an apostrophe; and

- the leading characters are not numeric followed by an asterisk.

In this case, the constant is terminated when a blank, comma, slash, or end of record is encountered, and apostrophes or quotation marks appearing within the constant must not be doubled.

Whenever a character value has a different length from the corresponding list item, the value is truncated or padded on the right with blanks, as in the character assignment statement.

It is possible to use a repeat count for a given constant, for example 6*10 to specify six occurrences of the integer value 10. If it is possible to interpret the constant as either a literal constant or an undelimited character constant, the first corresponding list item determines which it is.

The (optionally repeated) constants are separated in the input by *separators*. A separator is one of the following, appearing other than in a character constant:

- a comma, optionally preceded and optionally followed by one or more contiguous blanks;

- a slash (/), optionally preceded and optionally followed by one or more contiguous blanks; or

- one or more contiguous blanks between two non-blank values or following the last non-blank value.

An end of record not within a character constant is regarded as a blank and, therefore, forms part of a separator. A blank embedded in a complex constant or delimited character constant is not a separator. An input record may be terminated by a slash separator, in which case all the following values in the record are ignored, and the input statement terminates.

If there are no values between two successive separators, or between the beginning of the first record and the first separator, this is taken to represent a *null value* and the corresponding item in the input list is left unchanged, defined or undefined as the case may be. A null value must not be used for the real or imaginary part of a complex constant, but a single null value may be used for the whole complex value. A series of null values may be represented by a repeat count without a constant: `, 6*,`. When a slash separator is encountered, null values are given to any remaining list items.

An example of this form of the read statement is:

```
integer           ::  i
real              ::  a
complex           ::  field(2)
logical           ::  flag
character (len=12) :: title
character (len=4)  :: word
    :
read *, i, a, field, flag, title, word
```

If this reads the input record

10*b*6.4*b*(1.,0.)*b*(2.,0.)*btbt*est/

(in which *b* stands for a blank, and blanks are used as separators), then i, a, field, flag, and title will acquire the values 10, 6.4, (1.,0.) and (2.,0.), .true., and test, respectively, while word remains unchanged. For the input records

```
10,.64e1,2*,.true.
'histogramb10'/val1
```

(in which commas are used as separators), the variables i, a, flag, and title will acquire the values 10, 6.4, .true., and histogram*b*10, respectively. The variables field and word remain unchanged, and the input string val1 is ignored as it follows a slash. (Note the apostrophes, which are required as the string contains a blank. Without delimiters, this string would appear to be a string followed by the integer value 10.) Because of this slash, the read statement does not continue with the next record and the list is thus not fully satisfied.

9.10   Namelist I/O

It can be useful, especially for program testing, to input or output an annotated list of values. The values required are specified in a namelist group (Section 7.15), and the I/O is performed by a read or write statement that does not have an I/O list, and in which either

- the format is replaced by a namelist-group name as the second positional parameter, or

- the `fmt=` specifier is replaced by a `nml=` specifier with that name.

When reading, only those objects which are specified in the input record and which do not have a null value become defined. All other list items remain in their existing state of definition or undefinition. It is possible to define the value of an array element or section without affecting the other portions of the array. When writing, all the items in the group are written to the file specified. This form of I/O is not available for internal files.

The value for a scalar object or list of values for an array is preceded in the records by the name or designator and an equals sign which may optionally be preceded or followed by blanks. The form of the list of values and null values in the input and output records is as that for list-directed I/O (Section 9.9), except that character constants must *always* be delimited in input records and logical constants must not contain an equals sign. A `namelist` input statement terminates on the appearance of a slash in the list outside a character constant. A simple example is

```
integer   :: no_of_eggs, litres_of_milk, kilos_of_butter
namelist/food/no_of_eggs, litres_of_milk, kilos_of_butter
read (5, nml=food)
```

to read the record

```
&food litres_of_milk=5, no_of_eggs=12 /
```

where we note that the order of the two values given is not the same as their order in the `namelist` group — the orders need not necessarily match. The value of `kilos_of_butter` remains unchanged. The first non-blank item in the record is an ampersand followed without an intervening blank by the group name. The slash is obligatory as a terminator. On output, a similar annotated list of values is produced, starting with the name of the group and ending with a slash. Here the order is that of the `namelist` group. Thus, the statements

```
integer   :: number, list(10)
namelist/out/number, list
write (6, nml=out)
```

might produce the record

```
&OUT NUMBER=1, LIST=14, 9*0 /
```

On output, the names are always in upper case.

Where a subobject designator appears in an input record, all substring expressions, subscripts, and strides must be scalar integer literal constants without specified kind parameters. All group names, object names, and component names are interpreted without regard to case. Blanks may precede or follow the name or designator, but must not appear within it.

If the object is scalar and of intrinsic type, the equals sign must be followed by one value. If it is of derived type or is an array, the equals sign must be followed by a list of values of intrinsic type corresponding to the replacement of each derived-type value by its ultimate components and each array by its elements in array element order.

The list of values must not be too long, but it may be too short, in which case trailing null values are regarded as having been appended. If an object is of type character, the corresponding item must be of the same kind.

Zero-sized objects must not appear in a `namelist` input record. In any multiple occurrence of an object in a sequence of input records, the final value is taken.

Input records for `namelist` input may bear a comment following an object name/value separator other than a slash. This allows programmers to document the structure of a `namelist` input file line by line. The comment is in the usual format for comments. The input record of this section might be documented thus:

```
&food litres_of_milk=5,          ! For camping holiday
no_of_eggs=12 /
```

A comment line, with ! as the first non-blank character in an input record, is also permitted, but may not occur in a character context.

9.11 Non-advancing I/O

So far we have considered each `read` or `write` statement to perform the input or output of a complete record. There are, however, many applications, especially in screen management, where this would become an irksome restriction. What is required is the ability to read and write without always advancing the file position to ahead of the next record. This facility is provided by *non-advancing* I/O. To gain access to this facility, the optional `advance=` specifier must appear in the `read` or `write` statement and be associated with a scalar default character expression *advance* which evaluates, after suppression of any trailing blanks and conversion of any upper-case letters to lower case, to the value no. The only other allowed value is yes, which is the default value if the specifier is absent; in this case, normal (advancing) I/O occurs.

The following optional specifiers are available for a non-advancing `read` statement:

> `eor=`*eor-label*
> `size=`*size*

where *eor-label* is a statement label in the same scoping unit and *size* is a default integer scalar variable. The *eor-label* may be the same as an *end-label* or *error-label* of the `read` statement.

An advancing I/O statement always repositions the file after the last record accessed, but a non-advancing I/O statement usually leaves the file positioned within the record. However, if a non-advancing input statement attempts to transfer data from beyond the end of the *current* record, an end-of-record condition occurs and the file is repositioned to follow the record. The `iostat` variable, if present, will acquire a different negative value to the one indicating an end-of-file condition; and, if the `eor=` specifier is present, control is transferred to the statement specified by its associated *eor-label*. In order to provide a means of controlling this process, the `size=` specifier, when present, sets *size* to the number of characters actually read. A full example is thus

```
      character(len=3) :: key
      integer          :: unit, size
      read (unit, '(a3)', advance='no', size=size, eor=66) key
      :
  ! key is not in one record
66  key(size+1:) = ''
      :
```

As for error and end-of-file conditions, the program terminates when an end-of-record condition occurs if neither eor= nor iostat= is specified.

If encountering an end-of-record on reading results in the input list not being satisfied, the pad= specifier described in Section 10.3 will determine whether any padding with blank characters occurs. Blanks inserted as padding are not included in the size= count.

It is possible to perform normal and non-advancing I/O on the same record or file. For instance, a non-advancing read might read the first few characters of a record and a normal read the remainder.

A particular application of this facility is to write a prompt to a terminal screen and to read from the next character position on the screen without an intervening line-feed:

```
write (*, '(a)', advance='no') 'enter next prime number:'
read  (*, '(i10)') prime_number
```

Non-advancing I/O may be performed only on an external file, and may not be used for namelist or list-directed I/O. Note that, as for advancing input/output, several records may be processed by a single statement.

9.12   Edit descriptors

In the description of the possible forms of a format specification in Section 9.4, a few examples of the edit descriptors were given. As mentioned there, edit descriptors give a precise specification of how values are to be converted into a character string on an output device or internal file, or converted from a character string on an input device or internal file to internal representations.

With certain exceptions noted in the following text, edit descriptors in a list are separated by commas, and only in the case where an input/output list is empty or specifies only zero-sized arrays may there be no edit descriptor at all in the format specification.

On a processor that supports upper- and lower-case letters, edit descriptors are interpreted without regard to case. This is also true for numerical and logical input fields; an example is 89AB as a hexadecimal input value. In output fields, any alphabetic characters are in upper case.

9.12.1   Repeat counts

Edit descriptors fall into three classes: *data*, *control*, and *character-string*. The data edit descriptors may be preceded by a repeat count (a nonzero unsigned default integer literal constant), as in the example

```
10f12.3
```

Of the remaining edit descriptors, only the slash edit descriptor (Section 9.12.5) may have an associated repeat count. A repeat count may be applied to a group of edit descriptors, enclosed in parentheses:

```
print '(4(i5,f8.2))', (i(j), a(j), j=1,4)
```

(for integer i and real a). This is equivalent to writing

```
print '(i5,f8.2,i5,f8.2,i5,f8.2,i5,f8.2)', (i(j), a(j), j=1,4)
```

Repeat counts such as this may be nested:

```
print '(2(2i5,2f8.2))', i(1),i(2),a(1),a(2),i(3),i(4),a(3),a(4)
```

If a format specification without components in parentheses is used with an I/O list that contains more elements than the number of edit descriptors, taking account of repeat counts, then a new record will begin, and the format specification will be repeated. Further records begin in the same way until the list is exhausted. To print an array of 100 integer elements, 10 elements to a line, the following statement might be used:

```
print '(10i8)', (i(j), j=1,100)
```

Similarly, when reading from an input file, new records will be read until the list is satisfied, a new record being taken from the input file each time the specification is repeated *even if the individual records contain more input data than specified by the format specification*. These superfluous data will be ignored. For example, reading the two records (*b* again stands for a blank)

```
bbb10bbb15bbb20
bbb25bbb30bbb35
```

under control of the read statement

```
read '(2i5)', i,j,k,l
```

will result in the four integer variables i, j, k, and l acquiring the values 10, 15, 25, and 30, respectively.

If a format contains components in parentheses, as in

```
'(2i5, 3(i2,2(i1,i3)), 2(2f8.2,i2))'
```

whenever the format is exhausted, a new record is taken and format control reverts to the repeat factor preceding the left parenthesis corresponding to the last-but-one right parenthesis, here 2(2f8.2,i2), or to the parenthesis itself if it has no repeat factor. This we call *reversion*.

9.12.2 Data edit descriptors

Values of all the intrinsic data types may be converted by the g edit descriptor. However, for reasons of clarity, it is described last.

Integer values may be converted by means of the i edit descriptor. This comes in a basic form, iw, where w is a nonzero unsigned default integer literal constant that defines the width of the field. The integer value will be read from or written to this field, adjusted to its right-hand side. If we again designate a blank position by b then the value -99 printed under control of the edit descriptor i5 will appear as bb-99, the sign counting as one position in the field.

For output, an alternative form of this edit descriptor allows the number of digits that are to be printed to be specified exactly, even if some are leading zeros. The form i$w.m$ specifies the width of the field, w, and that at least m digits are to be output, where m is an unsigned default integer literal constant. The value 99 printed under control of the edit descriptor i5.3 would appear as bb099. The value of m is even permitted to be zero, and the field will be then filled with blanks if the value printed is 0. On input, i$w.m$ is interpreted in exactly the same way as iw.

For the i and all other numeric edit descriptors, if the output field is too narrow to contain the number to be output, it is filled with asterisks.

Integer values may also be converted by the bw, b$w.m$, ow, o$w.m$, zw, and z$w.m$ edit descriptors. These are similar to the i form, but are intended for integers represented in the binary, octal, and hexadecimal number systems, respectively (Section 2.6.1). The external form does not contain the leading letter (b, o, or z) or the delimiters.

Real values may be converted by either e, en, es, or f edit descriptors. The f descriptor we have met in earlier examples. Its general form is f$w.d$, where w and d are unsigned default integer literal constants which define, respectively, the field width and the number of digits to appear after the decimal point in the output field. The decimal point counts as one position in the field. On input, if the input string has a decimal point, the value of d is ignored. Reading the input string b9.3729b with the edit descriptor f8.3 would cause the value 9.3729 to be transferred. All the digits are used, but roundoff may be inevitable because of the actual physical storage reserved for the value on the computer being used.

There are, in addition, two other forms of input string that are acceptable to the f edit descriptor. The first is an optionally signed string of digits without a decimal point. In this case, the d rightmost digits will be taken to be the fractional part of the value. Thus b-14629 read under control of the edit descriptor f7.2 will transfer the value -146.29. The second form is the standard default real form of literal constant, as defined in Section 2.6.2, and the variant in which the exponent is signed and e is omitted. In this case, the d part of the descriptor is again ignored. Thus the value 14.629e-2 (or 14.629-2), under control of the edit descriptor f9.1, will transfer the value 0.14629. The exponent letter may also be written in upper case.

Values are rounded on output following the normal rules of arithmetic. Thus, the value 10.9336, when output under control of the edit descriptor f8.3, will appear as bb10.934, and under the control of f4.0 as b11.

The e edit descriptor has two forms, e$w.d$ and e$w.d$ee, and is more appropriate for numbers with a magnitude below about 0.01, or above 1000. The rules for these two forms for input are identical to those for the f$w.d$ edit descriptor. For output with the e$w.d$ form of the descriptor, a different character string will be transferred, containing a significand with absolute value less than 1 and an exponent field of four characters that consists of either E followed by a sign and two digits or of a sign and three digits. Thus, for 1.234×10^{23} converted by the edit descriptor e10.4, the string b.1234E+24 or b.1234+024 will be transferred. The form containing the exponent letter E is not used if the magnitude of the exponent exceeds 99. For instance, e10.4 would cause the value 1.234×10^{-150} to be transferred as b.1234-149. Some processors print a zero before the decimal point.

In the second form of the e edit descriptor, e$w.d$ee, e is an unsigned, nonzero default integer literal constant that determines the number of digits to appear in the exponent field. This form is obligatory for exponents whose magnitude is greater than 999. Thus the value 1.234×10^{1234} with the edit descriptor e12.4e4 is transferred as the string b.1234E+1235. An increasing number of computers are able to deal with these very large exponent ranges. It can also be used if only one exponent digit is desired. For example, the value 1.211 with the edit descriptor e9.3e1 is transferred as the string b0.121E+1.

The en (***engineering***) edit descriptor is identical to the e edit descriptor except that on output the decimal exponent is divisible by three, a nonzero significand is greater than or equal to 1 and less than 1000, and the scale factor (Section 9.12.5) has no effect. Thus, the value 0.0217 transferred under an en9.2 edit descriptor would appear as 21.70E-03 or 21.70-003.

The es (***scientific***) edit descriptor is identical to the e edit descriptor, except that on output the absolute value of a nonzero significand is greater than or equal to 1 and less than 10, and the scale factor (Section 9.12.5) has no effect. Thus, the value 0.0217 transferred under an es9.2 edit descriptor would appear as 2.17E-02 or 2.17-002.

Complex values may be edited under control of pairs of f, e, en, or es edit descriptors. The two descriptors do not need to be identical. The complex value (0.1,100.) converted under control of f6.1,e8.1 would appear as bbb0.1b0.1E+03. The two descriptors may be separated by character string and control edit descriptors (to be described in Sections 9.12.4 and 9.12.5, respectively).

Logical values may be edited using the lw edit descriptor. This defines a field of width w which on input consists of optional blanks, optionally followed by a decimal point, followed by t or f (or T or F), optionally followed by additional characters. Thus a field defined by l7 permits the strings .true. and .false. to be input. The characters t or f will be transferred as the values true or false, respectively. On output, the character T or F will appear in the rightmost position in the output field.

Character values may be edited using the a edit descriptor in one of its two forms, either a or aw. In the first of the two forms, the width of the input or output field is determined by the actual width of the item in the I/O list, measured in number of characters of whatever kind. Thus, a character variable of length 10, containing the value STATEMENTS, when written under control of the a edit descriptor would appear in a field 10 characters wide, and the non-default character variable of length 4 containing the value 国際標準 would appear in a field 4 characters wide. If, however, the first variable were converted under an a11 edit descriptor, it would be printed with a leading blank: bSTATEMENTS. Under control of a8, the eight leftmost characters only would be written: STATEMEN.

Conversely, with the same variable on input, an a11 edit descriptor would cause the 10 rightmost characters in the 11-character-wide input field to be transferred, so that *b*STATEMENTS would be transferred as STATEMENTS. The a8 edit descriptor would cause the eight characters in the field to be transferred to the eight leftmost positions in the variable, and the remaining two would be filled with blanks: STATEMEN would be transferred as STATEMEN*bb*.

All characters transferred under the control of an a or a*w* edit descriptor have the kind of the I/O list item, and we note that this edit descriptor is the *only* one which can be used to transmit non-default characters to or from a record. In the non-default case, the blank padding character is processor dependent.

The g*w.d* and g*w.dee* (**general**) edit descriptor may be used for any intrinsic data type. When used for real or complex types, it is identical to the e edit descriptor except that an output value with magnitude n in the range

$$0.1 - 0.5 \times 10^{-d-1} \le n < 10^d - 0.5$$

or zero when $d = 0$ is converted as if by an f edit descriptor, and followed by the same number of blanks as the e edit descriptor would have used for the exponent part. The equivalent f edit descriptor is f$w'.d'$, where $w' = w - 4$ for g$w.d$ or $w - e - 2$ for g$w.dee$, and $d' = d - k$ when n lies in the range

$$10^{k-1}(1 - 0.5 \times 10^{-d}) \le n < 10^k(1 - 0.5 \times 10^{-d})$$

for $k = 0, 1, \ldots, d$ and $d' = d - 1$ when $n = 0$ and $d > 0$. This form is useful for printing values whose magnitudes are not well known in advance, and where an f conversion is preferred where possible, and an e otherwise.

When the g edit descriptor is used for integer, logical, or character types, it follows the rules of the iw, lw, and aw edit descriptors, respectively.

Finally, values of **derived types** are edited by the appropriate sequence of edit descriptors corresponding to the intrinsic types of the ultimate components of the derived type. An example is:

```
type string
   integer              :: length
   character(len=20)  :: word
end type string
type(string) :: text
read(*, '(i2, a)') text
```

Fortran 2003 offers enhanced facilities for derived-type input/output (Section 19.2).

9.12.3 Minimal field width editing

In order to allow output records to contain as little unused space as possible, the i, f, b, o, and z edit descriptors (Section 9.12.2) may specify a field width of zero, as in i0 or f0.3. This does not denote a zero-width field, but a field that is of the minimum width necessary to contain the output value in question. The programmer does not need to worry that a field with too narrow a width will cause output values to overflow and contain only asterisks.

9.12.4   Character string edit descriptor

A *default character* literal constant without a specified kind parameter can be transferred to an output file by embedding it in the format specification itself, as in the example

```
print "(' This is a format statement')"
```

The string will appear each time the statement is executed. In this descriptor, case is significant. Character string edit descriptors must not be used on input.

9.12.5   Control edit descriptors

It is sometimes necessary to give other instructions to an I/O device than just the width of fields and how the contents of these fields are to be interpreted. For instance, it may be that one wishes to position fields at certain columns or to start a new record without issuing a new `write` command. For this type of purpose, the control edit descriptors provide a means of informing the processor which action has to be taken. Some of these edit descriptors contain information that is used as it is processed; others are like switches, which change the conditions under which I/O takes place from the point where they are encountered, until the end of the processing of the I/O statement containing them (including reversions, Section 9.12.1). These latter descriptors we shall deal with first.

Control edit descriptors setting conditions

Embedded blanks in numeric input fields are treated in one of two ways, either as zero, or as null characters that are squeezed out by moving the other characters in the input field to the right, and adding leading blanks to the field (unless the field is totally blank, in which case it is interpreted as zero). The default is given by the `blank=` specifier (Section 10.3) currently in effect for the unit or is null for an internal file. Whatever the default may then be for a file, it may be overridden during a given format conversion by the `bn` (blanks null) and `bz` (blanks zero) edit descriptors. Let us suppose that the mode is that blanks are treated as zeros. The input string *bb1b4* converted by the edit descriptor `i5` would transfer the value 104. The same string converted by `bn,i5` would give 14. A `bn` or `bz` edit descriptor switches the mode for the rest of that format specification, or until another `bn` or `bz` edit descriptor is met. The `bn` and `bz` edit descriptors have no effect on output.

Negative numerical values are always written with *leading signs* on output. For positive quantities other than exponents, whether the signs are written depends on the processor. The `ss` (sign suppress) edit descriptor suppresses leading plus signs, that is the value 99 printed by `i5` is *bbb99* and 1.4 is printed by `e10.2` as *bb0.14E+01*. To switch on plus sign printing, the `sp` (sign print) edit descriptors may be used; the same numbers written by `sp,i5,e10.2` become *bb+99* and *b+0.14E+01*. The `s` edit descriptor restores the option to the processor. An `ss`, `sp`, or `s` will remain in force for the remainder of the format specification, unless another `ss`, `sp`, or `s` edit descriptor is met. These edit descriptors provide complete control over sign printing, and are useful for producing coded outputs which have to be compared automatically, on two different computers.

Scale factors apply to the input of real quantities under the e, f, en, es, and g edit descriptors, and are a means of scaling the input values. Their form is kp, where k is a default integer literal constant specifying the scale factor. The value is zero at the beginning of execution of the statement. The effect is that any quantity which does not have an exponent field will be reduced by a factor 10^k. Quantities with an exponent are not affected.

The scale factor kp also affects output with e, f, or g editing, but has no effect with en or es editing. Under control of an f edit descriptor, the quantity will be multiplied by a factor 10^k. Thus, the number 10.39 output by an f6.0 edit descriptor following the scale factor 2p will appear as b1039.. With the e edit descriptor, and with g where the e style editing is taken, the quantity is transferred with the exponent reduced by k, and the significand multiplied by 10^k. Thus 0.31×10^3, written after a 2p edit descriptor under control of e9.2, will appear as 31.00E+01. This gives a better control over the output style of real quantities which otherwise would have no significant digits before the decimal point.

The comma between a scale factor and an immediately following f, e, en, es, or g edit descriptor (without a repeat count) may be omitted, but we do not recommend that practice since it suggests that the scale factor applies only to the next edit descriptor, whereas in fact it applies throughout the format until another scale factor is encountered.

Control edit descriptors for immediate processing

Tabulation in an input or output field can be achieved using the edit descriptors tn, tr$n$ (and nx), and tl$n$, where n is a positive default integer literal constant. These state, respectively, that the next part of the I/O should begin at position n in the current record (where the *left tab limit* is position 1), or at n positions to the right of the current position, or at n positions to the left of the current position (the left tab limit if the current position is less than or equal to n). Let us suppose that, following an advancing read, we read an input record bb9876 with the following statement:

```
read (*, '(t3, i4, tl4, i1, i2)') i, j, k
```

The format specification will move a notional pointer firstly to position 3, whence i will be read. The variable i will acquire the value 9876, and the notional pointer is then at position 7. The edit descriptor tl4 moves it left four positions, back to position 3. The quantities j and k are then read, and they acquire the values 9 and 87, respectively. These edit descriptors cause replacement on output, or multiple reading of the same items in a record on input. On output, any gaps ahead of the last character actually written are filled with spaces. If any character that is skipped by one of the descriptors is of other than default type, the positioning is processor dependent.

If the current record is the first one processed by the I/O statement and follows non-advancing I/O that left the file positioned within a record, the next character is the left tab limit; otherwise, the first character of the record is the left tab limit.

The nx edit descriptor is equivalent to the tr$n$ edit descriptor. It is often used to place spaces in an output record. For example, to start an output record with a blank by this method, one writes

```
fmt= '(1x,....)'
```

Spaces such as this can precede a data edit descriptor, but 1x, i5 is not, for instance, exactly equivalent to i6 on output, as any value requiring the full six positions in the field will not have them available in the former case.

The t and x edit descriptors never cause replacement of a character already in an output record, but merely cause a change in the position within the record such that such a replacement might be caused by a subsequent edit descriptor.

New records may be started at any point in a format specification by means of the slash (/) edit descriptor. This edit descriptor, although described here, may in fact have repeat counts; to skip, say, three records one can write either /,/,/ or 3/. On input, a new record will be started each time a / is encountered, even if the contents of the current record have not all been transferred. Reading the two records

```
bbb99bbb10
bb100bbb11
```

with the statement

```
read '(bz,i5,i3,/,i5,i3,i2)', i, j, k, l, m
```

will cause the values 99, 0, 100, 0, and 11 to be transferred to the five integer variables, respectively. This edit descriptor does not need to be separated by a comma from a preceding edit descriptor, unless it has a repeat count; it does not ever need to be separated by a comma from a succeeding edit descriptor.

The result of writing with a format containing a sequence of, say, four slashes, as represented by

```
print '(i5,4/,i5)', i, j
```

is to separate the two values by three blank records (the last slash starts the record containing j); if i and j have the values 99 and 100, they would appear as

```
bbb99
b
b
b
bb100
```

A slash edit descriptor written to an internal file will cause the following values to be written to the next element of the character array specified for the file. Each such element corresponds to a record, and the number of characters written to a record must not exceed its length.

Colon editing is a means of terminating format control if there are no further items in an I/O list. In particular, it is useful for preventing further output of character strings used for annotation if the output list is exhausted. Consider the following output statement, for an array l(3):

```
print '(" l1 = ", i5, :, " l2 = ", i5, :," l3 = ", i5)', &
       (l(i) ,i=1,n)
```

If n has the value 3, then three values are printed. If n has the value 1, then, without the colons, the following output string would be printed:

```
l1 = 59 l2 =
```

The colon, however, stops the processing of the format, so that the annotation for the absent second value is not printed. This edit descriptor need not be separated from a neighbour by a comma. It has no effect if there are further items in the I/O list.

9.13 Unformatted I/O

The whole of this chapter has so far dealt with formatted I/O. The internal representation of a value may differ from the external form, which is always a character string contained in an input or output record. The use of formatted I/O involves an overhead for the conversion between the two forms, and often a roundoff error too. There is also the disadvantage that the external representation usually occupies more space on a storage medium than the internal representation. These three actual or potential drawbacks are all absent when unformatted I/O is used. In this form, the internal representation of a value is written exactly as it stands to the storage medium, and can be read back directly with neither roundoff nor conversion overhead. Here, a value of derived type is treated as a whole and is not equivalent to a list of its ultimate components. This is another reason for the rule (Section 9.3) that it must not have a pointer component at any level of component selection.

This type of I/O should be used in all cases where the records are generated by a program on one computer, to be read back on the same computer or another computer using the same internal number representations. Only when this is not the case, or when the data have to be visualized in one form or another, should formatted I/O be used. The records of a file must all be formatted or all be unformatted (apart from the endfile record).

Unformatted I/O has the incidental advantage of being simpler to program since no complicated format specifications are required. The forms of the read and write statements are the same as for formatted I/O, but without any fmt= or nml= specifier:

```
read(4) q
write(nout, iostat=ios, err=110) a
```

Non-advancing I/O is not available (in fact, an advance= specifier is not allowed).

Each read or write statement transfers exactly one record. The file must be an external file. The number of values specified by the input list of a read statement must not exceed the number of values available in the current record.

On output to a file connected for sequential access, a record of sufficient length is created. On input, the type and type parameters of each entity in the list must agree with those of the value in the record, except that two reals may correspond to one complex when all three have the same kind parameter.

9.14 Direct-access files

The only type of file organization that we have so far dealt with is the sequential file, which has a beginning and an end, and which contains a sequence of records, one after the other.

Fortran permits another type of file organization known as *direct access* (or sometimes as random access or indexed). All the records have the same length, each record is identified by an index number, and it is possible to write, read, or rewrite any specified record without regard to position. (In a sequential file, only the last record may be rewritten without losing other records; in general, records in sequential files cannot be replaced.) The records are either all formatted or all unformatted.

By default, any file used by a Fortran program is a sequential file, unless declared to be direct access. This declaration has to be made using the access= 'direct' and recl=*rl* specifiers of the open statement, which is described in the next chapter (*rl* is the length of a record in the file). Once this declaration has been made, reading and writing, whether formatted or unformatted, proceeds as described for sequential files, except for the addition of a rec=*i* specifier to the read and write statements, where *i* is a scalar integer expression whose value is the index number of the record concerned. An end= specifier is not permitted. Usually, a data transfer statement for a direct-access file accesses a single record, but during formatted I/O any slash edit descriptor increases the record number by one and causes processing to continue at the beginning of this record. A sequence of statements to write, read, and replace a given record is given in Figure 9.5.

Figure 9.5

```
      integer, parameter :: nunit=2, len=100
      integer            :: i, length
      real               :: a(len), b(len+1:2*len)
      :
      inquire (iolength=length) a          ! See Section 10.5
      open (nunit, access='direct', recl=length)
                                           ! See Section 10.3
      :
!   Write array B to direct-access file in record 14
      write (nunit, rec=14) b
      :
!
!   Read the array back into array a
      read (nunit, rec=14) a
      :
      do i = 1, len/2
         a(i) = i
      end do
!
!   Replace modified record
      write (nunit, rec=14) a
```

The file must be an external file and namelist formatting, list-directed formatting, and non-advancing I/O are all unavailable.

Direct-access files are particularly useful for applications which involve lots of hopping around inside a file, or where records need to be replaced, for instance in data base applications. A weakness is that the length of all the records must be the same, though, on formatted output, the record is padded with blanks if necessary. For unformatted output, if the record is not filled, the remainder is undefined.

This simple and powerful facility allows much clearer control logic to be written than is the case for a sequential file which is repeatedly read, backspaced, or rewound. Only when direct-access files become large may problems of long access times become evident on some computer systems, and this point should always be investigated before heavy investments are made in programming large direct-access file applications.

Some computer systems allow the same file to be regarded as sequential or direct access according to the specification in the open statement or its default. The standard, therefore, regards this as a property of the connection rather than of the file. In this case, the order of records, even for sequential I/O, is that determined by the direct-access record numbering.

9.15 Execution of a data transfer statement

So far, we have used simple illustrations of data transfer statements without dependencies. However, some forms of dependency are permitted and can be very useful. For example, the statement

```
read (*, *) n, a(1:n)              ! n is an integer
```

allows the length of an array section to be part of the data.

With dependencies in mind, the order in which operations are executed is important. It is as follows:

  i) identify the unit;

 ii) establish the format (if any);

iii) position the file ready for the transfer (if required);

 iv) transfer data between the file and the I/O list or namelist;

  v) position the file following the transfer (if required);

 vi) cause the iostat and size variables (if present) to become defined.

The order of transfer of namelist input is that in the input records. Otherwise, the order is that of the I/O list or namelist. Each input item is processed in turn, and may affect later subobjects and implied-do indices. All expressions within an I/O list item are determined at the beginning of the processing of the item. If an entity is specified more than once during execution of a namelist input statement, the later value overwrites the earlier value. Any zero-sized array or zero-length implied-do list is ignored.

When an input item is an array, no element of the array is permitted to affect the value of an expression within the item. For example, the cases shown in Figure 9.6 are not permitted. This prevents dependencies occurring within the item itself.

Figure 9.6

```
      integer :: j(10)
      :
      read *, j(j)                        ! Not permitted
      read *, j(j(1):j(10))               ! Not permitted
```

In the case of an internal file, an I/O item must not be in the file or associated with it. Nor may an input item contain or be associated with any portion of the established format.

Finally, a function reference must not appear in an expression anywhere in an I/O statement if it causes another I/O statement or a `stop` statement to be executed.

9.16 Summary

This chapter has begun the description of Fortran's extensive I/O facilities. It has covered the formatted I/O statements, and their associated format specifications, and then turned to unformatted I/O and direct-access files.

The syntax of the `read` and `write` statements has been introduced gradually. The full syntax is

    `read` *(control-list)* *[input-list]*

and

    `write` *(control-list)* *[output-list]*

where *control-list* contains one or more of the following:

```
[unit=] u
[fmt=] fmt
[nml=] nml-name
rec= i
iostat= ios
err= error-label
end= end-label
advance= advance
size= size
eor= eor-label
```

A *control-list* must include a unit specifier and must not include any specifier more than once. The `iostat` and `size` variables must not be associated with each other (for instance, be identical), nor with any entity being transferred, nor with any *do-var* of an implied-do list of the same statement. If either of these variables is an array element, the subscript value must not be affected by the data transfer, implied-do processing, or the evaluation of any other specifier in the statement.

9.17   Exercises

1. Write suitable `print` statements to print the name and contents of each of the following arrays:

   a) `real ::   grid d(10,10)`, ten elements to a line (assuming the values are between 1.0 and 100.0);

   b) `integer ::   list(50)`, the odd elements only;

   c) `character(len=10) ::   titles(20)`, two elements to a line;

   d) `real ::   power(10)`, five elements to a line in engineering notation;

   e) `logical ::   flags(10)`, on one line;

   f) `complex ::   plane(5)`, on one line.

2. Write statements to output the state of a game of tic-tac-toe (noughts and crosses) to a unit designated by the variable `unit`.

3. Write a program which reads an input record of up to 132 characters into an internal file and classifies it as a Fortran comment line with no statement, an initial line without a statement label, an initial line with a statement label, a continuation line, or a line containing multiple statements.

4. Write separate list-directed input statements to fill each of the arrays of Exercise 1. For each statement write a sample first input record.

5. Write a subroutine `get_char(unit,c,end_of_file)` to read a single character c from a formatted, sequential file `unit`, ignoring any record structure; `end_of_file` is a logical variable that is given the value `.true.` if the end of the file is reached and the value `.false.` otherwise.

10. Operations on external files

10.1 Introduction

So far we have discussed the topic of external files in a rather superficial way. In the examples of the various I/O statements in the previous chapter, an implicit assumption has always been made that the specified file was actually available, and that records could be written to it and read from it. For sequential files, the file control statements described in the next section further assume that it can be positioned. In fact, these assumptions are not necessarily valid. In order to define explicitly and to test the status of external files, three file status statements are provided: open, close, and inquire. Before beginning their description, however, two new definitions are required.

A computer system contains, among other components, a CPU and a storage system. Modern storage systems are usually based on some form of disc, which is used to store files for long or short periods of time. The execution of a computer program is, by comparison, a transient event. A file may exist for years, whereas programs run for only seconds or minutes. In Fortran terminology, a file is said to *exist* not in the sense we have just used, but in the restricted sense that it exists as a file *to which the program might have access*. In other words, if the program is prohibited from using the file because of a password protection system, or because some other necessary action has not been taken, the file 'does not exist'.

A file which exists for a running program may be empty and may or may not be *connected* to that program. The file is connected if it is associated with a unit number known to the program. Such connection is usually made by executing an open statement for the file, but many computer systems will *preconnect* certain files which any program may be expected to use, such as terminal input and output. Thus we see that a file may exist but not be connected. It may also be connected but not exist. This can happen for a preconnected new file. The file will only come into existence (be *created*) if some other action is taken on the file: executing an open, write, print, or endfile statement. A unit must not be connected to more than one file at once, and a file must not be connected to more than one unit at once.

There are a number of other points to note with respect to files.

- The set of allowed names for a file is processor dependent.

- Both sequential and direct access may be available for some files, but normally a file is limited to one or the other.

- A file never contains both formatted and unformatted records.

Finally, we note that no statement described in this chapter applies to internal files.

10.2   File positioning statements

When reading or writing an external file that is connected for sequential access, whether formatted or unformatted, it is sometimes necessary to perform other control functions on the file in addition to input and output. In particular, one may wish to alter the current position, which may be within a record, between records, ahead of the first record (at the *initial point*), or after the last record (at its *terminal point*). The following three statements are provided for these purposes.

10.2.1   The backspace statement

It can happen in a program that a series of records is being written and that, for some reason, the last record written should be replaced by a new one, that is be overwritten. Similarly, when reading records, it may be necessary to reread the last record read, or to check-read a record which has just been written. For this purpose, Fortran provides the backspace statement, which has the syntax

```
backspace u
```

or

```
backspace ([unit=]u [,iostat=ios] [,err=error-label])
```

where *u* is a scalar integer expression whose value is the unit number, and the other optional specifiers have the same meaning as for a read statement. Again, keyword specifiers may be in any order, but the unit specifier must come first as a positional specifier.

The action of this statement is to position the file before the current record if it is positioned within a record, or before the preceding record if it is positioned between records. An attempt to backspace when already positioned at the beginning of a file results in no change in the file's position. If the file is positioned after an endfile record (Section 10.2.3), it becomes positioned before that record. It is not possible to backspace a file that does not exist, nor to backspace over a record written by a list-directed or namelist output statement (Sections 9.9 and 9.10). A series of backspace statements will backspace over the corresponding number of records. This statement is often very costly in computer resources and should be used as little as possible.

10.2.2   The rewind statement

In an analogous fashion to rereading, rewriting, or check-reading a record, a similar operation may be carried out on a complete file. For this purpose the rewind statement,

```
rewind u
```

or

```
rewind ([unit=]u [,iostat=ios] [,err=error-label])
```

may be used to reposition a file, whose unit number is specified by the scalar integer expression *u*. Again, keyword specifiers may be in any order, but the unit specifier must come first as a positional specifier. If the file is already at its beginning, there is no change in its position. The statement is permitted for a file that does not exist, and has no effect.

10.2.3   The endfile statement

The end of a file connected for sequential access is normally marked by a special record which is identified as such by the computer hardware, and computer systems ensure that all files written by a program are correctly terminated by such an *endfile record*. In doubtful situations, or when a subsequent program step will reread the file, it is possible to write an endfile record explicitly using the endfile statement:

```
endfile u
```

or

```
endfile ([unit=]u [,iostat=ios] [,err=error-label])
```

where *u*, once again, is a scalar integer expression specifying the unit number. Again, keyword specifiers may be in any order, but the unit specifier must come first as a positional specifier. The file is then positioned after the endfile record. This endfile record, if subsequently read by a program, must be handled using the end=*end-label* specifier of the read statement, otherwise program execution will normally terminate. Prior to data transfer, a file must not be positioned after an endfile record, but it is possible to backspace or rewind across an endfile record, which allows further data transfer to occur. An endfile record is written automatically whenever either a backspace or rewind operation follows a write operation as the next operation on the unit, or the file is closed by execution of a close statement (Section 10.4), by an open statement for the same unit (Section 10.3), or by normal program termination.

If the file may also be connected for direct access, only the records ahead of the endfile record are considered to have been written and only these may be read during a subsequent direct-access connection.

Note that if a file is connected to a unit but does not exist for the program, it will be made to exist by executing an endfile statement on the unit.

10.2.4   Data transfer statements

Execution of a data transfer statement (read, write, or print) also affects the file position. If it is between records, it is moved to the start of the next record. Data transfer then takes place, which usually moves the position. No further movement occurs for non-advancing access. For advancing access, the position finally moves to follow the last record transferred.

10.3   The open statement

The open statement is used to connect an external file to a unit, create a file that is preconnected, create a file and connect it to a unit, or change certain properties of a connection. The syntax is

> open ([unit=]*u* [,*olist*])

where *u* is a scalar integer expression specifying the external file unit number, and *olist* is a list of optional specifiers. If the unit is specified with unit=, it may appear in *olist*. A specifier must not appear more than once. In the specifiers, all entities are scalar and all characters are of default kind. In character expressions, any trailing blanks are ignored and, except for file=, any upper-case letters are converted to lower case. The specifiers are as follows.

iostat= *ios*, where *ios* is a default integer variable which is set to zero if the statement is correctly executed, and to a positive value otherwise.

err= *error-label*, where *error-label* is the label of a statement in the same scoping unit to which control will be transferred in the event of an error occurring during execution of the statement.

file= *fln*, where *fln* is a character expression that provides the name of the file. If this specifier is omitted and the unit is not connected to a file, the status= specifier must be specified with the value scratch and the file connected to the unit will then depend on the computer system. Whether the interpretation is case sensitive varies from system to system.

status= *st*, where *st* is a character expression that provides the value old, new, replace, scratch, or unknown. The file= specifier must be present if new or replace is specified or if old is specified and the unit is not connected; the file= specifier must not be present if scratch is specified. If old is specified, the file must already exist; if new is specified, the file must not already exist, but will be brought into existence by the action of the open statement. The status of the file then becomes old. If replace is specified and the file does not already exist, the file is created; if the file does exist, the file is deleted, and a new file is created with the same name. In each case the status is changed to old. If the value scratch is specified, the file is created and becomes connected, but it cannot be kept after completion of the program or execution of a close statement (Section 10.4). If unknown is specified, the status of the file is system dependent. This is the default value of the specifier, if it is omitted.

access= *acc*, where *acc* is a character expression that provides one of the values sequential or direct. For a file which already exists, this value must be an allowed value. If the file does not already exist, it will be brought into existence with the appropriate access method. If this specifier is omitted, the value sequential will be assumed.

form= *fm*, where *fm* is a character expression that provides the value formatted or unformatted, and determines whether the file is to be connected for formatted or unformatted I/O. For a file which already exists, the value must be an allowed value. If the file does not already exist, it will be brought into existence with an allowed set of forms that includes the specified form. If this specifier is omitted, the default is formatted for sequential access and unformatted for direct-access connection.

recl= *rl*, where *rl* is an integer expression whose value must be positive. For a direct-access file, it specifies the length of the records, and is obligatory. For a sequential file, it specifies the maximum length of a record, and is optional with a default value that is processor dependent. For formatted files, the length is the number of characters for records that contain only default characters; for unformatted files it is system dependent but the inquire statement (Section 10.5) may be used to find the length of an I/O list. In either case, for a file which already exists, the value specified must be allowed for that file. If the file does not already exist, the file will be brought into existence with an allowed set of record lengths that includes the specified value.

blank= *bl*, where *bl* is a character expression that provides the value null or zero. This connection must be for formatted I/O. This specifier sets the default for the interpretation of blanks in numeric input fields, as discussed in the description of the bn and bz edit descriptors (Section 9.12.5). If the value is null, such blanks will be ignored (except that a completely blank field is interpreted as zero). If the value is zero, such blanks will be interpreted as zeros. If the specifier is omitted, the default is null.

position= *pos*, where *pos* is a character expression that provides the value asis, rewind, or append. The access method must be sequential, and if the specifier is omitted the default value asis will be assumed. A new file is positioned at its initial point. If asis is specified and the file exists and is already connected, the file is opened without changing its position; if rewind is specified the file is positioned at its initial point; if append is specified and the file exists, it is positioned ahead of the endfile record if it has one (and otherwise at its terminal point). For a file which exists but is not connected, the effect of the asis specifier on the file's position is unspecified.

action= *act*, where *act* is a character expression that provides the value read, write, or readwrite. If read is specified, the write, print and endfile statements must not be used for this connection; if write is specified, the read statement must not be used (and backspace and position='append' may fail on some systems); if readwrite is specified, there is no restriction. If the specifier is omitted, the default value is processor dependent.

delim= *del*, where *del* is a character expression that provides the value quote, apostrophe, or none. If apostrophe or quote is specified, the corresponding character will be used to delimit character constants written with list-directed or namelist formatting, and it will be doubled where it appears within such a character constant; also, non-default character values will be preceded by kind values. No delimiting character is used if none is specified, nor does any doubling take place. The default value if the specifier is omitted is none. This specifier may appear only for formatted files.

pad= *pad*, where *pad* is a character expression that provides the value yes or no. If yes is
specified, a formatted input record will be regarded as padded out with blanks whenever
an input list and the associated format specify more data than appear in the record. (If
no is specified, the length of the input record must not be less than that specified by
the input list and the associated format, except in the presence of an advance='no'
specifier and either an eor= or an iostat= specification.) The default value if the
specifier is omitted is yes. For non-default characters, the blank padding character is
processor dependent.

An example of an open statement is

```
open (2, iostat=ios, err=99, file='cities',                          &
      status='new', access='direct', recl=100)
```

which brings into existence a new, direct-access, unformatted file named cities, whose
records have length 100. The file is connected to unit number 2. Failure to execute the
statement correctly will cause control to be passed to the statement labelled 99, where the
value of ios may be tested.

The open statements in a program are best collected together in one place, so that any
changes which might have to be made to them when transporting the program from one
system to another can be carried out without having to search for them. Regardless of where
they appear, the connection may be referenced in any program unit of the program.

The purpose of the open statement is to connect a file to a unit. If the unit is, however,
already connected to a file then the action may be different. If the file= specifier is omitted,
the default is the name of the connected file. If the file in question does not exist, but is
preconnected to the unit, then all the properties specified by the open statement become part
of the connection. If the file is already connected to the unit, then of the existing attributes
only the blank=, delim=, pad=, err=, and iostat= specifiers may have values different
from those already in effect. If the unit is already connected to another file, the effect of the
open statement includes the action of a prior close statement on the unit (without a status=
specifier, see next section).

A file already connected to one unit must not be specified for connection to another unit.

In general, by repeated execution of the open statement on the same unit, it is possible to
process in sequence an arbitrarily high number of files, whether they exist or not, as long as
the restrictions just noted are observed.

10.4 The close statement

The purpose of the close statement is to disconnect a file from a unit. Its form is

```
close ([unit=]u [,iostat=ios] [,err=error-label] [,status=st])
```

where *u*, *ios*, and *error-label* have the same meanings as described in the previous section
for the open statement. Again, keyword specifiers may be in any order, but the unit specifier
must come first as a positional specifier.

The function of the status= specifier is to determine what will happen to the file once it
is disconnected. The value of *st*, which is a scalar default character expression, may be either

keep or delete, ignoring any trailing blanks and converting any upper-case letters to lower case. If the value is keep, a file that exists continues to exist after execution of the close statement, and may later be connected again to a unit. If the value is delete, the file no longer exists after execution of the statement. In either case, the unit is free to be connected again to a file. The close statement may appear anywhere in the program, and if executed for a non-existing or unconnected unit, acts as a 'do nothing' statement. The value keep must not be specified for files with the status scratch.

If the status= specifier is omitted, its default value is keep unless the file has status scratch, in which case the default value is delete. On normal termination of execution, all connected units are closed, as if close statements with omitted status= specifiers were executed.

An example of a close statement is

```
close (2, iostat=ios, err=99, status='delete')
```

10.5 The inquire statement

The status of a file can be defined by the operating system prior to execution of the program, or by the program itself during execution, either by an open statement or by some action on a preconnected file which brings it into existence. At any time during the execution of a program it is possible to inquire about the status and attributes of a file using the inquire statement. Using a variant of this statement, it is similarly possible to determine the status of a unit, for instance whether the unit number exists for that system (that is, whether it is an allowed unit number), whether the unit number has a file connected to it and, if so, which attributes that file has. Another variant permits an inquiry about the length of an output list when used to write an unformatted record.

Some of the attributes that may be determined by use of the inquire statement are dependent on others. For instance, if a file is not connected to a unit, it is not meaningful to inquire about the form being used for that file. If this is nevertheless attempted, the relevant specifier is undefined.

The three variants are known as inquire by file, inquire by unit, and inquire by output list. In the description of the inquire statement which follows, the first two variants will be described together. Their forms are

```
inquire ([unit=]u, ilist)
```

for inquire by unit, where *u* is a scalar integer expression specifying an external unit, and

```
inquire ( file=fln, ilist)
```

for inquire by file, where *fln* is a scalar character expression whose value, ignoring any trailing blanks, provides the name of the file concerned. Whether the interpretation is case sensitive is system dependent. If the unit or file is specified by keyword, it may appear in *ilist*. A specifier must not occur more than once in the list of optional specifiers, *ilist*. All assignments occur following the usual rules, and all values of type character, apart from that for the name= specifier, are in upper case. The specifiers, in which all variables are scalar and of default kind, are as follows.

iostat= *ios* and **err=** *error-label*, have the meanings described for them in the open statement in Section 10.3. The iostat= variable is the only one which is defined if an error condition occurs during the execution of the statement.

exist= *ex*, where *ex* is a logical variable. The value true is assigned to *ex* if the file (or unit) exists, and false otherwise.

opened= *open*, where *open* is a logical variable. The value true is assigned to *open* if the file (or unit) is connected to a unit (or file), and false otherwise.

number= *num*, where *num* is an integer variable that is assigned the value of the unit number connected to the file, or -1 if no unit is connected to the file.

named= *nmd* and **name=** *nam*, where *nmd* is a logical variable that is assigned the value true if the file has a name, and false otherwise. If the file has a name, the character variable *nam* will be assigned the name. This value is not necessarily the same as that given in the file specifier, if used, but may be qualified in some way. However, in all cases it is a name which is valid for use in a subsequent open statement, and so the inquire can be used to determine the actual name of a file before connecting it. Whether the file name is case sensitive is system dependent.

access= *acc*, where *acc* is a character variable that is assigned one of the values SEQUENTIAL or DIRECT depending on the access method for a file that is connected, and UNDEFINED if there is no connection.

sequential= *seq* and **direct=** *dir*, where *seq* and *dir* are character variables that are assigned the value YES, NO, or UNKNOWN, depending on whether the file *may* be opened for sequential or direct access, respectively, or whether this cannot be determined.

form= *frm*, where *frm* is a character variable that is assigned one of the values FORMATTED or UNFORMATTED, depending on the form for which the file is actually connected, and UNDEFINED if there is no connection.

formatted= *fmt* and **unformatted=** *unf*, where *fmt* and *unf* are character variables that are assigned the value YES, NO, or UNKNOWN, depending on whether the file *may* be opened for formatted or unformatted access, respectively, or whether this cannot be determined.

recl= *rec*, where *rec* is an integer variable that is assigned the value of the record length of a file connected for direct access, or the maximum record length allowed for a file connected for sequential access. The length is the number of characters for formatted records containing only characters of default type, and system dependent otherwise. If there is no connection, *rec* becomes undefined.

nextrec= *nr*, where *nr* is an integer variable that is assigned the value of the number of the last record read or written, plus one. If no record has been yet read or written, it is assigned the value 1. If the file is not connected for direct access or if the position is indeterminate because of a previous error, *nr* becomes undefined.

blank= *bl*, where *bl* is a character variable that is assigned the value NULL or ZERO, depending on whether the blanks in numeric fields are by default to be interpreted as null fields or zeros, respectively, and UNDEFINED if there is either no connection, or if the connection is not for formatted I/O.

position= *pos*, where *pos* is a character variable that is assigned the value REWIND, APPEND, or ASIS, as specified in the corresponding open statement, if the file has not been repositioned since it was opened. If there is no connection, or if the file is connected for direct access, the value is UNDEFINED. If the file has been repositioned since the connection was established, the value is processor dependent (but must not be REWIND or APPEND unless that corresponds to the true position).

action= *act*, where *act* is a character variable that is assigned the value READ, WRITE, or READWRITE, according to the connection. If there is no connection, the value assigned is UNDEFINED.

read= *rd*, where *rd* is a character variable that is assigned the value YES, NO, or UNKNOWN, according to whether read is allowed, not allowed, or is undetermined for the file.

write= *wr*, where *wr* is a character variable that is assigned the value YES, NO, or UNKNOWN, according to whether write is allowed, not allowed, or is undetermined for the file.

readwrite= *rw*, where *rw* is a character variable that is assigned the value YES, NO, or UNKNOWN, according to whether read/write is allowed, not allowed, or is undetermined for the file.

delim= *del*, where *del* is a character variable that is assigned the value QUOTE, APOSTROPHE, or NONE, as specified by the corresponding open statement (or by default). If there is no connection, or if the file is not connected for formatted I/O, the value assigned is UNDEFINED.

pad= *pad*, where *pad* is a character variable that is assigned the value YES or NO, as specified by the corresponding open statement (or by default). If there is no connection, or if the file is not connected for formatted I/O, the value assigned is UNDEFINED.

A variable that is a specifier in an inquire statement or is associated with one must not appear in another specifier in the same statement.

The third variant of the inquire statement, inquire by I/O list, has the form

```
inquire (iolength=length) olist
```

where *length* is a scalar integer variable of default kind and is used to determine the length of an unformatted output list in processor-dependent units, and might be used to establish whether, for instance, an output list is too long for the record length given in the recl= specifier of an open statement, or be used as the value of the length to be supplied to a recl= specifier (see Figure 9.5 in Section 9.14).

An example of the inquire statement, for the file opened as an example of the open statement in Section 10.3, is

```
logical              :: ex, op
character (len=11) :: nam, acc, seq, frm
integer              :: irec, nr
inquire (2, err=99, exist=ex, opened=op, name=nam, access=acc, &
    sequential=seq, form=frm, recl=irec, nextrec=nr)
```

After successful execution of this statement, the variables provided will have been assigned the following values:

ex	.true.
op	.true.
nam	cities*bbbbb*
acc	DIRECT*bbbbb*
seq	NO*bbbbbbbbb*
frm	UNFORMATTED
irec	100
nr	1

(assuming no intervening read or write operations).

The three I/O status statements just described are perhaps the most indigestible of all Fortran statements. They provide, however, a powerful and portable facility for the dynamic allocation and deallocation of files, completely under program control, which is far in advance of that found in any other programming language suitable for scientific applications.

10.6 Summary

This chapter has completed the description of the input/output features begun in the previous chapter, and together they provide a complete reference to all the facilities available.

10.7 Exercises

1. A direct-access file is to contain a list of names and initials, to each of which there corresponds a telephone number. Write a program which opens a sequential file and a direct-access file, and copies the list from the sequential file to the direct-access file, closing it for use in another program.

Write a second program which reads an input record containing either a name or a telephone number (from a terminal if possible), and prints out the corresponding entry (or entries) in the direct-access file if present, and an error message otherwise. Remember that names are as diverse as Wu, O'Hara and Trevington-Smythe, and that it is insulting for a computer program to corrupt or abbreviate people's names. The format of the telephone numbers should correspond to your local numbers, but the actual format used should be readily modifiable to another.

11. Floating-point exception handling

11.1 Introduction

Exception handling is required for the development of robust and efficient numerical software, a principal application of Fortran. Indeed, the existence of such a facility makes it possible to develop more efficient software than would otherwise be possible. The clear need for exception handling, something that had been left out of Fortran 95, led to a facility being developed on a 'fast track' as a Technical Report,[1] suitable for immediate implementation as an extension to Fortran 95. In this chapter, we describe the extensions to Fortran 95 that were detailed in this Report and which are all now part of Fortran 2003. We also describe the few related Fortran 2003 features that were not in the Report, with a clear indication of this in each case.

Most computers nowadays have hardware based on the IEEE standard for binary floating-point arithmetic,[2] which later became an ISO standard.[3] Therefore, the Fortran exception handling features are based on the ability to test and set the five flags for floating-point exceptions that the IEEE standard specifies. However, non-IEEE computers have not been ignored; they may provide support for some of the features and the programmer is able to find out what is supported or state that certain features are essential.

Few (if any) computers support every detail of the IEEE standard. This is because considerable economies in construction and increases in execution performance are available by omitting support for features deemed to be necessary to few programmers. It was therefore decided to include inquiry facilities for the extent of support of the standard, and for the programmer to be able to state which features are essential.

The mechanism finally chosen by the committees is based on a set of procedures for setting and testing the flags and inquiring about the features, collected in an intrinsic module called `ieee_exceptions`.

Given that procedures were being provided for the IEEE flags, it seemed sensible to provide procedures for other aspects of the IEEE standard. These are collected in a separate intrinsic module, `ieee_arithmetic`, which contains a `use` statement for `ieee_exceptions`.

To provide control over which features are essential, there is a third intrinsic module, `ieee_features` containing named constants corresponding to the features. If a named constant is accessible in a scoping unit, the corresponding feature must be available there.

---

[1]Technical Report ISO/IEC TR 15580 : 1998(E).
[2]IEEE 754-1985, Standard for binary floating-point arithmetic.
[3]IEC 559 : 1989, Binary floating-point arithmetic for microprocessor systems.

11.2 The IEEE standard

In this section, we explain those aspects of the IEEE standard that the reader needs to know in order to understand the features of this extension of Fortran 95. We do not attempt to give a complete description of the standard.

Two floating-point data formats are specified, one for real and one for double precision arithmetic. They are supersets of the Fortran model, repeated here (see Section 8.7.1),

$$x = 0$$

and

$$x = s \times b^e \times \sum_{k=1}^{p} f_k \times b^{-k}$$

where s is ± 1, p and b are integers exceeding one, e is an integer in a range $e_{\min} \le e \le e_{\max}$, and each f_k is an integer in the range $0 \le f_k < b$ except that f_1 is also nonzero. Both IEEE formats are binary, with $b = 2$. The precisions are $p = 24$ and $p = 53$, and the exponent ranges are $-125 \le e \le 128$ and $-1021 \le e \le 1024$, for real and double precision, respectively.

In addition, there are numbers with $e = e_{\min}$ and $f_1 = 0$, which are known as *denormalized* numbers; note that they all have absolute values less than that returned by the intrinsic tiny since it considers only numbers within the Fortran model. Also, zero has a sign and both 0 and -0 have inverses, ∞ and $-\infty$. Within Fortran, -0 is treated as the same as a zero in all intrinsic operations and comparisons, but it can be detected by the sign function and is respected on formatted output.

The IEEE standard also specifies that some of the binary patterns that do not fit the model be used for the results of exceptional operations, such as 0/0. Such a number is known as a *NaN* (Not a Number). A NaN may be *signaling* or *quiet*. Whenever a signaling NaN appears as an operand, the invalid exception signals and the result is a quiet NaN. Quiet NaNs propagate through almost every arithmetic operation without signaling an exception.

The standard specifies four rounding modes.

nearest rounds the exact result to the nearest representable value.

to-zero rounds the exact result towards zero to the next representable value.

up rounds the exact result towards $+\infty$ to the next representable value.

down rounds the exact result towards $-\infty$ to the next representable value.

Some computers perform division by inverting the denominator and then multiplying by the numerator. The additional roundoff that this involves means that such an implementation does not conform with the IEEE standard. The IEEE standard also specifies that sqrt properly rounds the exact result and returns -0 for $\sqrt{-0}$. The Fortran facilities include inquiry functions for IEEE division and sqrt.

The presence of -0, ∞, $-\infty$, and the NaNs allows IEEE arithmetic to be closed, that is, every operation has a result. This is very helpful for optimization on modern hardware since several operations, none needing the result of any of the others, may actually be progressing in parallel. If an exception occurs, execution continues with the corresponding flag signaling, and the flag remains signaling until explicitly set quiet by the program. The flags are therefore called *sticky*.

There are five flags.

overflow occurs if the exact result of an operation with two normal values is too large for the data format. The stored result is ∞, huge (x), -huge (x), or $-\infty$, according to the rounding mode in operation, always with the correct sign.

divide_by_zero occurs if a finite nonzero value is divided by zero. The stored result is ∞ or $-\infty$ with the correct sign.

invalid occurs if the operation is invalid, for example, $\infty \times 0$, 0/0, or when an operand is a signaling NaN.

underflow occurs if the result of an operation with two finite nonzero values cannot be represented exactly and is too small to represent with full precision. The stored result is the best available, depending on the rounding mode in operation.

inexact occurs if the exact result of an operation cannot be represented in the data format without rounding.

The standard specifies the possibility of exceptions being trapped by user-written handlers, but this inhibits optimization and is not supported by the Fortran feature. Instead it supports the possibility of halting program execution after an exception signals. For the sake of optimization, such halting need not occur immediately.

The standard specifies several functions which are implemented in this Fortran 95 extension as ieee_copy_sign, ieee_logb, ieee_next_after, ieee_rem, ieee_rint, ieee_scalb, and ieee_unordered, and which are described in Section 11.9.3.

11.3   Access to the features

To access the features of this chapter, we recommend that the user employ use statements for one or more of the intrinsic modules ieee_exceptions, ieee_arithmetic (which contains a use statement for ieee_exceptions), and ieee_features. If the processor does not support a module accessed in a use statement, the compilation must, of course, fail.

If a scoping unit does not access ieee_exceptions or ieee_arithmetic, the level of support is processor dependent, and need not include support for any exceptions. If a flag is signaling on entry to such a scoping unit, the processor ensures that it is signaling on exit. If a flag is quiet on entry to such a scoping unit, whether it is signaling on exit is processor dependent.

The module ieee_features contains the derived type

```
ieee_features_type
```

for identifying a particular feature. The only possible values objects of this type may take are those of named constants defined in the module, each corresponding to an IEEE feature. If a scoping unit has access to one of these constants, the compiler must support the feature in the scoping unit or reject the program. For example, some hardware is much faster if denormalized numbers are not supported and instead all underflowed values are flushed to zero. In such a case, the statement

```
use, intrinsic :: ieee_features, only: ieee_denormal
```

will ensure that the scoping unit is compiled with (slower) code supporting denormalized numbers.

The module is unusual in that all a code ever does is to access it with use statements, which affect the way the code is compiled in the scoping units with access to one or more of the module's constants. There is no purpose in declaring data of type ieee_features_type, though it is permitted; the components of the type are private, no operation is defined for it, and only intrinsic assignment is available for it. In a scoping unit containing a use statement, the effect is that of a compiler directive, but the other properties of use make the feature more powerful than would be possible with a directive.

The complete set of named constants in the module and the effect of their accessibility is:

ieee_datatype The scoping unit must provide IEEE arithmetic for at least one kind of real.

ieee_denormal The scoping unit must support denormalized numbers for at least one kind of real.

ieee_divide The scoping unit must support IEEE divide for at least one kind of real.

ieee_halting The scoping unit must support control of halting for each flag supported.

ieee_inexact_flag The scoping unit must support the inexact exception for at least one kind of real.

ieee_inf The scoping unit must support ∞ and $-\infty$ for at least one kind of real.

ieee_invalid_flag The scoping unit must support the invalid exception for at least one kind of real.

ieee_nan The scoping unit must support NaNs for at least one kind of real.

ieee_rounding The scoping unit must support control of the rounding mode for all four rounding modes on at least one kind of real.

ieee_sqrt The scoping unit must support IEEE square root for at least one kind of real.

ieee_underflow_flag The scoping unit must support the underflow exception for at least one kind of real.

Execution may be slowed on some processors by the support of some features. If ieee_exceptions is accessed but ieee_features is not accessed, the vendor is free to choose which subset to support. The processor's fullest support is provided when all of ieee_features is accessed:

```
use, intrinsic :: ieee_arithmetic
use, intrinsic :: ieee_features
```

but execution may then be slowed by the presence of a feature that is not needed. In all cases, the extent of support may be determined by the inquiry functions of Sections 11.8.2 and 11.9.2.

11.4 The Fortran flags

There are five Fortran exception flags, corresponding to the five IEEE flags. Each has a value that is either quiet or signaling. The value may be determined by the function `ieee_get_flag` (Section 11.8.3). Its initial value is quiet and it signals when the associated exception occurs in a real or complex operation. Its status may also be changed by the subroutine `ieee_set_flag` (Section 11.8.3) or the subroutine `ieee_set_status` (Section 11.8.4). Once signaling, it remains signaling unless set quiet by an invocation of the subroutine `ieee_set_flag` or the subroutine `ieee_set_status`. For invocation of an elemental procedure, it is as if the procedure were invoked once for each set of corresponding elements; if any of the invocations return with a flag signaling, it will be signaling in the caller on completion of the call.

If a flag is signaling on entry to a procedure, the processor will set it to quiet on entry and restore it to signaling on return. This allows exception handling within the procedure to be independent of the state of the flags on entry, while retaining their 'sticky' properties: within a scoping unit, a signaling flag remains signaling until explicitly set quiet. Evaluation of a specification expression may cause an exception to signal.

If a scoping unit has access to `ieee_exceptions` and references an intrinsic procedure that executes normally, the values of the overflow, divide-by-zero and invalid flags are as on entry to the intrinsic procedure, even if one or more signals during the calculation. If a real or complex result is too large for the intrinsic procedure to handle, overflow may signal. If a real or complex result is a NaN because of an invalid operation (for example, `log(-1.0)`), invalid may signal. Similar rules apply to format processing and to intrinsic operations: no signaling flag shall be set quiet and no quiet flag shall be set signaling because of an intermediate calculation that does not affect the result.

An implementation may provide alternative versions of an intrinsic procedure; for example, one might be rather slow but be suitable for a call from a scoping unit with access to `ieee_exceptions`, while an alternative faster one might be suitable for other cases.

If it is known that an intrinsic procedure will never need to signal an exception, there is no requirement for it to be handled — after all, there is no way that the programmer will be able to tell the difference. The same principle applies to a sequence of in-line code with no invocations of `ieee_get_flag`, `ieee_set_flag`, `ieee_get_status`, `ieee_set_status`, or `ieee_set_halting`. If the code, as written, includes an operation that would signal a flag, but after execution of the sequence no value of a variable depends on that operation, whether the exception signals is processor dependent. Thus, an implementation is permitted to optimize such an operation away. For example, when y has the value zero, whether the code

```
x = 1.0/y
x = 3.0
```

signals divide-by-zero is processor dependent. Another example is:

```
real, parameter :: x=0.0, y=6.0
   :
if (1.0/x == y) print *,'Hello world'
```

where the processor is permitted to discard the `if` statement since the logical expression can never be true and no value of a variable depends on it.

An exception does not signal if this could arise only during execution of code not required or permitted by the standard. For example, the statement

```
if (f(x) > 0.0) y = 1.0/z
```

must not signal divide-by-zero when both `f(x)` and `z` are zero and the statement

```
where(a > 0.0) a = 1.0/a
```

must not signal divide-by-zero. On the other hand, when x has the value 1.0 and y has the value 0.0, the expression

```
x > 0.00001 .or. x/y > 0.00001
```

is permitted to cause the signaling of divide-by-zero.

The processor need not support the invalid, underflow, and inexact exceptions. If an exception is not supported, its flag is always quiet. The function `ieee_support_flag` (Section 11.8.2) may be used to inquire whether a particular flag is supported. If invalid is supported, it signals in the case of conversion to an integer (by assignment or an intrinsic procedure) if the result is too large to be representable.

11.5   Halting

Some processors allow control during program execution of whether to abort or continue execution after an exception has occurred. Such control is exercised by invocation of the subroutine `ieee_set_halting_mode` (Section 11.8.3). Halting is not precise and may occur any time after the exception has occurred. The function `ieee_support_halting` (Section 11.8.2) may be used to inquire whether this facility is available. The initial halting mode is processor dependent.

In a procedure other than `ieee_set_halting_mode`, the processor does not change the halting mode on entry, and on return ensures that the halting mode is the same as it was on entry.

11.6   The rounding mode

Some processors support alteration of the rounding mode during execution. In this case, the subroutine `ieee_set_rounding_mode` (Section 11.9.4) may be used to alter it. The function `ieee_support_rounding` (Section 11.9.2) may be used to inquire whether this facility is available for a particular mode.

In a procedure other than `ieee_set_rounding_mode`, the processor does not change the rounding mode on entry, and on return ensures that the rounding mode is the same as it was on entry.

Note that the value of a literal constant is not affected by the rounding mode.

11.7 The underflow mode (Fortran 2003 only)

Some processors support alteration of the underflow mode during execution, that is, whether small values are represented as denormalized values or are set to zero. The reason is likely to be that such a processor executes much faster without denormalized values. The underflow mode is said to be *gradual* if denormalized values are employed. If the underflow mode may be altered at run time, the subroutine ieee_set_underflow_mode (Section 11.9.4) may be used to alter it. The function ieee_support_underflow_control (Section 11.9.2) may be used to inquire whether this facility is available for a particular kind of reals.

In a procedure other than ieee_set_underflow_mode, the processor does not change the underflow mode on entry, and on return ensures that it is the same as it was on entry.

11.8 The module ieee_exceptions

When the module ieee_exceptions is accessible, the overflow and divide-by-zero flags are supported in the scoping unit for all available kinds of real and complex data. This minimal level of support has been designed to be possible also on a non-IEEE computer. Which other exceptions are supported may be determined by the function ieee_support_flag, see Section 11.8.2. Whether control of halting is supported may be determined by the function ieee_support_halting, see Section 11.8.2. The extent of support of the other exceptions may be influenced by the accessibility of the named constants ieee_inexact_flag, ieee_invalid_flag, and ieee_underflow_flag of the module ieee_features, see Section 11.3.

The module contains two derived types (Section 11.8.1), named constants of these types (Section 11.8.1), and a collection of generic procedures (Sections 11.8.2, 11.8.3, and 11.8.4). None of the procedures is permitted as an actual argument.

11.8.1 Derived types

The module ieee_exceptions contains two derived types.

ieee_flag_type for identifying a particular exception flag. The only values that can be taken by objects of this type are those of named constants defined in the module

```
ieee_overflow    ieee_divide_by_zero   ieee_invalid
ieee_underflow   ieee_inexact
```

and these are used in the module to define the named array constants

```
type(ieee_flag_type), parameter ::                       &
ieee_usual(3) =                                          &
    (/ieee_overflow, ieee_divide_by_zero, ieee_invalid/), &
ieee_all(5) = (/ieee_usual, ieee_underflow, ieee_inexact/)
```

These array constants are convenient for inquiring about the state of several flags at once by using elemental procedures. Besides convenience, such elemental calls may be more efficient than a sequence of calls for single flags.

ieee_status_type for saving the current floating-point status. It includes the values of all the flags supported, and also the current rounding mode if dynamic control of rounding is supported and the halting mode if dynamic control of halting is supported.

The components of both types are private. No operation is defined for them and only intrinsic assignment is available for them.

11.8.2   Inquiry functions for IEEE exceptions

The module ieee_exceptions contains two inquiry functions, both of which are pure. Their argument flag must be of type type(ieee_flag_type) with one of the values ieee_invalid, ieee_overflow, ieee_divide_by_zero, ieee_inexact, and ieee_underflow. The inquiries are in terms of reals, but the same level of support is provided for the corresponding kinds of complex type.

ieee_support_flag (flag [,x]) returns .true. if the processor supports the exception flag for all reals (x absent) or for reals of the same kind type parameter as the real argument x. Otherwise, it returns .false..

ieee_support_halting (flag) returns .true. if the processor supports the ability to change the mode by call ieee_set_halting(flag). Otherwise, it returns .false..

11.8.3   Subroutines for the flags and halting modes

The module ieee_exceptions contains the following elemental subroutines.

call ieee_get_flag (flag, flag_value) where:

> **flag** is of type type(ieee_flag_type) and has intent in. It specifies a flag.
>
> **flag_value** is of type default logical and has intent out. If the value of flag is ieee_invalid, ieee_overflow, ieee_divide_by_zero, ieee_underflow, or ieee_inexact, flag_value is given the value true if the corresponding exception flag is signaling and false otherwise.

call ieee_get_halting_mode (flag, halting) where:

> **flag** is of type type(ieee_flag_type) and has intent in. It must have one of the values ieee_invalid, ieee_overflow, ieee_divide_by_zero, ieee_underflow, or ieee_inexact.
>
> **halting** is of type default logical and has intent out. If the exception specified by flag will cause halting, halting is given the value true; otherwise, it is given the value false.

Elemental subroutines would not be appropriate for the corresponding 'set' actions since an invocation might ask for a flag or mode to be set more than once. The module therefore contains the following subroutines that are pure but not elemental:

`call ieee_set_flag (flag, flag_value)` which may be called only if the value returned by ieee_support_halting(flag) is true:

flag is of type type(ieee_flag_type) and has intent in. It may be scalar or array valued. If it is an array, no two elements may have the same value.

flag_value is of type default logical and has intent in. It must be conformable with flag. Each flag specified by flag is set to be signaling if the corresponding flag_value is true, and to be quiet if it is false.

`call ieee_set_halting_mode (flag, halting)` where:

flag is of type type(ieee_flag_type) and has intent in. It may be scalar or array valued. If it is an array, no two elements may have the same value.

halting is of type default logical and has intent in. It must be conformable with flag. Each exception specified by flag will cause halting if the corresponding value of halting is true and will not cause halting if the value is false.

11.8.4 Subroutines for the whole of the floating-point status

The module ieee_exceptions contains the following non-elemental subroutines.

`call ieee_get_status (status_value)` where:

status_value is scalar and of type type(ieee_status_type) and has intent out. It returns the floating-point status, including all the exception flags, the rounding mode, and the halting mode.

`call ieee_set_status (status_value)` where:

status_value is scalar and of type type(ieee_status_type) and has intent in. Its value must have been set in a previous invocation of ieee_get_status. The floating-point status, including all the exception flags, the rounding mode, and the halting mode, is reset to as it was then.

Figure 11.1

```
use, intrinsic        :: ieee_exceptions
type(ieee_status_type) :: status_value
   :
call ieee_get_status(status_value)   ! Get the flags
call ieee_set_flag(ieee_all,.false.) ! Set the flags quiet
   :  ! Calculation involving exception handling
call ieee_set_status(status_value)   ! Restore the flags
```

These subroutines have been included for convenience and efficiency when a subsidiary calculation is to be performed, and one wishes to resume the main calculation with exactly the same environment, as shown in Figure 11.1. There are no facilities for finding directly the value held within such a variable of a particular flag, rounding mode, or halting mode.

11.9   The module ieee_arithmetic

The module `ieee_arithmetic` behaves as if it contained a use statement for the module `ieee_exceptions`, so all the features of `ieee_exceptions` are also features of `ieee_arithmetic`.

The module contains two derived types (Section 11.9.1), named constants of these types (Section 11.9.1), and a collection of generic procedures (Sections 11.9.2, 11.9.3, 11.9.4, and 11.9.5). None of the procedures is permitted as an actual argument.

11.9.1   Derived types

The module `ieee_arithmetic` contains two derived types.

ieee_class_type for identifying a class of floating-point values. The only values objects of this type may take are those of the named constants defined in the module

```
ieee_signaling_nan    ieee_quiet_nan
ieee_negative_inf     ieee_negative_normal
ieee_negative_denormal ieee_negative_zero
ieee_positive_zero    ieee_positive_denormal
ieee_positive_normal  ieee_positive_inf
```

with obvious meanings and (**Fortran 2003 only**)

```
ieee_other_value
```

for any cases that cannot be so identified, for example, if an unformatted file were written with gradual underflow enabled and read with it disabled.

ieee_round_type for identifying a particular rounding mode. The only possible values objects of this type may take are those of the named constants defined in the module

```
ieee_nearest ieee_to_zero
ieee_up      ieee_down
```

for the IEEE modes and

```
ieee_other
```

for any other mode.

The components of both types are private. The only operations defined for them are `==` and `/=` for comparing values of one of the types; they return a value of type default logical. Intrinsic assignment is also available.

11.9.2 Inquiry functions for IEEE arithmetic

The module `ieee_arithmetic` contains the following inquiry functions, all of which are pure. The inquiries are in terms of reals, but the same level of support is provided for the corresponding kinds of complex type.

ieee_support_datatype ([x]) returns .true. if the processor supports IEEE arithmetic for all reals (x absent) or for reals of the same kind type parameter as the real argument x. Otherwise, it returns .false.. Complete conformance with the IEEE standard is not required for .true. to be returned, but the normalized numbers must be exactly those of IEEE single or IEEE double; the binary arithmetic operators +, −, and * must be implemented with at least one of the IEEE rounding modes; and the functions ieee_copy_sign, ieee_scalb, ieee_logb, ieee_next_after, ieee_rem, and ieee_unordered must implement the corresponding IEEE functions.

ieee_support_denormal ([x]) returns .true. if the processor supports the IEEE denormalized numbers for all reals (x absent) or for reals of the same kind type parameter as the real argument x. Otherwise, it returns .false..

ieee_support_divide ([x]) returns .true. if the processor supports divide with the accuracy specified by the IEEE standard for all reals (x absent) or for reals of the same kind type parameter as the real argument x. Otherwise, it returns .false..

ieee_support_inf ([x]) returns .true. if the processor supports the IEEE infinity facility for all reals (x absent) or for reals of the same kind type parameter as the real argument x. Otherwise, it returns .false..

ieee_support_nan ([x]) returns .true. if the processor supports the IEEE Not-A-Number facility for all reals (x absent) or for reals of the same kind type parameter as the real argument x. Otherwise, it returns .false..

ieee_support_rounding (round_value [,x]) for a round_value of the type ieee_round_type returns .true. if the processor supports that rounding mode for all reals (x absent) or for reals of the same kind type parameter as the argument x. Otherwise, it returns .false.. Here, support includes the ability to change the mode by the invocation

```
call ieee_set_rounding_mode (round_value)
```

ieee_support_sqrt ([x]) returns .true. if sqrt implements IEEE square root for all reals (x absent) or for reals of the same kind type parameter as the real argument x. Otherwise, it returns .false..

ieee_support_standard ([x]) returns .true. if the processor supports all the IEEE facilities defined in this chapter for all reals (x absent) or for reals of the same kind type parameter as the real argument x. Otherwise, it returns .false..

ieee_support_underflow_control ([x]) (**Fortran 2003 only**) returns .true.
   if the processor supports control of the underflow mode for all reals (x absent) or for
   reals of the same kind type parameter as the real argument x. Otherwise, it returns
   .false..

11.9.3   Elemental functions

The module ieee_arithmetic contains the following elemental functions for the reals x and
y for which the values of ieee_support_datatype(x) and ieee_support_datatype(y)
are true. If x or y is an infinity or a NaN, the behaviour is consistent with the general rules
of the IEEE standard for arithmetic operations. For example, the result for an infinity is
constructed as the limiting case of the result with a value of arbitrarily large magnitude, when
such a limit exists.

ieee_class (x) is of type type(ieee_class_type) and returns the IEEE class of the
   real argument x. The possible values are explained in Section 11.9.1.

ieee_copy_sign (x, y) returns a real with the same type parameter as x, holding the
   value of x with the sign of y. This is true even for the IEEE special values, such as
   NaN and ∞ (on processors supporting such values).

ieee_is_finite (x) returns the value .true. if ieee_class (x) has one of the
   values

```
ieee_negative_normal   ieee_negative_denormal
ieee_negative_zero     ieee_positive_zero
ieee_positive_denormal ieee_positive_normal
```

and .false. otherwise.

ieee_is_nan (x) returns the value .true. if the value of x is an IEEE NaN and
   .false. otherwise.

ieee_is_negative (x) returns the value .true. if ieee_class (x) has one of the
   values

```
ieee_negative_normal ieee_negative_denormal
ieee_negative_zero   ieee_negative_inf
```

and .false. otherwise.

ieee_is_normal (x) returns the value .true. if ieee_class (x) has one of the
   values

```
ieee_negative_normal   ieee_negative_zero
ieee_positive_zero     ieee_positive_normal
```

and .false. otherwise.

ieee_logb (x) returns a real with the same type parameter as x. If x is neither zero, infinity, nor NaN, the value of the result is the unbiased exponent of x, that is, exponent(x)-1. If x==0, the result is $-\infty$ if ieee_support_inf(x) is true and -huge(x) otherwise; ieee_divide_by_zero signals.

ieee_next_after (x, y) returns a real with the same type parameter as x. If x==y, the result is x, without an exception ever signaling. Otherwise, the result is the neighbour of x in the direction of y. The neighbours of zero (of either sign) are both nonzero. If either x or y is a NaN, the result is one of the input NaNs. Overflow is signaled when x is finite but ieee_next_after (x, y) is infinite; underflow is signaled when ieee_next_after (x, y) is denormalized; in both cases, ieee_inexact signals.

ieee_rem (x, y) returns a real with the type parameter of whichever argument has the greater precision and value exactly x-y*n, where n is the integer nearest to the exact value x/y; whenever $|n - x/y| = 1/2$, n is even. If the result value is zero, the sign is that of x.

ieee_rint (x, y) returns a real with the same type parameter as x whose value is that of x rounded to an integer value according to the current rounding mode.

ieee_scalb (x, i) returns a real with the same type parameter as x whose value is $2^i x$ if this is within the range of normalized numbers. If $2^i x$ is too large, ieee_overflow signals; if ieee_support_inf(x) is true, the result value is infinity with the sign of x; otherwise, it is sign(huge(x),x). If $2^i x$ is too small and cannot be represented exactly, ieee_underflow signals; the result is the nearest representable number with the sign of x.

ieee_unordered (x, y) returns .true. if x or y is a NaN or both are, and .false. otherwise.

ieee_value (x, class) returns a real with the same type parameter as x and a value specified by class. The argument class may have value

ieee_signaling_nan or ieee_quiet_nan if ieee_support_nan(x) is true,

ieee_negative_inf or ieee_positive_inf if ieee_support_inf(x) is true,

ieee_negative_denormal or ieee_positive_denormal if the value of ieee_support_denormal(x) is true, or

ieee_negative_normal, ieee_negative_zero, ieee_positive_zero, or ieee_positive_normal.

Although in most cases the value is processor dependent, it does not vary between invocations for any particular kind type parameter of x and value of class.

11.9.4 Non-elemental subroutines

The module `ieee_arithmetic` contains the following non-elemental subroutines.

call `ieee_get_rounding_mode` (`round_value`) where:

> **`round_value`** is scalar, of type `type(ieee_round_type)`, and has intent `out`. It returns the floating-point rounding mode, with value `ieee_nearest`, `ieee_to_zero`, `ieee_up`, or `ieee_down` if one of the IEEE modes is in operation, and `ieee_other` otherwise.

call `ieee_get_underflow_mode` (`gradual`) (**Fortran 2003 only**) where:

> **`gradual`** is scalar, of type default `logical`, and has intent `out`. It returns `.true.` if gradual underflow is in effect, and `.false.` otherwise.

call `ieee_set_rounding_mode` (`round_value`) where:

> **`round_value`** is scalar, of type `type(ieee_round_type)`, and has intent `in`. It specifies the mode to be set. The value of `ieee_support_rounding` (`round_value`, x) must be true for some x such that the value of `ieee_support_datatype(x)` is true.

call `ieee_set_underflow_mode` (`gradual`) (**Fortran 2003 only**) where:

> **`gradual`** is scalar, of type default `logical`, and has intent `in`. If its value is `.true.`, gradual underflow comes into effect; otherwise gradual underflow ceases to be in effect.

The example in Figure 11.2 shows the use of these subroutines to store all the exception flags, perform a calculation involving exception handling, and restore them later.

Figure 11.2

```
use, intrinsic :: ieee_arithmetic
type(ieee_round_type) round_value
   :
call ieee_get_rounding_mode(round_value) ! Store the rounding mode
call ieee_set_rounding_mode(ieee_nearest)
   : ! Calculation with round to nearest
call ieee_set_rounding_mode(round_value) ! Restore the rounding mode
```

11.9.5 Transformational function for kind value

The module `ieee_arithmetic` contains the following transformational function that is permitted in an initialization expression (Section 7.4):

ieee_selected_real_kind ([p][, r]) is just like selected_real_kind (Section 8.7.4) except that the result is the kind value of a real x for which ieee_support_datatype(x) is true.

11.10 Examples

11.10.1 Dot product

Our first example, Figure 11.3, is of a module for the dot product of two real arrays of rank 1. It contains a logical scalar dot_error, which acts as an error flag. If the sizes of the arrays are different, an immediate return occurs with dot_error true. If overflow occurs during the actual calculation, the overflow flag will signal and dot_error is set true. If all is well, its value is unchanged.

Figure 11.3

```
module dot ! Module for dot product of two real rank-1 arrays.
   ! The caller must ensure that exceptions do not cause halting.
   use, intrinsic :: ieee_exceptions
   implicit none
   private        :: mult
   logical        :: dot_error = .false.
   interface operator(.dot.)
      module procedure mult
   end interface
contains
   real function mult(a,b)
      real, intent(in) :: a(:), b(:)
      integer          :: i
      logical          :: overflow
      if (size(a)/=size(b)) then
         dot_error = .true.
         return
      end if
! The processor ensures that ieee_overflow is quiet
      mult = 0.0
      do i = 1, size(a)
         mult = mult + a(i)*b(i)
      end do
      call ieee_get_flag(ieee_overflow,overflow)
      if (overflow) dot_error = .true.
   end function mult
end module dot
```

11.10.2　Calling alternative procedures

Suppose the function `fast_inv` is a code for matrix inversion that 'lives dangerously' and may cause a condition to signal. The alternative function `slow_inv` is far less likely to cause a condition to signal, but is much slower. The following code, Figure 11.4, tries `fast_inv` and, if necessary, makes another try with `slow_inv`. If this still fails, a message is printed and the program stops. Note, also, that it is important to set the flags quiet before the second try. The state of all the flags is stored and restored.

Figure 11.4

```fortran
use, intrinsic :: ieee_exceptions
use, intrinsic :: ieee_features, only: ieee_invalid_flag
! The other exceptions of ieee_usual (ieee_overflow and
! ieee_divide_by_zero) are always available with ieee_exceptions
type(ieee_status_type) :: status_value
logical, dimension(3)  :: flag_value
   :
call ieee_get_status(status_value)
call ieee_set_halting_mode(ieee_usual,.false.) ! Needed in case the
!                 default on the processor is to halt on exceptions.
call ieee_set_flag(ieee_usual,.false.)         ! Elemental
! First try the "fast" algorithm for inverting a matrix:
matrix1 = fast_inv(matrix) ! This must not alter matrix.
call ieee_get_flag(ieee_usual,flag_value)      ! Elemental
if (any(flag_value)) then
! "Fast" algorithm failed; try "slow" one:
   call ieee_set_flag(ieee_usual,.false.)
   matrix1 = slow_inv(matrix)
   call ieee_get_flag(ieee_usual,flag_value)
   if (any(flag_value)) then
      write (*, *) 'Cannot invert matrix'
      stop
   end if
end if
call ieee_set_status(status_value)
```

11.10.3　Calling alternative in-line code

This example, Figure 11.5, is similar to the inner part of the previous one, but here the code for matrix inversion is in line, we know that only overflow can signal, and the transfer is made more precise by adding extra tests of the flag.

Figure 11.5

```
use, intrinsic :: ieee_exceptions
logical        :: flag_value
   :
call ieee_set_halting_mode(ieee_overflow,.false.)
call ieee_set_flag(ieee_overflow,.false.)
! First try a fast algorithm for inverting a matrix.
do k = 1, n
   :
   call ieee_get_flag(ieee_overflow,flag_value)
   if (flag_value) exit
end do
if (flag_value) then
! Alternative code which knows that k-1 steps have
! executed normally.
:
end if
```

11.10.4   Reliable hypotenuse function

The most important use of a floating-point exception handling facility is to make possible the development of much more efficient software than is otherwise possible. The code in Figure 11.6 for the 'hypotenuse' function, $\sqrt{x^2 + y^2}$, illustrates the use of the facility in developing efficient software.

An attempt is made to evaluate this function directly in the fastest possible way. This will work almost every time, but if an exception occurs during this fast computation, a safe but slower way evaluates the function. This slower evaluation may involve scaling and unscaling, and in (very rare) extreme cases this unscaling can cause overflow (after all, the true result might overflow if x and y are both near the overflow limit). If the overflow or underflow flag is signaling on entry, it is reset on return by the processor, so that earlier exceptions are not lost.

Figure 11.6

```fortran
real function hypot(x, y)
   implicit none
! In rare circumstances this may lead to the signaling of
! ieee_overflow.
! The caller must ensure that exceptions do not cause halting.
   use, intrinsic :: ieee_exceptions
   use, intrinsic :: ieee_features, only: ieee_underflow_flag
! ieee_overflow is always available with ieee_exceptions
   real                   :: x, y
   real                   :: scaled_x, scaled_y, scaled_result
   logical, dimension(2) :: flags
   type(ieee_flag_type), parameter, dimension(2) ::          &
         out_of_range = (/ ieee_overflow, ieee_underflow /)
   intrinsic :: sqrt, abs, exponent, max, digits, scale
! The processor clears the flags on entry
   call ieee_set_halting_mode(out_of_range, .false.) ! Needed in
!     case the default on the processor is to halt on exceptions.
! Try a fast algorithm first
   hypot = sqrt( x**2 + y**2 )
   call ieee_get_flag(out_of_range, flags)
   if ( any(flags) ) then
     call ieee_set_flag(out_of_range, .false.)
     if ( x==0.0 .or. y==0.0 ) then
       hypot = abs(x) + abs(y)
     else if ( 2*abs(exponent(x)-exponent(y)) > digits(x)+1 ) then
       hypot = max( abs(x), abs(y) )! We can ignore one of x and y
     else     ! Scale so that abs(x) is near 1
       scaled_x = scale( x, -exponent(x) )
       scaled_y = scale( y, -exponent(x) )
       scaled_result = sqrt( scaled_x**2 + scaled_y**2 )
       hypot = scale(scaled_result, exponent(x)) ! May cause
     end if                                      ! overflow
   end if
! The processor resets any flag that was signaling on entry
end function hypot
```

11.10.5   Access to IEEE arithmetic values

The program in Figure 11.7 illustrates how the `ieee_arithmetic` module can be used to
test for special IEEE values. It repeatedly doubles a and halves b, testing for overflowed,
denormalized, and zero values. It uses `ieee_set_halting_mode` to prevent halting. The
beginning and end of a sample output are shown. Note the warning messages; the processor
is required to produce some such output if any exceptions are signalling at termination.

Figure 11.7

```
program test
   use ieee_arithmetic; use ieee_features
   real    :: a=1.0, b=1.0
   integer :: i
   call ieee_set_halting_mode(ieee_overflow, .false.)
   do i = 1,1000
      a = a*2.0
      b = b/2.0
      if(.not. ieee_is_finite(a)) then
         write(*,*) '2.0**',i,' is infinite'
         a = 0.0
      end if
      if(.not. ieee_is_normal(b)) write(*,*) '0.5**', i,    &
                                      ' is denormal'
      if(b==0.0) exit
   end do
   write(*,*) '0.5**',i,' is zero'
end program test

 0.5** 127  is denormal
 2.0** 128  is infinite
 0.5** 128  is denormal
 0.5** 129  is denormal
 :
 0.5** 148  is denormal
 0.5** 149  is denormal
 0.5** 150  is zero
Warning: Floating overflow occurred during execution
Warning: Floating underflow occurred during execution
```

12. Allocatable array extensions

12.1 Introduction

The subject of this chapter is another standardized extension[1] of Fortran 95. It involves the use of allocatable arrays as dummy arguments, function results, and components of structures. Pointer arrays may be used instead, but there are significant advantages for memory management and execution speed in using allocatable arrays when the added functionality of pointers is not needed. We describe the extensions to Fortran 95 that were detailed in the Technical Report and which are all now part of Fortran 2003. We also describe the few related Fortran 2003 features that were not in the Technical Report, with a clear indication of this in each case.

Why is this extension needed? Firstly, code for a pointer array is likely to be less efficient because allowance has to be made for strides other than unity. For example, its target might be the section vector(1:n:2) or the section matrix(i,1:n) with non-unit strides, whereas most computers hold allocatable arrays in contiguous memory.

Secondly, if a defined operation involves a temporary variable of a derived type with a pointer component, the compiler will probably be unable to deallocate its target when storage for the variable is freed. Consider, for example, the statement

```
a = b + c*d        ! a, b, c, and d are of the same derived type
```

This will create a temporary for c*d, which is not needed once b + c*d has been calculated. The compiler is unlikely to be sure that no other pointer has the component or part of it as a target, so is unlikely to deallocate it.

Thirdly, intrinsic assignment is often unsuitable for a derived type with a pointer component because the assignment

```
a = b
```

will leave a and b sharing the same target for their pointer component. Therefore, a defined assignment that allocates a fresh target and copies the data will be used instead. However, this is very wasteful if the right-hand side is a temporary such as that of the assignment of the previous paragraph.

Fourthly, similar considerations apply to a function invocation within an expression. The compiler will be unlikely to be able to deallocate the pointer after the expression has been calculated.

---

[1] Technical Report ISO/IEC TR 15581 : 1998(E).

Although the Fortran standard does not mention descriptors, it is very helpful to think of an allocatable array as being held as a descriptor that records whether it is allocated and, if so, its address and its bounds in each dimension. This is like a descriptor for a pointer, but no strides need be held since these are always unity. As for pointers, the expectation is that the array itself is held separately.

12.2   Allocatable dummy arguments

A dummy argument is permitted to have the allocatable attribute. In this case, the corresponding actual argument must be an allocatable array of the same type, kind parameters, and rank; also, the interface must be explicit. The dummy argument always receives the allocation status (descriptor) of the actual argument on entry and the actual argument receives that of the dummy argument on return. In both cases, this includes the bounds and may be 'not currently allocated'.

Our expectation is that some compilers will perform copy-in / copy-out of the descriptor. Rule i) of Section 5.7.2 is applicable and is designed to permit compilers to do this. In particular, this means that no reference to the actual argument (for example, through it being a module variable) is permitted from the invoked procedure if the dummy array is allocated or deallocated there.

For the array itself, the situation is just like the case when the actual and dummy arguments are both explicit-shaped arrays (see Section 6.7.3). Copy-in / copy-out is permitted unless both arrays have the `target` attribute.

An allocatable dummy argument is permitted to have intent and this applies both to the allocation status (the descriptor) and to the array itself. If the intent is `in`, the array is not permitted to be allocated or deallocated and the value is not permitted to be altered. If the intent is `out` and the array is allocated on entry, it becomes deallocated. An example of the application of an allocatable dummy argument to reading arrays of variable bounds is shown in Figure 12.1.

Figure 12.1

```
subroutine load(array, unit)
    real, allocatable, intent(out), dimension(:,:,:) :: array
    integer, intent(in)          :: unit
    integer                      :: n1, n2, n3
    read(unit) n1, n2, n3
    allocate(array(n1, n2, n3))
    read(unit) array
end subroutine load
```

12.3   Allocatable functions

A function result is permitted to have the allocatable attribute. The allocation status on each entry to the function is 'not currently allocated'. The result may be allocated and deallocated any number of times during execution of the procedure, but it must be allocated and have a defined value on return.

The interface must be explicit in any scoping unit in which the function is referenced. The result array is automatically deallocated after execution of the statement in which the reference occurs, even if it has the target attribute. We can thus recast the example in Section 5.10, and safely use the function result in an expression as shown in Figure 12.2, without fearing a memory leak.

Figure 12.2

```
program no_leak
    real, dimension(100) :: x, y
    :
    y(:size(compact(x)) = compact(x)**2
    :
contains
    function compact(x)  ! To remove duplicates from the array x
        real, allocatable, dimension(:) :: compact
        real, dimension(:), intent(in)  :: x
        integer                         :: n
        :                   ! Find the number of distinct values, n
        allocate(compact(n))
        :                   ! Copy the distinct values into compact
    end function compact
end program no_leak
```

12.4 Allocatable components

Components of derived type are permitted to have the allocatable attribute. For example, for each scalar variable of type type(stack) with the type declaration

```
type stack
    integer :: index
    integer, allocatable :: content(:)
end type stack
```

the bounds of the component content are determined by an allocate statement, by assignment, or by argument association.

In Section 9.3, we used the term ultimate component when a sequence of component selections involves no pointer components of derived type and ends with an intrinsic type. It is convenient to extend the term to include the case that ends with a component of derived type that is allocatable or is a pointer. For example, if the components called alloc are allocatable and the components called point are pointers, the components obj%point and obj%alloc are ultimate components, but obj%point%comp and obj%alloc%comp are not. The parent object (obj in our example) may be allocatable or a pointer.

Just as for an ordinary allocatable array, the initial state of an allocable component is 'not currently allocated'. This is also true for an ultimate allocatable component of an object created by an allocate statement. Hence, there is no need for default initialization of allocatable components. In fact, initialization in a derived-type definition (Section 7.11) of an allocatable component is not permitted.

In a structure constructor (Section 3.8), an expression corresponding to an allocatable component must be an array or a reference to the intrinsic function `null` with no arguments. If it is an allocatable array, the component takes the same allocation status and, if allocated, the same bounds and value. If it is an array, but not an allocatable array, the component is allocated with the same bounds and is assigned the same value. If it is a reference to the intrinsic function `null` with no arguments, the component receives the allocation status of 'not currently allocated'.

Allocatable components are illustrated in Figure 12.3, where code to manipulate polynomials with variable numbers of terms is shown.

Just as an allocatable array is not permitted to have the `parameter` attribute (be a constant), so an object of a type having an ultimate allocatable component is not permitted by the Technical Report to have the `parameter` attribute; further, a structure constructor of such a type cannot be a constant and thus an initialization expression cannot have such a type. However, all of these are permitted in Fortran 2003 provided the component is specifed as 'not currently allocated' explicitly with `null()` or implicitly by not being given a value. The component will always be 'not currently allocated'.

In an array subobject (Section 6.13), a *part-ref* to the right of a *part-ref* with nonzero rank must not be an element of an allocatable component, for example,

```
type(stack) :: a(10)   ! The type was declared at the
    :                  ! start of this section.
... a(:)%content(1)    ! Not permitted.
```

This is because such an object would not be an ordinary array — its elements are likely to be stored without any regular pattern, each having been separately given storage by an `allocate` statement.

When a variable of derived type is deallocated, any ultimate allocatable component that is currently allocated is also deallocated, as if by a deallocate statement. The variable may be a pointer or an allocatable array, and the rule applies recursively, so that all allocated allocatable components at all levels (apart from any lying beyond pointer components) are deallocated. Such deallocations of components also occur when a variable is associated with an `intent(out)` dummy argument. Note the convenience to the programmer of this feature; to avoid memory leakage with pointer components, the programmer would need to deallocate each one explicitly and be careful to order the deallocations correctly.

Intrinsic assignment

$$variable = expr$$

for a type with an ultimate allocatable component (as in r = p + q in Figure 12.3) consists of the following steps for each such component.

i) If the component of *variable* is currently allocated, it is deallocated.

Figure 12.3

```
module real_polynomial_module
    type real_polynomial
        real, allocatable, dimension(:) :: coeff
    end type real_polynomial
    interface operator(+)
        module procedure rp_add_rp
    end interface operator(+)
contains
    function rp_add_rp(p1, p2)
        type(real_polynomial)              :: rp_add_rp
        type(real_polynomial), intent(in) :: p1, p2
        integer                            :: m, m1, m2
        m1 = ubound(p1%coeff,1)
        m2 = ubound(p2%coeff,1)
        allocate(rp_add_rp%coeff(max(m1,m2)))
        m = min(m1,m2)
        rp_add_rp%coeff(:m) = p1%coeff(:m) +p2%coeff(:m)
        if (m1 > m) rp_add_rp%coeff(m+1:) = p1%coeff(m+1:)
        if (m2 > m) rp_add_rp%coeff(m+1:) = p2%coeff(m+1:)
    end function rp_add_rp
end module real_polynomial_module
program example
    use real_polynomial_module
    type(real_polynomial) :: p, q, r
    p = real_polynomial((/4.0, 2.0, 1.0/))  ! Set p to 4+2x+x**2
    q = real_polynomial((/-1.0, 1.0/))
    r = p + q
    print *, 'Coefficients are: ', r%coeff
end program example
```

ii) If the component of *expr* is currently allocated, the component of *variable* is allocated with the same bounds and the value is then transferred using intrinsic assignment.

If the allocatable component of *expr* is 'not currently allocated', nothing happens in step ii), so the component of *variable* is left 'not currently allocated'. Note that if the component of *variable* is already allocated with the same shape, the compiler may choose to avoid the overheads of deallocation and reallocation. Note also that if the compiler can tell that there will be no subsequent reference to *expr*, because it is a function reference or a temporary variable holding the result of expression evaluation, no allocation or assignment is needed — all that has to happen is the deallocation of any allocated ultimate allocatable components of *variable* followed by the copying of the descriptor.

If an actual argument and the corresponding dummy argument have an ultimate allocatable component, rule i) of Section 5.7.2 is applicable and requires all allocations and deallocations of the component to be performed through the dummy argument, in case copy-in / copy-out is in effect.

If a statement contains a reference to a function whose result is of a type with an ultimate allocatable component, any allocated ultimate allocatable components of the function result are deallocated after execution of the statement. This parallels the rule for allocatable function results (Section 12.3).

Just as for pointer components (see Section 9.3), a structure with an ultimate allocatable component is not permitted in an I/O list. In Fortran 2003, however, programmers are able to write procedures that define edit descriptors for data structures and are called as part of the I/O processing (see Chapter 19). Such a procedure will be able to handle structures whose size and composition vary dynamically, the usual case with allocatable components.

Similarly, such a structure is not permitted in a namelist group (Section 7.15). This is entirely consistent with not permitting allocatable arrays or structures with pointer components here.

A sequence type (Section 20.2.1) is permitted to have an allocatable component, which permits independent declarations of the same type in different scopes; but such a type has an unspecified storage unit, that is, does not have numeric or character storage association (as for a type with a pointer component).

This dynamic feature is ill-adapted to the fixed storage model implied by storage association, and so, just as for pointer components (see Section 20.2.2), a structure with an ultimate allocatable component is not permitted as an `object` in an `equivalence` statement. Just as for allocatable arrays (see Section 20.2.3), a structure with an ultimate allocatable component is not permitted in a `common` block. Thus, such a structure is not permitted at all in a storage association context.

12.5 Exercises

1. Using the type `stack` of Section 12.4, write code to define a variable of that type with an allocatable component length of four and then to extend that allocatable array with two additional values.

2. Given the type

```
type emfield
    real, allocatable :: strength(:,:)
end type
```

initialise a variable of type `emfield` so that its component has bounds (1:4,1:6) and value 1 everywhere. Extend this variable so that the component has bounds (0:5,0:8), keeping the values of the old elements and setting the values of the new elements to zero.

3. As 2., but with new bounds (1:6,1:9) and using the `reshape` intrinsic function.

13. Enhanced module facilities

13.1 Introduction

The module facilities of Fortran 95, while adequate for programs of modest size, have some shortcomings for very large programs. The extent of these shortcomings was not properly appreciated when the main features of Fortran 2003 were chosen and a straightforward solution was not devised until the development of Fortran 2003 was nearly complete. Therefore, instead of risking a delay to the whole of Fortran 2003, it was decided to define the submodule feature as an extension in a Technical Report,[1] with the promise that the next revision of Fortran would include it, apart from correcting any defects found in the field. Since the formal approval procedures for a Technical Report are simpler than those for a Standard, we expect its final approval and publication to take place at about the same time as the Standard.

The publication of this Technical Report will enable vendors to implement the submodule feature, secure in the knowledge that no frivolous changes to it will occur in the next revision of the language. Since there is wide agreement that it is important, we expect a number of vendors to implement it without waiting until they have implemented the whole of Fortran 2003, which is why this chapter appears here.

The shortcomings of the module feature all arise from the fact that, although modules are an aid to modularization of the program, they are themselves difficult to modularize. As a module grows larger, perhaps because the concept it is encapsulating is large, the only way of modularization is to break it into several modules. This exposes the internal structure of the concept, raising the potential for unnecessary global name clashes and giving the user of the module access to what ought to be private data and/or procedures. Worse, if the subfeatures of the module are interconnected, they must remain together in a single module, however large.

Another significant shortcoming is that if a change is made to the code inside a module procedure, even a private one, typical use of make or similar tools results in the recompilation of every file which used that module, directly or indirectly. (A method of avoiding this for some compilers is described in Appendix D.)

The solution is to allow modules to be split into separate program units called *submodules*, which can be in separate files. Module procedures can then be split so that the interface information remains in the module, but the bodies can be placed in the submodules. A change

---

[1] Technical Report ISO/IEC TR 19767.

in a submodule cannot alter an interface, and so does not cause the recompilation of program units that use the module.

The introduction of submodules gives other benefits, which we can explain more easily once we have described the feature.

13.2   Submodules

Submodules provide a way of structuring a module into component parts, which may be in separate files. All module procedures continue to have their interface defined in the module, but their implementation can be deferred to a submodule. A submodule has access via host association to entities in the module, and may have entities of its own in addition to providing implementations of module procedures.

13.2.1   Separate module procedures

The essence of the feature is to separate the definition of a module procedure into two parts: the interface, which is defined in the module; and the body, which is defined in the submodule. Such a module procedure is known as a *separate module procedure*. A simple example is shown in Figure 13.1. The keyword module in the prefix of the function statement indicates in the interface block that this is the interface to a module procedure rather than an external procedure and in the submodule that this is the implementation part of a module procedure. The submodule specifies the name of its parent. Both the interface and the submodule gain access to the type point by host association.

Figure 13.1

```
module points
    type :: point
       real :: x,y
    end type point
    interface
       real module function point_dist (a,b)
          type(point), intent(in) :: a,b
       end function point_dist
    end interface
end module points

submodule (points) points_a
contains
    real module function point_dist (a,b)
       type(point), intent(in) :: a,b
       point_dist = sqrt((a%x-b%x)**2+(a%y-b%y)**2)
    end function point_dist
end submodule points_a
```

The interface specified in the submodule must be exactly the same as that specified in the interface block. For an external procedure, the interface is permitted to differ in respect of the names of the arguments, whether it is pure, and whether it is recursive (see Section 5.11); such variations are not permitted for a submodule since the intention is simply to separate the definition of the procedure into two parts. The name of the result variable is not part of the interface and so is permitted to be different in the two places; in this case, the name in the interface block is ignored.

There is also a syntax that avoids the redeclaration altogether:

```
submodule (points) points_a
contains
    module procedure point_dist
        point_dist = sqrt((a%x-b%x)**2+(a%y-b%y)**2)
    end procedure point_dist
end submodule points_a
```

In this case, the whole interface is taken from the interface block, including whether it is a function or a subroutine and the name of the result variable if it is a function.

13.2.2 Submodules of submodules

Submodules are themselves permitted to have submodules, which is useful for very large programs. The module or submodule of which a submodule is a direct subsidiary is called its *parent* and it is called a *child* of its parent. We do not expect the number of levels of submodules often to exceed two (that is, a module with submodules that themselves have submodules) but there is no limit and we refer to *ancestors* and *descendants* with the obvious meanings. Each module or submodule is the root of a tree whose other nodes are its descendants and have access to it by host association. No other submodules have such access, which is helpful for developing parts of large modules independently. Furthermore, there is no mechanism for accessing anything declared in a submodule from elsewhere — it is effectively private.

If a change is made to a submodule, only it and its descendants will need recompilation.

A submodule is identified by the combination of the name of its ancestor module and the name of its parent, for example, `points:points_a` for the submodule of Figure 13.1. This allows two submodules to have the same name if they are descendants of different modules. This identifier is needed only to specify it as the parent in the `submodule` statement, as in

```
submodule (points:points_a) points_b
```

13.2.3 Submodule entities

A submodule can also contain entities of its own. These are not module entities and so are neither public nor private; they are, however, inaccessible outside of the defining submodule except to its descendants.

Typically, these will be variables, types, named constants, etc., for use in the implementation of some separate module procedure. As per the usual rules of host association, if any submodule entity has the same name as a module entity, the module entity is hidden.

A submodule can also contain procedures, which we will call *submodule procedures*. A submodule procedure is only accessible in the submodule and its descendants, and so can be invoked only there. In particular, a submodule procedure with the bind attribute (see Section 14.7) does not have a binding label, and cannot have a name= specifier. This is because a user of a module might write a submodule with the module as its parent and containing a procedure that accesses private module entities by host association. However, without a binding label, there is no mechanism for the user to invoke such a procedure.

Like a module procedure, a submodule procedure can also be *separate*; a separate submodule procedure has its interface declared in one submodule and its body in a descendant.

13.2.4   Submodules and use association

A submodule is not permitted to access its ancestor module by use association; there is, after all, no need since it has access by host association. It may, however, access any other module by use association. In particular, it is possible for a submodule of module a to access module b and a submodule of module b to access module a. A simple example is where a procedure of module a calls a procedure of module b and a procedure of module b calls a procedure of module a. Because circular dependencies between modules are not permitted, without submodules this would require that a and b were the same module, or that a third module c be used (containing those parts which were mutually dependent).

13.3   The advantages of submodules

A major benefit of submodules is that if a change is made to one, only it and its descendants are affected. Thus a large module may be divided into small submodule trees, improving modularity (and thus maintainability) and avoiding unnecessary recompilation cascades (but see also Appendix D). We now summarize other benefits.

Entities declared in a submodule are private to that submodule and it descendants, which controls their name management and accidental use within a large module.

Separate concepts with circular dependencies can be separated into different submodules in the common case where it is just the implementations that reference each other (because circular dependencies are not permitted between modules, this was impossible before).

Where a large task has been implemented as a set of modules, it may be appropriate to replace this by a single module and a collection of submodules. Entities that were public only because they are needed by other modules of the set can become private to the module or to a submodule and its descendants.

Once the implementation details of a module have been separated into submodules, the text of the module itself can be published to provide authoritative documentation of the interface without exposing any trade secrets contained in the implementation.

On many systems, each source file produces a single object file that must be loaded in its entirety into the executable program. Breaking the module into several files will allow the loading of only those procedures that are actually invoked into a user program. This makes modules more attractive for building large libraries.

14. Interoperability with C

14.1 Introduction

Fortran 2003 provides a standardized mechanism for interoperating with C. Clearly, any entity involved must be such that equivalent declarations of it may be made in the two languages. This is enforced within the Fortran program by requiring all such entities to be *interoperable*. We will explain in turn what this requires for types, variables, and procedures. They are all requirements on the syntax so that the compiler knows at compile time whether an entity is interoperable. We continue with examining interoperability for global data and then discuss some examples. We conclude with a new syntax for defining sets of integer constants that is useful in this context.

14.2 Interoperability of intrinsic types

There is an intrinsic module named `iso_c_binding` that contains named constants of type default integer holding kind type parameter values for intrinsic types. Their names are shown in Table 14.1, together with the corresponding C types. The processor is required to support only `int`. Lack of support is indicated with a negative value of the constant. If the value is positive, it indicates that the Fortran type and kind type parameter interoperate with the corresponding C type.

The negative values are as follows. For the integer types, the value is -1 if there is such a C type but no interoperating Fortran kind or -2 if there is no such C type. For the real types, the value is -1 if the C type does not have a precision equal to the precision of any of the Fortran real kinds, -2 if the C type does not have a range equal to the range of any of the Fortran real kinds, -3 if the C type has neither the precision nor range of any of the Fortran real kinds, and equal to -4 if there is no interoperating Fortran kind for other reasons. The values of `c_float_complex`, `c_double_complex`, and `c_long_double_complex` are the same as those of `c_float`, `c_double`, and `c_long_double`, respectively. For logical, the value of `c_bool` is -1 if there is no Fortran kind corresponding to the C type `_Bool`. For character, the value of `c_char` is -1 if there is no Fortran kind corresponding to the C type `char`.

For character type, interoperability also requires that the length type parameter be omitted or be specified by an initialization expression whose value is one. The following named constants (with the obvious meanings) are provided: `c_null_char`, `c_alert`, `c_backspace`, `c_form_feed`, `c_new_line`, `c_carriage_return`, `c_horizontal_tab`, `c_vertical_tab`.

They are all of type character with length one and kind c_char (or default kind if c_char has
the value −1).

Table 14.1. Interoperability between Fortran and C types.

Type	Named constant	C type or types
integer	c_int	int
	c_short	short int
	c_long	long int
	c_long_long	long long int
	c_signed_char	signed char, unsigned char
	c_size_t	size_t
	c_int8_t	int8_t
	c_int16_t	int16_t
	c_int32_t	int32_t
	c_int64_t	int64_t
	c_int_least8_t	int_least8_t
	c_int_least16_t	int_least16_t
	c_int_least32_t	int_least32_t
	c_int_least64_t	int_least64_t
	c_int_fast8_t	int_fast8_t
	c_int_fast16_t	int_fast16_t
	c_int_fast32_t	int_fast32_t
	c_int_fast64_t	int_fast64_t
	c_intmax_t	intmax_t
	c_intptr_t	intptr_t
real	c_float	float
	c_double	double
	c_long_double	long double
complex	c_float_complex	float _Complex
	c_double_complex	double _Complex
	c_long_double_complex	long double _Complex
logical	c_bool	_Bool
character	c_char	char

14.3 Interoperability with C pointer types

For interoperating with C pointers (which are just addresses), the module contains the derived types c_ptr and c_funptr that are interoperable with C object and function pointer types, respectively. Their components are private. There are named constants c_null_ptr and c_null_funptr for the corresponding null values of C.

The module also contains the following procedures.

c_loc(x) is an inquiry function that returns a scalar of type c_ptr that holds the C address of its argument x, which must

    i) have interoperable type and type parameters and be

        a) a variable that has the target attribute and is interoperable,

        b) an allocated allocatable variable that has the target attribute and is not an array of zero size, or

        c) an associated scalar pointer,

    or

    ii) be a non-polymorphic scalar, have no length type parameters, and be

        a) a non-allocatable, non-pointer variable that has the target attribute,

        b) an allocated allocatable variable that has the target attribute, or

        c) an associated pointer.

c_funloc(x) is an inquiry function that returns the C address of a procedure. The argument x is permitted to be a procedure that is interoperable (see Section 14.7) or a pointer associated with such a procedure.

c_associated (c_ptr1[, c_ptr2]) is an inquiry function for scalars of type c_ptr or for scalars of type c_funptr. It returns a default logical scalar. It has the value false if c_ptr1 is a C null pointer or if c_ptr2 is present with a different value; otherwise, it has the value true.

c_f_pointer (cptr, fptr [, shape]) is a subroutine with arguments

    cptr is a scalar of type c_ptr with intent(in). Its value is either

        i) the C address of an interoperable data entity or

        ii) the result of a reference to c_loc with a non-interoperable argument.

    It must not be the C address of a Fortran variable that does not have the target attribute.

    fptr is a pointer with intent(out).

        i) If cptr is the C address of an interoperable entity, fptr must be a data pointer of the type and type parameters of the entity and it becomes pointer associated with the target of cptr. If it is an array, its shape is specified by shape and each lower bound is 1.

ii) If cptr was returned by a call of c_loc with a non-interoperable argument
    x, fptr must be a non-polymorphic scalar pointer of the type and type
    parameters of x. x or its target if it is a pointer shall not have since been
    deallocated or have become undefined due to execution of a return or an
    end statement. fptr becomes pointer-associated with x or its target.

shape (optional) is a rank-one array of type integer with intent(in). If present, its
size is equal to the rank of fptr. It must be present if fptr is an array.

c_f_procpointer (cptr, fptr)) is a subroutine with arguments

cptr is a scalar of type c_funptr with intent(in). Its value is the C address of a
procedure that is interoperable.

fptr is a procedure pointer with intent(out). Its interface must be interoperable
with the target of cptr and it becomes pointer-associated with that target.

A Fortran pointer or allocatable variable, and most Fortran arrays, do not interoperate
directly with any C entity because C does not have quite the same concepts; for example,
unlike a Fortran array pointer, a C array pointer cannot describe a non-contiguous array
section. However, this does not prevent such entities being passed to C via argument
association since Fortran compilers already perform copy-in copy-out when this is necessary.
Also, the function c_loc may be used to obtain the C address of an allocated allocatable
array, which is useful if the C part of the program wishes to maintain a pointer to this array.
Similarly, the address of an array allocated in C may be passed to Fortran and c_f_pointer
used to construct a Fortran pointer whose target is the C array. There is an illustration of this
in Section 14.9.

Case ii) of c_loc allows the C program to receive a pointer to a Fortran scalar that is not
interoperable. It is not intended that any use of it be made within C except to pass it back
to Fortran, where c_f_pointer is available to reconstruct the Fortran pointer. There is an
illustration of this in Section 14.10.

14.4 Interoperability of derived types

For a derived type to be interoperable, it must have the bind attribute:

```
type, bind(c) :: mytype
  :
end type mytype
```

It must not be a sequence type (Section 20.2.1), have type parameters, have the extends
attribute (Section 16.2), or have any type-bound procedures (Section 16.6). Each component
must have interoperable type and type parameters, must not be a pointer, and must not be
allocatable.

These restrictions allow the type to interoperate with a C struct type that has the same
number of components. The components correspond by position in their definitions. Each
Fortran component must be interoperable with the corresponding C component. Here is a
simple example:

```
typedef struct {
  int m, n;
  float r;
} myctype;
```

is interoperable with

```
use iso_c_binding
type, bind(c) :: myftype
  integer(c_int) :: i, j
  real(c_float) :: s
end type myftype
```

The name of the type and the names of the components are not significant for interoperability. If two equivalent definitions of an interoperable derived type are made in separate scoping units, they interoperate with the same C type (but it is usually preferable to define one type in a module and access it by use statements).

No Fortran type is interoperable with a C union type, a C struct type that contains a bit field, or a C struct type that contains a flexible array member.

14.5 Interoperability of variables

A scalar Fortran variable is interoperable if it is of interoperable type and type parameters, and is neither a pointer nor allocatable. It is interoperable with a C scalar if the Fortran type and type parameters are interoperable with the C type.

An array Fortran variable is interoperable if it is of interoperable type and type parameters and it is of explicit shape or assumed size (Section 20.2.5).

For a Fortran array of rank one to interoperate with a C array, the Fortran array elements must be interoperable with the C array elements. If the Fortran array is of explicit size, the C array must have the same size. If the Fortran array is of assumed size, the C array must not have a specified size.

A Fortran array a of rank greater than one and of shape $(e_1, e_2, \ldots, e_r)$ is interoperable with a C array of size e_r with elements that are interoperable with a Fortran array of the same type as a and of shape $(e_1, e_2, \ldots, e_{r-1})$. For ranks greater than two, this rule is applied recursively. For example, the Fortran arrays declared as

```
integer(c_int) :: fa(18, 3:7),  fb(18, 3:7, 4)
```

are interoperable with C arrays declared as

```
int ca[5][18], cb[4][5][18];
```

and the elements correspond if one set of subscripts is reversed.

An assumed-size Fortran array of rank greater than one is interoperable with a C array of unspecified size if its elements are related to the Fortran array in the same way as in the explicit-size case. For example, the Fortran arrays declared as

```
integer(c_int) :: fa(18, *),  fb(18, 3:7, *)
```

are interoperable with C arrays declared as

```
int ca[ ][18], cb[ ][5][18];
```

14.6   The value attribute

For the sake of interoperability, a new attribute, value, has been introduced for scalar dummy arguments. It may be specified in a type declaration statement for the argument or separately in a value statement:

```
function func(a, i, j, a) bind(c)
      real(c_float) func, a
      integer(c_int), value :: i
      value :: a, j
```

When the procedure is invoked, a copy of the actual argument is made. The dummy argument is a variable that may be altered during execution of the procedure, but on return no copy back takes place. The only restriction on the type is that, if it is character, the character length must be known at compile time. The argument must not be a pointer, be allocatable, have intent out or inout, be a procedure, or have the volatile attribute (Section 18.3).

The value attribute is not limited to procedures with the bind attribute, it may be used in any procedure. This is useful for a particular programming style; for example, in

```
integer function nth_word_position(string, n) result(pos)
   character(*), intent(in) :: string
   integer, value           :: n
   integer                  :: next_nonblank

   pos = 1
   do
      next_nonblank = verify(string(pos:),' ')
      if (next_nonblank==0) then
        pos = 0
        return
      end if
      pos = next_nonblank + pos - 1
      if (n<=1) exit
      n = n - 1
   end do
end function
```

the argument n is locally decreased until it reaches zero, without affecting the actual argument or requiring an extra temporary variable. Because the attribute alters the argument passing mechanism, a procedure with a value dummy argument is required to have an explicit interface.

In the context of a call from C, the absence of the value attribute indicates that it expects the actual argument to be an object pointer to an object of the specified type or a function pointer whose target has a prototype that is interoperable with the specified interface (see next section).

14.7 Interoperability of procedures

A Fortran procedure is interoperable if it has an explicit interface and is declared with the bind attribute:

```
function func(i, j, k, l, m) bind(c)
subroutine subr () bind(c)
```

Note that for a subroutine with no arguments, the parentheses are required. The procedure may be an external or module procedure, but is not permitted to be an internal procedure. All the dummy arguments must be non-optional and interoperable. For a function, the result must be scalar and interoperable.

The procedure usually has a *binding label*, which has global scope and is the name by which it is known to the C processor. By default, it is the lower-case version of the Fortran name. For example, the function in the previous paragraph has the binding label func. An alternative binding label may be specified:

```
function func(i, j, k, l, m) bind(c, name='c_func')
```

The value following the name= must be a scalar default character initialization expression. Ignoring leading and trailing blanks, this must be a valid C identifier and case is significant.

A binding label is not an alias for the procedure name for an ordinary Fortran invocation. It is for use only from C. Two different entitities must not have the same binding label.

If the name has zero length or is all blanks, there is no binding label. The procedure may still be invoked from C through a procedure pointer and, if this is the only way it will be invoked, it is not appropriate to give it a binding label. In particular, a private module procedure must not have a binding label.

An interoperable Fortran procedure interface is interoperable with a C function prototype that has the same number of arguments and does not have variable arguments denoted by the ellipsis (...). For a function, the result must be interoperable with the prototype result. For a subroutine, the prototype must have a void result. A dummy argument with the value attribute must be interoperable with the corresponding formal parameter. A dummy argument without the value attribute must correspond to a formal parameter of a pointer type and be interoperable with an entity of the referenced type of the formal parameter. Note that a Fortran array is not permitted to have the value attribute, but it can interoperate with a C array since this is automatically of a pointer type.

Here is an example of procedure interface interoperability. The Fortran interface in Figure 14.1 is interoperable with the C function prototype

```
short func(int i, double *j, int *k, int l[10], void *m);
```

If a C function with this prototype is to be called from Fortran, the Fortran code must access an interface such as this. The call itself is handled in just the same way as if an external Fortran procedure with an explicit interface were being called. This means, for example, that the array section `larray(1:20:2)` might be the actual argument corresponding to the dummy array `1`; in this case, copy-in copy-out takes place.

Figure 14.1

```
   interface
      function func(i, j, k, l, m) bind(c)
      use, intrinsic          :: iso_c_binding
         integer(c_short)     :: func
         integer(c_int), value :: i
         real(c_double)       :: j
         integer(c_int)       :: k, l(10)
         type(c_ptr), value   :: m
      end function func
   end interface
```

Similarly, if a Fortran function with the interface of the previous paragraph is to be called from C, the C code must have a prototype such as that of the previous paragraph.

If a C function is called from Fortran, it must not use signal (C standard, 7.14.1) to change the handling of any exception that is being handled by the Fortran processor, and it must not alter the floating-point status (Section 11.8.4) other than by setting an exception flag to signaling. The values of the floating-point exception flags on entry to a C function are processor dependent.

14.8   Interoperability of global data

An interoperable module variable (or a common block, Section 20.2.3, with interoperable members) may be given the `bind` attribute in a type declaration statement or in a `bind` statement:

```
            use iso_c_binding
            integer(c_int), bind(c) :: c_extern
            integer(c_long) :: c2
            bind(c, name='myvariable') :: c2
            common /com/ r, s
            real(c_float) :: r, s
            bind(c) :: /com/
```

It has a binding label defined by the same rules as for procedures and interoperates with a C variable with external linkage that is of a corresponding type. If a binding label is specified in a statement, the statement must define a single variable.

A variable with the `bind` attribute also has the `save` attribute (which may be confirmed explicitly). A change to the variable in either language affects the value of the corresponding variable in the other language. More than one Fortran variable is not permitted to interoperate with a single C variable.

The bind statement is available only for this purpose; it is not available, for instance, to specify the bind attribute for a module procedure. Also, the bind attribute must not be specified for a variable that is not a module variable (that is, it is not available to confirm that a variable is interoperable), and it must not be specified for a module variable that is in a common block.

If a common block is specified in a bind statement, it must be specified in a bind statement with the same binding label in every scoping unit in which it is declared. It interoperates with a variable of struct type whose components are each interoperable with the corresponding member of the common block. If the common block has only one member, it also interoperates with a variable that is interoperable with the member.

The equivalence statement (Section 20.2.2) is not permitted to specify a variable that has the bind attribute or is a member of a common block that has the bind attribute.

The double colon in a bind statement is optional.

14.9   Invoking a C function from Fortran

If a C function is to be invoked from Fortran, it must have external linkage and be describable by a C prototype that is interoperable with an accessible Fortran interface that has the same binding label.

If it is required to pass a Fortran array to C, the interface may specify the array to be of explicit or assumed size and the usual Fortran mechanisms, perhaps involving copy-in copy-out, ensure that a contiguous array is received by the C code. Here is an example involving both an assumed-size array and an allocatable array. The C prototype is

```
int C_Library_Function(int expl[100], float alloc[], int len_alloc);
```

and the Fortran code is shown in Figure 14.2.

The rules on shape and character length disagreement (Section 20.3) allow entities specified as character(kind=c_char) of any length to be associated with an assumed-size or explicit-shape array, and thus to be passed to and from C. For example, the C function with prototype

```
void Copy(char in[], char out[]);
```

may be invoked by the Fortran code in Figure 14.3.

This code works because Fortran allows the character variable digit_string to be associated with the assumed-size dummy array in. We have also taken the opportunity here to illustrate the use of a binding label to call a C procedure whose name includes an upper-case letter.

14.10   Invoking Fortran from C

A reference in C to a procedure that has the bind attribute, has the same binding label, and is defined by means of Fortran, causes the Fortran procedure to be invoked.

Figure 14.4 shows an example of a Fortran procedure that is called from C and uses a structure to enable arrays allocated in C to be accessed in Fortran. The corresponding C struct declaration is:

Figure 14.2

```
      use iso_c_binding
         interface
            integer (c_int) function c_library_function  &
            (expl, alloc, len_alloc) bind(c)
            use iso_c_binding
            integer (c_int) :: expl(100)
            real (c_float)  :: alloc(*)
            integer (c_int), value :: len_alloc
         end interface
      integer (c_int) :: expl(100)
      integer (c_float), allocatable :: alloc(:)
      integer (c_int)         ::  len_alloc
         :
      len_alloc = 200
      allocate( alloc(len_alloc) )
         :
      call c_library_function(expl, alloc, len_alloc)
         :
```

Figure 14.3

```
     use, intrinsic :: iso_c_binding, only: c_char, c_null_char
     interface
       subroutine copy(in, out) bind(c,name='Copy')
          use, intrinsic :: iso_c_binding, only: c_char
          character(kind=c_char), dimension(*) :: in, out
       end subroutine copy
     end interface
     character(len=10, kind=c_char) :: &
                 digit_string = c_char_'123456789' // c_null_char
     character(kind=c_char) :: digit_arr(10)
     call copy(digit_string, digit_arr)
     print '(1x, a1)', digit_arr(1:9)
     end
```

```
struct pass {
  int lenc, lenf;
  float *c, *f;
};
```

the C function prototype is:

```
void simulation(struct pass *arrays);
```

and the C calling statement might be:

```
simulation(&arrays);
```

Figure 14.4

```
subroutine simulation(arrays) bind(c)
    use iso_c_binding
    type, bind(c) :: pass
        integer (c_int) :: lenc, lenf
        type (c_ptr)    :: c, f
    end type pass
    type (pass), intent(in) :: arrays
    real (c_float), pointer :: c_array(:)
    ...
    ! associate c_array with an array allocated in C
    call c_f_pointer(arrays%c, c_array, (/arrays%lenc/) )
    ...
end subroutine simulation
```

It is not uncommon for a Fortran library module to have an initialization procedure that establishes a data structure to hold all the data for a particular problem that is to be solved. Subsequent calls to other procedures in the module provide data about the problem or receive data about its solution. The data structure is likely to be of a type that is not interoperable, for example, because it has components that are allocatable arrays.

The procedures c_loc and c_f_pointer have been designed to support this situation. Here is an illustration; the Fortran code is as in Figure 14.5. The type pass holds the size of the problem, an allocatable array of this size, and lots more. When the C code calls initialize, it passes the size. The Fortran code allocates a structure and inside it stores the size and allocates an array component; it then returns a pointer to the structure. The C code later calls add and passes additional data together with the pointer that it received from initialize. The Fortran procedure add uses c_f_pointer to establish a Fortran pointer for the relevant structure. Note that the C code may call initialize several times if it wishes to work simultaneously with several problems; each will have a separate structure of type pass and be accessible through its own 'handle' of type(c_ptr).

Figure 14.5

```
module lib_code
    use iso_c_binding
    type :: pass
        integer :: n
        real, allocatable :: a(:)
          :   ! More stuff
    end type pass
    type(pass), pointer :: struct
contains
    subroutine initialize(n,data) bind(c)
        integer(c_int), value :: n
        type(c_ptr), intent(out) :: data
        allocate (struct)
        struct%n = n
        allocate (struct%a(n))
        data = c_loc(struct)
    end subroutine initialize
    subroutine add(data,...) bind(c)
        type(c_ptr), intent(in) :: data
          :
        call c_f_pointer(data, struct)
          :
    end subroutine add
end module lib_code
```

14.11   Enumerations

An enumeration is a set of integer constants (enumerators) that is appropriate for interoperating with C. The kind of the enumerators corresponds to the integer type that C would choose for the same set of constants. Here is an example:

```
enum, bind(c)
    enumerator :: red = 4, blue = 9
    enumerator yellow
end enum
```

This declares the named constants red, blue, and yellow with values 4, 9, and 10, respectively.

If a value is not specified for an enumerator, it is taken as one greater than the previous enumerator or zero if it is the first.

15. Type parameters and procedure pointers

15.1 Introduction

This chapter combines the separate topics of type parameter extensions and procedure pointers.

The type parameter extensions consist of the addition of deferred type parameters, type parameter enquiry, and the ability to parameterize derived types.

The procedure pointer extension provides the ability to associate a pointer with a procedure, similar to the way dummy procedures become associated with actual procedures.

15.2 Deferred type parameters

A `len` type parameter value is permitted to be a colon in a type declaration statement such as

```
character(len=:), pointer :: varchar
```

for a pointer or an allocatable entity. It indicates a *deferred type parameter*; such a type parameter has no defined value until it is given one by allocation or pointer assignment.

For intrinsic types, only character length may be deferred. Derived types that are parameterized may have type parameters which can be deferred, see Section 15.4.2. For example, in

```
character(:), pointer :: varchar
character(100), target :: name
character(200), target :: address
 :
varchar => name
 :
varchar => address
```

the character length of `varchar` after each pointer assignment is the same as that of its target; that is, 100 after the first pointer assignment and 200 after the second.

Deferred type parameters can be altered by the `allocate` statement; see Section 17.4.1 for details. For allocatable variables, they can also be altered by assignment; see Section 17.5.2 for details.

15.3   Type parameter enquiry

The (current) value of a type parameter of a variable can be discovered by a *type parameter enquiry*. This uses the same syntax as for component access, but the value is always scalar, even if the object is an array; for example, in

```
real(selected_real_kind(10,20)) :: z(100)
    :
print *,z%kind
```

a single value is printed, that being the result of executing the reference to the intrinsic function selected_real_kind. This particular case is equivalent to kind(z). However, the type parameter enquiry may be used even when the intrinsic function is not available; for example, in

```
subroutine write_centered(ch,len)
   character(*), intent(inout) :: ch
   integer, intent(in)         :: len
   integer                     :: i
   do i=1,(len-ch%len)/2
```

it would not be possible to replace the type parameter enquiry ch%len with the reference to the intrinsic function len(ch) because len is the name of a dummy argument.

   Note that this syntax must not be used to alter the value of a type parameter, say by appearing on the left-hand side of an assigment statement.

15.4   Parameterized derived types

Type parameters have been introduced for derived types, in exact analogy with type parameters of intrinsic types. Like intrinsic type parameters, derived type parameters come in two flavours; those that must be known at compile time (like the kind parameter for type real), and those whose evaluation may be deferred until run time (like the len parameter for type character). The former are known as *kind* type parameters (because, for the intrinsic types, these are all named kind), and the latter as *length* type parameters (by analogy with character length).

15.4.1   Defining a parameterized derived type

To define a derived type that has type parameters, the type parameters are listed on the type definition statement and must also be explicitly declared at the beginning of the type definition. For example,

```
type matrix(real_kind,n,m)
   integer, kind :: real_kind
   integer, len  :: n,m
   real(real_kind) :: value(n,m)
end type matrix
```

defines a derived type `matrix` with one kind type parameter named `real_kind` and two length type parameters named n and m. All type parameters must be explicitly declared to be of type `integer` with the attribute `kind` or `len` to indicate a kind or length parameter, respectively. Within the type definition, a kind type parameter may be used in both initialization and specification expressions, but a length type parameter may only be used in a specification expression (that is, for array bounds and for other length type parameters such as character length). There is, however, no requirement that a type parameter be used at all. For example, see Figure 15.1.

Figure 15.1

```
type goodtype(p1, p2, p3, p4)
   integer, kind      :: p1, p3
   integer, len       :: p2, p4
   real(kind=p1)      :: c1     ! ok, p1 is a kind type parameter
   character(len=p2)  :: c2     ! ok, this is a specification expr
   complex            :: c3(p3) ! ok, p3 can be used anywhere
   integer            :: c4 = p1 ! ok, p1 can be used anywhere
   ! p4 has not been used, but that is ok.
end type goodtype

type badtype(p5)
   integer, len  :: p5
   real(kind=p5) :: x     ! Invalid, p5 is not a kind type parameter
   integer       :: y = p5 ! Invalid, p5 is not a kind type parameter
end type badtype
```

When declaring an entity of a parameterized derived type, its name is qualified by the type parameters. Thus, a *derived-type-spec* is now

> *derived-type-name* (*type-param-spec-list*)

where *derived-type-name* is the name of the derived type and *type-param-spec* is

> [*keyword* =] *type-param-value*

The keyword must be the name of one of the type parameters of the type. Like keyword arguments in procedure calls, after a *type-param-spec* that includes a *keyword* = clause, any further type parameter specifications must include a keyword. Note that this is consistent with the syntax for specifying type parameters for intrinsic types. Here are some examples for variables of our type `matrix`:

```
type(matrix(kind(0.0),10,20)) :: x
type(matrix(real_kind=kind(0d0),n=n1,m=n2)) :: y
```

15.4.2   Assumed and deferred type parameters

As for the intrinsic type character, an assumed derived type parameter is indicated by a *type-param-value* that is an asterisk. An assumed type parameter specification must be for a length type parameter, and can be used in the declaration of a dummy argument:

```
subroutine print_matrix(z)
   type(matrix(selected_real_kind(30,999),n=*,m=*)) :: z
   :
```

in which case the type parameter value is taken to be that of the actual argument (just as for assumed-length character arguments). An assumed type parameter may also be used in the allocate statement (see Section 17.4) and the select type statement (see Section 16.5).

As for the intrinsic type character, a length *type-param-value* may indicate a deferred type parameter. For example, in

```
type(matrix(selected_real_kind(30,999),n=:,m=:)), pointer :: mp
type(matrix(selected_real_kind(30,999),n=100,m=200)), target :: x
mp => x
```

the values for both n and m are deferred until association or allocation. After execution of the pointer assignment, the n and m type parameter values of mp are equal to those of x (100 and 200, respectively).

15.4.3   Default type parameter values

All type parameters for intrinsic types have default values. Similarly, a type parameter for a derived type may have a default value; this is declared using the same syntax as for default initialization of components, for example

```
type char_with_max_length(maxlen,kind)
   integer, len        :: maxlen = 255
   integer, kind       :: kind = kind('a')
   integer             :: len
   character(maxlen,kind) :: value
end type char_with_max_length
```

When declaring objects of type char_with_max_length, it is not necessary to specify the kind or maxlen parameters if the default values are acceptable. This also illustrates that, in many simple cases that have only one kind type parameter, the natural name for the type parameter may be kind (just as it is for the intrinsic types). That name was chosen in this particular example because char_with_max_length was meant to be as similar to the intrinsic type character as possible. Note that this choice does not conflict with the attribute keyword (kind), nor does it conflict with the use of the intrinsic function kind within the type definition.

15.4.4 Derived type parameter enquiry

As with intrinsic types, the value of a type parameter of a variable can be discovered by a type parameter enquiry. For example, in

```
type(char_with_max_length(...,...)) :: x, y(100)
:
print *,x%kind
print *,y%maxlen
```

the values of the `kind` type parameter of `x` and the `maxlen` type parameter of `y` will be printed.

Because component syntax is used to access the value of a type parameter, it is not allowed to have a component whose name is the same as one of the parameters of the type.

15.5 Abstract interfaces

In Fortran 95, to declare a dummy or an external procedure with an explicit interface one needs to use an interface block. This is fine for a single procedure, but is somewhat verbose for declaring several procedures that have the same interface (apart from the procedure names). Furthermore, in Fortran 2003, there are several situations where this becomes either excessively verbose (declaring several procedure pointers with the same interface) or impossible (procedure pointer components or abstract type-bound procedures).

For these reasons the *abstract interface* is introduced in Fortran 2003. An abstract interface gives a name to a set of characteristics and argument keyword names which would constitute an explicit interface to a procedure, without declaring any actual procedure to have those characteristics. This abstract interface name may be used in the `procedure` statement to declare procedures which might be external procedures, dummy procedures, procedure pointers, or deferred type-bound procedures.

An abstract interface block contains the `abstract` keyword, and each procedure body declared therein defines a new abstract interface. For example, given the abstract interface block

```
abstract interface
   subroutine boring_sub_with_no_args
   end subroutine boring_sub_with_no_args
   real function r2_to_r(a,b)
      real, intent(in) :: a, b
   end function r2_to_r
end interface
```

the declaration statements

```
procedure(boring_sub_with_no_args) :: sub1, sub2
procedure(r2_to_r) :: modulus, xyz
```

declare `sub1` and `sub2` to be subroutines with no actual arguments, and `modulus` and `xyz` to be `real` functions of two `real` arguments. The names `boring_sub_with_no_args` and r2_to_r are local to the scoping unit in which the abstract interface block is declared, and do not represent procedures or other global entities in their own right.

The procedure statement need not be used with abstract interfaces; if fun is any procedure that has an explicit interface,

```
procedure(fun) :: fun2
```

declares fun2 to be a procedure with an identical interface to that of fun. However, if fun is an intrinsic procedure name, it may only be used in this way if it is one of those which may be passed as an actual argument (see Table 20.2).

In addition, the procedure statement can be used to declare procedures that have implicit interfaces; instead of putting the name of a procedure inside the parentheses, either nothing or a type specification is used. For example,

```
procedure() x
procedure(real) y
```

declares x to be a procedure (which might be a subroutine or a function), and y to be a real function. This is exactly equivalent to

```
external :: x
real, external :: y
```

For these cases the procedure statement offers no useful functionality over the external or type declaration statement; it really only comes into its own when declaring procedure pointers (see next section).

The full syntax of the procedure statement is

```
procedure ( [ proc-interface ] ) [[, proc-attr-spec] ... ::] proc-decl-list
```

where a *proc-attr-spec* is one of

```
public
private
bind ( c [, name=character-string] )
intent ( inout )
optional
pointer
save
```

and a *proc-decl* is

```
procedure-name [ => null-init ]
```

where *null-init* is a reference to the intrinsic function null with no arguments. (The bind attribute for procedures is described in Section 14.7.)

Each *proc-attr-spec* gives all the procedures declared in that statement the corresponding attribute. The initialization (to being a null pointer) may only appear if a procedure is a pointer.

15.6 Procedure pointers

A procedure pointer is a pointer that, instead of being associated with a data object, is associated with a procedure. It may have an explicit or implicit interface and its association with a target is as for a dummy procedure, so its interface is not permitted to be generic or elemental.

15.6.1 Procedure pointer variables

A procedure pointer is declared by specifying that it is both a procedure and has the `pointer` attribute. For example,

```
pointer :: sp
interface
    subroutine sp(a,b)
        real,intent(inout) :: a
        real,intent(in) :: b
    end subroutine sp
end interface
real, external, pointer :: fp
```

declares sp to be a pointer to a subroutine with the specified explicit interface and declares fp to be a pointer to a scalar `real` function with an implicit interface. More usually, a procedure pointer is declared with the `procedure` statement specifying the `pointer` attribute:

```
procedure(sp), pointer :: p1 ! Pointer with the interface of sp
procedure(), pointer :: p2 ! Pointer with an implicit interface
```

If a procedure pointer is currently associated (is neither disassociated nor undefined), its target may be invoked by referencing the pointer. For example,

```
fp => cos
sp => sub
print *,fp(x) ! prints cos(x)
call sp(a,b)  ! calls sub
```

15.6.2 Procedure pointer components

A component of a derived type is permitted to be a procedure pointer. It must be declared using the `procedure` statement. For example, to define a type for representing a list of procedures (each with the same interface) to be called at some time, a procedure pointer component can be used, see Figure 15.2.

Figure 15.2

```
type process_list
    procedure(process_interface), pointer :: process
    type(process_list), pointer           :: next => null()
end type process_list
abstract interface
    subroutine process_interface( ... )
        :
    end subroutine process_interface
end interface
```

A procedure pointer component may be pointer-assigned to a procedure pointer, passed as an actual argument, or invoked directly. For example,

```
type(process_list) :: x, y(10)
procedure(process_interface), pointer :: p
:
p => x%process
call another_subroutine(x%process)
call y(i)%process(...)
```

Note that just as with data pointer components, the object to the left of the procedure pointer component name must be scalar (because there are no arrays of pointers in Fortran).

When a procedure is called through a pointer component of an object, there is often a need to access the object itself; this is the topic of Section 15.6.3.

15.6.3 The pass attribute

When a procedure pointer component (or a type-bound procedure, Section 16.6) is invoked, the object through which it is invoked is normally passed to the procedure as its first actual argument and the items in the parenthesized list are the other actual arguments. This could be undesirable; for instance, it might be wished to pass the object to a dummy argument other than the first, or not to pass it at all.

To pass the invoking object to a different dummy argument, the pass attribute is used. An example is shown in Figure 15.3. The dummy argument to which the object is to be passed is known as the *passed-object dummy argument*.

Note that the pass attribute applies to the procedure pointer component (or type-bound procedure), and not to the procedure with which it is associated. For example, the procedure pointer might be associated from time to time with components of two different types; the object might be passed as the first argument in the first case and as the second argument in the second case. However, if the associated procedure is invoked through some other means, there is no passed-object dummy argument, so an explicit actual argument must be provided in the reference (as in 'call my_obp_sub(32,a)' in Figure 15.3).

Figure 15.3

```
type t
   procedure(obp), pointer, pass(x) :: p
end type
abstract interface
   subroutine obp(w,x)
      import  :: t
      integer :: w
      type(t) :: x
   end subroutine
end interface
:
type(t) a
a%p => my_obp_sub
:
call a%p(32)    ! equivalent to 'call my_obp_sub(32,a)'
```

Figure 15.4

```
module utility_module
   private
   type, public :: utility_access_type
   contains
      procedure, nopass :: startup
      procedure, nopass :: shutdown
   end type
contains
   subroutine startup
      print *,'Process started'
   end subroutine
   subroutine shutdown
      stop 'Process stopped'
   end subroutine
end module
:
use utility_module
type(utility_access_type) :: process_control
call process_control%startup
```

The pass attribute may also be used to confirm the default (of passing the invoking object to the first dummy argument), by using the name of the first dummy argument.

If it is not desired to pass the invoking object to the procedure at all, the nopass attribute is used. An example for type-bound procedures is shown in Figure 15.4.

15.7 Exercises

1. Write an input procedure that reads a variable number of characters from a file, stopping on encountering a character in a user-specified set or at end of record, returning the input in a deferred-length allocatable character string.

2. Write a replacement for the intrinsic type complex, which is opaque (has private components), uses polar representation internally, and has a single kind parameter that has the same default as the intrinsic type.

3. Write replacements for the character concatenation operator (//) and the intrinsic function index which work on type char_with_max_length (defined in Section 15.4.4).

4. Write an event queue (data structure) and event dispatcher (procedure) using procedure pointer components. Each event should have a time and an action (procedure to be invoked); the action procedures should take the time as an argument. There should be a schedule procedure which, given a time and a procedure, queues an event for that time. If the time has already passed, the procedure should still be enqueued for immediate activation. The dispatcher procedure itself should, on invocation, process each event in the queue in time order (including extra events scheduled during this process) until the queue is empty.

16. Object-oriented programming

16.1 Introduction

The object-oriented approach to programming and design is characterized by its focus on the data structures of a program rather than the procedures. Often, invoking a procedure with a data object as its principal argument is thought of as 'sending a message' to the object. Typically, special language support is available for collecting these procedures (sometimes known as 'methods') together with the definition of the type of the object.

This approach is supported in Fortran 2003 by type extension, polymorphic variables, and type-bound procedures.

16.2 Type extension

Type extension creates new derived types by extending pre-existing derived types. To create a new type extending an old one, the `extends` attribute is used on the type definition statement. For example, given an old type such as

```
type person
   character(len=10)  :: name
   real               :: age
   integer            :: id
end type person
```

this can be extended to form a new type with

```
type, extends(person) :: employee
   integer :: national_insurance_number
   real    :: salary
end type employee
```

The new type inherits all of the components of the old type and may have additional components. So an `employee` variable has the inherited components of `name`, `age`, and `id`, and the additional components of `number` and `salary`.

Additionally, an extended type has a *parent component*; this is a component that has the type and type parameters of the old type and its name is that of the old type. It allows the inherited portion to be referenced as a whole. Thus, an `employee` variable has a component called `person` of type `person`, associated with the inherited components. For example, given

```
type(employee) :: director
```

the component director%name is the same as director%person%name, and so on. The parent component is particularly useful when invoking procedures that operate on the parent type but which were not written with type extension in mind. For example, the procedure

```
subroutine display_older_people(parray, min_age)
   type(person), intent(in) :: parray(:)
   integer, intent(in)      :: min_age
   intrinsic                :: size
   do i=1, size(parray)
      if (parray(i)%age >= min_age) print *, parray(i)%name
   end do
end subroutine display_older_people
```

may be used with an array of type(employee) by passing it the parent component of the array, for example

```
type(employee) :: staff_list(:)
   :
   !
   ! Show the employees eligible for early retirement
   !
   call display_older_people(staff_list%person, 55)
```

The parent component is itself inherited if the type is further extended (becoming a 'grandparent component'); for example, with

```
type, extends(employee) :: salesman
   real :: commission_rate
end type salesman
type(salesman) :: traveller
```

the traveller has both the employee and person components, and traveller%person is exactly the same as traveller%employee%person.

A type can be extended without adding components, for example

```
type, extends(employee) :: clerical_staff_member
end type clerical_staff_member
```

Although a clerical_staff_member has the same ultimate components as an employee, it is nonetheless considered to be a different type.

Extending a type without adding components can be useful in several situations, in particular:

- to create a new type with extra operations (as type-bound procedures), when it is impossible or inappropriate to change the old type;

- for classification, that is, when the only extra information about the new type is the fact that it is of that type (for example, as in the clerical_staff_member type above).

Any derived type can be extended provided it does not have the sequence attribute (see Section 20.2.1) or the bind attribute (see Section 14.4).

16.2.1   Type extension and type parameters

When a type is extended, the new type inherits all of the type parameters. New type parameters may also be added, for example:

```
type matrix(real_kind,n,m)
   integer, kind   :: real_kind
   integer, len    :: n,m
   real(real_kind) :: value(n,m)
end type matrix

type,extends(matrix) :: labelled_matrix(max_label_length)
   integer, len                 :: max_label_length
   character(max_label_length) :: label = ''
end type labelled_matrix

type(labelled_matrix(kind(0.0),10,20,200)) :: x
```

The variable x has four type parameters: real_kind, n, m, and max_label_length.

16.3   Polymorphic entities

A polymorphic variable is a variable whose data type may vary at run time. It must be a pointer or allocatable variable, or a dummy data object, and is declared using the class keyword in place of the type keyword. For example,

```
type point
   real :: x, y
end type point
class(point), pointer :: p
```

declares a pointer p that may point to any object whose type is in the class of types consisting of type(point) and all of its extensions.

We say that the polymorphic object is *type-compatible* with such objects. A polymorphic pointer may only be pointer-associated with a type-compatible target, a polymorphic allocatable variable may only be allocated to have a type-compatible allocation (see Section 17.4), and a polymorphic dummy argument may only be argument-associated with a type-compatible actual argument. Furthermore, if a polymorphic dummy argument is allocatable or a pointer, the actual argument must be of the same declared type; this is to ensure that the type-compatibility relationship is enforced.

The type named in the class attribute must be an extensible derived type — it cannot be a sequence derived type, a bind derived type, or an intrinsic type. This type is called the *declared type* of the polymorphic entity, and the type of the object to which it refers is called the *dynamic type*.

However, even when a polymorphic entity is referring to an object of a more extended type, it only provides direct access (that is, via component notation) to components, type parameters, and bindings that appear in the declared type. This is because the compiler only knows about the declared type of the object, it cannot know about the dynamic type (which may vary at run time). Access to components, etc. that are in the dynamic type but not the declared type is provided by the select type construct (see Section 16.5).

A polymorphic dummy argument that is neither allocatable nor a pointer assumes its dynamic type from the actual argument. This provides a convenient means of writing a function that applies to any extension of a type, for example

```
real function distance(a,b)
  class(point) :: a, b
  distance = sqrt((a%x-b%x)**2 + (a%y-b%y)**2)
end function distance
```

This function will work unchanged, for example, not only on a scalar of type point but also on a scalar of type

```
type, extends(point) :: data_point
  real, allocatable :: data_value(:)
end type data_point
```

16.3.1 Unlimited polymorphic entities

Sometimes one wishes to have a pointer that may refer not just to objects in a class of extended types, but to objects of any type, perhaps even including non-extensible or intrinsic types. For example, one might wish to have a 'universal' list of variables (pointer targets), each of which might be of any type.

This can be done with an *unlimited polymorphic* pointer. These are declared using * as the class specifier, for example

```
class(*), pointer :: up
```

declares up to be an unlimited polymorphic pointer. This could be associated with a real target, for instance:

```
real, target :: x
:
up => x
```

An unlimited polymorphic object cannot be referenced in any normal way; it can only be used as an actual argument, as the pointer or target in pointer assignment, or as the selector in a select type statement (see Section 16.5).

Type information is maintained for an unlimited polymorphic pointer while it is associated with an intrinsic type or an extensible derived type, but not when it is associated with a non-extensible derived type. (This is because different non-extensible types are considered to be the same if they have the same structure and names.) To prevent a pointer of intrinsic or extensible type from becoming associated with an incompatible target, such a pointer is not permitted to be the left-hand side of a pointer assignment when the target is unlimited polymorphic. For example,

```
use iso_c_binding
type, bind(c) :: triplet
   real(c_double_t) :: values(3)
end type triplet
class(*), pointer       :: univp
type(triplet), pointer :: tripp
real, pointer          :: realp
:
univp => tripp                    ! Valid
univp => realp                    ! Valid
:
tripp => univp                    ! Valid
realp => univp                    ! Invalid
```

Instead of the invalid pointer assignment, a select type construct must be used to associate a pointer of intrinsic or extensible type with an unlimited polymorphic target. A longer example showing the use of unlimited polymorphic pointers, together with select type, is shown in Figure 16.2.

16.4   The associate construct

The associate construct allows one to associate a name either with a variable, or with the value of an expression, for the duration of a block. During execution of the block, the *associate-name* remains associated with the variable (or retains the value) specified, and takes its type, type parameters, and rank from its association. This construct is useful for simplifying multiple accesses to a variable which has a lengthy description (subscripts and component names). For example, given a nested set of derived-type definitions, the innermost of which is

```
type one
   real, allocatable, dimension(:) :: xvec, levels
   logical                         :: tracing
end type one
```

then the association as specified in

```
associate(point_qfstate => master_list%item(n)%qfield%posn(i,j)%state)
   point_qfstate%xvec = matmul(transpose_matrix,point_qfstate%xvec)
   point_qfstate%levels = timestep(point_qfstate%levels,input_field)
   if (point_qfstate%tracing) call show_qfstate(point_qfstate,stepno)
end associate
```

would be even harder to understand if point_qfstate were written out in full in each occurrence.

Formally, the syntax is

```
associate ( association-list )
    block
end associate
```

where each *association* is either

> *associate-name* => *variable*

or

> *associate-name* => *expr*

and the construct can be named just as can the do construct (Section 4.5).

If the association is with a variable, the *associate-name* may be used as a variable within .the block. The association is as for argument association of a dummy argument that does not have the *pointer* or *allocate* attribute but the *associate-name* has the *target* attribute if the variable does. If the association is with an expression, the *associate-name* may be used only for its value.

Multiple associations may be established within a single associate construct. For example, in

```
associate ( x => arg(i)%ground%coordinates(1), &
             y => arg(i)%ground%coordinates(2) )
    distance = sqrt((myloc%x-x)**2+(myloc%y-y)**2)
    bearing = atan2(myloc%y-y,myloc%x-x)
end associate
```

the simplifying names x and y improve the readability of the code.

Without this construct, to make this kind of code readable either a procedure would need to be used, or pointers (requiring, in addition, the target attribute on the affected variables). This could adversely affect the performance of the program (and indeed would probably still not attain the readability shown here).

The construct may be nested with other constructs in the usual way.

16.5   The select type construct

To execute alternative code depending on the dynamic type of a polymorphic entity and to gain access to the dynamic parts, the select type construct is provided. This construct has the form

```
select type ( [associate-name =>] selector)
[type-guard-stmt
    block]...
end select
```

where each type guard statement is one of

```
type is (derived-type-spec)
class is (derived-type-spec)
class default
```

and the construct can be named just as can the `if` construct (Section 4.3.2).

The selector is a variable or an expression and the *associate-name* is associated with it within the block in exactly the same way as for an associate construct (previous section). However, the body is now divided into parts, at most one of which is executed.

The block following a `type is` guard is executed if the dynamic type of the selector is exactly the derived type specified, and the kind type parameter values match.

Failing this, the block following a `class is` guard is executed if it is the only one for which the dynamic type is the derived type specified, or an extension thereof, and the kind type parameter values match. If there is more than one such guard, one of them must be of a type that is an extension of the types of all the others, and its block is executed.

Failing this, the block following a `class default` guard is executed.

In the (frequently occurring) case where the *selector* is a simple name and the same name is suitable for the *associate-name*, the '*associate-name*=>' may be omitted.

The example in Figure 16.1 shows a typical use of `select type`.

Figure 16.1

```
subroutine describe_particle(p)
   class(particle) :: p

   ! These attributes are common to all particles.
   call describe_vector('Position:',p%position)
   call describe_vector('Velocity:',p%velocity)
   print *,'Mass:',p%mass

   ! Check for other attributes.
   select type (p)
   type is (charged_particle)
      print *,'Charge:',p%charge
   class is (charged_particle)
      print *,'Charge:',p%charge
      print *,'... may have other (unknown) attributes.'
   type is (particle)
      ! Just the basic particle type, there is nothing extra.
   class default
      print *,'... may have other (unknown) attributes.'
   end select
end subroutine describe_particle
```

If the *derived-type-spec* contains a *type-param-spec-list*, values corresponding to kind type parameters must be initialization expressions and those for length type parameters must be asterisks. This is so that length type parameters do not participate in type parameter matching, but are always assumed from the *selector*.

If the selector is unlimited polymorphic, a type guard statement is permitted to specify an intrinsic type:

```
type is (intrinsic-type[(type-parameter-value-list)])
```

For example, if the unlimited polymorphic pointer up is associated with the real target x, the execution of

```
select type(up)
type is (real)
   up = 3.5
   rp => up
end select
```

assigns the value of 3.5 to x and associates the real pointer rp with x.   (The pointer assignment would not have been allowed outside of the select type construct.)

Figure 16.2 Generic vector list and type selection.

```
type generic_vector_pointer_list_elt
   class(*), pointer                :: element_vector(:) => null()
   procedure(gvp_processor), pointer :: default_processor => null()
   type(generic_vector_pointer_list_elt),pointer :: next => null()
end type generic_vector_pointer_list_elt
abstract interface
   subroutine gvp_processor(gvp)
      import :: generic_vector_pointer_list_elt
      class(generic_vector_pointer_list_elt) :: gvp
   end subroutine gvp_processor
end interface
type(generic_vector_pointer_list_elt), pointer :: p
:
do
   if (.not.associated(p)) exit
   select type(q => p%element_vector)
   type is (integer(selected_int_kind(9)))
      call special_process_i9(q)
   type is (real)
      call special_process_default_real(q)
   type is (double precision)
      call special_process_double_precision(q)
   type is (character(*))
      call special_process_character(q)
   class default
      if (associated(q%default_procesor)) call q%default_processor
   end select
   p => next(p)
end do
```

When an unlimited polymorphic pointer is allocated, the required type and type parameter values must be specified in the `allocate` statement (Section 17.4).

A longer example, showing the use of unlimited polymorphic in constructing a generic vector list package, is shown in Figure 16.2.

16.6 Type-bound procedures

Often, in object-oriented programming, one wishes to invoke a procedure to perform a task whose nature varies according to the dynamic type of a polymorphic object.

This is the purpose of *type-bound procedures*. These are procedures which are invoked through an object, and the actual procedure executed depends on the dynamic type of the object.

They are called type-bound because the selection of the procedure depends on the type of the object, in contrast to procedure pointer components which depend on the value of the object (one might call the latter object-bound).

In some other languages type-bound procedures are known as *methods*, and invocation of a method is thought of as 'sending a message' to the object.

However, type-bound procedures can be used even when there is no intention to extend the type. We will first describe how to define and use type-bound procedures in the simple case, and later explain how they are affected by type extension.

16.6.1 Specific type-bound procedures

The type-bound procedure section of a type definition is separated from the component section by the `contains` statement, analogous to the way that module variables are separated from the module procedures. The default accessibility of type-bound procedures is separate from the default accessibility for components; that is, even with `private` components, each type-bound procedure is `public` unless a `private` statement appears in the type-bound procedure section or unless it is explicitly declared to be `private`.

Each type-bound procedure declaration specifies the name of the binding, and the name of the actual procedure to which it is bound. (The latter may be omitted if it is the same as the type-bound procedure name.) For example, in Figure 16.3 objects of type `mytype` have two type-bound procedures, `write` and `reset`. These are invoked as if they were component procedure pointers of the object, and the invoking object is normally passed to the procedure as its first argument. For example, the procedure references

```
call x%write(6)
call x%reset
```

are equivalent to

```
call write_mytype(x,6)
call reset(x)
```

However, because they are public, the type-bound procedures (`write` and `reset`) can be referenced anywhere in the program that has a `type(mytype)` variable, whereas, because

Figure 16.3

```
module mytype_module
   type mytype
      private
      real :: myvalue(4) = 0.0
   contains
      procedure :: write => write_mytype
      procedure :: reset
   end type mytype
   private :: write_mytype, reset
contains
   subroutine write_mytype(this,unit)
      class(mytype)    :: this
      integer,optional :: unit
      if (present(unit)) then
         write (unit,*) this%myvalue
      else
         print *,this%myvalue
      end if
   end subroutine write_mytype
   subroutine reset(variable)
      class(mytype) :: variable
      variable%myvalue = 0.0
   end subroutine reset
end module mytype_module
```

the module procedures (write_mytype and reset) are private, they can only be directly referenced from within mytype_module.

The full syntax of the statement declaring a specific type-bound procedure is

procedure[(*interface-name*)] [[, *binding-attr-list*]::] *tbp-name* [=>*procedure-name*]

where each *binding-attr* is one of

access-spec
deferred
nopass
non_overridable
pass [(*arg-name*)]

The pass and nopass attributes are described in Section 15.6.3. The (*interface-name*) appears if and only if the deferred attribute also appears; these are described in Section 16.7.

If the non_overridable attribute appears, that type-bound procedure cannot be overridden during type extension (see Section 16.6.3).

16.6.2 Generic type-bound procedures

Type-bound procedures may be generic. A generic type-bound procedure is defined with the `generic` statement within the type-bound procedure part. This statement takes the form

```
generic [[ , access-spec ] ::] generic-spec => tbp-name-list
```

and can be used for named generics as well as for operators, assignment, and user-defined derived-type input/output specifications. Each *tbp-name* specifies an individual (specific) type-bound procedure to be included in the generic set.

For example, in Figure 16.4 the type-bound procedure `extract` is generic, being resolved to one of the specific type-bound procedures `xi` or `xc`, depending on the data type of the argument.

Figure 16.4

```
module container_module
   private
   type, public :: container
   contains
      private
      procedure :: xi => extract_integer_from_container
      procedure :: xc => extract_complex_from_container
      generic, public :: extract => xi, xc
   end type
contains
   subroutine extract_integer_from_container(this, val)
      class(container), intent(in) :: this
      integer, intent(out)         :: val
      :
   end subroutine extract_integer_from_container
   subroutine extract_complex_from_container(this, val)
      class(container), intent(in) :: this
      complex, intent(out)         :: val
      :
   end subroutine extract_complex_from_container
end module container_module
```

Thus, in

```
use container_module
type(container) v
integer ix
complex cx
:
call v%extract(ix)
call v%extract(cx)
```

one of the 'extract_*something*_from_container' procedures will be invoked.

A generic type-bound procedure need not be named; it may be an operator, assignment, or a user-defined derived-type input/output specification. In this case, the object through which the type-bound procedure is invoked is whichever of the operands corresponds to the passed-object dummy argument. For this reason, the specific type-bound procedures for an unnamed generic must not have the nopass attribute. Like other type-bound procedures, unnamed generics are accessible wherever the type or an object of the type is accessible.

This is useful for packaging-up a type and its operations, because the only clause of a use statement does not block type-bound operators, unlike operators defined by an interface block. This prevents the accidental omission of required operators by making a mistake in the use statement.

For example, Figure 16.5 shows the overloading of the operator (+) for operations on type(mycomplex); these operations are available even if the user has done 'use mycomplex_module, only: mycomplex'.

Figure 16.5 Generic type-bound operators.

```
module mycomplex_module
   type mycomplex
      private
      : ! data components not shown
   contains
      private
      procedure          :: mycomplex_plus_mycomplex
      procedure          :: mycomplex_plus_real
      procedure, pass(b) :: real_plus_mycomplex
      generic, public :: operator(+) => mycomplex_plus_mycomplex, &
                         mycomplex_plus_real, real_plus_mycomplex
      : ! many other operations and functions...
   end type
contains
   : ! procedures which implement the operations
end module
```

16.6.3   Type extension and type-bound procedures

When a type is extended, the new type usually inherits all the type-bound procedures of the old type, as is illustrated in Figure 16.6, where the new type charged_particle inherits not only the components of particle, but also its type-bound procedures momentum and energy.

Specific type-bound procedures defined by the new type are either additional bindings (with a new name), or may *override* type-bound procedures that would have been inherited from the old type. (However, overriding a type-bound procedure is not permitted if the inherited one has the non_overridable attribute.) An overriding type-bound procedure binding must have exactly the same interface as the overridden procedure except for the

Figure 16.6

```
type particle
    type(vector) :: position, velocity
    real         :: mass
contains
    procedure :: momentum => particle_momentum
    procedure :: energy => particle_energy
end type particle

type,extends(particle) :: charged_particle
    real :: charge
end type charged_particle
```

type of the passed-object dummy argument; if there is a passed-object dummy argument, the overriding procedure must specify its type to be class(*new-type*).

Generic type-bound procedures defined by the new type always extend the generic set; the complete set of generic bindings for any particular generic identifier (including both the inherited and newly defined generic bindings) must satisfy the usual rules for generic disambiguation (Section 5.18). A procedure that is part of an inherited generic set may be overridden using its specific name.

For example, in Figure 16.7 the three specific type-bound procedures have been overridden; when the generic operation of (+) is applied to entities of type instrumented_mycomplex, one of the overriding procedures will be invoked.

Figure 16.7

```
type mycomplex
    private
contains
    procedure           :: mycomplex_plus_mycomplex
    procedure           :: mycomplex_plus_real
    procedure, pass(b)  :: real_plus_mycomplex
    generic             :: operator(+) => mycomplex_plus_mycomplex, &
                           mycomplex_plus_real, real_plus_mycomplex
end type mycomplex

type, extends(mycomplex) :: instrumented_mycomplex
    integer, public :: plus_operation_count = 0
contains
    procedure :: mycomplex_plus_mycomplex => instrumented_myc_plus_myc
    procedure :: mycomplex_plus_real => instrumented_myc_plus_r
    procedure :: real_plus_mycomplex => instr_r_p_myc
end type instrumented_mycomplex
```

16.7   Deferred bindings and abstract types

Sometimes a type is defined not for the purpose of creating objects of that type, but only to serve as a base type for extension. In this situation, a type-bound procedure in the base type might not have a default or natural implementation, but rather only a well-defined purpose and interface. This is supported by the abstract keyword on the type definition and the deferred keyword in the procedure statement.

Here is a simple example:

```
type, abstract :: file_handle
contains
   procedure (open_file), deferred, pass :: open
   :
end type file_handle
abstract interface
   subroutine open_file(handle)
      import                           :: file_handle
      class(file_handle), intent(inout) :: handle
   end subroutine open_file
end interface
```

Here, the intention is that extensions of the type would have components that hold data about the file and open would be overridden by a procedure that uses these data to open it.

The procedure is known as a *deferred* type-bound procedure. An interface is required, which may be an abstract interface or that of a procedure with an explicit interface.

No ordinary variable is permitted to be of an abstract type, but a polymorphic variable may have it as its declared type. When an abstract type is extended, the new type may be a normal extended type or may itself be abstract.

Deferred bindings are allowed only in abstract types. (But an abstract type is not required to have any deferred binding.)

Figure 16.8 shows the definition of an abstract type my_numeric_type, and the creation of the normal type my_integer_type as an extension of it. Variables that are declared to be my_numeric_type must be polymorphic, and if they are pointer or allocatable the allocate statement must specify a normal type to allocate them to.

The use of the abstract and deferred attributes ensures that objects of insufficient type cannot be created, and that when extending the abstract type to create a normal type, the programmer can expect a warning from the compiler if he or she has forgotten to override any inherited deferred type-bound procedures.

16.8   Finalization

When variables are deallocated or otherwise cease to exist, it is sometimes desirable to execute some procedure which 'cleans up' after the variable, perhaps releasing some resource (such as closing a file or deallocating a pointer component). This process is known as *finalization* and is provided by 'final subroutines'. Finalization is only available for derived types that do not have the sequence or bind attributes (see Sections 20.2.1 and 14.4).

Figure 16.8 Abstract numeric type.

```
type, abstract :: my_numeric_type
contains
   private
   procedure(op2), deferred :: add
   procedure(op2), deferred :: subtract
   : ! procedures for other operations not shown
   generic, public :: operator(+) => add, ...
   generic, public :: operator(-) => subtract, ...
   : ! generic specs for other operations not shown
end type my_numeric_type
abstract interface
   function op2(a,b) result(r)
      import :: my_numeric_type
      class(my_numeric_type), intent(in) :: a, b
      class(my_numeric_type), allocatable :: r
   end function op2
end interface
:
type, extends(my_numeric_type) :: my_integer
   integer, private :: value
contains
   procedure :: add => add_my_integer
   procedure :: subtract => subtract_my_integer
   :
end type my_integer
```

The set of final subroutines for a derived type is specified in the type-bound procedure section; however, unlike normal type-bound procedures, they are not normally invoked by the user but execute automatically when an object of that type ceases to exist.

A final subroutine for a type must be a module procedure with a single dummy argument of that type. All the final subroutines for that type form a generic set and must satisfy the rules for unambiguous generic references; since they each have exactly one dummy argument of the same type, this simply means that the dummy arguments must have different kind type parameter values or rank. These dummy arguments cannot be pointers or allocatable, and all length type parameters must be assumed (the value must be '*').

A nonpointer object is finalizable if its type has a final subroutine whose dummy argument matches the object. When a finalizable object is about to cease to exist (for example, by being deallocated or from execution of a `return` statement), the final subroutine is invoked with the object as its actual argument. This also occurs when the object is passed to an intent out dummy argument, or is the variable on the left-hand side of an intrinsic assignment statement. In the latter case, the final subroutine is invoked after the expression on the right-hand side has been evaluated, but before it is assigned to the variable.

An example is shown in Figure 16.9. When subroutine s returns, the subroutine `close_scalar_file_handle` will be invoked with x as its actual argument, and `close_rank1_file_handle` will be invoked with y as its actual argument. The order in which these will be invoked is processor dependent.

Figure 16.9

```
module file_handle_module
   type file_handle
      private
      :
   contains
      final :: close_scalar_file_handle, close_rank1_file_handle
   end type file_handle
contains
   subroutine close_scalar_file_handle(h)
      type(file_handle) :: h
      :
   end subroutine close_scalar_file_handle
   :
end module file_handle_module
:
subroutine s(n)
   type(file_handle) :: x, y(n)
   :
end subroutine s
```

Termination of a program by an error condition, by execution of a `stop` statement or the end statement in the main program, does not invoke any final subroutines.

If an object contains any (non-pointer) finalizable components, the object as a whole will be finalized before the individual components. That is, in Figure 16.10, when ovalue is finalized, `destroy_outer_ftype` will be invoked with ovalue as its argument before `destroy_inner_ftype` is invoked with ovalue%ivalue as its argument.

16.8.1 Type extension and final subroutines

When a type is extended, the new type does not inherit any of the final subroutines of the old type. The new type is, however, still finalizable, and when it is finalized any applicable final subroutines of the old type are invoked on the parent component.

If the new type defines any final subroutine, it will be invoked before any final subroutines of the old type are invoked. (Which is to say, the object as a whole is finalized, then its parent component is finalized, etc.) This operates recursively, so that when x is deallocated in the code of Figure 16.11, `destroy_bottom_type` will be invoked with x as its argument, then `destroy_top_type` will be invoked with x%top_type as its argument.

Figure 16.10

```
type inner_ftype
   :
contains
   final :: destroy_inner_ftype
end type inner_ftype
type outer_ftype
   type(inner_ftype) :: ivalue
contains
   final :: destroy_outer_ftype
end type outer_ftype
   :
type(outer_ftype) :: ovalue
```

Figure 16.11

```
type top_type
   :
contains
   final :: destroy_top_type
end type
type, extends(top_type) :: middle_type
   :
end type
type, extends(middle_type) :: bottom_type
   :
contains
   final :: destroy_bottom_type
end type
   :
type(bottom_type), pointer :: x
allocate(x)
   :
deallocate(x)
```

16.9   Procedure encapsulation example

This example is intended to show how type extension and type-bound procedures can be used to encapsulate a procedure with user-defined data in a convenient way. The problem chosen is multi-dimensional quadrature of a user-defined function.

Figure 16.12

```
module quadrature_module
  ! Working precision
  integer, parameter :: wp = selected_real_kind(15)

  type, abstract :: bound_user_function
    ! No data components
  contains
    procedure(user_function_interface), deferred :: eval
  end type bound_user_function

  abstract interface
    real(wp) function user_function_interface(data, coords)
      import                     :: wp, bound_user_function
      class(bound_user_function) :: data
      real(wp), intent(in)       :: coords(:)
    end function user_function_interface
  end interface
  :
contains
  real(wp) function ndim_integral(hyper_rect, userfun, options, &
                                  status)
    real(wp), intent(in)                :: hyper_rect(:)
    class(bound_user_function)          :: userfun
    type(quadrature_options), intent(in) :: options
    type(quadrature_status), intent(out) :: status
    :
    ! This is how the user function is invoked
    single_value = userfun%eval(coordinates)
    :
  end function ndim_integral
  :
end module
```

When solving problems of this kind, involving user-defined functions, it is often desirable for the functions to be determined partly by some data. One difficulty that arises is that a general quadrature routine cannot know in advance what kind of data the user-defined function needs in order to produce its results.

Previously available solutions have been:

i) for the quadrature routine to accept an extra argument, typically a `real` vector, and pass that to the user-defined function when it is called;

ii) for the program to pass the information to the function via `module` variables or common blocks; or

iii) the use of 'reverse communication' techniques, where the program repeatedly calls the quadrature routine giving it extra information each time, until the quadrature routine is satisfied.

These all have disadvantages; the first is not very flexible (a `real` vector might be a poor way of representing the data), the second requires global data (recognized as being poor practice) and is not thread-safe, while the third is flexible and thread-safe but very complicated to use, particularly for the writer of the quadrature routine.

With type extension, the user can package up a procedure with any kind of required data, and the quadrature routine will pass it through. Figure 16.12 shows the definition of the types concerned and an outline of the quadrature routine. Details not relevant to the function evaluation (such as the definition of the types for passing options to the routine, and for receiving the status of the integration) have been omitted.

Figure 16.13

```
module polynomial_integration
   use quadrature_module

   type, extends(bound_user_function) :: my_bound_polynomial
      integer                :: degree, dimensionality
      real(wp),allocatable :: coeffs(:,:)
   contains
      procedure :: eval => polynomial_evaluation
   end type
contains
   real(wp) function polynomial_evaluation(data, coords) result(r)
      class(my_bound_polynomial) :: data
      real(wp), intent(in)       :: coords(:)
      integer                    :: i, j
      r = 0
      do i=1, data%dimensionality
         r = r + sum([ (data%coeffs(i,j)*coords(i)**j, &
                                       j=1,data%degree) ])
      end do
   end function polynomial_evaluation
end module polynomial_integration
```

To use `ndim_integral`, the user needs to extend the abstract type to include any necessary data components and to bind his or her function to the type. Figure 16.13 shows how the user could do this for an arbitrary polynomial function.

To actually perform an integration, the user merely needs a local variable of this type to be loaded with the required data, and calls the quadrature routine as shown in Figure 16.14.

Figure 16.14

```
use polynomial_integration
type(my_bound_polynomial)  :: poly
real(wp)                   :: integral
real(wp), allocatable      :: hyper_rectangle(:)
type(quadrature_options)   :: options
type(quadrature_status)    :: status

! Read the data into the local variable
read (...) poly%degree, poly%dimensionality
allocate(poly%coeffs(poly%dimensionality,poly%degree))
read (...) poly%coeffs

! Read the hyper-rectangle information
allocate(hyper_rectangle(poly%dimensionality))
read (...) hyper_rectangle
: ! Option-setting omitted
! Evaluate the integral
integral = ndim_integral(hyper_rectangle, poly, options, status)
```

16.10   Type inquiry functions

Two new intrinsic functions have been added which compare dynamic types. These are intended for use on polymorphic variables but may also be used on non-polymorphic variables.

extends_type_of(a, mold) returns, as a scalar default logical, whether the dynamic type of a is an extension of the dynamic type of mold. Both a and mold must be of extensible type. If mold is unlimited polymorphic and either a disassociated pointer or an unallocated allocatable variable, the result is true.

same_type_as(a, b) returns, as a scalar default logical, whether the dynamic type of a is the same as the dynamic type of b. Both a and b must be of extensible type.

These two functions are not terribly useful, because knowing the dynamic type of a (or how it relates to the dynamic type of b or mold) does not in itself allow access to the extended components. Therefore, we recommend that `select type` be used for testing the dynamic types of polymorphic entities.

16.11   Exercises

1. Define a polygon type where each point is defined by a component of class `point` (defined in Section 16.3). A function to test whether a position is within the polygon would be useful. A typical extension of such a type could have a label and some associated data; define such an extension.

2. Define a data logging type. This should contain type-bound procedures to initialize logging to a particular file, and to write a log entry. The file should automatically be closed if the object ceases to exist.

17. Establishing and moving data

17.1 Introduction

Many relatively minor improvements have been made for manipulating data objects.

17.2 Mixed component accessibility

It is now possible for some components of a type to be `private` while others remain `public`. The `private` statement in a type, which previously set all components to be private, now merely sets the default accessibility of components to be private. The default accessibility for each component may be overridden or confirmed in the component definition statement, by specifying the `public` or `private` attributes. For example, in

```
module mytype_module
   type mytype
      private
      character(20), public :: debug_tag = ''
      : ! private components omitted
   end type mytype
   :
end module mytype_module
```

although some of the components of `mytype` are private, the `debug_tag` field is public, exposing itself to the user of the module `mytype_module`.

If any component of a derived type is private, the structure constructor can be used outside the module in which it is defined only if the value for that component is omitted.

17.3 Structure constructors

In Fortran 95, structure constructors look like function calls, except that keyword arguments are not allowed. In Fortran 2003, structure constructors can have keyword arguments and optional arguments; moreover, a generic procedure name can be the same as the structure constructor name (which is the same as the type name), with any specific procedures in the generic set taking precedence over the structure constructor if there is any ambiguity. This can be used effectively to produce extra 'constructors' for the type, as shown in Figure 17.1.

Figure 17.1

```
module mycomplex_module
   type mycomplex
      real :: argument, modulus
   end type
   interface mycomplex
      module procedure complex_to_mycomplex, two_reals_to_mycomplex
   end interface
   :
contains
   type(mycomplex) function complex_to_mycomplex(c)
      complex, intent(in) :: c
      :
   end function complex_to_mycomplex
   type(mycomplex) function two_reals_to_mycomplex(x,y)
      real, intent(in)           :: x
      real, intent(in), optional :: y
      :
   end function two_reals_to_mycomplex
   :
end module mycomplex_module
:
use mycomplex_module
type(mycomplex) :: a, b, c
:
a = mycomplex(argument=5.6, modulus=1.0) ! The structure constructor
c = mycomplex(x=0.0, y=1.0)              ! A function reference
```

If a component of a type has default initialization, its value may be omitted in the structure constructor as if it were an optional argument. For example, in

```
type real_list_element
   real                            :: value
   type(real_list_element), pointer :: next => null()
end type real_list_element
:
type(real_list_element) :: x = real_list_element(3.5)
```

the omitted value for the next component means that it takes on its default initialization value — that is, a null pointer.

If the derived type has type parameters, these are specified in parentheses immediately after the type name in its structure constructor. Again, if the type parameters have default values, they may be omitted, as in the example in Figure 17.2.

Figure 17.2

```
type character_with_max_length(maxlen, kind)
    integer, len    :: maxlen
    integer, kind   :: kind = kind('a')
    integer         :: length = 0
    character(kind) :: value(maxlen)
end type character_with_max_length
:
type(character_with_max_length(100)) :: name
:
name = character_with_max_length(100)('John Hancock')
```

17.4   The allocate statement

As well as determining array size, the `allocate` statement can now determine type parameter values, type, and value. This is controlled either by the inclusion of a type specification in the `allocate` statement, or by use of the `source=` clause. The syntax of the `allocate` is thus extended to be:

allocate([*type-spec* ::] *allocation-list* [,source=*source-expr*][,stat=*stat*])

where *type-spec* is the type name followed by the type parameter values in parentheses, if any, for both intrinsic and derived types; and the *source-expr* is any expression that is type-compatible (see Section 16.3) with the allocation.

An `allocate` statement with a *type-spec* is *typed allocation*, and an `allocate` statement with a `source=` clause is *sourced allocation*. Only one of these clauses is allowed, so an `allocate` statement cannot both be a typed allocation and a sourced allocation. We now explain the new features.

17.4.1   Typed allocation and deferred type parameters

A length type parameter that is deferred (indicated by a colon in the *type-spec*) has no defined value until it is given one by an `allocate` statement or by pointer assignment (a type parameter that is not deferred cannot be altered by `allocate` or pointer assignment). For example, in

```
character(:), allocatable :: x(:)
:
allocate(character(n) :: x(m))
```

the array x will have m elements and each element will have character length n after execution of the `allocate` statement.

If a length parameter of an item being allocated is assumed, it must be specified as an asterisk in the *type-spec*. For example, the type parameter `string_dim` in Figure 17.3 must be specified as * because it is assumed.

Figure 17.3

```
type string_vector(string_dim,space_dim)
   integer, len              :: string_dim, space_dim
   type(string(string_dim)) :: value(space_dim)
end type string_vector
:
subroutine allocate_string_vectors(vp,n,m)
   type(string_vector(*,:)), pointer :: vp(:)
   integer, intent(in)               :: n, m
   allocate(string_vector(string_dim=*, space_dim=n) :: vp(m))
end subroutine allocate_string_vectors
```

Note that there is only one *type-spec* in an allocate statement, so it must be suitable for all the items being allocated. In particular, if any one of them is a dummy argument with an assumed type parameter, they must all be dummy arguments that assume this type parameter.

If any type parameter is neither assumed nor deferred, the value specified for it by the *type-spec* must be the same as its current value. For example, in

```
subroutine allocate_string3_vectors(vp,n,m)
   type(string_vector(3,:)), pointer :: vp(:)
   integer, intent(in)               :: n, m
   allocate(string_vector(string_dim=3, space_dim=n) :: vp(m))
end subroutine allocate_string3_vectors
```

the expression provided for the string_dim type parameter must be equal to 3.

17.4.2 Polymorphic variables and typed allocation

For polymorphic variables, the *type-spec* specifies not only the values of any deferred type parameters, but also the dynamic type to allocate. If an item is unlimited polymorphic, it can be allocated to be any type (including intrinsic types); otherwise the type specified in the allocate statement must be an extension of the declared type of the item.

For example,

```
class(*), pointer :: ux, uy(:)
class(t), pointer :: x, y(:)
:
allocate(t2 :: ux, x, y(10))
allocate(real :: uy(100))
```

allocates ux, x, and y to be of type t2 (an extension of t), and uy to be of type default real.

17.4.3 Sourced allocation

Instead of allocating a variable with an explicitly specified type (and type parameters), it is possible to take the type, type parameters, and value from another variable or expression. This effectively produces a 'clone' of the source expression, and is done by using the source= clause in the `allocate` statement. For example, in

```
subroutine s(b)
  class(t), allocatable :: a
  class(t)              :: b
  allocate(a, source=b)
```

the variable a is allocated with the same dynamic type and type parameters as b, and will have the same value.

This is useful for copying heterogeneous data structures such as lists and trees, as in the example in Figure 17.4.

Figure 17.4

```
type singly_linked_list
  class(singly_linked_list), pointer :: next => null()
  ! No data - the user of the type should extend it to include
  ! desired data.
end type singly_linked_list
:
recursive function sll_copy(source) result(copy)
  class(singly_linked_list), pointer     :: copy
  class(singly_linked_list), intent(in) :: source
  allocate(copy, source=source)
  if (associated(source%next)) copy%next => sll_copy(source%next)
end function sll_copy
```

If source= appears, only one item is allowed in the `allocate` statement. If the allocated item is an array, its bounds and shape are specified in the usual way and are not taken from the source. This allows the source to be a scalar whose value is given to every element of the array. Alternatively, it may be an array of the same shape.

Because the bounds and shape of the allocated item are not taken from the source, making a clone of an array has to be done as follows:

```
class(t), allocatable :: a(:), b(:)
:
allocate(a(lbound(b,1):ubound(b,1)), source=b)
```

17.5 Allocatable entities

There are several extensions to the `allocatable` attribute in Fortran 2003, beyond those described in the Technical Report (Chapter 12). We will now describe each of these in turn.

17.5.1 Allocatable scalars

The `allocatable` attribute (and hence the `allocated` function) may now also be applied to scalar variables and components. This is particularly useful when combined with deferred type parameters, for example, in

```
character(:), allocatable :: chdata
integer                   :: unit, reclen
:
read(unit) reclen
allocate(character(reclen) :: chdata)
read(unit) chdata
```

where `reclen` allows the length of `character` to be specified at run time.

Allocatable scalar components can also be used to construct data structures which do not leak memory (because they get deallocated automatically).

17.5.2 Assignment to an allocatable array

In Fortran 95, before assigning an array value to an allocatable array, the allocatable variable must be allocated with the same shape as the value. This was considered to be too onerous a requirement for variables containing allocatable components, as this would need to be coded separately for each allocatable component. Thus the standardized allocatable component extension to Fortran 95 (see Chapter 12) instead specified that any allocatable components were automatically (re)allocated to be the right shape if they were not already of that shape.

In Fortran 2003, for consistency with allocatable components, this automatic reallocation is extended to ordinary allocatable variables as well. This simplifies the use of array functions which return a variable-sized result (such as the intrinsic functions `pack` and `unpack`).

For example, in

```
subroutine process(x)
    real(wp), intent(inout) :: x
    real(wp), allocatable   :: nonzero_values(:)
    nonzero_values = pack(x,x/=0)
```

the variable `nonzero_values` is automatically allocated to be of the correct length to contain the results of the `pack` function, instead of the user having to allocate it manually (which would necessitate counting the number of nonzeros separately). It also permits a simple extension of an existing allocatable array whose lower bounds are all 1. To add some extra values to such an integer array a of rank 1, it sufficient to write, for example,

```
a = (/ a, 5, 6 /)
```

This automatic reallocation also occurs if the allocatable variable has a deferred type parameter which does not already have the same value as the corresponding parameter of the expression. This applies to allocatable scalars as well as to allocatable arrays, as in

```
character(:), allocatable :: quotation
:
quotation = 'Now is the winter of our discontent.'
:
quotation = "This ain't the summer of love."
```

In each of the assignments to quotation, it is reallocated to be the right length (unless it is already of that length) to hold the desired quotation. If instead the normal truncation or padding is required in an assignment to an allocatable-length character, substring notation can be used to suppress the automatic reallocation. For example,

```
quotation(:) = ''
```

leaves quotation at its current length, setting all of it to blanks.

17.5.3 Transferring an allocation

The intrinsic subroutine move_alloc has been introduced to move an allocation from one allocatable object to another.

call move_alloc (from, to) where:

> **from** is allocatable and of any type. It has intent inout.
>
> **to** is allocatable and of the same type and rank as from. It has intent out.
>
> After the call, the allocation status and target (if any) of to is that of from beforehand and from becomes deallocated.

It provides what is essentially the allocatable array equivalent of pointer assignment: allocation transfer. However, unlike pointer assignment, the allocatable array semantics of having a one-to-one mapping between the variable and the allocation are maintained; therefore the original variable becomes unallocated. For example,

```
real, allocatable :: a1(:), a2(:)
allocate(a1(0:10))
a1(3) = 37
call move_alloc(from=a1, to=a2)
! a1 is now unallocated,
! a2 is allocated with bounds (0:10) and a2(3)==37.
```

This can be used to minimize the amount of copying required when one wishes to expand or contract an allocatable array; the canonical sequence for this is:

```
real, allocatable :: a(:,:), temp(:,:)
:
! Increase size of a to (n,m)
allocate(temp(n,m))
temp(1:size(a,1),1:size(a,2)) = a
call move_alloc(temp,a)
! a is now (n,m), and temp is unallocated
```

This sequence only requires one copying operation instead of the two that would have been required without move_alloc. Because the copy is controlled by the user, pre-existing values will end up where the user wants them (which might be at the same subscripts, or all at the beginning, or all at the end, etc.).

17.6   Pointer assignment

Two improvements have been made to the array pointer assignment statement. The first is that it is now possible to set the desired lower bounds to any value. This can be desirable in situations like the following. Consider

```
real, target   :: annual_rainfall(1700:2003)
real, pointer :: rp1(:), rp2(:)
:
rp1 => annual_rainfall
rp2 => annual_rainfall(1800:1856)
```

The bounds of rp1 will be (1700:2003), however those of rp2 will be (1:57). To be able to have a pointer to a subsection of an array have the appropriate bounds, they may be set on the pointer assignment as follows:

```
rp2(1800:) => annual_rainfall(1800:1856)
```

This statement will set the bounds of rp2 to (1800:1856).

The second new facility for array pointer assignment is that the target of a multi-dimensional array pointer may be one-dimensional. The syntax is similar to that of the lower-bounds specification above, except that in this case one specifies each upper bound as well as the lower bound. This can be used, for example, to provide a pointer to the diagonal of an array:

```
real, pointer :: base_array(:), matrix(:,:), diagonal(:)
allocate(base_array(n*n))
matrix(1:n,1:n) => base_array
diagonal => base_array(::n+1)
```

After execution of the pointer assignments, diagonal is now a pointer to the diagonal elements of matrix.

17.7   More control of access from a module

It is sometimes desirable to allow the user of a module to be able to reference the value of a module variable without allowing it to be changed. Such control is provided by the protected attribute. This attribute does not affect the visibility of the variable, which must still be public to be visible, but confers the same protection against modification that intent(in) does for dummy arguments.

The protected attribute may be specified with the protected keyword in a type declaration statement. For example, in

```
module m
  public
  real, protected    :: v
  integer, protected :: i
```

both v and i have the `protected` attribute. The attribute may also be specified separately, in a `protected` statement, just as for other attributes (see Section 7.7).

Variables with this attribute may only be modified within the defining module. Outside the module they are not allowed to appear in a context in which they would be altered, such as on the left-hand side of an assignment statement.

For example, in the code of Figure 17.5, the `protected` attribute allows users of `thermometer` to read the temperature in either Fahrenheit or Celsius, but the variables can only be changed via the provided subroutines which ensure that both values agree.

Figure 17.5

```
module thermometer
  real, protected :: temperature_celsius    = 0
  real, protected :: temperature_fahrenheit = 32
contains
  subroutine set_celsius(new_celsius_value)
    real, intent(in) :: new_celsius_value
    temperature_celsius = new_celsius_value
    temperature_fahrenheit = temperature_celsius*(9.0/5.0) + 32
  end subroutine set_celsius
  subroutine set_fahrenheit(new_fahrenheit_value)
    real, intent(in) :: new_fahrenheit_value
    temperature_fahrenheit = new_fahrenheit_value
    temperature_celsius = (temperature_fahrenheit - 32)*(5.0/9.0)
  end subroutine set_fahrenheit
end module thermometer
```

17.8 Renaming operators on the use statement

User-defined operators may now be renamed on the use statement, just as variable and procedure names may be. For example,

```
use fred, operator(.nurke.) => operator(.banana.)
```

renames the `.banana.` operator located in module `fred` so that it may be referenced by using `.nurke.` as an operator.

However, this only applies to user-defined operators. Intrinsic operators cannot be renamed, so all of the following are invalid

```
use fred, only: operator(.equal.) => operator(.eq.)      ! Invalid
use fred, only: operator(.ne.) => operator(.notequal.) ! Invalid
use fred, only: operator(*) => assignment(=)             ! Invalid
```

17.9 Array constructor syntax

A well-recognized deficiency of array constructors in Fortran 95 is that they are somewhat inconvenient to use for `character` type; each element must have exactly the same character length. This is irritating to the user, who is thus required to pad character constants with blanks manually, to make them all the same length. For array constructors involving variables, this requirement is often not checkable at compile time, leading to potential run time errors or strange results.

Another deficiency is that for zero-sized array constructors, it can be difficult if not impossible for the compiler to deduce the value of any length type parameters (in Fortran 95 this is limited to `character` type).

A less serious deficiency is that one cannot mix items of different type even when those items would be assignable to a common type (for example, having integer or real items in a complex array constructor).

Finally, when parenthesized expressions are array constructor items, and when array constructors are items inside parenthesized expressions and function references, it can be difficult to match the parentheses so that the array constructors end with /).

All of these deficiencies have been addressed in Fortran 2003. To make it easier to match parentheses, an array constructor may be bracketed with [ ] instead of (/ /).

To overcome the type deficiencies, an array constructor may now begin with an explicit specification of its type and type parameters. The syntax for an array constructor with a type specification is:

> (/ *type-spec* :: *ac-value-list* /)

where the *type-spec* is the short form used in the `allocate` statement (Section 17.4). In this case, the array constructor values may have any type (and type parameters) that is assignment-compatible with the specified type and type parameters, and the values are converted to that type by the usual assignment conversions.

Here are some examples:

```
[ character(len=33) :: 'the good', 'the bad', 'and', &
                       'the appearance-challenged' ]
[ complex(kind(0d0)) :: 1, (0,1), 3.1415926535897932384626433827d0 ]

[ matrix(kind=kind(0.0), n=10, m=20) :: ] ! zero-sized array
```

If *type-spec* is absent, the rules of Fortran 95 continue to apply: all items must have the same type and type parameters. This rule applies to parameterized derived types, too.

17.10   Specification and initialization expressions

A specification expression (used for an array bound or length type parameter) may now reference a recursive function, so long as the function does not invoke the procedure containing that specification expression. It may contain a type parameter enquiry (Section 15.3) or a reference to an IEEE inquiry function (Section 11.9.2). Inside a derived-type definition, a specification expression may also reference any type parameter of the type being defined.

An initialization expression is not as restricted as in Fortran 95. It may reference any elemental or transformational standard intrinsic function, or the function ieee_selected_real_kind of the intrinsic module ieee_arithmetic, as long as its arguments are all initialization expressions. This includes the mathematical intrinsic functions (sin, cos, etc.). For example,

```
real :: root2 = sqrt(2.0)
```

is now a valid initialization. The exponentiation operator is not limited to an integer power.

All the inquiry functions may be referenced in an initialization expression with the restrictions on their arguments that are given in item vii) of the list in Section 7.4. A type parameter enquiry (Section 15.3) may be used as long as the type parameter is not assumed, deferred, or defined by an expression other than an initialization expression.

An initialization expression may reference the null intrinsic function as long as it does not have an argument with a type parameter that is assumed or defined by an expression that is not an initialization expression.

Finally, within a derived-type definition, an initialization expression may reference a *kind* type parameter of the type being defined.

17.11   Exercise

1. Write a statement that makes an existing rank-2 integer array b, that has lower bounds of 1, two rows and two columns larger, with the old elements' values retained in the middle of the array. (Hint: Use the reshape intrinsic function.)

18. Miscellaneous enhancements

18.1   Introduction

This chapter collects together a number of miscellaneous enhancements made in Fortran 2003 that do not fit into any convenient category.

18.2   Pointer intent

The `intent` attribute has been extended to include pointers. For a pointer, the intent refers to the pointer association and not to the value of the target; that is, it refers to the descriptor. An `intent(out)` pointer has undefined association status on entry to the procedure; an `intent(in)` pointer cannot be nullified or associated during execution of the procedure; and the actual argument for an `intent(inout)` pointer must be a pointer variable (that is, it cannot be a reference to a pointer-valued function).

Note that, although an intent in pointer cannot have its pointer association status changed inside the procedure, if it is associated with a target the value of its target may be changed. For example,

```
subroutine maybe_clear(p)
   real, pointer, intent(in) :: p(:)
   if (associated(p)) p = 0.0
end subroutine maybe_clear
```

18.3   The volatile attribute

The `volatile` attribute is a new attribute which may be applied only to variables. It is conferred either by the `volatile` attribute in a type declaration statement, or by the `volatile` statement, which has the form

```
volatile [::]  variable-name-list
```

For example,

```
integer, volatile :: x
real              :: y
volatile          :: y
```

declares two volatile variables x and y.

18.3.1   Volatile semantics

Being volatile indicates to the compiler that, at any time, the variable might be changed and/or examined from outside the Fortran program. This means that each reference to the variable will need to load its value from main memory (so, for example, it cannot be kept in a register in an inner loop). Similarly, each assignment to the variable must write the data to memory. Essentially, this disables most optimizations that might have been applicable to the object, making the program run slower but, one hopes, making it work with some special hardware or multi-processing software.

However, it is the responsibility of the programmer to effect any necessary synchronization; this is particularly relevant to multi-processor systems. Even if only one process is writing to the variable and the Fortran program is reading from it, because the variable is not automatically protected by a critical section it is possible to read a partially updated (and thus an inconsistent or impossible) value. For example, if the variable is an IEEE floating-point variable, reading a partially updated value could return a signalling NaN; or if the variable is a pointer, its descriptor might be invalid. In either of these cases the program could be abruptly terminated, so this facility must be used with care.

Similarly, if two processes are both attempting to update a single `volatile` variable, the effects are completely processor dependent. The variable might end up with its original value, one of the values from an updating process, a partial conglomeration of values from the updating processes, or the program could even crash.

A simple use of this feature might be to handle some external (interrupt-driven) event, such as the user typing Control-C, in a controlled fashion. For example,

```
logical, target, volatile :: event_has_occurred
:
event_has_occurred = .false.
call register_event_flag(event_has_occurred, ...)
:
do
   :                              ! some calculations
   if (event_has_occurred) exit ! exit loop if event happened
   :                              ! some more calculations
   if (...) exit                 ! Finished our calculations yet?
end do
:
```

where `register_event_flag` is a routine, possibly written in another language, which ensures that `event_has_occurred` becomes true when the specified event occurs.

If the variable is a pointer, the `volatile` attribute applies both to the descriptor and to the target. Even if the target does not have the `volatile` attribute, it is treated as having it when accessed via a pointer that has it. If the variable is allocatable, it applies both to the allocation and to the value. In both cases, if the variable is polymorphic (Section 16.3), the dynamic type may change by non-Fortran means.

If a variable has the `volatile` attribute, so do all of its subobjects.

For example, in

```
logical, target              :: signal_state(100)
logical, pointer, volatile :: signal_flags(:)
:
signal_flags => signal_state
:
signal_flags(10) = .true.    ! A volatile reference
:
write (20) signal_state      ! A nonvolatile reference
```

the pointer (descriptor) of signal_flags is volatile, and access to each element of signal_flags is volatile; however, signal_state itself is not volatile.

The raison d'être for volatile is for interoperating with parallel processing packages such as MPI, which have procedures for asynchronously transferring data from one process to another. For example, without the volatile attribute on the array data in Figure 18.1, a compiler optimization could move the assignment prior to the call to mpi_wait. The use of mpi_module provides access to MPI constants and explicit interfaces for MPI routines; in particular, mpi_isend which requires the volatile attribute on its first dummy argument.

Figure 18.1

```
subroutine transfer_while_producing(...)
    use mpi_module ! Access interfaces for mpi_isend etc.
    double precision, allocatable              :: newdata(:)
    double precision, allocatable, volatile :: data(:)
    : ! Produce data here
    call mpi_isend(data, size(data), mpi_double_precision, dest, &
                   tag, comm, request, ierr)
    : ! Produce newdata here
    call mpi_wait(request, status)
    data = newdata
    :
end subroutine transfer_while_producing
```

18.3.2 Volatile scoping

If a variable only needs to be treated as volatile for a short time, the programmer has two options: either to pass it to a procedure to be acted on in a volatile manner (see next section), or to access it by use or host association, using a volatile statement to declare it to be volatile only in the accessing scope. For example, in the code of Figure 18.2, the data array is not volatile in data_processing, but is in data_transfer. Note that this is an exception to the usual rules of use association, which prohibit other attributes from being changed in the accessing scope. Similarly, declaring a variable that is accessed by host association to be volatile is allowed, and unlike other specification statements, does not cause the creation of a new local variable.

Figure 18.2

```
module data_module
    double precision, allocatable :: data(:,:), newdata(:,:)
    :
contains
    subroutine data_processing
        :
    end subroutine data_processing
    subroutine data_transfer
        volatile :: data
        :
    end subroutine data_transfer
end module data_module
```

18.3.3 Volatile arguments

The volatility of an actual argument and its associated dummy argument may differ. This is important since volatility may be needed in one but not in the other. In particular, a volatile variable may be used as an actual argument in a call to an intrinsic procedure. However, while a volatile variable is associated with a non-volatile dummy argument, the programmer must ensure that the value is not altered by non-Fortran means. Note that, if the volatility of an actual argument persists through a procedure reference, as for example in the MPI call in Figure 18.1, this means that the procedure referenced must have an explicit interface and the corresponding dummy argument must be declared to be volatile.

If the dummy argument is volatile, the actual argument is permitted to be an array section only if the dummy argument is assumed-shape or a pointer, and it is not permitted to have a vector subscript. These restrictions are designed to allow the argument to be passed by reference; in particular, to avoid the need for a local copy being made as this would interfere with the volatility.

A dummy argument with intent in or the value attribute (Section 14.6) is not permitted to be volatile. This is because the value of such an argument is expected to remain fixed during the execution of the procedure.

If a dummy argument of a procedure is volatile, the interface must be explicit whenever it is called and the dummy argument must be declared as volatile in any interface body for the procedure.

18.4 The import statement

One problem with procedure interface blocks in Fortran 95 is that an interface body does not access its environment by host association, and therefore cannot use named constants and derived types defined therein.

In particular, it is desirable in a module procedure to be able to describe a dummy procedure that uses types defined in the module. For example, in Figure 18.3, the interface body is invalid, because it has no access either to type t or to the constant wp.

Figure 18.3

```
module m
    integer, parameter :: wp = kind(0.0d0)
    type t
        :
    end type t
contains
    subroutine apply(fun,...)
        interface
            type(t) function fun(f)  ! Not allowed
                real(wp) :: f        ! Not allowed
            end function fun
        end interface
    end subroutine apply
end module m
```

This problem has been addressed by the import statement. This statement can be used only in an interface body, and gives access to named entities of the containing scoping unit. Figure 18.4 shows a correct interface body to replace the incorrect one in Figure 18.3.

Figure 18.4

```
interface
    function fun(f)
        import   :: t, wp
        type(t)  :: fun
        real(wp) :: f
    end function fun
end interface
```

The statement must be placed after any use statements but ahead of any other statements of the body. It has the general form:

```
import [ [::]  import-name-list ]
```

where each *import-name* is that of an entity that is accessible in the containing scoping unit. If an imported entity is defined in the containing scoping unit, it must be explicitly declared prior to the interface body.

An import statement without a list imports all entities from the containing scoping unit that are not declared to be local entities of the interface body; this works the same way as normal host association.

18.5   Intrinsic modules

Like an intrinsic function, an intrinsic module is one that is provided by the Fortran processor instead of by the user or a third party. A Fortran 2003 processor provides at least five intrinsic modules: `ieee_arithmetic`, `ieee_exceptions`, `ieee_features`, `iso_c_binding`, and `iso_fortran_env`, and may provide additional intrinsic modules.

Also like intrinsic procedures, it is possible for a program to use an intrinsic module and a user-defined module of the same name, though they cannot both be referenced from the same scoping unit. To use an intrinsic module in preference to a user-defined one of the same name, the `intrinsic` keyword is specified on the `use` statement, for example

```
use, intrinsic :: ieee_arithmetic
```

Similarly, to ensure that a user-defined module is accessed in preference to an intrinsic module, the `non_intrinsic` keyword is used, for example:

```
use, non_intrinsic :: random_numbers
```

If both an intrinsic module and a user-defined module are available with the same name, a `use` statement without either of these keywords accesses the user-defined module. However, should the compiler not be able to find the user's module it would access the intrinsic one instead without warning; therefore we recommend that programmers avoid using the same name for a user-defined module as that of a known intrinsic module (or that the `non_intrinsic` keyword be used).

The IEEE modules provide access to facilities from the IEEE arithmetic standard and are described in Chapter 11. The intrinsic module `iso_c_binding` provides support for interoperability with C and is described in Chapter 14.

The intrinsic module `iso_fortran_env` provides information about the Fortran environment, in the form of named constants as follows.

`character_storage_size` The size in bits of a character storage unit (only applicable to storage association contexts, see Section 20.2.1).

`error_unit` The unit number for a preconnected output unit suitable for reporting errors.

`file_storage_size` The size in bits of a file storage unit (the unit of measurement for the record length of an external file, as used in the `recl=` clause of an `open` or `inquire` statement).

`input_unit` The unit number for the preconnected standard input unit (the same one that is used by `read` without a unit number, or with a unit specifier of `*`).

`iostat_end` The value returned by `iostat=` to indicate an end-of-file condition.

`iostat_eor` The value returned by `iostat=` to indicate an end-of-record condition.

`numeric_storage_size` The size in bits of a numeric storage unit (only applicable to storage association contexts, see Section 20.2.1).

output_unit The unit number for the preconnected standard output unit (the same one that is used by print, or by write with a unit specifier of *).

Unlike normal unit numbers, the special unit numbers might be negative, but they will not be −1 (this is because −1 is used by the number= clause of the inquire statement to mean that there is no unit number). The error reporting unit error_unit might be the same as the standard output unit output_unit.

Intrinsic modules should always be used with an only clause, as vendors or future standards could make additions to the module.

18.6 Access to the computing environment

Intrinsic functions have been added to provide information about environment variables, and about the command by which the program was executed.

18.6.1 Environment variables

Most operating systems have some concept of an *environment variable*, associating names with values. Access to these is provided by an intrinsic subroutine.

call get_environment_variable (name [,value] [,length] [,status] [,trim_name]) where the arguments are defined as follows.

> **name** has intent in and is a scalar default character string containing the name of the environment variable to be retrieved. Trailing blanks are not significant unless trim_name is present and false. Case may or may not be significant.

> **value** has intent out and is a scalar default character variable; it receives the value of the environment variable (truncated or padded if the value argument is shorter or longer than the environment variable's value). If there is no such variable, there is such a variable but it has no value, or the processor does not support environment variables, this argument is set to blanks.

> **length** has intent out and is a scalar default integer variable; if the specified environment variable exists and has a value, the length argument is set to the length of that value; otherwise it is set to zero.

> **status** has intent out and is a scalar default integer; it receives the value 1 if the environment variable does not exist, 2 if the processor does not support environment variables, a number greater than 2 if an error occurs, −1 if the value argument is present but too short, and zero otherwise (indicating that no error or warning condition has occurred).

> **trim_name** has intent in and is a scalar of type logical; if this is false, trailing blanks in name will be considered significant if the processor allows environment variable names to contain trailing blanks.

18.6.2 Command arguments and the command line

Two different methods of retrieving information about the command are provided, reflecting the two approaches in common use.

The Unix-like method is provided by two procedures: a function which returns the number of command arguments and a subroutine which returns an individual argument. These are:

command_argument_count () returns, as a scalar default integer, the number of command arguments. If the result is zero, either there were no arguments or the processor does not support the facility. If the command name is available as an argument, it is not included in this count.

call get_command_argument (number [,value] [,length] [,status]) where

> **number** has intent in and is a scalar default integer indicating the number of the argument to return. If the command name is available as an argument, it is number zero.
>
> **value** has intent out and is a scalar default character variable; it receives the value of the indicated argument (truncated or padded if the character variable is shorter or longer than the command argument).
>
> **length** has intent out and is a scalar default integer variable; it receives the length of the indicated argument.
>
> **status** has intent out and is a scalar default integer variable; it receives a positive value if that argument cannot be retrieved, −1 to indicate that the value variable was shorter than the command argument, and zero otherwise.

The other paradigm for command processing provides a simple command line, not broken up into arguments. This is retrieved by the intrinsic subroutine

call get_command ([command] [, length] [, status]) where

> **command** has intent out and is a scalar default character variable; it receives the value of the command line (truncated or padded if the variable is shorter or longer than the actual command line).
>
> **length** has intent out and is a scalar default integer variable; it receives the length of the actual command line, or zero if the length cannot be determined.
>
> **status** has intent out and is a scalar default integer variable; it receives a positive value if the command line cannot be retrieved, −1 if command was present but the variable was shorter than the length of the actual command line, and zero otherwise.

18.7 Support for internationalization

The internationalization capabilities have been improved by additional requirements on the processor's basic character set, decimal symbol control for floating-point input/output, and many improvements to the support for other character sets, in particular for the universal character set ISO/IEC 10646-1 : 2000 (also known as Unicode).

18.7.1 Character sets

The Fortran character set now includes all the lower-case letters and many additional special characters from the ASCII character set. The additional special characters are

$$\sim \quad \wedge \quad \backslash \quad \{ \quad \} \quad ' \quad [\quad] \quad | \quad \# \quad @$$

Square brackets may be used to delimit array constructors (see Section 17.9); the others may appear only in comments, character literals, and character string edit descriptors.

The intrinsic function `achar` now takes an optional `kind` argument. This argument specifies the kind of the result. For instance, if the processor had an extra character kind 37 for EBCDIC, `achar(iachar('h'),37)` would return the EBCDIC lower-case `'h'` character.

Similarly, the intrinsic function `iachar` now accepts a character of any kind, returning the ASCII code for that character if it is in the ASCII character set and a processor-dependent value otherwise.

The new intrinsic function `selected_char_kind` can be used to select a specific character set.

selected_char_kind (name) returns the kind value for the character set whose name is given by the character string name, or -1 if it is not supported (or if the name is not recognized). In particular, if name is

DEFAULT, the result is the kind of the default character type (equal to `kind('A')`);

ASCII, the result is the kind of the ASCII character type;

ISO_10646, the result is the kind of the ISO/IEC 10646-1 : 2000 UCS-4 character type.

Other character set names are processor dependent. The character set name is not case sensitive (lower case is treated as upper case), and any trailing blanks are ignored.

Note that the only character set which is guaranteed to be supported is the default character set; a processor is not required to support ASCII or ISO 10646.

18.7.2 ASCII character set

If the default character set for a processor is not ASCII, but ASCII is supported on that processor, intrinsic assignment is defined between them to convert characters appropriately. For example, on an EBCDIC machine, in

```
integer, parameter :: ascii = selected_char_kind('ASCII')
character          :: ce
character(ascii)   :: ca
ce = ascii_'X'
ca = 'X'
```

the first assignment statement will convert the ASCII upper-case X to an EBCDIC upper-case X, and the second assignment statement will do the reverse.

18.7.3 ISO 10646 character set

ISO/IEC 10646-1 : 2000 UCS-4 is a 4-byte character set designed to be able to represent every character in every language in the world, including all special characters in use in other coded character sets. It is a strict superset of 7-bit ASCII; that is, its first 128 characters are the same as those of ASCII.

Assignment of default characters or ASCII characters to ISO 10646 is allowed, and the characters are converted appropriately. Assignment of ISO 10646 characters to default or ASCII characters is also allowed; however, if any ISO 10646 character is not representable in the destination character set, the result is processor dependent (information will be lost). For example, in

```
integer, parameter :: ascii = selected_char_kind('ASCII')
integer, parameter :: iso10646 = selected_char_kind('ISO_10646')
character(ascii) :: x = ascii_'X'
character(iso10646) :: y
y = x
```

the ISO 10646 character variable y will be set to the correct value for the upper-case letter X.

ISO 10646 character variables may be used as internal files; numeric, logical, default character, ASCII character, and ISO 10646 character values may all be read from or written to such a variable. For example,

```
subroutine japanese_date_stamp(string)
   integer, parameter ::  ucs4 = selected_char_kind('ISO_10646')
   character(*,ucs4), intent(out) ::  string
   integer                ::  values(8)
   call date_and_time(values=values)
   write(string,100) values(1), '年', values(2), '月', values(3), '日'
100 format(I0,A,I0,A,I0,A)
 end subroutine japanese_date_stamp
```

Note that, although reading from an ISO 10646 internal file into a default character or ASCII character variable is possible, it is only allowed when the data being read is representable in default character or ASCII character.

18.7.4 UTF-8 files

The ISO 10646 standard specifies a standard encoding of UCS-4 characters into a stream of bytes, called UTF-8. Formatted files in UTF-8 format are supported in Fortran 2003 by the encoding= specifier on the open statement. For example,

```
open(20, name='output.file', action='write', encoding='utf-8')
```

The encoding= specifier on the inquire statement returns the encoding of a file, which will be UTF-8 if the file is connected for UTF-8 input/output or the processor can detect the format in some way, UNKNOWN if the processor cannot detect the format, or a processor-dependent value if the file is known to be in some other format (for example, UTF-16LE).

For the most part, UTF-8 files can be treated as ordinary formatted files. On output, all data is effectively converted to ISO 10646 characters for UTF-8 encoding.

On input, if data is being read into an ASCII character variable each input character must be in the range 0-127 (the ASCII subset of ISO 10646); if data is being read into a default character variable each input character must be representable in the default character set. These conditions will be satisfied if the data were written by numeric or logical formatting, or by character formatting from an ASCII or default character value; otherwise it would be safer to read the data into an ISO 10646 character variable for processing.

Figure 18.5 shows the i/o routines for a data processing application using these facilities.

Figure 18.5

```
subroutine write_id(unit, name, id)
  character(kind=ucs4,len=*), intent(in) :: name
  integer, intent(in)                     :: id, unit
  write(unit,'(1x,i6,3a)') 'Customer number ', id, ' is ', name
end subroutine write_id
:
subroutine read_id(unit, name, id)
  character(kind=ucs4,len=*), intent(out) :: name
  integer, intent(in)                      :: unit
  integer, intent(out)                     :: id
  character(kind=ucs4,len=20)              :: string
  integer                                  :: stringlen
  read(unit,'(1x,a16)',advance='no') string
  if (string/=ucs4_'Customer number ') stop 'Bad format'
  do stringlen=1, len(string)
    read(unit,'(3x,a)',advance='no') string(stringlen:stringlen)
    if (string(stringlen:stringlen)==ucs4_' ') exit
  end do
  read(string(1:stringlen),*) id
  read(unit,'(3x,a)') name
end subroutine read_id
```

18.7.5 Decimal comma for input/output

Many countries use a decimal comma instead of a decimal point. Support for this is provided by the decimal= input/output specifier and by the dc and dp edit descriptors. These affect the *decimal edit mode* for the unit. While the decimal edit mode is *decimal point*, decimal points are used in input/output just as in Fortran 95.

While the mode is *decimal comma*, commas are used in place of decimal points both for input and for output. For example,

```
x = 22./7
print '(1x,f6.2)', x
```

would produce the output

```
3,14
```

in decimal comma mode.

The decimal= clause may appear on the open, read, and write statements, and has the form

> decimal=*scalar-character-expr*

where the *scalar-character-expr* evaluates either to point or to comma. On the open statement it specifies the default decimal edit mode for the unit. If there is no decimal= clause on the open statement, the mode for the unit defaults to decimal point. The default for internal files is also decimal point. For the read and write statements, the decimal= clause specifies the default mode for the duration of that input/output statement only.

The dc and dp edit descriptors change the decimal edit mode to decimal comma and decimal point, respectively. They take effect when they are encountered during format processing and continue in effect until another dc or dp edit descriptor is encountered or until the end of the current input/output statement. For example,

```
     write (*,10) x, x, x
10 format(1x,'Default ',f5.2,', English ',dp,f5.2,'Français',dc,f5.2)
```

would produce the value of x first with the default mode, then with a decimal point for English, and a decimal comma for French.

If the decimal edit mode is decimal comma during list-directed or namelist input/output, a semicolon acts as a value separator instead of a comma.

18.8 Lengths of names and statements

The maximum length for names (Section 2.7) has been increased to 63 characters.

Statements were previously limited to 40 lines (20 lines in fixed form, see Section B.1.1); the maximum length in either form is now 256 lines. That is, up to 255 continuation lines are allowed.

One of the reasons for allowing longer statements is to handle source code that is automatically generated.

18.9 Binary, octal, and hexadecimal constants

Binary, octal, and hexadecimal ('boz') constants, previously only allowed in data statements, are also allowed as a principal argument in a call of the intrinsic functions cmplx, dble, int, and real (not for an optional argument that specifies the kind).

For int, the 'boz' constant is treated as if it were an integer constant of the kind with the largest range supported by the processor. Thus,

```
integer :: i, j
data i/z'3f7'/
j = int(z'3f7')
```

gives both i and j the same value (in decimal, 1015).

For dble and real, it is treated as having the value that a variable of the same type and kind type parameter as the result would have if its internal representation were the bit pattern specified. This interpretation of the bit pattern is processor dependent. For cmplx with result of kind value kind, a 'boz' argument for either x or y provides the same value as real(x,kind) or real(y,kind), so that it specifies the internal representation of one component of the result.

The advantage of allowing 'boz' constants in expressions only as arguments to these intrinsics is that there is no ambiguity in the way they are interpreted. There are vendor extensions that allow them directly in expressions, but the ways that values are interpreted differ.

18.10   Other changes to intrinsic functions

The intrinsic functions max, maxval, min, and minval may now be used on values of type character.

If a set of array elements examined by maxloc or minloc is empty, the location of its maximum or minimum element is now deemed to have all subscripts zero (it was processor dependent in Fortran 95).

The following intrinsic functions now have an optional kind argument at the end of the argument list: count, iachar, ichar, index, lbound, len, len_trim, maxloc, minloc, scan, shape, size, ubound, and verify. This argument specifies the kind of integer result the function returns, in case a default integer is not big enough to contain the correct value (which may be the case on 64-bit machines).

For example, in the code

```
real, allocatable :: a(:,:,:,:)
allocate(a(64,1024,1024,1024))
    :
print *,size(a,kind=selected_int_kind(12))
```

the array a has a total of 2^{36} elements; on most machines this is bigger than huge(0), so the kind argument is needed to get the right answer from the reference to the intrinsic function size.

The count, count_rate, and count_max arguments of the intrinsic subroutine system_clock may now be of any kind of integer; this is to accommodate systems with a clock rate that is too high to be represented in a default integer. Additionally, the count_rate argument may now be of type real as well as integer; this is to accommodate systems whose clock does not tick an integral number of times each second.

Changes have been made to the intrinsic functions atan2, log, and sqrt for processors that distinguish between positive and negative real zero (on most computers, now that IEEE arithmetic is widespread). The intrinsic function atan2(y, x) now returns an approximation to $-\pi$ if x< 0 and y is a negative zero since this is the limit as y $\rightarrow$ 0 from below (previously it returned an approximation to π). For similar reasons, the intrinsic function log(x) now returns an approximation to $-\pi$ if x is of type complex with a real part that is less than zero and a negative zero imaginary part; and the intrinsic function sqrt(x) for complex x now returns a negative imaginary result if the real part of the result is zero and the imaginary part of x is less than zero.

18.11   Error message retrieval

The disadvantage of using the stat= clause on an allocate or deallocate statement is that it is impossible for the program to provide a sensible report of the error, because error codes are processor dependent.

To overcome this, the errmsg= clause has been added to these two statements. This takes a scalar default character string variable, and if an error condition occurs that is handled by stat=, an explanatory message is assigned to the errmsg= variable.

For example,

```
character(200) :: error_message ! Probably long enough
:
allocate(x(n), stat=allocate_status, errmsg=error_message)
if (allocate_status>0) then
  print *, 'Allocation of X failed:', trim(error_message)
  :
end if
```

18.12   Enhanced complex constants

A complex constant may now be written with a named constant of type real or integer for its real part, imaginary part, or both. For example,

```
real, parameter    :: zero = 0, one = 1
complex, parameter :: i = (zero, one)
```

However, no sign is allowed with a name, so although (0,-1) is a perfectly good complex constant, (zero,-one) is invalid.

Since the intrinsic function cmplx is now permitted to appear in an initialization expression, and provides all this functionality and more, there is very little use for this feature.

18.13   Interface block extensions

The module procedure statement (see Section 5.18) has been changed in Fortran 2003. The keyword module is now optional; for example,

```
interface gamma
   procedure :: sgamma, dgamma
end interface
```

If the keyword `module` is omitted, the named procedures need not be module procedures but may also be external procedures, dummy procedures, or procedure pointers. Each named procedure must already have an explicit interface to be used in this way.

This can be used to avoid the Fortran 95 limitation that an external procedure could not appear in more than one interface block. For example, in

```
type bitstring
   :
end type
:
interface operator(*)
   elemental type(bitstring) function bitwise_and(a,b)
      import :: bitstring
      type(bitstring), intent(in) :: a, b
   end function bitwise_and
end interface
interface operator(.and.)
   procedure :: bitwise_and
end interface
```

this allows the use of both the `*` and `.and.` operators for 'bitwise and' on values of type `bitstring`.

18.14   Public entities of private type

Entities of private type are no longer themselves required to be private; this applies equally to procedures with arguments that have private type. This means that a module writer can provide very limited access to values or variables without thereby giving the user the power to create new variables of the type.

For example, the widely-used LAPACK library requires character arguments such as `uplo`, a character variable that must be given the value `'L'` or `'U'` according to whether the matrix is upper or lower triangular. The value is checked at run time and an error return occurs if it is invalid. This could be replaced by values `lower` and `upper` of private type. This would be clearer and the check would be made at compile time.

19. Input/output enhancements

19.1 Introduction

In this chapter, we explain the enhancements to input/output processing that have been made in Fortran 2003. Non-default derived-type input/output (Section 19.2) allows the programmer to provide formatting specially tailored to a type and to transfer structures with pointer components. Asynchronous input/output (Sections 19.3 and 19.4) has been available as compiler extensions for many years and is now standardized. Since the advent of IEEE arithmetic many compilers have provided facilities for input/output of the exceptional values; this is now standardized (Section 19.5). Stream access (Section 19.6) allows great flexibility for both formatted and unformatted input/output. The remaining sections detail miscellaneous simple enhancements.

19.2 Non-default derived-type input/output

It may be arranged that, when a derived-type object is encountered in an input/output list, a Fortran subroutine is called. This either reads some data from the file and constructs a value of the derived type or accepts a value of the derived type and writes some data to the file.

For formatted input/output, the dt edit descriptor specifies a character string and an integer array to control the action. An example is

```
dt 'linked-list' (10, -4, 2)
```

The character string may be omitted; this case is treated as if a string of length zero had been given. The parenthetical list of integers may be omitted, in which case an array of length zero is passed.

Such subroutines may be bound to the type as generic bindings (see Section 16.6.3) of the forms

```
generic :: read(formatted) => r1, r2
generic :: read(unformatted) => r3, r4, r5
generic :: write(formatted) => w1
generic :: write(unformatted) => w2, w3
```

which makes them accessible wherever an object of the type is accessible. An alternative is an interface block such as

```
interface read(formatted)
   module procedure r1, r2
end interface
```

The form of such a subroutine depends on whether it is for formatted or unformatted I/O:

subroutine formatted_io (dtv,unit,iotype,v_list,iostat,iomsg)
subroutine unformatted_io(dtv,unit,   iostat,iomsg)

dtv is a scalar of the derived type. It may be polymorphic (so that it can be called for the type or any extension of it). All length type parameters must be assumed. For output, it is of intent(in) and holds the value to be written. For input, it is of intent(inout) and is altered in accord with the values read.

unit is a scalar of intent(in) and type default integer. Its value is the unit on which input/output is taking place or negative if on an internal file.

iotype is a scalar of intent(in) and type character(*). Its value is 'LISTDIRECTED', 'NAMELIST', or 'DT'//*string*, where *string* is the character string from the dt edit descriptor.

v_list is a rank-one assumed-shape array of intent(in) and type default integer. Its value comes from the parenthetical list of the edit descriptor.

iostat is a scalar of intent(out) and type default integer. If an error condition occurs, it must be given a positive value. Otherwise, if an end-of-file or end-of-record condition occurs it must be given, respectively, the value iostat_end or iostat_eor of the intrinsic module iso_fortran_env (see Section 18.5). Otherwise, it must be given the value zero.

iomsg is a scalar of intent(inout) and type character(*). If iostat is given a nonzero value, iomsg must be set to an explanatory message. Otherwise, it must not be altered.

The names of the subroutine and its arguments are not significant when they are invoked as part of input/output processing.

Within the subroutine, input/output to external files is limited to the specified unit and in the specified direction. Such a data transfer statement is called a *child* data transfer statement and the original statement is called the *parent*. No file positioning takes place before or after the execution of a child data transfer statement. Input/output to an internal file is permitted. An input/output list may include a dt edit descriptor for a component of the dtv argument, with the obvious meaning. Execution of any of the statements open, close, backspace, endfile, and rewind is not permitted. Also, the procedure must not alter any aspect of the parent input/output statement, except through the dtv argument.

The file position on entry is treated as a left tab limit and there is no record termination on return. Therefore, positioning with rec= (for a direct-access file, Section 9.15) or pos= (for stream access, Section 19.7) is not permitted in a child data transfer statement.

This feature is not available in combination with asynchronous input/output (next section).

A simple example of derived-type formatted output follows. The derived-type variable chairman has two components. The type and an associated write-formatted procedure are defined in a module called person_module and might be invoked as shown in Figure 19.1.

Figure 19.1

```
program
  use person_module
  integer id, members
  type (person) :: chairman
    :
  write(6, fmt="(i2, dt(15,6), i5)" ) id, chairman, members
! This writes a record with four fields, with lengths 2, 15, 6, 5,
! respectively
end program
```

Figure 19.2

```
module person_module
  type :: person
     character (len=20) :: name
     integer :: age
  contains
     generic :: write(formatted) => pwf
  end type person
contains
  subroutine pwf (dtv,unit,iotype,vlist,iostat,iomsg)
  ! Arguments
     class(person), intent(in)       :: dtv
     integer, intent(in)             :: unit
     character (len=*), intent(in)   :: iotype
     integer, intent(in)             :: vlist(:)
     ! vlist(1) and (2) are to be used as the field widths
     ! of the two components of the derived type variable.
     integer, intent(out)            :: iostat
     character (len=*), intent(inout) :: iomsg
     ! Local variable
     character (len=9) :: pfmt
     ! Set up the format to be used for output
     write(pfmt, '(a,i2,a,i2,a)' ) &
        '(a', vlist(1), ',i', vlist(2), ')'
     ! Now the child output statement
     write(unit, fmt=pfmt, iostat=iostat) dtv%name, dtv%age
  end subroutine pwf
end module person_module
```

The module that implements this is shown in Figure 19.2. From the edit descriptor dt(15,6), it constructs the format (a15,i 6) in the local character variable pfmt and applies it.

It would also be possible to check that iotype indeed has the value 'DT' and to set iostat and iomsg accordingly.

In the following example, Figure 19.3, we illustrate the output of a structure with a pointer component and show a child data transfer statement itself invoking derived-type input/output. Here, we show the case where the same (recursive) subroutine is invoked in both cases. The variables of the derived type node form a chain, with a single value at each node and terminating with a null pointer. The subroutine pwf is used to write the values in the list, one per line.

Figure 19.3

```
module list_module
    type node
        integer               :: value = 0
        type (node), pointer :: next_node => null ( )
    contains
        generic :: write(formatted) => pwf
    end type node
contains
    recursive subroutine pwf (dtv,unit,iotype,vlist,iostat,iomsg)
    ! Write the chain of values, each on a separate line in I9 format.
        class(node), intent(in) :: dtv
        integer, intent(in)      :: unit
        character (len=*), intent(in) :: iotype
        integer, intent(in)      :: vlist(:)
        integer, intent(out)     :: iostat
        character (len=*), intent(inout) :: iomsg
        write(unit,'(i9,/)', iostat = iostat) dtv%value
        if(iostat/=0) return
        if(associated(dtv%next_node)) &
            write(unit,'(dt)', iostat=iostat) dtv%next_node
    end subroutine pwf
end module list_module
```

19.3   Asynchronous input/output

Input/output may be asynchronous, that is, other statements may execute while an input/output statement is in execution. It is permitted only for external files opened with asynchronous='yes' in the open statement and is indicated by an asynchronous='yes' specifier in the read or write statement. By default, execution is synchronous even for a file opened with asynchronous='yes', but it may be specified with asynchronous='no'.

Execution of an asynchronous input/output statement initiates a 'pending' input/output operation and execution of other statements continues until it reaches a statement involving a wait operation for the file. This may be an explicit `wait` statement such as

```
wait(10)
```

or an `inquire`, a `close`, or a file positioning statement for the file. The compiler is permitted to treat each asynchronous input/output statement as an ordinary input/output statement (this, after all, is just the limiting case of the input/output being fast). The compiler is, of course, required to recognize all the new syntax.

Here is a simple example

```
real :: a(100000), b(100000)
open(10,file='mydata',asynchronous='yes')
read(10,'(10f8.3)',asynchronous='yes')
   :  ! Computation involving the array b
wait(10)
   :  ! Computation involving the array a
```

Further asynchronous input/output statements may be executed for the file before the `wait` statement is reached. The input/output statements for each file are performed in the same order as they would have been if they were synchronous.

An execution of an asynchronous input/output statement may be identified by a scalar integer variable in an `id=` specifier. Successful execution of the statement causes the variable to be given a processor-dependent value which can be passed to a subsequent `wait` or `inquire` statement as a scalar integer variable in an `id=` specifier.

A `wait` statement may have `end=`, `eor=`, `err=`, and `iostat=` specifiers. These have the same meanings as for a data transfer statement and refer to situations that occur while the input/output operation is pending. If there is also an `id=` specifier, only the identified pending operation is terminated and the other specifiers refer to this; otherwise, all pending operations for the file are terminated in turn.

An `inquire` statement is permitted to have a `pending=` specifier for a scalar default logical variable. If an `id=` specifier is present, the variable is given the value true if the particular input/output operation is still pending and false otherwise. If no `id=` specifier is present, the variable is given the value true if any input/output operations for the unit are still pending and false otherwise. In the 'false' case, wait operations are performed for the file or files. Wait operations are not performed in the 'true' case, even if some of the input/output operations are complete.

Execution of a `wait` statement specifying a unit that does not exist, has no file connected to it, or was not opened for asynchronous input/output is permitted, provided that the `wait` statement has no `id=` specifier; such a `wait` statement has no effect.

A file positioning statement (`backspace`, `endfile`, `rewind`) performs wait operations for all pending input/output operations for the file.

Asynchronous input/output is not permitted in conjunction with user-defined derived-type input/output (previous section) because it is anticipated that the number of characters actually written is likely to depend on the values of the variables.

A variable in a scoping unit is said to be an *affector* of a pending input/output operation if any part of it is associated with any part of an item in the input/output list, namelist, or `size=` specifier. While an input/output operation is pending, an affector is not permitted to be redefined, become undefined, or have its pointer association status changed. While an input operation is pending, an affector is also not permitted to be referenced or associated with a dummy argument with the `value` attribute (Section 14.6).

19.4   The asynchronous attribute

The `asynchronous` attribute for a variable has been introduced to warn the compiler that optimizations involving movement of code across `wait` statements (or other statements that cause wait operations) might lead to incorrect results. If a variable appears in an executable statement or a specification expression in a scoping unit and any statement of the scoping unit is executed while the variable is an affector, it must have the `asynchronous` attribute in the scoping unit.

A variable is automatically given this attribute if it or a subobject of it is an item in the input/output list, namelist, or `size=` specifier of an asynchronous input/output statement. A named variable may be declared with this attribute:

```
integer, asynchronous :: int_array(10)
```

or given it by the `asynchronous` statement

```
asynchronous :: int_array, another
```

This statement may be used to give the attribute to a variable that is accessed by use or host association.

Like the `volatile` attribute (Section 18.3), whether an object has the `asynchronous` attribute may vary between scoping units. If a variable is accessed by use or host association, it may gain the attribute, but it never loses it. For dummy and corresponding actual arguments, there is no requirement for agreement in respect of the `asynchronous` attribute. This provides useful flexibility, but needs to be used with care. If the programmer knows that all asynchronous action will be within the procedure, there is no need for the actual argument to have the `asynchronous` attribute. Similarly, if the programmer knows that no operation will ever be pending when the procedure is called, there is no need for the dummy argument to have the `asynchronous` attribute.

All subobjects of a variable with the `asynchronous` attribute have the attribute.

There are restrictions that avoid any copying of an actual argument when the corresponding dummy argument has the `asynchronous` attribute: the dummy argument must not be an array section with a vector subscript; if the actual argument is an array section or an assumed-shape array, the dummy argument must be an assumed-shape array; and if the actual argument is a pointer array, the dummy argument must be an assumed-shape or pointer array.

19.5 Input and output of IEEE exceptional values

Input and output of IEEE infinities and NaNs, previously done in a variety of ways as extensions of Fortran 95, is specified. All the edit descriptors for reals treat these values in the same way and only the field width w is taken into account.

The output forms, each right justified in its field, are

i) `-Inf` or `-Infinity` for minus infinity,

ii) `Inf`, `+Inf`, `Infinity`, or `+Infinity` for plus infinity, and

iii) `NaN`, optionally followed by non-blank characters in parentheses (to hold additional information).

On input, upper- and lower-case letters are treated as equivalent. The forms are

i) `-Inf` or `-Infinity` for minus infinity,

ii) `Inf`, `+Inf`, `Infinity`, or `+Infinity` for plus infinity, and

iii) `NaN`, optionally followed by non-blank characters in parentheses for a NaN. With no such non-blank characters it is a quiet NaN.

19.6 Stream access input/output

Stream access is a new method of accessing an external file. It is established by specifying `access='stream'` on the open statement and may be formatted or unformatted.

The file is positioned by 'file storage units', normally bytes, starting at position 1. The current position may be determined from a scalar integer variable in a pos= specifier of an inquire statement for the unit. A required position may be indicated in a read or write statement by the pos= specifier which accepts a scalar integer expression. For formatted input/output, the value must be 1 or a value previously returned in an inquire statement for the file. In the absence of a pos= specifier, the file position is left unchanged.

It is the intention that unformatted stream input/output will read or write only the data to/from the file; that is, that there is no ancillary record length information (which is normally written for unformatted files). This allows easy interoperability with C binary streams, but the facility to skip or backspace over records is not available.

Here is a simple example of unformatted stream input/output:

```
double precision :: d
integer          :: before_d
   :
open (unit, ..., access='stream', form='formatted')
   :
inquire (unit, pos=before_d)
write (unit) d
   :
write (unit, pos=before_d) d + 1
```

Assuming d is a 64-bit floating-point type, the user could reasonably expect the first write to write exactly 8 bytes to the file. The use of the pos= specifier ensures that the second write will overwrite the previously written value of d, assuming that the file has the capability of positioning; the standard permits a processor to prohibit the use of pos= for particular files that do not have this capability, or to prohibit the use of pos= for forward positioning.

Formatted stream files are very similar to ordinary (record-oriented) stream files; the main difference is that there is no preset maximum record length (the recl= specifier in the open or inquire statements). Another difference is that data-driven record termination in the style of C text streams is allowed. The intrinsic inquiry function new_line(a) returns the character that can be used to cause record termination for formatted stream output (this is the equivalent of the C language '\n' character):

new_line (a) returns the newline character used for formatted stream output. The argument a must be of type character. The result is of type character with the same kind type parameter value as a. In the unlikely event that there is no suitable character for newline in that character set, a blank is returned.

For example, in

```
open(28, file='/dev/tty', access='stream', form='formatted')
write(28, '(a)') 'Hello'//newline('x')//'World'
```

two lines will be written to the file /dev/tty.

19.7   Recursive input/output

A recursive input/output statement is one that is executed while another input/output statement is in execution. We met this in connection with derived-type input/output (Section 19.3); a child data transfer statement is recursive since it always executes while its parent is in execution. The only other situation in which execution of a recursive input/output statement is allowed, and this is an extension from Fortran 95, is for input/output to/from an internal file where the statement does not modify any internal file other than its own.

19.8   The flush statement

Execution of a flush statement for an external file causes data written to it to be available to other processes, or causes data placed in it by means other than Fortran to be available to a read statement. The syntax is just like that of the file positioning statements.

In combination with advance='no' or stream access (Section 19.6), it permits the program to ensure that data written to one unit are sent to the file before requesting input on another unit; that is, that 'prompts' appear promptly.

19.9   Comma after a P edit descriptor

The comma after a P edit descriptor becomes optional when followed by a repeat specifier. For example, 1P2E12.4 is permitted (as it was in Fortran 66).

19.10   The iomsg= specifier

Any input/output statement is permitted to have an iomsg= specifier. This identifies a scalar variable of type default character into which the processor places a message if an error, end-of-file, or end-of-record condition occurs during execution of the statement. If no such condition occurs, the value of the variable is not changed.

19.11   The round= specifier

Rounding during formatted input/output may be controlled by the round= specifier on the open statement, which takes one of the values up, down, zero, nearest, compatible, or processor_defined. It may be overridden by a round= specifier in a read or write statement with one of these values. The meanings are obvious except for the difference between nearest and compatible. Both refer to a closest representable value. If two are equidistant, which is taken is processor dependent for nearest and the value away from zero for compatible.

The rounding mode may also be temporarily changed within a read or write statement by the corresponding ru, rd, rz, rn, rc, and rp edit descriptors.

There is a corresponding specifier in the inquire statement that is assigned the value UP, DOWN, ZERO, NEAREST, COMPATIBLE, PROCESSOR_DEFINED, or UNDEFINED, as approriate. The processor returns the value PROCESSOR_DEFINED only if the I/O rounding mode currently in effect behaves differently from the other rounding modes.

19.12   The sign= specifier

The sign= specifier has been added to the open statement. It can take the value suppress, plus, or processor_defined and controls the optional plus characters in formatted numeric output. It may be overridden by a sign= specifier in a write statement with one of these values. The mode may also be temporarily changed within a write statement by the ss, sp, and s edit descriptors, which are part of Fortran 95.

There is a corresponding specifier in the inquire statement that is assigned the value PLUS, SUPPRESS, PROCESSOR_DEFINED, or UNDEFINED, as appropriate.

19.13   Kind type parameters of integer specifiers

The integer specifiers that return a value (such as nextrec=) were limited to default kind in Fortran 95. Any kind of integer is permitted in Fortran 2003.

19.14   Intrinsic functions for I/O status testing

Two new elemental intrinsic functions are provided for testing the I/O status value returned through the iostat= specifier. Both functions accept an argument of type integer, and return a default logical result.

is_iostat_end(i) returns the value true if i is an I/O status value that corresponds to an end-of-file condition, and false otherwise.

is_iostat_eor(i) returns the value true if i is an I/O status value that corresponds to an end-of-record condition, and false otherwise.

19.15   Some inquire statement enhancements

We have already met a number of new specifiers for the inquire statement (Section 10.5): encoding= (Section 18.7.4), id= and pending= (Section 19.3), pos= (Section 19.6), iomsg= (Section 19.10), round= (Section 19.11), and sign= (Section 19.12). Further, one existing specifier, access=, now has the additional possible value for *acc* of STREAM if the file is connected for stream access.

The following new, optional specifiers have not so far been described, and complete our description of the input/output enhancements.

asynchronous= *asynch*, where *asynch* is a character variable that is assigned the value YES if the file is connected and asynchronous input/output on the unit is allowed; it is assigned the value NO if the file is connected and asynchronous input/output on the unit is not allowed. If there is no connection, it is assigned the value UNDEFINED.

decimal= *dec*, where *dec* is a character variable that is assigned the value COMMA or POINT, corresponding to the decimal edit mode in effect for a connection for formatted input/output. If there is no connection, or if the connection is not for formatted input/output, it is assigned the value UNDEFINED.

size= *size*, where *size* is an integer variable that is assigned the size of the file in file storage units. If the file size cannot be determined, the variable is assigned the value −1. For a file that may be connected for stream access, the file size is the number of the highest-numbered file storage unit in the file. For a file that may be connected for sequential or direct access, the file size may be different from the number of storage units implied by the data in the records; the exact relationship is processor-dependent.

stream= *stm*, where *stm* is a character variable that is assigned the value YES if STREAM is included in the set of allowed access methods for the file, NO if STREAM is not included in the set of allowed access methods for the file, and UNKNOWN if the processor is unable to determine whether or not STREAM is included in the set of allowed access methods for the file.

20. Other features

20.1 Introduction

This chapter describes features that are redundant within Fortran 95 and whose use we deprecate. They might become obsolescent in a future revision, but this is a decision that can be made only within the standardization process. We note again that this decision to group certain features into a final chapter and to deprecate their use is ours alone, and does not have the actual or implied approval of either WG5 or J3.

Each description mentions how the feature concerned may be effectively replaced by a newer feature.

20.2 Storage association

20.2.1 Storage units

Storage units are the fixed units of physical storage allocated to certain data. There is a storage unit called *numeric* for any non-pointer scalar of the default real, default integer, and default logical types, and a storage unit called *character* for any non-pointer scalar of type default character and character length 1. Non-pointer scalars of type default complex or double precision real (Section 20.7) occupy two contiguous numeric storage units. Non-pointer scalars of type default character and length *len* occupy *len* contiguous character storage units.

As well as numeric and character storage units, there are a large number of *unspecified* storage units. A non-pointer scalar object of type non-default integer, real other than default or double precision, non-default logical, non-default complex, or non-default character of any particular length occupies a single unspecified storage unit that is different for each case. An object with the `pointer` attribute has an unspecified storage unit, different from that of any non-pointer object and different for each combination of type, type parameters, and rank. The standard makes no statement about the relative sizes of all these storage units and permits storage association to take place only between objects with the same category of storage unit.

A non-pointer array occupies a sequence of contiguous storage sequences, one for each element, in array element order.

Objects of derived type have no storage association, each occupying an unspecified storage unit that is different in each case, except where a given type contains a `sequence` statement making it a *sequence type*:

```
type storage
   sequence
   integer i          ! First numeric storage unit;
   real a(0:999)      ! subsequent 1000 numeric storage units.
end type storage
```

Should any other derived types appear in such a definition, they too must be sequence types. In Fortran 2003, the type is allowed to have type parameters (Section 15.4) but no type-bound procedures (Section 16.6) are permitted.

A sequence type is a *numeric sequence type* if it has no type parameters, no component is a pointer or allocatable, and each component is of type default integer, default real, double precision real, default complex, or default logical. A component may also be of a previously defined numeric sequence type. This implies that the ultimate components occupy numeric storage units and the type itself has *numeric storage association*. Similarly, a sequence type is a *character sequence type* if it has no type parameters, no component is a pointer or allocatable, and each component is of type default character or a previously defined character sequence type. Such a type has *character storage association*.

A scalar of numeric or character sequence type occupies a storage sequence that consists of the concatenation of the storage sequences of its components. A scalar of any other sequence type occupies a single unspecified storage unit that is unique for each combination of type and type parameters.

A `private` statement may be added to a sequence type definition, making its components private. The `private` and `sequence` statements may be interchanged but must be the second and third statements of the type definition.

Two type definitions in different scoping units define the same data type if they have the same name,[1] both have the `sequence` attribute, and they have components that are not `private` and agree in order, name, and attributes. However, such a practice is prone to error and offers no advantage over having a single definition in a module that is accessed by use association.

20.2.2   The equivalence statement

The `equivalence` statement specifies that a given storage area may be shared by two or more objects. For instance,

```
real aa, angle, alpha, a(3)
equivalence (aa, angle), (alpha, a(1))
```

allows aa and angle to be used interchangeably in the program text, as both names now refer to the same storage location. Similarly, alpha and a(1) may be used interchangeably.

It is possible to equivalence arrays together. In

```
real a(3,3), b(3,3), col1(3), col2(3), col3(3)
equivalence (col1, a, b), (col2, a(1,2)), (col3, a(1,3))
```

---

[1]If one or both types have been accessed by use association and renamed, it is the original names that must agree.

the two arrays a and b are equivalenced, and the columns of a (and hence of b) are equivalenced to the arrays co11, etc. We note in this example that more than two entities may be equivalenced together, even in a single declaration.

It is possible to equivalence variables of the same intrinsic type and kind type parameter or of the same derived type having the sequence attribute. It is also possible to equivalence variables of different types if both have numeric storage association or both have character storage association (see Section 20.2.1). Default character variables need not have the same length, as in

```
character(len=4) a
character(len=3) b(2)
equivalence (a, b(1)(3:))
```

where the character variable a is equivalenced to the last four characters of the six characters of the character array b. Zero character length is not permitted. An example for different types is

```
integer i(100)
real x(100)
equivalence (i, x)
```

where the arrays i and x are equivalenced. This might be used, for instance, to save storage space if i is used in one part of a program unit and x separately in another part. This is a highly dangerous practice, as considerable confusion can arise when one storage area contains variables of two or more data types, and program changes may be made very difficult if the two uses of the one area are to be kept distinct.

Types with default initialization are permitted, provided each initialized component has the same type, type parameters, and value in any pair of equivalenced objects.

All the various combinations of types that may be equivalenced have been described. No other is allowed. Also, apart from double precision real and the default numeric types, equivalencing objects that have different kind type parameters is not allowed. The general form of the statement is

```
equivalence (object, object-list) [, (object, object-list)]...
```

where each *object* is a variable name, array element, or substring. An object must be a variable and must not be a dummy argument, a function result, a pointer, an object with a pointer component at any level of component selection, an allocatable object, an automatic object, a function, a structure component, or a subobject of such an object. Each array subscript and character substring range must be an initialization expression. The interpretation of an array name is identical to that of its first element. An equivalence object must not have the target attribute.

The objects in an equivalence set are said to be *storage associated*. Those of nonzero length share the same first storage unit. Those of zero length are associated with each other and with the first storage unit of those of nonzero length. An equivalence statement may cause other parts of the objects to be associated, but not such that different subobjects of the same object share storage. For example,

```
real a(2), b
equivalence (a(1), b), (a(2), b)   ! Prohibited
```

is not permitted. Also, objects declared in different scoping units must not be equivalenced. For example,

```
use my_module, only : xx
real bb
equivalence(xx, bb)                ! Prohibited
```

is not permitted.

The various uses to which the equivalence was put are replaced by automatic arrays, allocatable arrays, pointers (reuse of storage, Sections 6.4 and 6.5), pointers as aliases (storage mapping, Section 6.15), and the transfer function (mapping of one data type onto another, Section 8.9).

20.2.3   The common block

We have seen in Chapter 5 how two program units are able to communicate by passing variables, or values of expressions between them via argument lists or by using modules. It is also possible to define areas of storage known as common blocks. Each has a storage sequence and may be either named or unnamed, as shown by the simplified syntax of the common specification statement:

```
common [/[cname]/] vlist
```

in which *cname* is an optional name, and *vlist* is a list of variable names, each optionally followed by an array bounds specification. An unnamed common block is known as a *blank* common block. Examples of each are

```
common /hands/ nshuff, nplay, nhand, cards(52)
```

and

```
common // buffer(10000)
```

in which the named common block hands defines a data area containing the quantities which might be required by the subroutines of a card playing program, and the blank common defines a large data area which might be used by different routines as a buffer area.

The name of a common block has global scope and must differ from that of any other global entity (external procedure, program unit, or common block). It may, however, be the same as that of a local entity other than a named constant or intrinsic procedure.

No object in a common block may have the parameter attribute or be a dummy argument, an automatic object, an allocatable object, a polymorphic pointer, or a function. An array may have its bounds declared either in the common statement or in a type declaration or dimension statement. If it is a non-pointer array, the bounds must be declared explicitly and with initialization expressions. If it is a pointer array, however, the bounds may not be declared in the common statement itself. If an object is of derived type, the type must have the sequence or bind attribute and must not have default initialization.

In order for a subroutine to access the variables in the data area, it is sufficient to insert the common definition in each scoping unit which requires access to one or more of the entities in the list. In this fashion, the variables nshuff, nplay, nhand, and cards are made available to those scoping units. No variable may appear more than once in all the common blocks in a scoping unit.

Usually, a common block contains identical variable names in all its appearances, but this is not necessary. In fact, the shared data area may be partitioned in quite different ways in different routines, using different variable names. They are said to be storage associated. It is thus possible for one subroutine to contain a declaration

```
common /coords/ x, y, z, i(10)
```

and another to contain a declaration

```
common /coords/ i, j, a(11)
```

This means that a reference to i(1) in the first routine is equivalent to a reference to a(2) in the second. Through multiple references via use or host association, this can even happen in a single routine. This manner of coding is both untidy and dangerous, and every effort should be made to ensure that all declarations of a given common block declaration are identical in every respect. In particular, the presence or absence of the target attribute is required to be consistent, since otherwise a compiler would have to assume that everything in common has the target attribute, in case it has it in another program unit.

A further practice that is permitted but which we do not recommend is to mix different storage units in the same common block. When this is done, each position in the storage sequence must always be occupied by a storage unit of the same category.

The total number of storage units must be the same in each occurrence of a named common block, but blank common is allowed to vary in size and the longest definition will apply for the complete program.

Yet another practice to be avoided is to use the full syntax of the common statement:

```
common [/[cname]/]vlist [[,]/[cname]/vlist]...
```

which allows several common blocks to be defined in one statement, and a single common block to be declared in parts. A combined example is

```
common /pts/x,y,z /matrix/a(10,10),b(5,5) /pts/i,j,k
```

which is equivalent to

```
common /pts/ x, y, z, i, j, k
common /matrix/ a(10,10), b(5,5)
```

which is certainly a more understandable declaration of two shared data areas. The only need for the piecewise declaration of one block is when the limit of 39 continuation lines is otherwise too low.

The common statement may be combined with the equivalence statement, as in the example

```
real a(10), b
equivalence (a,b)
common /change/ b
```

In this case, a is regarded as part of the common block, and its length is extended appropriately. Such an equivalence must not cause data in two different common blocks to become storage associated, it must not cause an extension of the common block except at its tail, and two different objects or subobjects in the same common block must not become storage associated. It must not cause an object of a type with default initialization to become associated with an object in a common block.

A common block may be declared in a module, and its variables accessed by use association. Variable names in a common block in a module may be declared to have the private attribute, but this does not prevent associated variables being declared elsewhere through other common statements.

An individual variable in a common block may not be given the save attribute, but the whole block may. If a common block has the save attribute in any scoping unit other than the main program, it must have the save attribute in all such scoping units. The general form of the save statement is

```
save [[::] saved-entity-list]
```

where *saved-entity* is *variable-name* or *common-block-name*. A simple example is

```
save /change/
```

A blank common always has the save attribute.

Data in a common block without the save attribute become undefined on return from a subprogram unless the block is also declared in the main program or in another subprogram that is in execution.

The use of modules (Section 5.5) obviates the need for common blocks.

20.2.4 The block data program unit

Non-pointer variables in named common blocks may be initialized in data statements, but such statements must be collected into a special type of program unit, known as a block data program unit. It must have the form

```
block data [block-data-name]
    [specification-stmt] ...
end [block data [block-data-name]]
```

where each *specification-stmt* is an implicit, use, type declaration (including double precision), intrinsic, pointer, target, common, dimension, data, equivalence, parameter, or save statement or derived-type definition. A type declaration statement must not specify the allocatable, external, intent, optional, private, or public attributes. An example is

```
block data
    common /axes/ i,j,k
    data i,j,k /1,2,3/
end block data
```

in which the variables in the common block axes are defined for use in any other scoping unit which accesses them.

It is possible to collect many common blocks and their corresponding data statements together in one block data program unit. However, it may be a better practice to have several different block data program units, each containing common blocks which have some logical association with one another. To allow for this, block data program units may be named in order to be able to distinguish them. A complete program may contain any number of block data program units, but only one of them may be unnamed. A common block must not appear in more than one block data program unit. It is not possible to initialize blank common.

The name of a block data program unit may appear in an external statement. When a processor is loading program units from a library, it may need such a statement in order to load the block data program unit.

The use of modules (Section 5.5) obviates the need for block data.

20.3 Shape and character length disagreement

In Fortran 77, it was often convenient, when passing an array, not to have to specify the size of the dummy array. For this case, the *assumed-size* array declaration is available, where the last *bounds* in the *bounds-list* is

[*lower-bound*:] *

and the other bounds (if any) must be declared explicitly. Such an array must not be a function result.

Since an assumed-size array has no bounds in its last dimension, it does not have a shape and, therefore, must not be used as a whole array in an executable statement, except as an argument to a procedure that does not require its shape. However, if an array section is formed with an explicit upper bound in the last dimension, this has a shape and may be used as a whole array.

An assumed-size array of a derived type with default initialization or of a finalizable type is not permitted to have intent out, because this would require an action for every element of an array of unknown shape.

An object of one size or rank may be passed to an explicit-shape or assumed-size dummy argument array that is of another size or rank. If an array element is passed to an array, the actual argument is regarded as an array with elements that are formed from the parent array from the given array element onwards, in array element order. Figure 20.1 illustrates this. Here only the last 49 elements of a are available to sub, as the first array element of a which is passed to sub is a(52). Within sub, this element is referenced as b(1).

In the same example, it would also be perfectly legitimate for the declaration of b to be written as real b(7, 7) and for the last 49 elements of a to be addressed as though they were ordered as a 7×7 array. The converse is also true. An array dimensioned 10×10 in

---

Figure 20.1

```
real a(100)
  :
call sub (a(52), 49)
  :
subroutine sub(b,n)
  :
real b(n)
  :
```

---

a calling subroutine may be dimensioned as a singly-dimensioned array of size 100 in the called subroutine. Within `sub`, it is illegal to address `b(50)` in any way, as that would be beyond the declared length of `a` in the calling routine. In all cases, the association is by storage sequence, in array element order.

In the case of default character type, agreement of character length is not required. For a scalar dummy argument of character length *len*, the actual argument may have a greater character length and its leftmost *len* characters are associated with the dummy argument. For example, if `chasub` has a single dummy argument of character length 1,

```
call chasub(word(3:4))
```

is a valid `call` statement. For an array dummy argument, the restriction is on the total number of characters in the array. An array element or array element substring is regarded as a sequence of characters from its first character to the last character of the array. For an assumed-size array, the size is the number of characters in the sequence divided by the character length of the dummy argument.

Shape or character length disagreement cannot of course occur when the dummy argument is assumed-shape (by definition, the shape is assumed from the actual argument). It can occur for explicit-shape and assumed-size arrays. Implementations are likely to receive explicit-shape and assumed-size arrays in contiguous storage, but permit any uniform spacing of the elements of an assumed-shape array. They will need to make a copy of any array argument that is not stored contiguously (for example, the section `a(1:10:2)`), unless the dummy argument is assumed-shape. To avoid copies of this kind, a scalar actual argument is permitted to be associated with an array only if the actual argument is an element of an array that is not an assumed-shaped array, an array pointer, or is a subobject of such an element.

In Fortran 2003, these rules on character length disagreement have been extended to include `character(kind=c_char)` (which will often be the same as default character) and to treat any other scalar actual argument of type default character or `character(kind=c_char)` as if it were an array of size one. This includes the case where the argument is an element of an assumed-shape array or an array pointer, or a subobject thereof; note that just that element or subobject is passed, not the rest of the array.

When a procedure is invoked through a generic name, as a defined operation, or as a defined assignment, rank agreement between the actual and the dummy arguments is required. Note also that only a scalar dummy argument may be associated with a scalar actual argument.

Assumed-shape arrays (Section 6.3) supplant this feature.

20.4 The entry statement

A subprogram usually defines a single procedure, and the first statement to be executed is the first executable statement after the header statement. In some cases it is useful to be able to define several procedures in one subprogram, particularly when wishing to share access to some saved local variables or to a section of code. This is possible for external and module subprograms (but not for internal subprograms) by means of the entry statement. This is a statement that has the form

>   entry *entry-name* [([*dummy-argument-list*]) [result(*result-name*)]]

and may appear anywhere between the header line and contains (or end if it has no contains) statement of a subprogram, except within a construct. The entry statement provides a procedure with an associated dummy argument list, exactly as does the subroutine or function statement, and these arguments may be different from those given on the subroutine or function statement. Execution commences with the first executable statement following the entry statement.

In the case of a function, each entry defines another function, whose characteristics (that is, shape, type, type parameters, and whether a pointer) are given by specifications for the *result-name* (or *entry-name* if there is no result clause). If the characteristics are the same as for the main entry, a single variable is used for both results; otherwise, they must not be allocatable, must not be pointers, must be scalar, and must both be one of the default integer, default real, double precision real (Section 20.7), or default complex types, and they are treated as equivalenced. The result clause plays exactly the same rôle as for the main entry.

Each entry is regarded as defining another procedure, with its own name. The names of all these procedures and their result variables (if any) must be distinct. The name of an entry has the same scope as the name of the subprogram. It must not be the name of a dummy argument of any of the procedures defined by the subprogram. An entry statement is not permitted in an interface block; there must be another body for each entry whose interface is wanted, using a subroutine or function statement, rather than an entry statement.

An entry is called in exactly the same manner as a subroutine or function, depending on whether it appears in a subroutine subprogram or a function subprogram. An example is given in Figure 20.2 which shows a search function with two entry points. We note that looku and looks are synonymous within the function, so that it is immaterial which value is set before the return.

None of the procedures defined by a subprogram is permitted to reference itself, unless the keyword recursive is present on the subroutine or function statement. For a function, such a reference must be indirect unless there is a result clause on the function or entry statement. If a procedure may be referenced directly in the subprogram that defines it, the interface is explicit in the subprogram.

The name of an entry dummy argument that appears in an executable statement preceding the entry statement in the subprogram must also appear in a function, subroutine, or entry statement that precedes the executable statement. Also, if a dummy argument is used

Figure 20.2

```
        function looku(list, member)
        integer looku, list(:), member, looks
!
!       To locate member in an array list.
!       If list is unsorted, entry looku is used;
!       if list is sorted, entry looks is used.
!
!       list is unsorted
        do looku = 1, size(list)
            if list(looku) .eq. member) go to 9
        end do
        go to 3
!
!        entry for sorted list
        entry looks(list, member)
!
        do looku = 1, size(list)
            if (list(looku) .ge. member) go to 2
        end do
        go to 3
!
!        is member at position looku?
    2   if (list(looku) .eq. member) go to 9
!
!        member not in list
    3   looku = 0
!
    9   end function looku
```

to define the array size or character length of an object, the object must not be referenced unless the argument is present in the procedure reference that is active.

During the execution of one of the procedures defined by a subprogram, a reference to a dummy argument is permitted only if it is a dummy argument of the procedure referenced.

The entry statement is made unnecessary by the use of modules (Section 5.5), with each procedure defined by an entry becoming a module procedure. Its presence has substantially complicated the standard because the reader has to remember that a subprogram may define several procedures.

20.5   The include line

It is sometimes useful to be able to include source text from somewhere else into the source stream presented to the compiler. This facility is possible using an include line:

```
include char-literal-constant
```

where *char-literal-constant* must not have a kind parameter that is a named constant. This line is not a Fortran statement and must appear as a single source line where a statement may occur. It will be replaced by material in a processor-dependent way determined by the character string *char-literal-constant*. The included text may itself contain `include` lines, which are similarly replaced. An `include` line must not reference itself, directly or indirectly. When an `include` line is resolved, the first included line must not be a continuation line and the last line must not be continued. An `include` line may have a trailing comment, but may not be labelled nor, when expanded, may it contain incomplete statements.

The `include` line was available as an extension to many Fortran 77 systems and was often used to ensure that every occurrence of global data in a `common` block was identical. In modern Fortran, the same effect is better achieved by placing global data in a module (Section 5.5). This cannot lead to accidental declarations of local variables in each procedure.

This feature is useful when identical executable statements are needed for more than one type, for example in a set of procedures for sorting data values of various types. The executable statements can be maintained in an include file that is referenced inside each instance of the sort procedure.

20.6   The do while form of loop control

In Section 4.5, a form of the `do` construct was described that may be written as

```
do
    if (scalar-logical-expr) exit
    :
end do
```

An alternative, but redundant, form of this is its representation using a `do while` statement:

```
do [label] [,] while (.not.scalar-logical-expr)
```

We prefer the form that uses the `exit` statement because this can be placed anywhere in the loop, whereas the `do while` statement always performs its test at the loop start. If the *scalar-logical-expr* becomes false in the middle of the loop, the rest of the loop is still executed. Potential optimization penalties that the use of the `do while` entails are fully described in Chapter 10 of *Optimizing Supercompilers for Supercomputers*, M. Wolfe (Pitman, 1989).

20.7   Double precision real

Another *type* that may be used in a type declaration, `function`, `implicit`, or component declaration statement is double precision which specifies double precision real. The precision is greater than that of default real.

Literal constants written with the exponent letter `d` (or `D`) are of type double precision real by default; no kind parameter may be specified if this exponent letter is used. Thus, `1d0` is of type double precision real. If dp is an integer named constant with the value `kind(1d0)`, `double precision` is synonymous with `real(kind=dp)`.

There is a d (or D) edit descriptor that was originally intended for double precision quantities, but, now, it is identical to the e edit descriptor except that the output form may have a D instead of an E as its exponent letter. A double precision real literal constant, with exponent letter d, is acceptable on input whenever any other real literal constant is acceptable.

There are two elemental intrinsic functions which were not described in Chapter 8 because they have a result of type double precision real.

dble (a) for a of type integer, real, or complex returns the double precision real value
    real(a, kind(0d0)).

dprod (x, y) returns the product x*y for x and y of type default real as a double precision real result.

The double precision real data type has been replaced by the real type of kind kind(0.d0).

20.8   The dimension and parameter statements

To declare entities, we normally use type specifications. However, if all the entities involved are arrays, they may be declared *without* type specifications in a dimension statement:

    dimension i(10), b(50,50), c(n,m) ! n and m are dummy integer
                                      ! arguments or named constants

The general form is

    dimension [::] *array-name*(*array-spec*) [, *array-name*(*array-spec*)]...

Here, the type may either be specified in a type declaration statement such as

    integer i

that does not specify the dimension information, or may be declared implicitly. Our view is that neither of these is sound practice; the type declaration statement looks like a declaration of a scalar and we explained in Section 7.2 that we regard implicit typing as dangerous. Therefore, the use of the dimension statement is not recommended.

An alternative way to specify a named constant is by the parameter statement. It has the general form

    parameter (*named-constant-definition-list*)

where each *named-constant-definition* is

    constant-name = *initialization-expr*

Each constant named must either have been typed in a previous type declaration statement in the scoping unit, or take its type from the first letter of its name according to the implicit typing rule of the scoping unit. In the case of implicit typing, the appearance of the named constant in a subsequent type declaration statement in the scoping unit must confirm the type and type parameters, and there must not be an implicit statement for the letter subsequently in the scoping unit. Similarly, the shape must have been specified previously or be scalar. Each named constant in the list is defined with the value of the corresponding expression according to the rules of intrinsic assignment.

An example using implicit typing and an initialization expression including a named constant that is defined in the same statement is

```
implicit integer (a, p)
parameter (apple = 3, pear = apple**2)
```

For the same reasons as for `dimension`, we recommend avoiding the `parameter` statement.

20.9 Specific names of intrinsic procedures

There are a number of intrinsic functions that may have arguments that are all of one type and type parameters, or all of another. For instance, we may write

```
a = sqrt(b)
```

and the appropriate square-root function will be invoked, depending on whether the variable b is real or complex and on its type parameters. In this case, the name sqrt is known as a *generic name*, meaning that the appropriate function is supplied, depending on the type and type parameters of the actual arguments of the function, and that a single name may be used for what are, probably, different specific functions.

Some of the intrinsic functions have *specific names* and are specified by the standard. They are listed in Tables 20.1 and 20.2. In the tables, 'Character' stands for default character, 'Integer' stands for default integer, 'Real' stands for default real, 'Double' stands for double precision real, and 'Complex' stands for default complex. Those functions in Table 20.2 may be passed as actual arguments to a subprogram, provided they are specified in an `intrinsic` statement (Section 8.1.3).

All the procedures that we described in Chapter 8 are regarded as generic, even where there is only one version.

Table 20.1. Specific intrinsic functions not available as actual arguments.

Description	Generic Form	Specific Name	Argument Type	Function Type
Conversion to integer	`int(a)`	`int`	Real	Integer
		`ifix`	Real	Integer
		`idint`	Double	Integer
Conversion to real	`real(a)`	`real`	Integer	Real
		`float`	Integer	Real
		`sngl`	Double	Real
max(a1,a2,...)	`max(a1,a2,...)`	`max0`	Integer	Integer
		`amax1`	Real	Real
		`dmax1`	Double	Double
		`amax0`	Integer	Real
		`max1`	Real	Integer
min(a1,a2,...)	`min(a1,a2,...)`	`min0`	Integer	Integer
		`amin1`	Real	Real
		`dmin1`	Double	Double
		`amin0`	Integer	Real
		`min1`	Real	Integer
lge(string_a,string_b)	`lge(string_a,string_b)`	`lge`	Character	Logical
lgt(string_a,string_b)	`lgt(string_a,string_b)`	`lgt`	Character	Logical
lle(string_a,string_b)	`lle(string_a,string_b)`	`lle`	Character	Logical
llt(string_a,string_b)	`llt(string_a,string_b)`	`llt`	Character	Logical

Table 20.2. Specific intrinsic functions available as actual arguments.

Description	Generic Form	Specific Name	Argument Type	Function Type
Absolute value of a	`sign(a,b)`	`isign`	Integer	Integer
times sign of b		`sign`	Real	Real
		`dsign`	Double	Double
max(x-y,0)	`dim(x,y)`	`idim`	Integer	Integer
		`dim`	Real	Real
		`ddim`	Double	Double
x*y		`dprod(x,y)`	Real	Double
Truncation	`aint(a)`	`aint`	Real	Real
		`dint`	Double	Double
Nearest whole	`anint(a)`	`anint`	Real	Real
number		`dnint`	Double	Double
Nearest integer	`nint(a)`	`nint`	Real	Integer
		`idnint`	Double	Integer
Absolute value	`abs(a)`	`iabs`	Integer	Integer
		`abs`	Real	Real
		`dabs`	Double	Double
		`cabs`	Complex	Real
Remainder	`mod(a,p)`	`mod`	Integer	Integer
modulo p		`amod`	Real	Real
		`dmod`	Double	Double
Square root	`sqrt(x)`	`sqrt`	Real	Real
		`dsqrt`	Double	Double
		`csqrt`	Complex	Complex
Exponential	`exp(x)`	`exp`	Real	Real
		`dexp`	Double	Double
		`cexp`	Complex	Complex
Natural logarithm	`log(x)`	`alog`	Real	Real
		`dlog`	Double	Double
		`clog`	Complex	Complex
Common logarithm	`log10(x)`	`alog10`	Real	Real
		`dlog10`	Double	Double
Sine	`sin(x)`	`sin`	Real	Real
		`dsin`	Double	Double
		`csin`	Complex	Complex

Cosine	cos(x)	cos	Real	Real
		dcos	Double	Double
		ccos	Complex	Complex
Tangent	tan(x)	tan	Real	Real
		dtan	Double	Double
Arcsine	asin(x)	asin	Real	Real
		dasin	Double	Double
Arccosine	acos(x)	acos	Real	Real
		dacos	Double	Double
Arctangent	atan(x)	atan	Real	Real
		datan	Double	Double
	atan2(y,x)	atan2	Real	Real
		datan2	Double	Double
Hyperbolic sine	sinh(x)	sinh	Real	Real
		dsinh	Double	Double
Hyperbolic cosine	cosh(x)	cosh	Real	Real
		dcosh	Double	Double
Hyperbolic tangent	tanh(x)	tanh	Real	Real
		dtanh	Double	Double
Imaginary part	aimag(z)	aimag	Complex	Real
Complex conjugate	conjg(z)	conjg	Complex	Complex
Character length	len(s)	len	Character	Integer
Starting position	index(s,t)	index	Character	Integer

A. Intrinsic procedures

In this appendix, we list all the intrinsic procedures, giving the names of their arguments and a short description. Those that are part of Fortran 2003 only have an asterisk after their names and those Fortran 95 procedures that have an added optional kind argument have an asterisk after this argument.

Name	Section	Description
abs (a)	8.3.1	Absolute value.
achar (i [,kind*])	8.5.1	Character in position i of ASCII collating sequence.
acos (x)	8.4	Arc cosine (inverse cosine) function.
adjustl (string)	8.5.3	Adjust left, removing leading blanks and inserting trailing blanks.
adjustr (string)	8.5.3	Adjust right, removing trailing blanks and inserting leading blanks.
aimag (z)	8.3.1	Imaginary part of complex number.
aint (a [,kind])	8.3.1	Truncate to a whole number.
all (mask [,dim])	8.11	True if all elements are true.
allocated (array) or	8.12.1	True if the array is allocated.
allocated* (scalar)	17.5.1	True if the scalar is allocated.
anint (a [,kind])	8.3.1	Nearest whole number.
any (mask [,dim])	8.11	True if any element is true.
asin (x)	8.4	Arcsine (inverse sine) function.
associated (pointer [,target])	8.2	True if pointer is associated with target.
atan (x)	8.4	Arctangent (inverse tangent) function.
atan2 (y, x)	8.4	Argument of complex number (x, y).
bit_size (i)	8.8.1	Maximum number of bits that may be held in an integer.

btest (i, pos)	8.8.2	True if bit pos of integer i has value 1.
ceiling (a [, kind])	8.3.1	Least integer greater than or equal to its argument.
char (i [,kind])	8.5.1	Character in position i of the processor collating sequence.
cmplx (x [,y] [,kind])	8.3.1	Convert to complex type.
command_argument_count* ()	18.6.2	Number of command arguments.
conjg (z)	8.3.2	Conjugate of a complex number.
cos (x)	8.4	Cosine function.
cosh (x)	8.4	Hyperbolic cosine function.
count (mask [,dim] [,kind*])	8.11	Number of true elements.
cpu_time (time)	8.16.2	Processor time
cshift (array, shift [,dim])	8.13.5	Perform circular shift.
call date_and_time ([date] [,time] [,zone] [,values])	8.16.1	Real-time clock reading date and time.
dble (a)	11.4.1	Convert to double precision real.
digits (x)	8.7.2	Number of significant digits in the model for x.
dim (x, y)	8.3.2	max(x−y, 0).
dot_product (vector_a, vector_b)	8.10	Dot product.
dprod (x, y)	11.4.1	Double precision real product of two default real scalars.
eoshift (array, shift [,boundary] [,dim])	8.13.5	Perform end-off shift.
epsilon (x)	8.7.2	Number that is almost negligible compared with one in the model for numbers like x.
exp (x)	8.4	Exponential function.
exponent (x)	8.7.3	Exponent part of the model for x.
extends_type_of* (a, mold)	16.10	Type extension inquiry.
floor (a [, kind])	8.3.1	Greatest integer less than or equal to its argument.
fraction (x)	8.7.3	Fractional part of the model for x.
get_command* ([command] [,length] [,status])	18.6.2	Get command line.

get_command_argument* (number [, value] [,length] [,status])	18.6.2	Get single command argument.
get_environment_variable* (name [, value] [,length] [,status] [,trim_name])	18.6.1	Get environment variable.
huge (x)	8.7.2	Largest number in the model for numbers like x.
iachar (c [,kind*])	8.5.1	Position of character c in ASCII collating sequence.
iand (i, j)	8.8.2	Logical and on the bits.
ibclr (i, pos)	8.8.2	Clear bit pos to zero.
ibits (i, pos, len)	8.8.2	Extract a sequence of bits.
ibset (i, pos)	8.8.2	Set bit pos to one.
ichar (c [,kind*])	8.5.1	Position of character c in the processor collating sequence.
ieor (i, j)	8.8.2	Exclusive or on the bits.
index (string, substring [,back] [,kind*])	8.5.3	Starting position of substring within string.
int (a [,kind])	8.3.1	Convert to integer type.
ior (i, j)	8.8.2	Inclusive or on the bits.
ishft (i, shift)	8.8.2	Logical shift on the bits.
ishftc (i, shift [,size])	8.8.2	Logical circular shift on a set of bits on the right.
is_isostat_end* (i)	19.14	Test value for end-of-file condition.
is_isostat_eor* (i)	19.14	Test value for end-of-record condition.
kind (x)	8.2	Kind type parameter value.
lbound (array [,dim] [,kind*])	8.12.2	Array lower bounds.
len (string) [,kind*]	8.6.1	Character length.
len_trim (string) [,kind*]	8.5.3	Length of string without trailing blanks.
lge (string_a, string_b)	8.5.2	True if string_a equals or follows string_b in ASCII collating sequence.
lgt (string_a, string_b)	8.5.2	True if string_a follows string_b in ASCII collating sequence.

`lle (string_a, string_b)`	8.5.2	True if `string_a` equals or precedes `string_b` in ASCII collating sequence.
`llt (string_a, string_b)`	8.5.2	True if `string_a` precedes `string_b` in ASCII collating sequence.
`log (x)`	8.4	Natural (base *e*) logarithm function.
`log10 (x)`	8.4	Common (base 10) logarithm function.
`logical (l, [,kind])`	8.5.4	Convert between kinds of logicals.
`matmul (matrix_a, matrix_b)`	8.10	Matrix multiplication.
`max (a1, a2 [,a3,...])`	8.3.2	Maximum value.
`maxexponent (x)`	8.7.2	Maximum exponent in the model for numbers like x.
`maxloc (array [,mask] [,kind*])` or `maxloc (array, dim [,mask] [,kind*])`	8.14	Location of maximum array element.
`maxval (array [,mask])` or `maxval (array, dim [,mask])`	8.11	Value of maximum array element.
`merge (tsource, fsource, mask)`	8.13.1	`tsource` when `mask` is true and `fsource` otherwise.
`min (a1, a2 [,a3,...])`	8.3.2	Minimum value.
`minexponent (x)`	8.7.2	Minimum exponent in the model for numbers like x.
`minloc (array [,mask] [,kind*])` or `minloc (array, dim [,mask] [,kind*])`	8.14	Location of minimum array element.
`minval (array [,mask])` or `minval (array, dim [,mask])`	8.11	Value of minimum array element.
`mod (a, p)`	8.3.2	Remainder modulo p, that is `a-int(a/p)*p`.
`modulo (a, p)`	8.3.2	`a modulo p`.
`move_alloc* (from, to)`	17.6	Move allocation.

`call mvbits (from,`
`    frompos, len, to,`
`    topos)`
	8.8.3	Copy bits.

`nearest (x, s)`	8.7.3	Nearest different machine number in the direction given by the sign of s.
`new_line* (a)`	19.6	Newline character.
`nint (a [,kind])`	8.3.1	Nearest integer.
`not (i)`	8.8.2	Logical complement of the bits.
`null([mold])`	8.15	Disassociated pointer.
`pack (array, mask` `    [,vector])`	8.13.2	Pack elements corresponding to true elements of mask into rank-one result.
`precision (x)`	8.7.2	Decimal precision in the model for x.
`present (a)`	8.2	True if optional argument is present.
`product (array [,mask]) or`		
`product (array, dim` `    [,mask])`	8.11	Product of array elements.
`radix (x)`	8.7.2	Base of the model for numbers like x.
`call random_number` `    (harvest)`	8.16.3	Random numbers in range $0 \leq x < 1$.
`call random_seed ([size]` `    [put] [get])`	8.16.3	Initialize or restart random number generator.
`range (x)`	8.7.2	Decimal exponent range in the model for x.
`real (a [,kind])`	8.3.1	Convert to real type.
`repeat (string, ncopies)`	8.6.2	Concatenates ncopies of string.
`reshape (source, shape` `    [,pad] [,order])`	8.13.3	Reshape source to shape shape.
`rrspacing (x)`	8.7.3	Reciprocal of the relative spacing of model numbers near x.
`same_type_as* (a,b)`	16.10	Compare dynamic types.
`scale (x, i)`	8.7.3	$x \times b^i$, where b=radix(x).
`scan (string, set [,back]` `    [,kind*])`	8.5.3	Index of leftmost (rightmost if back is true) character of string that belongs to set; zero if none belong.
`selected_char_kind* (name)`	18.7.1	Kind of character set called name.
`selected_int_kind (r)`	8.7.4	Kind of type parameter for specified exponent range.
`selected_real_kind ([p]` `    [,r])`	8.7.4	Kind of type parameter for specified precision and exponent range.

set_exponent (x, i)	8.7.3	Model number whose sign and fractional part are those of x and whose exponent part is i.
shape (source [,kind*])	8.12.2	Array (or scalar) shape.
sign (a, b)	8.3.2	Absolute value of a times sign of b.
sin (x)	8.4	Sine function.
sinh (x)	8.4	Hyperbolic sine function.
size (array [,dim] [,kind*])	8.12.2	Array size.
spacing (x)	8.7.3	Absolute spacing of model numbers near x.
spread (source, dim, ncopies)	8.13.4	ncopies copies of source forming an array of rank one greater.
sqrt (x)	8.4	Square-root function.
sum (array [,mask]) or sum(array, dim [,mask])	8.11	Sum of array elements.
call system_clock ([count] [,count_rate] [,count_max])	8.16.1	Integer data from real-time clock.
tan (x)	8.4	Tangent function.
tanh (x)	8.4	Hyperbolic tangent function.
tiny (x)	8.7.2	Smallest positive number in the model for numbers like x.
transfer (source, mold [,size])	8.9	Same physical representation as source, but type of mold.
transpose (matrix)	8.13.6	Matrix transpose.
trim (string)	8.6.2	Remove trailing blanks from a single string.
ubound (array [,dim] [,kind*])	8.12.2	Array upper bounds.
unpack (vector, mask, field)	8.13.2	Unpack elements of vector corresponding to true elements of mask.
verify (string, set [,back] [,kind*])	8.5.3	Zero if all characters of string belong to set or index of leftmost (rightmost if back true) that does not.

B. Obsolescent features

B.1 Obsolescent in Fortran 95

The features of this section are described by the Fortran 95 standard to be obsolescent. Their replacements are described in the relevant subsections.

B.1.1 Fixed source form

In the old fixed source form, each statement consists of one or more *lines* exactly 72 characters long,[1] and each line is divided into three *fields*. The first field consists of positions 1 to 5 and may contain a *statement label*. A Fortran statement may be written in the second fields of up to 20 consecutive lines. The first line of a multi-line statement is known as the *initial line* and the succeeding lines as *continuation lines*.

A non-comment line is an initial line or a continuation line depending on whether there is a character, other than zero or blank, in position 6 of the line, which is the second field. The first field of a continuation line must be blank. The ampersand is not used for continuation.

The third field, from positions 7 to 72, is reserved for the Fortran statements themselves. Note that if a construct is named, the name must be placed here and not in the label field.

Except in a character context, blanks are insignificant.

The presence of an asterisk (*) or a character c in position 1 of a line indicates that the whole line is commentary. An exclamation mark indicates the start of commentary, except in position 6, where it indicates continuation.

Several statements separated by a semicolon (;) may appear on one line. The semicolon may not, in this case, be in column 6, where it would indicate continuation. Only the first of the statements on a line may be labelled. A semicolon that is the last non-blank character of a line, or the last non-blank character ahead of commentary, is ignored.

A program unit end statement must not be continued, and any other statement with an initial line that appears to be a program unit end statement must not be continued.

A processor may restrict the appearance of its defined control characters, if any, in this source form.

In applications where a high degree of compatibility between the old and the new source forms is required, observance of the following rules can be of great help:

- confine statement labels to positions 1 to 5 and statements to positions 7 to 72;

---

[1]This limit is processor dependent if the line contains characters other than those of the default type.

- treat blanks as being significant;

- use only ! to indicate a comment (but not in position 6);

- for continued statements, place an ampersand in both position 73 of a continued line and position 6 of a continuing line.

The fixed source form has been replaced by the free source form (Section 2.4). Also, a tool to facilitate the conversion of Fortran 77 code to the free source form can be obtained by anonymous ftp to *ftp.numerical.rl.ac.uk*; the directory is */pub/MRandC* and the file name is *convert.f90*. The tool has a number of other features, such as the ability to indent code.

B.1.2   Computed go to

A form of branch statement is the computed go to, which enables one path among many to be selected, depending on the value of a scalar integer expression. The general form is

```
go to (sl1, sl2, sl3,...) [,] intexpr
```

where *sl1*, *sl2*, *sl3*, etc. are labels of statements in the same scoping unit, and *intexpr* is any scalar integer expression. The same statement label may appear more than once. An example is

```
go to (6,10,20) i(k)**2+j
```

which references three statement labels. When the statement is executed, if the value of the integer expression is 1, the first branch will be taken, and control is transferred to the statement labelled 6. If the value is 2, the second branch will be taken, and so on. If the value is less than 1, or greater than 3, no branch will be taken, and the next statement following the go to will be executed.

This statement is replaced by the case construct (Section 4.4).

B.1.3   Character length specification character*

Alternatives for default characters to

```
character([len=]len-value)
```

as a *type* in a type declaration, function, implicit, or component definition statement are

```
character*(len-value)[,]
```
and
```
character*len[,]
```

where *len* is an integer literal constant without a specified kind value and the optional comma is permitted only in a type declaration statement and only when :: is absent:

```
character*20 word, letter*1
```

B.1.4 Data statements among executables

The data statement may be placed among the executable statements, but such placement is rarely used and not recommended, since data initialization properly belongs with the specification statements.

B.1.5 Statement functions

It may be that within a single program unit there are repeated occurrences of a computation which can be represented as a single statement. For instance, to calculate the parabolic function represented by

$$y = a + bx + cx^2$$

for different values of x, but with the same coefficients, there may be references to

```
y1 = 1. + x1*(2. + 3.*x1)
:
y2 = 1. + x2*(2. + 3.*x2)
:
```

etc. In Fortran 77, it was more convenient to invoke a so-called *statement function* (now better coded as an internal subroutine, Section 5.6), which must appear after any implicit and other relevant specification statements and before the executable statements. The example above would become

```
parab(x) = 1. + x*(2. + 3.*x)
:
y1 = parab(x1)
:
y2 = parab(x2)
```

Here, x is a dummy argument, which is used in the definition of the statement function. The variables x1 and x2 are actual arguments to the function.

The general form is

function-name ([*dummy-argument-list*]) = *scalar-expr*

where the *function-name* and each *dummy-argument* must be specified, explicitly or implicitly, to be scalar data objects. To make it clear that this is a statement function and not an assignment to a host array element, we recommend declaring the type by placing the *function-name* in a type declaration statement; this is *required* whenever a host entity has the same name. The *scalar-expr* must be composed of constants, references to scalar variables, references to functions, and intrinsic operations. If there is a reference to a function, the function must not be a transformational intrinsic nor require an explicit interface, the result must be scalar, and any array argument must be a named array. A reference to a non-intrinsic function must not require an explicit interface. A named constant that is referenced or an array of which an element is referenced must be declared earlier in the scoping unit or be accessed by use or host association. A scalar variable referenced may be a dummy argument of the statement function or a variable that is accessible in the scoping unit. A dummy argument of the host procedure must not be referenced unless it is a dummy argument of the main entry or of an `entry` that precedes the statement function. If any entity is implicitly typed, a subsequent type declaration must confirm the type and type parameters. The dummy arguments are scalar and have a scope of the statement function statement only.

A statement function always has an implicit interface and may not be supplied as a procedure argument. It may appear within an internal procedure, and may reference other statement functions appearing before it in the same scoping unit, but not itself nor any appearing after. A function reference in the expression must not redefine a dummy argument. A statement function is pure (Section 6.10) if it references only pure functions.

A statement function statement is not permitted in an interface block.

Note that statement functions are irregular in that use and host association are not available.

B.1.6   Assumed character length of function results

A non-recursive external function whose result is scalar, character, and non-pointer may have assumed character length, as in Figure B.1. Such a function is not permitted to specify a defined operation. In a scoping unit that invokes such a function, the interface must be implicit and there must be a declaration of the length, as in Figure B.2, or such a declaration must be accessible by use or host association.

Figure B.1

```
      function copy(word)
         character(len=*) copy, word
         copy = word
      end function copy
```

Figure B.2

```
      program main
         external copy                 ! Interface block not allowed.
         character(len=10) copy
         write(*, *) copy('This message will be truncated')
      end program main
```

This facility is included only for compatibility with Fortran 77 and is completely at variance with the philosophy of Fortran 90/95 that the attributes of a function result depend only on the actual arguments of the invocation and on any data accessible by the function through host or use association.

This facility may be replaced by use of a subroutine whose arguments correspond to the function result and the function arguments.

B.1.7 Arithmetic if statement

The arithmetic if provides a three-way branching mechanism, depending on whether an arithmetic expression has a value which is less than, equal to, or greater than zero. It is replaced by the if statement and construct (Section 4.3). Its general form is

    if (*expr*) *sl1*, *sl2*, *sl3*

where *expr* is any scalar expression of type integer or real, and *sl1*, *sl2*, and *sl3* are the labels of statements in the same scoping unit. If the result obtained by evaluating *expr* is negative then the branch to *sl1* is taken, if the result is zero the branch to *sl2* is taken, and if the result is greater than zero the branch to *sl3* is taken. An example is

```
      if (p-q) 1,2,3
    1 p = 0.
      go to 4
    2 p = 1.
      q = 1.
      go to 4
    3 q = 0.
    4 ...
```

in which a branch to 1, 2, or 3 is taken depending on the value of p-q. The arithmetic if may be used as a two-way branch when two of the labels are identical:

```
      if (x-y) 1,2,1
```

B.1.8 Shared do-loop termination

A do-loop may be terminated on a labelled statement other than an end do or continue. Such a statement must be an executable statement other than go to, a return or an end statement of a subprogram, a stop or an end statement of a main program, exit, cycle, arithmetic if, or assigned go to statement. Nested do-loops may share the same labelled terminal statement, in which case all the usual rules for nested blocks hold, but a branch to the label must be from within the innermost loop. Thus we may write a matrix multiplication as

```
      a(1:n, 1:n) = 0.
      do 1 i = 1,n
         do 1 j = 1,n
            do 1 l = 1,n
    1          a(i,j) = a(i,j)+b(i,l)*c(l,j)
```

Execution of a cycle statement restarts the loop without execution of the terminal statement.

This form of do-loop offers no additional functionality but considerable scope for unexpected mistakes.

B.1.9   Alternate return

When calling certain types of subroutines, it is possible that specific exceptional conditions will arise, which should cause a break in the normal control flow. It is possible to anticipate such conditions, and to code different flow paths following a subroutine call, depending on whether the called subroutine has terminated normally, or has detected an exceptional or abnormal condition. This is achieved using the alternate `return` facility which uses the argument list in the following manner. Let us suppose that a subroutine `deal` receives in an argument list the number of cards in a shuffled deck, the number of players, and the number of cards to be dealt to each hand. In the interests of generality, it would be a reasonable precaution for the first executable statement of `deal` to be a check that there is at least one player and that there are, in fact, enough cards to satisfy each player's requirement. If there are no players or insufficient cards, it can signal this to the main program which should then take the appropriate action. This may be written in outline as

```
    call deal(nshuff, nplay, nhand, cards, *2, *3)
    call play
    :
2   ........     ! Handle no-player case
    :
3   ........     ! Handle insufficient-cards case
    :
```

If the cards can be dealt, normal control is returned, and the call to `play` executed. If an exception occurs, control is passed to the statement labelled 2 or 3, at which point some action must be taken — to stop the game or shuffle more cards. The relevant statement label is defined by placing the statement label preceded by an asterisk as an actual argument in the argument list. It must be a label of an executable statement of the same scoping unit. Any number of such alternate returns may be specified, and they may appear in any position in the argument list. Since, however, they are normally used to handle exceptions, they are best placed at the end of the list.

   In the called subroutine, the corresponding dummy arguments are asterisks and the alternate `return` is taken by executing a statement of the form

```
    return intexpr
```

where *intexpr* is any scalar integer expression. The value of this expression at execution time defines an index to the alternate `return` to be taken, according to its position in the argument list. If *intexpr* evaluates to 2, the second alternate `return` will be taken. If *intexpr* evaluates to a value which is less than 1, or greater than the number of alternate `return`s in the argument list, a normal `return` will be taken. Thus, in `deal`, we may write simply

```
    subroutine deal(nshuff, nplay, nhand, cards, *, *)
    :
    if (nplay.le.0) return 1
    if (nshuff .lt. nplay*nhand) return 2
```

   This feature is also available for subroutines defined by `entry` statements. It is not available for functions or elemental subroutines.

This feature is replaced by use of an integer argument holding a return code used in a computed go to following the call statement. A following case construct is now an even better alternative.

B.2 Feature deleted in Fortran 2003: Carriage control

Fortran's formatted output statements were originally designed for line-printers, with their concept of lines and pages of output. On such a device, the first character of each output record must be of default kind. It is not printed but interpreted as a *carriage control character*. If it is a blank, no action is taken, and it is good practice to insert a blank as the first character of each record, either explicitly as ' ' or using the t2 edit descriptor (described in Section 9.12.5), in order to avoid inadvertent generation of spurious carriage control characters. This can happen when the first character in an output record is non-blank, and might occur, for instance, when printing integer values with the format '(i5)'. Here all output values between −999 and 9999 will have a blank in the first position, but all others will generate a character there which may be used mistakenly for carriage control.

The carriage control characters defined by the standard are:

b	to start a new line
+	to remain on the same line (overprint)
0	to skip a line
1	to advance to the beginning of the next page

As a precaution, the first character of each record produced by list-directed and namelist output is a blank, unless it is the continuation of a delimited character constant.

In this context, we note that execution of a print statement does not imply that any printing will actually occur, and nor does execution of a write statement imply that printing will not occur.

B.3 Features deleted in Fortran 95

The features listed in this section were deleted from the Fortran 95 language entirely. Although it can be expected that compilers will continue to support these features for some period, their use should be completely avoided to ensure very long-term portability and to avoid unnecessary compiler warning messages. They are fully described in previous editions of this book.

Non-integer do indices The do variable and the expressions that specify the limits and stride of a do construct or an implied-do in an I/O statement could be of type default real or double precision real.

Assigned go to and assigned formats Another form of branch statement is actually written in two parts, an assign statement and an assigned go to statement. One use of the assign statement is replaced by character expressions to define format specifiers (Section 9.4).

Branching to an end if statement It was permissible to branch to an end if statement from outside the construct that it terminates. A branch to the following statement is a replacement for this practice.

The pause statement At certain points in the execution of a program it was possible to pause, in order to allow some possible external intervention in the running conditions to be made.

H edit descriptor The H (or h) edit descriptor provided an early form of the character string edit descriptor.

C. Pointer example

A recurring problem in computing is the need to manipulate a linked data structure. This might be a simple linked list like the one encountered in Section 2.13, but often a more general tree structure is required.

The example in this appendix consists of a module that establishes and navigates one or more such trees, organized as a 'forest', and a short test program for it. Here, each node is identified by a name and has any number of children, any number of siblings, and (optionally) some associated real data. Each root node is regarded as having a common parent, the 'forest root' node, whose name is `forest_root`. Thus, every node has a parent. The module provides facilities for adding a named node to a specified parent, for enquiring about all the nodes that are offspring of a specified node, for removing a tree or subtree, and for performing I/O operations on a tree or subtree.

The user-callable interfaces are as follows.

start must be called to initialize a forest.

add_node stores the data provided at the node whose parent is specified and sets up pointers
   to the parent and siblings (if any).

remove_node deallocates all the storage occupied by a complete tree or subtree.

retrieve retrieves the data stored at a specified node and the names of the parent and children.

dump_tree writes a complete tree or subtree.

restore_tree reads a complete tree or subtree.

finish deallocates all the storage occupied by all the trees of the forest.

The source code can be obtained by anonymous ftp to *ftp.numerical.rl.ac.uk*. When prompted for a userid, reply with

```
anonymous
```

and give your name as password. The directory is */pub/MRandC* and the file name is *pointer.f90*.

```
module directory
 !
```

```
! Strong typing imposed
  implicit none
!
! Only subroutine interfaces, the length of the character
! component, and the I/O unit number are public
   public :: start, add_node, remove_node, retrieve,              &
             dump_tree, restore_tree, finish
   private :: find, remove
!
! Module constants
   character(len=*), private, parameter :: eot = "End-of-Tree....."
   integer, parameter, public :: unit = 4,   & ! I/O unit number
                                 max_char = 16 ! length of character
                                               ! component
!
! Define the basic tree type
   type, private :: node
        character(len=max_char)    :: name           ! name of node
        real, pointer, dimension(:) :: y              ! stored real data
        type(node), pointer     :: parent  => null() ! parent node
        type(node), pointer     :: sibling => null() ! next sibling node
        type(node), pointer     :: child   => null() ! first child node
   end type node

!
! Module variables
   type(node), pointer, private  :: current     ! current node
   type(node), pointer, private  :: forest_root ! the root of the forest
   integer,private               :: max_data    ! max size of data array
   character(len=max_char), private, allocatable, target, dimension(:)  &
                                               :: names
                                 ! for returning list of names
! The module procedures

contains

    subroutine start ()
!
! Initialize the tree.
      allocate (forest_root)
      current => forest_root
      forest_root%name = "forest_root"
      allocate(forest_root%y(0))
      max_data = 0
      allocate (names(0))
    end subroutine start

    subroutine find(name)
      character(len=*), intent(in) :: name
```

```
! Make the module variable current point to the node with given name,
! or be null if the name is not there.
      type(node), pointer     :: root
! For efficiency, we search the tree rooted at current, and if this
! fails try its parent and so on until the forest root is reached.
      if (associated(current)) then
         root => current
         nullify (current)
      else
         root => forest_root
      end if
      do
         call look(root)
         if (associated(current)) then
            return
         end if
         root => root%parent
         if (.not.associated(root)) then
            exit
         end if
      end do

   contains

      recursive subroutine look(root)
         type(node), intent(in), target    :: root
! Look for name in the tree rooted at root. If found, make the
! module variable current point to the node
         type(node), pointer               :: child
!
         if (root%name == name) then
            current => root
         else
            child => root%child
            do
               if (.not.associated(child)) then
                 exit
               end if
               call look(child)
               if (associated(current)) then
                 return
               end if
               child => child%sibling
            end do
         end if
      end subroutine look
   end subroutine find
```

```
   subroutine add_node(name, name_of_parent, data)
       character(len=*), intent(in)               :: name, name_of_parent
! For a root, name_of_parent = ""
       real, intent(in), optional, dimension(:) :: data
! Allocate a new tree node of type node, store the given name and
! data there, set pointers to the parent and to its next sibling
! (if any). If the parent is not found, the new node is treated as
! a root. It is assumed that the node is not already present in the
! forest.
       type(node), pointer :: new_node
!
       allocate (new_node)
       new_node%name = name
       if (present(data)) then
          allocate(new_node%y(size(data)))
          new_node%y = data
          max_data = max(max_data, size(data))
       else
          allocate(new_node%y(0))
       end if
!
! If name of parent is not null, search for it.
! If not found, print message.
       if (name_of_parent == "") then
          current => forest_root
       else
          call find (name_of_parent)
          if (.not.associated(current)) then
             print *, "no parent ", name_of_parent, " found for ", name
             current => forest_root
          end if
       end if
       new_node%parent => current
       new_node%sibling => current%child
       current%child => new_node
   end subroutine add_node

   subroutine remove_node(name)
       character(len=*), intent(in) :: name
! Remove node and the subtree rooted on it (if any),
! deallocating associated pointer targets.
       type(node), pointer :: parent, child, sibling
!
       call find (name)
       if (associated(current)) then
          parent => current%parent
          child => parent%child
          if (.not.associated(child, current)) then
! Make it the first child, looping through the siblings to find it
```

```
! and resetting the links
            parent%child => current
            sibling => child
            do
               if (associated (sibling%sibling, current)) then
                  exit
               end if
               sibling => sibling%sibling
            end do
            sibling%sibling => current%sibling
            current%sibling => child
         end if
         call remove(current)
      end if
   end subroutine remove_node

   recursive subroutine remove (old_node)
! Remove a first child node and the subtree rooted on it (if any),
! deallocating associated pointer targets.
      type(node), pointer :: old_node
      type(node), pointer :: child, sibling
!
      child => old_node%child
      do
         if (.not.associated(child)) then
            exit
         end if
         sibling => child%sibling
         call remove(child)
         child => sibling
      end do
! remove leaf node
      if (associated(old_node%parent)) then
         old_node%parent%child => old_node%sibling
      end if
      deallocate (old_node%y)
      deallocate (old_node)
   end subroutine remove

   subroutine retrieve(name, data, parent, children)
      character(len=*), intent(in)            :: name
      real, pointer, dimension(:)             :: data
      character(len=*), intent(out)           :: parent
      character(len=*), pointer, dimension(:) :: children
! Returns a pointer to the data at the node, the name of the
! parent, and a pointer to the names of the children.
      integer :: counter, i
      type(node), pointer :: child
!
```

```
      call find (name)
      if (associated(current)) then
         data => current%y
         parent = current%parent%name
! Count the number of children
         counter = 0
         child => current%child
         do
            if (.not.associated(child)) then
              exit
            end if
            counter = counter + 1
            child => child%sibling
         end do
         deallocate (names)
         allocate (names(counter))
! and store their names
         children => names
         child => current%child
         do i = 1, counter
            children(i) = child%name
            child => child%sibling
         end do
      else
         nullify(data)
         parent = ""
         nullify(children)
      end if
   end subroutine retrieve

   subroutine dump_tree(root)
      character(len=*), intent(in) :: root
! Write out a complete tree followed by an end-of-tree record
! unformatted on the file unit.
      call find (root)
      if (associated(current)) then
         call tree_out(current)
      end if
      write(unit = unit) eot, 0, eot

   contains

      recursive subroutine tree_out (root)
! Traverse a complete tree or subtree, writing out its contents
         type(node), intent(in) :: root      ! root node of tree
! Local variable
         type(node), pointer    :: child
!
         write(unit = unit) root%name, size(root%y), root%y, &
```

```
                         root%parent%name
          child => root%child
          do
              if (.not.associated(child)) then
                exit
              end if
              call tree_out (child)
              child => child%sibling
          end do
       end subroutine tree_out
    end subroutine dump_tree

    subroutine restore_tree ()
! Reads a subtree unformatted from the file unit.
       character(len=max_char)          :: name
       integer :: length_y
       real, allocatable, dimension(:) :: y
       character(len=max_char)          :: name_of_parent
!
       allocate(y(max_data))
       do
          read (unit= unit) name, length_y, y(:length_y), name_of_parent
          if (name == eot) then
            exit
          end if
          call add_node( name, name_of_parent, y(:length_y) )
       end do
       deallocate(y)
    end subroutine restore_tree

    subroutine finish ()
! Deallocate all allocated targets.
       call remove (forest_root)
       deallocate(names)
    end subroutine finish

end module directory

module tree_print

  use  directory
  implicit none
  private
  public :: print_tree

contains

    recursive subroutine print_tree(name)
! To print the data contained in a subtree
```

```
      character(len=*), intent(in)                      :: name
      integer                                           :: i
      real, pointer, dimension(:)                       :: data
      character(len=max_char)                           :: parent, self
      character(len=max_char), pointer, dimension(:)    :: children
      character(len=max_char), allocatable, dimension(:) :: siblings
!
      call retrieve(name, data, parent, children)
      if (.not.associated(data)) then
        return
      end if
      self = name
      write(unit=*,fmt=*) self, data
      write(unit=*,fmt=*) "  parent:   ", parent
      if (size(children) > 0 ) then
          write(unit=*,fmt=*) "   children: ", children
      end if
      allocate(siblings(size(children)))
      siblings = children
      do i = 1, size(children)
          call print_tree(siblings(i))
      end do
      deallocate(siblings)
    end subroutine print_tree
end module tree_print

program test
   use directory
   use tree_print
   implicit none
!
! Initialize a tree
   call start ()
! Fill it with some data
   call add_node("ernest","",(/1.0,2.0/))
   call add_node("helen","ernest",(/3.0,4.0,5.0/))
   call add_node("douglas","ernest",(/6.0,7.0/))
   call add_node("john","helen",(/8.0/))
   call add_node("betty","helen",(/9.0,10.0/))
   call add_node("nigel","betty",(/11.0/))
   call add_node("peter","betty",(/12.0/))
   call add_node("ruth","betty")
! Manipulate subtrees
   open(unit=unit, form="unformatted", status="scratch",     &
        action="readwrite", position="rewind")
   call dump_tree("betty")
   call remove_node("betty")
   write(unit=*,fmt=*)
   call print_tree("ernest")
```

```
   rewind (unit=unit)
   call restore_tree ()
   rewind (unit=unit)
   write(unit=*,fmt=*)
   call print_tree("ernest")
   call dump_tree("john")
   call remove_node("john")
   write(unit=*,fmt=*)
   call print_tree("ernest")
   rewind (unit=unit)
   call restore_tree ()
   write(unit=*,fmt=*)
   call print_tree("ernest")
! Return storage
   call finish ()

end program test
```

D. Avoiding compilation cascades

When compiling a module, most compilers produce two files: an object file, and a separate file containing the information for use of the module (we will call the latter the .mod file, as that is the most common suffix in use for it).

A program unit that uses a module depends on the .mod file, not on the object file or source file, but a recompilation cascade arises from any change to the module because

i) the .mod file depends on the source file, and

ii) the compiler updates the .mod file when compiling the source file even if there are no changes to it.

To avoid this cascade one must both break the connection between the source file and the .mod file, and avoid updating the .mod file when there are no changes to it.

We will describe how to do this using the make tool. Firstly, the Makefile needs a description of how to generate the .mod file when it does not exist. This should be done by a recursive make invocation. Secondly, the compiler needs to be prevented from updating the .mod file when there are no changes. This can be done by using a shell script to wrap the compiler invocation. We will show how to do these with the NAGWare f95 compiler.

In the simplest case we have a program, example.exe with two source files, one.f90 containing a module that is used by the other, two.f90. The Makefile is shown in Figure D.1, and the shell script is shown in Figure D.2 (f95 is the name by which the compiler is invoked).

The shell script uses the -M and -nomod options which cause the compiler only to produce the .mod files or not to produce any .mod files, respectively.

In the slightly more complicated case that one uses another module zero and does not make everything from zero private, then zero.mod must appear as a dependency of one.mod (as well as of one.o), that is

```
one.mod: zero.mod
```

This technique can be used for most compilers that store the module information in a separate file; for some of them, the time of compilation is written into the .mod file, so a more intelligent tool must be used to compare the new and old .mod files — this information can usually be obtained from the compiler vendor or from the World-Wide Web.

Figure D.1

```
# Makefile for example.exe

# Compilation options:
# (the -nocheck_modtime option suppresses the compiler's check for the
# .mod file being outofdate - since we are using make, we don't need
# this check.)
F90FLAGS = -O -nocheck_modtime

# Linking options:
F90LINKFLAGS =

# The executable depends on all the object files:
example.exe: one.o two.o
        f95 $F90LINKFLAGS -o example.exe one.o two.o

# Use mf95 to avoid .mod file updates
one.o: one.f90
        mf95 one one.f90

# No module(s) in two.f90, so can just use f95 directly
two.o: two.f90 one.mod
        f95 two.f90

# If there is no .mod file, 'make one.f90' will make sure we
# have an uptodate source file, then compile it asking for the
# .mod file only to be produced (this is very quick).
one.mod:
        make one.f90
        f95 -M one.f90
```

Figure D.2

```
#!/bin/sh
if [ -f $1.mod ]; then
#    Just produce the .mod file...
     mkdir $1.tmp
     f95 -M $F90FLAGS -mdir $1.tmp $2
     cmp -s $1.tmp/$1.mod $1.mod
     if [ $? != 0 ]; then
#        Different .mod file contents, so update it
         mv $1.tmp/$1.mod $1.mod
     fi
     rm -r $1.tmp
#    Now produce the object file and don't produce a .mod file
     f95 $F90FLAGS -nomod $2
else
# .mod file does not exist, just compile
     f95 $F90FLAGS $2
fi
```

E. Fortran terms

The following is a list of the principal technical terms used in this book and their definitions. To facilitate reference to the standard, we have kept closely to the meanings used there. We make no reference to obsolescent or deleted features (Appendix B) in this appendix.

abstract type : A type that has the `abstract` attribute. It can only be used as a basis for type extension.

action statement : A single statement specifying or controlling a computational action (*action-stmt*).

actual argument : An expression, a variable, or a procedure that is specified in a procedure reference.

allocatable variable : A variable having the `allocatable` attribute. It may be referenced or defined only when it is allocated. If it is an array, it has a shape only when it is allocated. It may be a named variable or a structure component.

ancestor : Of a submodule, its parent or an ancestor of its parent.

argument : An actual argument or a dummy argument.

argument association : The relationship between an actual argument and a dummy argument during the execution of a procedure reference.

array : A set of scalar data, all of the same type and type parameters, whose individual elements are arranged in a rectangular pattern. It may be a named array, an array section, a structure component, a function value, or an expression. Its rank is at least one.

array element : One of the scalar data that make up an array that is either named or is a structure component.

array pointer : A pointer to an array.

array section : A subobject that is an array and is not a structure component.

assignment statement : A statement of the form 'variable = expression'.

associate name : The name of the construct entity with which a selector of an `associate` or `select type` construct is associated within the construct.

association : Name association, pointer association, storage association, or inheritance association.

assumed-shape array : A non-pointer dummy array that takes its shape from the associated actual argument.

assumed-size array : A dummy array whose size is assumed from the associated actual argument. Its last upper bound is specified by an asterisk.

attribute : A property of a data object that may be specified in a type declaration statement.

automatic data object : A data object that is a local entity of a subprogram, that is not a dummy argument, and that has a length type parameter or array bound that is specified by an expression that is not an initialization expression.

base type : An extensible type that is not an extension of another type.

belong : If an `exit` or a `cycle` statement contains a construct name, the statement belongs to the `do` construct using that name. Otherwise, it belongs to the innermost `do` construct in which it appears.

binding label : A value of type default character that uniquely identifies how a variable, common block, subroutine, or function is known to a companion processor.

block : A sequence of executable constructs embedded in another executable construct, bounded by statements that are particular to the construct, and treated as an integral unit.

block data program unit : A program unit that provides initial values for data objects in named common blocks.

bounds : For a named array, the limits within which the values of the subscripts of its array elements shall lie.

character : A letter, digit, or other symbol.

character length parameter : The type parameter that specifies the number of characters for an entity of type character.

character storage unit : The unit of storage for holding a scalar that is not a pointer and is of type default character and character length one.

character string : A sequence of characters numbered from left to right 1, 2, 3, ...

characteristics :

   i) Of a procedure, its classification as a function or subroutine, whether it is pure, whether it is elemental, whether it has the bind attribute, the value of its binding label, the characteristics of its dummy arguments, and the characteristics of its function result if it is a function.

   ii) Of a dummy argument, whether it is a data object, is a procedure, is a procedure pointer, or has the optional attribute.

   iii) Of a dummy data object, its type, type parameters, shape, the exact dependence of an array bound or type parameter on other entities, intent, whether it is optional, whether it is a pointer or a target, whether it is allocatable, whether it has the value, asynchronous, or volatile attributes, whether it is polymorphic, and whether the shape, size, or a type parameter is assumed.

   iv) Of a dummy procedure or procedure pointer, whether the interface is explicit, the characteristics of the procedure if the interface is explicit, and whether it is optional.

   v) Of a function result, its type, type parameters, which type parameters are deferred, whether it is polymorphic, whether it is a pointer or allocatable, whether it is a procedure pointer, rank if it is a pointer or allocatable, shape if it is not a pointer or allocatable, and the exact dependence of an array bound or type parameter on other entities.

child : A submodule is a child of its parent.

class : A class named t is the set of types extended from the type named t.

collating sequence : An ordering of all the different characters of a particular kind type parameter.

common block : A block of physical storage that may be accessed by any of the scoping units in a program.

companion processor : A mechanism by which global data and procedures may be referenced or defined. It may be a mechanism that references and defines such entities by means other than Fortran. The procedures can be described by a C function prototype.

component : A constituent of a derived type.

component order : The ordering of the components of a derived type that is used for intrinsic formatted input/output, for structure constructors, and for interoperability.

conformable : Two arrays are said to be conformable if they have the same shape. A scalar is conformable with any array.

conformance : A program conforms to the standard if it uses only those forms and relationships described therein and if the program has an interpretation according to the standard. A program unit conforms to the standard if it can be included in a program in a manner that allows the program to be standard conforming. A processor conforms to the standard if it executes standard-conforming programs in a manner that fulfils the interpretations prescribed in the standard and contains the capability of detection and reporting as described in Section 1.8.

connected :

    i) For an external unit, the property of referring to an external file.

    ii) For an external file, the property of having an external unit that refers to it.

constant : A data object whose value shall not change during execution of a program. It may be a named constant or a literal constant.

construct : A sequence of statements starting with an `associate`, `do`, `forall`, `if`, `select case`, `select type`, or `where` statement and ending with the corresponding terminal statement.

construct association : The association between the selector of an `associate` or `select type` construct and the associated construct entity.

construct entity : An entity defined by a lexical token whose scope is a construct.

correspond : A module procedure interface body and a subprogram that defines a separate module procedure correspond if they have the same name, and the module procedure interface is declared in the same program unit as the separate module procedure or is declared in an ancestor of the program unit in which the separate module procedure is defined and is accessible by host association from that ancestor.

data : Plural of datum.

data entity : A data object, the result of the evaluation of an expression, or the result of the execution of a function reference (called the function result). A data entity has a type (either intrinsic or derived) and has, or may have, a data value (the exception is an undefined variable). Every data entity has a rank and is thus either a scalar or an array.

data object : A data entity that is a constant, a variable, or a subobject of a constant.

data type : See type.

datum : A single quantity that may have any of the set of values specified for its type.

decimal symbol : The character that separates the whole and fractional parts in the decimal representation of a real number in a file. By default, the decimal symbol is a decimal point (also known as a period). The current decimal symbol is determined by the current decimal edit mode.

declared type : The type that a data entity is declared to have. It may differ from the type during execution (the dynamic type) for polymorphic data entities.

default initialization : If initialization is specified in a type definition, an object of the type will be automatically initialized. Non-pointer components may be initialized with values by default; pointer components may be initially disassociated by default. Default initialization is not provided for objects of intrinsic type.

default-initialized : A subcomponent is said to be default-initialized if it will be initialized by default initialization.

deferred binding : A binding with the `deferred` attribute. A deferred binding shall appear only in an abstract type definition.

deferred type parameter : A length type parameter whose value is not specified in the declaration of an object, but instead is specified when the object is allocated or pointer-assigned.

definable : A variable is definable if its value may be changed by the appearance of its designator on the left of an assignment statement. An allocatable variable that has not been allocated is an example of a data object that is not definable. An example of a subobject that is not definable is `c(i)` when `c` is an array that is a constant and `i` is an integer variable.

defined : For a data object, the property of having or being given a valid value.

defined assignment statement : An assignment statement that is not an intrinsic assignment statement; it is defined by a subroutine and a generic interface that specifies `assignment (=)`.

defined operation : An operation that is not an intrinsic operation and is defined by a function that is associated with a generic identifier.

derived type : A type whose data have components, each of which is either of intrinsic type or of another derived type.

descendant : Of a module or submodule, one of its children or a descendant of one of its children.

designator : A name, followed by zero or more component selectors, array section selectors, array element selectors, and substring selectors.

disassociated : A disassociated pointer is not associated with a target. A pointer is disassociated following execution of a `nullify` statement, following pointer assignment with a disassociated pointer, by default initialization, or by explicit initialization. A data pointer may also be disassociated by execution of a `deallocate` statement.

dummy argument : An entity by which an associated actual argument is accessed during execution of a procedure.

dummy array : A dummy argument that is an array.

dummy data object : A dummy argument that is a data object.

dummy pointer : A dummy argument that is a pointer.

dummy procedure : A dummy argument that is specified or referenced as a procedure.

dynamic type : The type of a data entity during execution of a program. The dynamic type of a data entity that is not polymorphic is the same as its declared type.

effective item : A scalar object resulting from expanding an input/output list.

elemental : An adjective applied to an operation, procedure, or assignment statement that is applied independently to elements of an array or corresponding elements of a set of conformable arrays and scalars.

entity : The term used for any of the following: a program unit, procedure, abstract interface, operator, generic interface, common block, external unit, type, data entity, statement label, construct, or namelist group.

executable construct : An action statement (*action-stmt*) or an `associate`, `case`, `do`, `forall`, `if`, `select type`, or `where` construct.

executable statement : An instruction to perform or control one or more computational actions.

explicit initialization : Explicit initialization may be specified for objects of intrinsic or derived type in type declaration statements or `data` statements. An object of a derived type that specifies default initialization shall not appear in a `data` statement.

explicit interface : If a procedure has an explicit interface at the point of a reference to it, the processor is able to verify that the characteristics of the reference and declaration are related as required by the standard. A procedure has an explicit interface if it is an internal procedure, a module procedure, an intrinsic procedure, an external procedure that has an interface body, a procedure reference in its own scoping unit, or a dummy procedure that has an interface body.

explicit-shape array : A named array that is declared with explicit bounds.

expression : A sequence of operands, operators, and parentheses (*expr*). It may be a variable, a constant, a function reference, or may represent a computation.

extended type : An extensible type that is an extension of another type. A type that is declared with the `extends` attribute.

extensible type : A type from which new types may be derived using the `extends` attribute. A non-sequence type that does not have the `bind` attribute.

extension type : A base type is an extension type of itself only. An extended type is an extension type of itself and of all types for which its parent type is an extension.

extent : The size of one dimension of an array.

external file : A sequence of records that exists in a medium external to the program.

external linkage : The characteristic describing that a C entity is global to the program; defined in clause 6.2.2 of the C standard.

external procedure : A procedure that is defined by an external subprogram or by a means other than Fortran.

external subprogram : A subprogram that is not in a main program, module, or another subprogram. Note that a module is not called a subprogram.

external unit : A mechanism that is used to refer to an external file. It is identified by a non-negative integer.

file : An internal file or an external file.

file storage unit : The unit of storage for an unformatted or stream file.

final subroutine : A subroutine that is called automatically by the processor during finalization.

finalizable : A type that has final subroutines, or that has a finalizable component. An object of finalizable type.

finalization : The process of calling user-defined final subroutines immediately before destroying an object.

function : A procedure that is invoked in an expression and computes a value which is then used in evaluating the expression.

function result : The data object that returns the value of a function.

function subprogram : A sequence of statements beginning with a `function` statement that is not in an interface block and ending with the corresponding `end` statement.

generic identifier : A lexical token that appears in an `interface` statement and is associated with all the procedures in the interface block, or that appears in a `generic` statement and is associated with the specific type-bound procedures.

generic interface : An interface specified by a generic procedure binding or a generic interface block.

generic interface block : An interface block with a generic specification.

global entity : An entity with an identifier whose scope is a program.

host : A host scoping unit.

host association : The process by which a contained scoping unit accesses entities of its host.

host scoping unit : A scoping unit that immediately surrounds another scoping unit.

implicit interface : For a procedure referenced in a scoping unit, the property of not having an explicit interface.

inherit : To acquire from a parent. Type parameters, components, or procedure bindings of an extended type that are automatically acquired from its parent type without explicit declaration in the extended type are said to be inherited.

inheritance association : The relationship between the inherited components and the parent component in an extended type.

inquiry function : A function that is either intrinsic or is defined in an intrinsic module and whose result depends on properties of one or more of its arguments instead of their values.

instance of a subprogram : The copy of a subprogram that is created when a procedure defined by the subprogram is invoked.

intent : An attribute of a dummy data object that indicates whether it is used to transfer data into the procedure, out of the procedure, or both.

interface block : A sequence of statements from an `interface` statement to the corresponding `end interface` statement.

interface body : A sequence of statements in an interface block from a `function` or `subroutine` statement to the corresponding `end` statement.

interface of a procedure : See procedure interface.

internal file : A character variable that is used to transfer and convert data from internal storage to internal storage.

internal procedure : A procedure that is defined by an internal subprogram.

internal subprogram : A subprogram in a main program or in another subprogram.

interoperable : The property of a Fortran entity that ensures that an equivalent entity may be defined by means of C.

intrinsic : An adjective applied to types, operations, assignment statements, procedures, and modules that are defined in the standard and may be used in any scoping unit without definition or specification. Additionally, some processors provide non-standard intrinsic procedures and modules which can be used in the same way.

invoke :

    i) To call a subroutine by a `call` statement or by a defined assignment statement.

    ii) To call a function by a reference to it by name or operator during the evaluation of an expression.

iii) To call a final subroutine by finalization.

keyword : A word that is part of the syntax of a statement or a name that is used to identify an item in a list.

kind type parameter : A parameter whose values label the available kinds of an intrinsic type, or a type parameter of a derived type whose value must be known at compile time.

label : See statement label.

length of a character string : The number of characters in the character string.

lexical token : A sequence of one or more characters with a specified interpretation.

line : A sequence of 0 to 132 characters, which may contain Fortran statements, a comment, or an `include` line.

literal constant : An unnamed constant whose value is literally written down in the program text.

local entity : An entity identified by a lexical token whose scope is a scoping unit.

local variable : A variable local to a particular scoping unit; not imported through use or host association, not a dummy argument, and not a variable in common.

main program : A Fortran main program or a replacement defined by means other than Fortran.

many–one array section : An array section with a vector subscript having two or more elements with the same value.

module : A program unit that contains or accesses definitions to be accessed by other program units.

module procedure : A procedure that is defined by a module subprogram.

module procedure interface : An interface defined by an interface body in which `module` appears in the prefix of the initial function or subroutine statement. It declares the interface for a separate module procedure.

module subprogram : A subprogram that is in a module but is not an internal subprogram.

name : A lexical token consisting of a letter followed by up to 62 alphanumeric characters (letters, digits, and underscores).

name association : Argument association, use association, host association, or construct association.

named : Having a name. That is, in a phrase such as 'named variable,' the word 'named' signifies that the variable name is not qualified by a subscript list, substring specification, and so on. For example, if x is an array variable, the reference 'x' is a named variable while the reference 'x(1)' is an object designator.

named constant : A constant that has a name.

NaN : A Not-a-Number value of IEEE arithmetic. It represents an undefined value or a value created by an invalid operation.

nonexecutable statement : A statement used to configure the program environment in which computational actions take place.

numeric storage unit : The unit of storage for holding a scalar that is not a pointer and is of type default real, default integer, or default logical.

numeric type : Integer, real, or complex type.

object : Data object.

object designator : A designator for a data object.

operand : An expression that precedes or succeeds an operator.

operation : A computation involving one or two operands.

operator : A lexical token that specifies an operation.

override : When explicit initialization or default initialization overrides default initialization, it is as if only the overriding initialization were specified. If a procedure is bound to an extensible type, it overrides the one that would have been inherited from the parent type.

parent : Of a submodule, the module or submodule specified in parentheses in its submodule statement.

parent component : The component of an entity of extended type that corresponds to its inherited portion.

parent type : The extensible type from which an extended type is derived.

passed-object dummy argument : The dummy argument of a type-bound procedure or procedure pointer component that becomes associated with the object through which the procedure was invoked.

pointer : An entity that has the `pointer` attribute.

pointer assignment : The pointer association of a pointer with a target by the execution of a pointer assignment statement or the execution of an assignment statement for a data object of derived type having the pointer as a subobject.

pointer assignment statement : A statement of the form *pointer => target.*

pointer associated : The relationship between a pointer and a target following a pointer assignment or a valid execution of an `allocate` statement.

pointer association : The process by which a pointer becomes pointer associated with a target.

polymorphic : Able to be of differing types during program execution. An object declared with the `class` keyword is polymorphic.

preconnected : A property describing a unit that is connected to an external file at the beginning of execution of a program. Such a unit may be specified in input/output statements without an `open` statement being executed for that unit.

procedure : A computation that may be invoked during program execution. It may be a function or a subroutine. It may be an intrinsic procedure, an external procedure, a module procedure, an internal procedure, or a dummy procedure. A subprogram may define more than one procedure if it contains `entry` statements.

procedure designator : A designator for a procedure.

procedure interface : The characteristics of a procedure, the name of the procedure, the name of each dummy argument, and the generic identifiers (if any) by which it may be referenced.

processor : The combination of a computing system and the mechanism by which programs are transformed for use on that computing system.

processor dependent : The designation given to a facility that is not completely specified by the standard. Such a facility shall be provided by a processor, with methods or semantics determined by the processor.

program : A set of program units that includes exactly one main program.

program unit : The fundamental component of a program. A sequence of statements, comments, and `include` lines. It may be a main program, a module, an external subprogram, or a block data program unit.

prototype : The C analogue of a function interface body; defined in clause 6.7.5.3 of the C standard.

pure procedure : A procedure that is a pure intrinsic procedure is defined by a pure subprogram, or is a statement function that references only pure functions.

rank : The number of dimensions of an array (zero for a scalar).

record : A sequence of values or characters that is treated as a whole within a file.

reference : The appearance of an object designator in a context requiring the value at that point during execution, the appearance of a procedure designator, its operator symbol, or a defined assignment statement in a context requiring execution of the procedure at that point, or the appearance of a module name in a use statement. Neither the act of defining a variable nor the appearance of the name of a procedure as an actual argument is regarded as a reference.

result variable : The variable that returns the value of a function.

rounding mode : The method used to choose the result of an operation that cannot be represented exactly. In IEEE arithmetic, there are four modes: nearest, towards zero, up (towards ∞), and down (towards $-\infty$). In addition, for input/output the two additional modes compatible and processor_defined are provided.

scalar :

    i) A single datum that is not an array.

    ii) Not having the property of being an array.

scope : That part of a program within which a lexical token has a single interpretation. It may be a program, a scoping unit, a construct, a single statement, or a part of a statement.

scoping unit : One of the following.

    i) A program unit or subprogram, excluding any scoping units in it.

    ii) A derived-type definition.

    iii) An interface body, excluding any scoping units in it.

section subscript : A subscript, vector subscript, or subscript triplet in an array section selector.

selector : A syntactic mechanism for designating one of the following.

    i) Part of a data object. It may designate a substring, an array element, an array section, or a structure component.

    ii) The set of values for which a case block is executed.

    iii) The object whose type determines which branch of a select type construct is executed.

    iv) The object that is associated with the *associate-name* in an associate construct.

separate module procedure : A module procedure defined by a subprogram in which module appears in the prefix of the initial function or subroutine statement.

shape : The rank and extents of an array. The shape may be represented by the rank-one array whose elements are the extents in each dimension.

size : The total number of elements of an array.

specification expression : An expression with limitations that make it suitable for use in specifications such as length type parameters or array bounds.

specification function : A non-intrinsic function that may be used in a specification expression.

standard-conforming program : A program that uses only those forms and relationships described in the standard, and that has an interpretation according to the standard.

statement : A sequence of lexical tokens. It usually consists of a single line, but a statement may be continued from one line to another and the semicolon symbol may be used to separate statements within a line.

statement entity : An entity identified by a lexical token whose scope is a single statement or part of a statement.

statement label : A lexical token consisting of up to five digits that precedes a statement and may be used to refer to the statement.

storage association : The relationship between two storage sequences if a storage unit of one is the same as a storage unit of the other.

storage sequence : A sequence of contiguous storage units.

storage unit : A character storage unit, a numeric storage unit, a file storage unit, or an unspecified storage unit.

stride : The increment specified in a subscript triplet.

struct : The C analogue of a sequence derived type; defined in clause 6.2.5 of the C standard.

structure : A scalar data object of derived type.

structure component : A part of an object of derived type. It may be referenced by an object designator.

structure constructor : A syntactic mechanism for constructing a value of derived type.

subcomponent : A subcomponent of an object of derived type is a component of that object or of a subobject of that object.

submodule : A program unit that depends on a module or another submodule; it extends the program unit on which it depends.

submodule identifier : Identifier of a submodule, consisting of the ancestor module name together with the submodule name.

subobject : A portion of a data object that may be referenced or defined independently of other portions. It may be an array element, an array section, a structure component, a substring, or the real or imaginary part of a complex object.

subprogram : A function subprogram or a subroutine subprogram.

subroutine : A procedure that is invoked by a `call` statement or by a defined assignment statement.

subroutine subprogram : A sequence of statements beginning with a `subroutine` statement that is not in an interface block and ending with the corresponding end statement.

subscript : One of the list of scalar integer expressions in an array element selector.

subscript triplet : An item in the list of an array section selector that contains a colon and specifies a regular sequence of integer values.

substring : A contiguous portion of a scalar character string. Note that an array section can include a substring selector; the result is called an array section and not a substring.

target : A data entity that has the `target` attribute, or an entity that is associated with a pointer.

transformational function : A function that is either intrinsic or is defined in an intrinsic module and that is neither an elemental function nor an inquiry function.

type : A named category of data that is characterized by a set of values, together with a way to denote these values and a collection of operations that interpret and manipulate the values. The set of data values depends on the values of the type parameters.

type compatible : All entities are type compatible with other entities of the same type. Unlimited polymorphic entities are type compatible with all entities. A polymorphic entity of declared type `t` is type compatible with entities whose dynamic type is an extension of `t`.

type declaration statement : An `integer`, `real`, `double precision`, `complex`, `logical`, `character`, or `type` (*type-name*) statement.

type parameter : A parameter of a data type. `kind` and `len` are the type parameters of intrinsic types. The type parameters of a derived type are defined in the derived-type definition.

type parameter order : The ordering of the type parameters of a derived type that is used for derived-type specifiers.

type-bound procedure : A procedure binding in a type definition. The procedure may be referenced by the *binding-name* via any object of that dynamic type, as a defined operator, by defined assignment, or as part of the finalization process.

ultimate component : For a structure, a component that is of intrinsic type, has the `allocatable` attribute, or has the `pointer` attribute, or an ultimate component of a derived-type component that does not have the `pointer` attribute or the `allocatable` attribute.

undefined : For a data object, the property of not having a determinate value.

unspecified storage unit : A unit of storage for holding a pointer or a scalar that is not a pointer and is of type other than default integer, default character, default real, double precision real, default logical, or default complex.

use association : The association of names in different scoping units specified by a use statement.

variable : A data object whose value can be defined and redefined during the execution of a program. It may be a named data object, an array element, an array section, a structure component, or a substring.

vector subscript : A section subscript that is an integer expression of rank one.

void : A C type comprising an empty set of values; defined in clause 6.2.5 of the C standard. There is nothing analogous in Fortran.

whole array : A named array.

F. Solutions to exercises

Note: A few exercises have been left to the reader.

Chapter 2

1.

b is less than m	true
8 is less than 2	false
* is greater than T	not determined
$ is less than /	not determined
blank is greater than A	false
blank is less than 6	true

2.

```
   x = y                      correct
 3 a = b+c ! add              correct, with commentary
   word = 'string'            correct
   a = 1.0; b = 2.0           correct
   a = 15. ! initialize a; b = 22. ! and b
                              incorrect (embedded commentary)
   song = "Life is just&      correct, initial line
      & a bowl of cherries"   correct, continuation
   chide = 'Waste not,        incorrect, trailing & missing
      want not!'              incorrect, leading & missing
 0 c(3:4) = 'up"              incorrect (invalid statement
                                  label; invalid form of
                                  character constant)
```

3.

−43	integer	'word'	character
4.39	real	1.9−4	not legal
0.0001e+20	real	'stuff & nonsense'	character
4 9	not legal	(0.,1.)	complex
(1.e3,2)	complex	'I can''t'	character
'(4.3e9, 6.2)'	character	.true._1	legal logical
			provided kind=1 available
e5	not legal	'shouldn' 't'	not legal

```
1_2                legal integer    "O.K."                character
   provided kind=2 available
z10                not legal        z'10'                 hexadecimal
```

4.

```
name       legal        name32      legal
quotient   legal        123         not legal
a182c3     legal        no-go       not legal
stop!      not legal    burn_       legal
no_go      legal        long__name  legal
```

5.

```
real, dimension(11)      :: a    a(1), a(10), a(11), a(11)
real, dimension(0:11)    :: b    b(0), b(9), b(10), b(11)
real, dimension(-11:0)   :: c    c(-11), c(-2), c(-1), c(0)
real, dimension(10,10)   :: d    d(1,1), d(10,1), d(1,2), d(10,10)
real, dimension(5,9)     :: e    e(1,1), e(5,2), e(1,3), e(5,9)
real, dimension(5,0:1,4) :: f    f(1,0,1), f(5,1,1), f(1,0,2),
                                                     f(5,1,4)
```

Array constructor: (/ (i, i = 1,11) /)

6.

```
c(2,3)      legal        c(4:3)(2,1)   not legal
c(6,2)      not legal    c(5,3)(9:9)   legal
c(0,3)      legal        c(2,1)(4:8)   legal
c(4,3)(:)   legal        c(3,2)(0:9)   not legal
c(5)(2:3)   not legal    c(5:6)        not legal
c(5,3)(9)   not legal    c(,)          not legal
```

7.

a) ```
    type vehicle_registration
        character(len=3) :: letters
        integer   :: digits
    end type vehicle_registration
    ```

b)  ```
    type circle
        real                 ::  radius
        real, dimension(2) ::  centre
    end type circle
    ```

c) ```
    type book
        character(len=20)   :: title
        character(len=20), dimension(2) :: author
        integer   :: no_of_pages
    end type book
    ```
    ```

Derived type constants:

```
vehicle_registration('PQR', 123)
circle(15.1, (/ 0., 0. /))
book("Pilgrim's Progress", (/ 'John ', 'Bunyan' /), 250 )
```

8.

t	array	t(4)%vertex(1)	scalar
t(10)	scalar	t(5:6)	array
t(1)%vertex	array	t(5:5)	array (size 1)

9.

a) ```
    integer, parameter ::   twenty = selected_int_kind(20)
    integer (kind = twenty) :: counter
    ```
b)  ```
    integer, parameter :: high = selected_real_kind(12,100)
    real(kind = high)   :: big
    ```
c) ```
    character(kind=2)   :: sign
    ```

## Chapter 3

**1.**

| | | | |
|---|---|---|---|
| a+b | valid | -c | valid |
| a+-c | invalid | d+(-f) | valid |
| (a+c)**(p+q) | valid | (a+c)(p+q) | invalid |
| -(x+y)**i | valid | 4.((a-d)-(a+4.*x)+1) | invalid |

**2.**

```
c+(4.*f)
((4.*g)-a)+(d/2.)
a**(e**(c**d))
((a*e)-((c**d)/a))+e
(i .and. j) .or. k
((.not. l) .or. ((.not. i) .and. m)) .neqv. n
((b(3).and.b(1)).or.b(6)).or.(.not.b(2))
```

3.

```
3+4/2   = 5       6/4/2   = 0
3.*4**2 = 48.     3.**3/2 = 13.5
-1.**2  = -1.     (-1.)**3 = -1.
```

4.

```
ABCDEFGH
ABCD0123
ABCDEFGu           u = unchanged
ABCDbbuu           b = blank
```
```

5.

```
.not.b(1).and.b(2)  valid    .or.b(1)                    invalid
b(1).or..not.b(4)   valid    b(2)(.and.b(3).or.b(4))     invalid
```

6.

```
d .le. c           valid     p .lt. t > 0               invalid
x-1 /= y           valid     x+y < 3 .or. > 4.          invalid
d.lt.c.and.3.0     invalid   q.eq.r .and. s>t           valid
```

7.

a) 4*1
b) b*h/2.
c) 4./3.*pi*r**3

        (assuming pi has value π).

8.

```
integer :: n, one, five, ten, twenty_five
twenty_five = (100-n)/25
ten         = (100-n-25*twenty_five)/10
five        = (100-n-25*twenty_five-10*ten)/5
one         = 100-n-25*twenty_five-10*ten-5*five
```

9.

```
a = b + c      valid
c = b + 1.0    valid
d = b + 1      invalid
r = b + c      valid
a = r + 2      valid
```

10.

```
a = b          valid    c = a(:,2) + b(5,:5)    valid
a = c+1.0      invalid  c = a(2,:) + b(:,5)     invalid
a(:,3) = c     valid    b(2:,3) = c + b(:5,3)   invalid
```

Chapter 4

1.

```
integer               :: i, j, k, temp
integer, dimension(100) :: reverse
do i = 1,100
   reverse(i) = i
end do
read *, i, j
do k= i, i+(j-i-1)/2
   temp = reverse(k)
   reverse(k) = reverse(j-k+i)
```

```
      reverse(j-k+i) = temp
   end do
   end
```

Note: A simpler method for performing this operation will become apparent in Section 6.13.

2.

```
   integer :: limit, f1, f2, f3
   read *, limit
   f1 = 1
   if (limit.ge.1) print *, f1
   f2 = 1
   if (limit.ge.2) print *, f2
   do i = 3, limit
      f3 = f1+f2
      print *, f3
      f1 = f2
      f2 = f3
   end do
   end
```

6.

```
   real x
   do
      read *, x
      if (x.eq.-1.) then
         print *, 'input value -1. invalid'
      else
         print *, x/(1.+x)
         exit
      end if
   end do
   end
```

7.

```
type(entry), pointer :: first, current, previous
current => first
if (current%index == 10) then
   first => first%next
else
   do
      previous => current
      current => current%next
      if (current%index == 10) exit
   end do
   previous%next => current%next
end if
```

Chapter 5

1.

```
subroutine calculate(x, n, mean, variance, ok)
   integer, intent(in)             :: n
   real, dimension(n), intent(in) :: x
   real, intent(out)               :: mean, variance
   logical, intent(in)             :: ok
   integer :: i
   mean = 0.
   variance = 0.
   ok = n > 1
   if (ok) then
      do i = 1, n
         mean = mean + x(i)
      end do
      mean = mean/n
      do i = 1, n
         variance = variance + (x(i) - mean)**2
      end do
      variance = variance/(n-1)
   end if
end subroutine calculate
```

Note: A simpler method will become apparent in Chapter 8.

2.

```
subroutine matrix_mult(a, b, c, i, j, k)
   integer, intent(in)             :: i, j, k
   real, dimension(i,j), intent(in)  :: a
   real, dimension(j,k), intent(in)  :: b
   real, dimension(i,k), intent(out) :: c
   integer :: l, m, n
   c(1:i, 1:k) = 0.
   do n = 1, k
      do l = 1, j
         do m = 1, i
            c(m, n) = c(m, n) + a(m,l)*b(l, n)
         end do
      end do
   end do
end subroutine matrix_mult
```

3.

```fortran
subroutine shuffle(cards)
   integer, dimension(52), intent(in) :: cards
   integer                            :: left, choice, i, temp
   real                               :: r
   cards = (/ (i, i=1,52) /)      ! Initialize deck.
   do left = 52,1,-1              ! Loop over number of cards left.
      call random_number(r)       ! Draw a card
      choice = r*left + 1         !    from remaining possibilities
      temp = cards(left)          !    and swap with last
      cards(left) = cards(choice) !    one left.
      cards(choice) = temp
   end do
end subroutine shuffle
```

4.

```fortran
character function earliest(string)
   character(len=*), intent(in) :: string
   integer                      :: j, length
   length = len(string)
   if (length <= 0) then
      earliest = ''
   else
      earliest = string(1:1)
      do j = 2, length
         if (string(j:j) < earliest) earliest = string(j:j)
      end do
   end if
end function earliest
```

5.

```fortran
subroutine sample
   real :: r, l, v, pi
   pi = acos(-1.)
   :
   r = 3.
   l = 4.
   v = volume(r, l)
   :
contains
   function volume(radius, length)
      real, intent(in) :: radius, length
      real             :: volume
      volume = pi*radius**2*length
   end function volume
end subroutine sample
```

7.

```
module string_type
   type string
      integer :: length
      character(len=80)    :: string_data
   end type string
   interface assignment(=)
      module procedure c_to_s_assign, s_to_c_assign
   end interface (=)
   interface len
      module procedure string_len
   end interface
   interface operator(//)
      module procedure string_concat
   end interface (//)
contains
   subroutine c_to_s_assign(s, c)
      type (string), intent(out)   :: s
      character(len=*), intent(in) :: c
      s%string_data = c
      s%length = len(c)
      if (s%length > 80) s%length = 80
   end subroutine c_to_s_assign
   subroutine s_to_c_assign(c, s)
      type (string), intent(in)    :: s
      character(len=*), intent(out) :: c
      c = s%string_data(1:s%length)
   end subroutine s_to_c_assign
   function string_len(s)
      integer       :: string_len
      type(string) :: s
      string_len = s%length
   end function string_len
   function string_concat(s1, s2)
      type (string), intent(in) :: s1, s2
      type (string)             :: string_concat
      string_concat%string_data =                    &
                  s1%string_data(1:s1%length) // &
                  s2%string_data(1:s2%length)
      string_concat%length = s1%length + s2%length
      if (string_concat%length > 80)                 &
                  string_concat%length = 80
   end function string_concat
end module string_type
```

Note: The intrinsic len function, used in subroutine c_to_s_assign, is first described in Section 8.6.

Chapter 6

1.

   i) `a(1, :)`

  ii) `a(:, 20)`

 iii) `a(2:50:2, 2:20:2)`

 iv) `a(50:2:-2, 20:2:-2)`

  v) `a(1:0, 1)`

2.

```
where (z.gt.0) z = 2*z
```

3.

```
integer, dimension(16) :: j
```

4.

```
w       explicit-shaped
a, b    assumed-shape
d       pointer
```

5.

```
real, pointer :: x(:, :, :)
x => tar(2:10:2, 2:20:2, 2:30:2)%du(3)
```

6.

```
ll = ll + ll
ll = mm + nn + n(j:k+1, j:k+1)
```

7.

```
program backwards
   integer                   :: i, j
   integer, dimension(100) :: reverse
   reverse = (/ (i, i=1, 100) /)
   read *, i, j
   reverse(i:j) = reverse(j:i:-1)
end program backwards
```

Chapter 7

1.

   i) `integer, dimension(100) :: bin`

  ii) `real(selected_real_kind(6, 4)), dimension(0:20, 0:20) :: &`
     `iron_temperature`

 iii) `logical, dimension(20) :: switches`

iv) `character(len=70), dimension(44) ::  page`

2.
Value of i is 3.1, but may be changed;
value of i is 3.1, but may not be changed.

3.

i) `integer, dimension(100) ::  i=(/ (0, k=1, 100) /)`

ii) `integer, dimension(100) ::  i=(/ (0, 1, k=1, 50) /)`

iii) `real, dimension(10, 10) ::  x=reshape((/ (1.0, k=1, 100) /), &`
`(/10, 10/) )`

iv) `character(len=10) ::  string = '0123456789'`

Note: the reshape function will be met in Section 8.13.3.

4.

	mod	outer	inner	fun
a–b	character(10,2)	–	–	–
c,d,e	real	–	–	–
f	real	–	–	real
g,h	real	–	–	–
i–n	integer	–	–	–
o–w	real	–	–	–
x	real	–	–	real
y	real	–	–	–
z	real	–	complex	–

5.

i) `type(person) boss = person('Smith', 48.7, 22)`

ii) a) This is impossible because a pointer component cannot be a constant.
b)
`type(entry) current`
`data current%value, current%index /1.0, 1/`

6.
The following are not:
iv) because of the real exponent, and
viii) because of the pointer component.

Chapter 8

1.

```
program qroots        ! Solution of quadratic equation.
!
    real :: a, b, c, d, x1, x2
!
    read(*, *) a, b, c
    write( *, *) ' a = ', a, 'b = ', b, 'c = ', c
    if (a == 0.) then
        if (b /= 0.) then
            write(*, *) ' Linear: x = ', -c/b
        else
            write(*, *) ' No roots!'
        endif
    else
        d = b**2 - 4.*a*c
        if (d < 0.) then
            write (*, *) ' Complex', -b/(2.*a), '+-',      &
                        sqrt(-d)/(2.*a)
        else
            x1 = -(b + sign(sqrt(d), b))/(2.*a)
            x2 = c/(x1*a)
            write(*, *) ' Real roots', x1, x2
        endif
    endif
end program qroots
```

Historical note: A similar problem was set in one of the first books on Fortran programming —
A FORTRAN Primer, E. Organick (Addison-Wesley, 1963). It is interesting to compare Organick's
solution, written in FORTRAN II, on p. 122 of that book, with the one above. (It is reproduced in the
Encyclopedia of Physical Science & Technology (Academic Press, 1987), vol. 5, p. 538.)

2.

```
subroutine calculate(x, mean, variance, ok)
    real, intent(in)    :: x(:)
    real, intent(out)   :: mean, variance
    logical, intent(out) :: ok
    ok = size(x) > 1
    if (ok) then
        mean = sum(x)/size(x)
        variance = sum((x-mean)**2)/(size(x)-1)
    end if
end subroutine calculate
```

3.

F		p1 and p2 are associated with the same array elements, but in reverse order
T		p1 and p2(4:1:-1) are associated with exactly the same array elements, a(3), a(5), a(7), a(9)

4.

5	1	a has bounds 5:10 and a(:) has bounds 1:6
5	1	p1 has bounds 5:10 and p2 has bounds 1:6
1	1	x and y both have bounds 1:6

Chapter 9

1.

```
a) print '(a/ (t1, 10f6.1))', ' grid', grid
b) print '(a, " ", 25i5)', ' list', (list(i), i = 1, 49, 2)
or                         list(1:49:2)
c) print '(a/ (" ", 2a12))', ' titles', titles
d) print '(a/ (t1, 5en15.6))', ' power', power
e) print '(a, 10l2)', ' flags', flags
f) print '(a, 5(" (", 2f6.1, ")"))', ' plane', plane
```

2.

```
        character, dimension(3,3) :: tic_tac_toe
        integer                   :: unit
        :
        write(unit, '(t1, 3a2)' ) tic_tac_toe
```

4.

```
a) read(*, *) grid
1.0 2.0 3.0 4.0 5.0 6.0 7.0 8.0 9.0 10.0

b) read(*, *) list(1:49:2)
25*1

c) read(*, *) titles
data transfer

d) read(*, *) power
1.0 1.e-03

e) read(*, *) flags
t f t f t f f t f t

f) read(*, *) plane
(0.0, 1.0),(2.3, 4)
```

5.

```
subroutine get_char(unit,c,end_of_file)
    integer, intent(in)    :: unit
    character, intent(out) :: c
    logical, intent(out)   :: end_of_file
    integer :: ios
    end_of_file = .false.
    do
        read(unit, '(a1)', advance='no', iostat=ios, end=10) c
        if(ios == 0) return
    end do
10  c = ' '
    end_of_file = .true.
end subroutine get_char
```

Chapter 12

1.

```
type(stack) a
allocate(a%content(4))
a%index = 1
a%content = (/ 1, 2, 3, 4 /)
a = stack(2, (/a%content, 5, 6 /))
```

2.

```
type(emfield) a, temp
allocate(a%strength(4, 6))
a%strength = 1.0
temp = a                     ! automatic allocation of temp%content
deallocate(a%strength)
allocate(a%strength(0:5, 0:8))
a%strength(1:4, 1:6) = temp%strength
a%strength(0:5:5, :) = 0
a%strength(1:4, 0) = 0
a%strength(1:4, 7:8) = 0
```

3.

```
type(emfield) a
allocate(a%strength(4, 6))
a%strength = 1.0
a = emfield(reshape( (/ (a%strength(:,i),0.,0.,i=1,6),          &
                        (0.,0.,0.,0.,0.,0.,0.,0.,i=7,9) /), &
                        (/6, 9/)))
```

Chapter 17

1.

```
b = reshape( [ (0,i=1,size(b,1)+2), (0,b(:,i),0,i=1,size(b,2)), &
              (0,i=1,size(b,1)+2) ], [size(b,1)+2, size(b,2)+2 ] )
```

Index